ANTIPODEAN RIFFS

ANTIPODEAN RIFFS
ESSAYS ON AUSTRALASIAN JAZZ

EDITED BY BRUCE JOHNSON

SHEFFIELD UK   BRISTOL CT

Published by Equinox Publishing Ltd.

UK: Office 415, The Workstation, 15 Paternoster Row, Sheffield, South Yorkshire, S1 2BX
USA: ISD, 70 Enterprise Drive, Bristol, CT 06010

www.equinoxpub.com

The Introduction and chapters 1–14 were first published in *Jazz Research Journal*, Volume 8, Number 1-2 (2014). This collection in book form first published 2016.

© Bruce Johnson and contributors 2016

All rights reserved. No part of this publication may be reproduced or transmitted in any form or by any means, electronic or mechanical, including photocopying, recording or any information storage or retrieval system, without prior permission in writing from the publishers.

British Library Cataloguing-in-Publication Data
A catalogue record for this book is available from the British Library.

Library of Congress Cataloging-in-Publication Data
Antipodean riffs : essays on Australasian jazz / edited by Bruce Johnson.
   pages cm
 Includes bibliographical references and index.
 ISBN 978-1-78179-280-3 (hb) -- ISBN 978-1-78179-281-0 (pb)
 1. Jazz--Australia--History and criticism. I. Johnson, Bruce, 1943- editor.
 ML3509.A92A67 2016
 781.650994--dc23
                    2015031543

ISBN: 978 1 78179 280 3   (hardback)
        978 1 78179 281 0   (paperback)

eISBN: 978 1 78179 363 3   (PDF)

Typeset by CA Typesetting Ltd, www.publisherservices.co.uk
Printed and bound in the UK by Lightning Source UK Ltd., Milton Keynes and Lightning Source Inc., La Vergne, TN

Contents

Acknowledgements   vii

Introduction
Bruce Johnson   1

Cultural Contexts

1. Demons of discord down under:
   'Jump Jim Crow' and 'Australia's first jazz band'
   John Whiteoak   19

2. Early jazz in Australia as oriental exotica
   Aline Scott-Maxwell   47

3. Got a little rhythm?
   The Australian influence on swing in New Zealand
   during the 1930s and 1940s
   Aleisha Ward   65

4. The reception of jazz in Adelaide and Melbourne and the
   creation of an Australian sound in the *Angry Penguins* decade
   Bruce Clunies Ross   84

5. Cuba Street parade:
   Identity, authenticity and self-expression in
   contemporary Australasian jazz scenes
   Nick Tipping   103

6. The lost history of jazz on early Australian popular
   music television
   Liz Giuffre   117

Infrastructures

7. Shotgun weddings and bohemian dreams:
   Jazz, family values and storytelling in Australian film
   Christopher Coady   135

8   Perspectives on the Melbourne International Women's
    Jazz Festival
    Louise Denson   155

9   'A tale of five festivals':
    Exploring the cultural intermediary function of Australian
    jazz festivals
    Brent Keogh   173

10 'I wouldn't change skins with anybody'
    Dulcie Pitt/Georgia Lee, a pioneering Indigenous Australian
    jazz, blues and community singer
    Karl Neuenfeldt   192

Musicians

11 Examining the legend and music of Australian saxophonist,
    Frank Smith
    Ralph Whiteoak   215

12 Lydia in Oz:
    The reception of George Russell in 1960s Australia
    Pierre-Emmanuel Seguin   229

13 Expressive identity in the voices of three Australian
    saxophonists: McGann, Sanders and Gorman
    Sandy Evans   248

14 *Sex* and the sonic smorgasbord:
    The Necks—extending the 'jazz' piano trio format
    Jane Galbraith   267

    Index   285

Acknowledgements

I could not have prepared this collection without invaluable assistance of various kinds from a number of individuals, whose contribution I wish to acknowledge: Denis Crowdy, Nicholas Gebhardt, Glen Hodges, Andrew Hurley, George McKay, Graeme Smith, Catherine Tackley, Sherrie Tucker, Tim Wall, Michael Webb, John Whiteoak and Tony Whyton. I also want to make special mention of the patient and wonderfully efficient assistance of friend and colleague Liz Giuffre. Many thanks to you all.

Bruce Johnson

Introduction

Bruce Johnson*

As one of the first musics mediated by modern technologies, jazz was circulated globally with a rapidity unprecedented for any other new music. As early as 1922, US journalist Burnet Hershey reported that in his recent journey around the world he found jazz everywhere (Walser 1999: 26). The speed of its international circulation tells us as much about modernity itself as about the music that became its anthem. Curious, then, that it has taken so long for the history of diasporic jazz to be taken seriously. The jazz narrative has been overwhelmingly US-centric for most of the music's history, with jazz outside the US generally neglected as some kind of inauthentic reflection of the 'real thing'. This is a deeply conservative approach to the study of a modern cultural form, telling us, for example, very little about the dynamics of globalization/glocalization in relation to a genre that may be regarded as having created the modern musical template. Indeed, that jazz came to be regarded as the quintessential new music of the twentieth century was itself a phenomenon of its diasporic process. On the basis of their own reports (see for example Shapiro and Hentoff 1955, especially 3–74) musicians in what is regarded as the birthplace of the music, New Orleans, thought of themselves as bearers of a local semi-folk tradition, not as harbingers of internationalist modernity. It was the new audiences in diasporic sites that made the music the anthem of all that was modern, emancipative and thus threatening to tradition.

The further from the source, the more comprehensively was that association defined, and this is partly because of the primary diasporic media. Jazz was a music disseminated, especially beyond the US, largely by recordings, radio and film. It was thus delivered via the medium not of provincial folk traditions but by technologies that coded it as of an increasingly internationalized New World that represented the future. It was in the diasporic process that

---

* Bruce Johnson holds honorary Professorships at the Universities of New South Wales and Macquarie in Sydney; Glasgow, and Turku in Finland, where he co-founded of the International Institute for Popular Culture. His current research lies in music, acoustic cultural history and modernity. Recent publications include *Dark Side of the Tune: Music and Violence*, (with Martin Cloonan); *They Do Things Differently There: Essays on Cultural History* (ed. with Harri Kiiskinen).

jazz became, internationally, the soundtrack to modernity (see further Johnson 2000: 7–27; Johnson forthcoming). Jazz was not invented then exported, arriving in some contaminated and enervated form, but was continuously invented in the diasporic process, which thus contributes to, rather than compromises, the jazz tradition (see further Johnson 2002a: passim). Even where diasporic jazz has attracted attention, what are in many ways the most instructive forms have been overlooked and even scorned for their embarrassing *gaucherie*—that is, the earliest attempts to make local sense of the music, before its international, placeless codification from the 1960s through such infrastructures as the LP, its cover notes, jazz education programmes and fake books. To me there are more telling lessons in a non-US recording from the 1920s of Edwardian dance-band or vaudeville trained musicians still trying to find their feet, than a diasporic 1960s performance by musicians whose greatest pride is to be indistinguishable from their New York counterparts.

But from the late twentieth century the situation has been changing, with studies of jazz in Europe, including the early general study, Goddard (1979) and later Atkins (2003), and specific regional studies including, inter alia, the USSR (Starr 1983); the UK (Godbolt 1984); the Third Reich (Kater 1992); South Africa (Ballantine 1993); Finland (Haavisto 1996); Japan (Atkins 2001) and France (Nettelbeck 2004). The flow of such studies now gains impetus yearly. This shift has been given momentum by the 'New Jazz Studies', and the current centre of gravity of its diasporic interests may be seen as the Hera-funded research project Rhythm Changes (see http://heranet.info/rhythm-changes/index). Australia was among the first regions to receive such attention. Following the 'registry' style privately printed publication by Hayes, Scribner and Magee (1976), extended scholarly monographs began with Andrew Bisset (1979, updated 1987) followed by Johnson (1987), Whiteoak (1999) and more focused, anecdotal and interview-based surveys as exemplified by Williams (1981), Clare/Brennan (1995), Sharpe (2001, 2006, 2008), Boldiston (2007), Shand (2009), Newton (2009), James (2014) and Hopgood (2014). There are also discographical resources by Dean (2005), and most comprehensively by Mitchell (1988, 1998, 2002). There are several essay-length overviews of Australian jazz history including Johnson (2008) from which much of the following is condensed. There is also a growing library of jazz in New Zealand, including Hardie and Thomas (2009); Ward (2009, 2013) (see also Ward's website nzjazz.wordpress.com); and there is coverage in Bourke (2010).

Thus far I have been identifying nation(s) as a regional descriptor, since that is the most succinct way to tell a potential reader what to expect, and given that the nation is not the US this situates the volume very much with the 'New Jazz Studies' that have emerged since the late twentieth century. But I want to take that alignment further along a chain of logic. The idea embodied in the term 'Australian jazz' or 'Australasian jazz' overlooks internal regionalisms and micro-communities that challenge that monolithic idea of nation, as indicated dramatically by the titles of the texts listed above in the category of Australasian jazz studies. One of the thrusts of 'New Jazz' and diasporic jazz studies is to challenge the schematic models of entrenched jazz narratives, by breaking down simplistic binaries such as 'centre (US)/margins (the rest)', or based on essentialisms of place, gender and race. This process discovers continuities where, before, there had been ruptures, but also micro-differences elided in conceptions of jazz based on, for example, nation. 'Australian jazz' occupies the greater space in this collection, and for discursive convenience in this Introduction, I shall focus on that component of Australasia. The term certainly has some coherence as a subject, but it is also intersected by lines of force that range from the regional to the personal. When Europeans began to speak of Australian jazz in the wake of our successive exports, perhaps what they were really noticing was a regional flavour or even the personal signatures of particular musicians such as Ade Monsbourgh and Roger and Graeme Bell, which happened to coalesce for them with other supposed markers of 'Australian-ness' (see further Johnson 2000: 141–64). Without losing a bigger picture, the current enquiries into diasporic jazz often involve delicate nuancing and cross-hatchings that force us to reconsider schematic models of the music and its history.

I have arranged the chapters in this collection into three sections that more or less constitute thematic categories, and within each the order is more or less chronological. It will help to contextualize the individual studies if we situate them in the historical narrative.

Cultural contexts

Jazz began to be spoken of in Australia towards the close of World War I, but this was not our first exposure to entertainment derived from African-American sources, and the transition was by no means clearly marked, largely because the performances identified by the term jazz were understood so differently from later interpretations. 'Australia's First Jazz Band', led by a female singer Belle Sylvia, was presented in mid-1918 on a Sydney theatre stage, a vaudeville setting that had hosted a broad range of light entertainments including minstrelsy, a pattern evident in other diasporic sites including England (see, for example, Parsonage 2005; Rye 2014). The collection begins, then, with John Whiteoak's discussion of what might be called the 'prehistory' of jazz in Australia, including African-American minstrel companies, musicians, dancers, brass bands and ragtime artists from the late nineteenth century and the 1910s, which introduced certain social, cultural and musical practices that evolved into those of early so-called 'jazz' in Australia. Contemporary reviews suggest that one understanding of jazz by audiences and performers was as a form of comic anarchy, with novelty instruments, *sons trouvés*, extravagant animation and a general zaniness (Johnson 1987: 1–2). Low culture in Australia was far more irredeemably 'low' than it was in the US where, only six years after the first recordings proclaimed the emergence of jazz from its vernacular origins, jazz was toying with 'symphonic form' through the premiere of Gershwin's *Rhapsody in Blue* with Paul Whiteman's Orchestra in 1924. There is little evidence of any courtship across the high/low divide for perhaps the first fifty years of Australian jazz history, and still today relatively little acknowledgement of the dignity and significance of the music on its own terms, with corresponding attempts to seek a haven in the category of 'art', averting the eyes from its low-rent associations (see Johnson 2002b).

From the beginning, Australian writers noted that the origins of jazz were 'negroid' and embodied a challenge to authorized notions of musicality. In every way jazz represented a reaction against pre-twentieth-century Anglo-European high-cultural orientations. Cacophonous, raucous, literally brazen, jazz represented part of a larger 'otherness' to the civilizing arts of Europe. As such it became entwined with broader notions of alien-ness. The 1920s saw an ambivalent fascination on the part of the West with exotic cultures, including one of its periodic flirtations with *chinoiserie* and other exotic motifs apparent in new art movements. There was also the lure of the desert as represented in Lowell Thomas's film presentations on T. E. Lawrence and the imagery of the 1921 Valentino film *The Sheik* (which enjoyed a world record run in Australia, where, as a verb, the word also became a euphemism for seduction). An interest in ancient Egypt was also given impetus by Carter's excavations in the early 1920s in the Valley of the Kings. Aline Scott-Maxwell documents the ways in which this fascination with the exotic was also refracted through 1920s jazz, and while this was an international fashion, she discusses the reasons that it had a distinctive inflection in Australia, so remote from Europe and so anxiously conscious of the proximity of the orient. In the process, she also throws new light that challenges some of the more schematic Euro-US centric formulae about orientalization, but also it discloses an early Australian jazz style—'Chinese jazz'—that draws on a non-US imaginary (albeit drawing on unappealing stereotypes).

As in all countries affected by the onset of the Great Depression, the insouciant high spirits of jazz deprived it of its appeal in the parlous times beginning at the end of the 1920s. In Australia this process was intensified by virtue of a strain of racism and xenophobia which forms a significant component of its cultural history. Throughout the 1920s the unions lobbied against jazz, and especially the importation of bands from the US and England, which had begun in 1923. It was argued that these imports stole work from local musicians; furthermore as a primitive 'negroid' music it was shamelessly degrading. These economic and moral imperatives obligingly converged when the first visiting African-American jazz band toured with the revue 'The Coloured Idea' in 1928. During its season in Melbourne, collusion between the local yellow press, the intelligence organization the Commonwealth Investigation Branch, and the local police, led to members of the band being caught in drug and alcohol-fuelled frolics with several local women. The band was deported, the last African-American jazz band allowed into the country for decades (see further Bisset 1987: 23, 43–45, 85; Hall 1997: passim; Sutcliffe 1997: passim, Johnson 2010: passim).

From the end of the 1920s, the word 'jazz' itself virtually disappeared from the public sphere, and when its influence began to make itself felt again in Australian popular music from about the mid-1930s, it first did so under the name 'swing'. Like jazz in the 1920s, the word was understood in various ways, but also like jazz, it became a descriptor for the US-sourced music that swept the world in the 1930s. A victim of its own popularity, swing had become all but a stale formula when it was suddenly re-invigorated by the entry into the war of the US in 1941. In Australia, with around one million US service personnel passing through a country of about seven million, this, the biggest single invasion in the country's history, transformed popular culture (see further Potts and Potts 1985: passim). The same pattern was evident throughout Europe and the UK, where swing was the musical expression of the crucial intervention of the US into the war. But in the antipodes a unique line of force traversed the way in which swing developed. Both Australians and New Zealanders enjoyed levels of exposure to US swing musicians during the war when US service bands were stationed around both countries. The Red Arrows, for example, were stationed in Adelaide where they made still-extant private recordings that cast instructive light on the development of local musicians. Artie Shaw's navy band performed in Sydney and although they played officially only to US service personnel, Australian musicians were also able to hear the band by Shaw's personal invitation (Johnson 2008: 127). Local jazz musicians mingled with the US players, and one member of Shaw's band, Max Kaminsky, cut a number of tracks with Roger Bell's band. New Zealanders hosted 150,000 wartime US servicemen, including US service bands who significantly influenced local approaches to dance music, of which swing was a major component (Bourke 2010: 117–19; also on New Zealand jazz see Whiteoak 2009). But prior to the war, a network was already built up that exemplifies one of the most interesting developments in the diffusion of jazz: a diasporic path that in important respects bypassed the source. In this collection, Aleisha Ward documents these linkages between Australia and New Zealand during the swing era. Since then, there have been transforming developments in jazz support systems, including the burgeoning of formal education programmes, and Nick Tipping explores the way in which these trans-Tasman linkages have developed in the contemporary scene, and the implications for national jazz styles.

With the end of the war, the dam burst on two jazz streams that had built up for nearly a decade and which, under the names 'traditional' and 'modern', would define Australian jazz topography for the coming decades. The year 1946 may be taken as the beginning of the deluge. It was in December of that year that the revivalist or traditional jazz community inaugurated the world's first, and now longest surviving annual festival of jazz, the Australian Jazz Convention. Initially held for some years in Melbourne, it confirmed the city's centrality to the traditional movement, with three figures of particular importance. They were the Bell brothers, Roger (mainly trumpet) and Graeme (piano), and multi-instrumentalist Ade Monsbourgh; all were also prolific composers. I believe these three are the most durably influential figures to emerge in Australian jazz, both locally and internationally. As members of the same band, they were central to the incubation of the revivalist movement, they virtually established the jazz movement in parts of Europe, and transformed the social function of jazz in the UK (see further Johnson 2000: 147–57). Apart from providing the nucleus around which the traditional jazz community formed, each made a decisive contribution to what has come to be regarded internationally as a distinctive Australian jazz sound (see further: on Graeme Bell, Bell 1988; on the 'Australian jazz sound' debate, the benchmark scholarly essay is by Clunies Ross 1979 [at that time, Clunies-Ross], and see also for example Johnson 1981, 1982a, 1982b, 1982c, 2000: 157–63; Linehan 1983; Clunies Ross 1983 and below).

The idea that Australia has made a distinctive contribution to the world's jazz tradition goes back to Ross's Jazz Band from Melbourne who, in 1924, embarked on what became nine years' touring as the Three Australian Boys, embracing the UK and the US, recording and playing prestigious engagements. In the early 1930s, Australian bandleader Cec Morrison visited the US where his broadcasts of 'Kangaroo Jazz' prompted the suggestion that he should stay to 'educate our own jazz leaders into what jazz might be' (Johnson 2000: 147). The UK-published international compendium *Jazz: The Essential Companion* refers to the 'disturbingly original compositions of such Bell sidemen as Ade Monsbourgh', and asserts that 'in Australia itself a jazz scene flourishes which (it could be argued) produces the most stimulating music of any outside America' (Carr *et al.* 1987: 17). The tributes continue in the extraordinary international acclaim accorded the group The Necks (see further below). Among Australian commentators, the idea of an 'Australian style' is more contested than overseas. In any event, the Bells, Monsbourgh, Dallwitz, and their coteries, are central to any such discussion.

Also important in this development were musicians from two other centres, Hobart in Tasmania and, to a greater extent, Adelaide in South Australia, particularly the group to which painter, musician and composer Dave Dallwitz was central. All of those mentioned were also prominent in the major Australian modernist movement involving overlap between jazz and radical arts and politics which centred on the journal *Angry Penguins* during the 1940s. This moment in Australian cultural history is unparallelled, an intellectual ferment that marked a major transition in our cultural history, for which jazz was the soundtrack. These events are in my view the most significant in the history of jazz in this country. They are not only unique locally: there seems to me to be no equivalent anywhere either in US or diasporic jazz. Not only has this complicity of jazz with the country's major moment in literary, artistic and political radicalism been generally overlooked, it is especially noteworthy that the conjunction should have been made with the revivalist rather than the progressive jazz sector. This instructively challenges received assumptions about the culturally progressive impetus of 'modern jazz', and has very important lessons that resonate with the whole avant-garde sector of 'art music', the relationship between popular culture (especially as construed in the Adorno tradition) and modernity, and the role of jazz in Australia's cultural history. In particular, it throws further light on the importance of the Bell/Monsbourgh coterie. The importance of and reasons for its emergence at this time have been argued in various studies, pioneered by Bruce Clunies Ross's 1979 essay. In this collection he elaborates and reflects on those arguments of nearly forty years ago in the contemporary context.

Infrastructures

Two jazz platforms are explored in this section: moving image and jazz festivals. Australia was a pioneer in both. The earliest appearance of jazz on film in Australia was a locally made feature, *Does the Jazz Lead to Destruction?* Tantalisingly, all that remains are posters from the press, themselves rich in implications, including, as the title suggests, a very early marketing of transgressive alternativity. It was exhibited as part of what, as far as I can discover, was the world's first jazz festival, the 'Jazz Week' at the Globe theatre in Sydney in 1919. That this elaborate convergence of media (film, stage and the press) could be organized profitably (the 'Jazz Week' was extended by popular demand) in less than two years of the first jazz recordings, is in itself a study of modernity and the media. The relationship between jazz and moving image (film and later television) has remained close in Australia, and included a feature film with a major acting appearance by Miles Davis (*Dingo* 1991, dir. Rolph de Heer).

The convergence has provided a site for the exploration of national identity as well as the way in which popular music itself has been understood. With the advent of television in 1956 jazz became eclipsed in the discourses of music and the media. This was especially so because of the simultaneous arrival of rock and youth music television shows, in both of which one of the major figures was the legendary performer Johnny O'Keefe, who fronted the show *Six O'Clock Rock*. When John Lennon reportedly declared a loathing of forms of jazz, he helped to consolidate a narrative of antagonistic disruption between the pre- and post-rock moment, and this model has broadly persisted. Recent research is beginning to disclose continuities between those two moments; in generic terms, continuities between the jazz and the rock cultures. In many cases, these continuities are established by cross-over musicians of the period. Yet the perception of the iconic programme *Six O'Clock Rock* as being wholly dominated by the new youth music and, as such, an abrupt rupture with the earlier jazz culture is, as Liz Giuffre demonstrates in this collection, seriously misleading. Her study suggests that the continuities are more deeply and systemically embedded, in the mediascape and its management itself. I have a clip of the opening of the show in which O'Keefe's backing vocal quartet and some of his group (probably the Dee-Jays) are in shot during the sequence, but so is the jazz group, a potent visual symbol of the more or less equal presence of rock and jazz in the show at that time. The connection is further documented in Liz Giuffre's study, in which, by drawing on previously unpublished documents including correspondence and financial records from the national public broadcaster, the Australian Broadcasting Commission (later 'Corporation'), who presented the show, she demonstrates important continuities and overlaps between jazz and rock in the early presentation of youth music on Australian television. Her chapter urges further research into primary sources that question the powerful mythology of disruption between jazz and rock cultures in the mid-twentieth century.

The convergence of jazz and film, in the meantime, remained an unbroken pattern from the earliest days of Australian cinema. As both a diegetic subject and an extradiegetic narrative device, jazz shadowed and gave meaning to the shifting understandings of Australian identity and value systems. Jazz became a standard marker of modern relationships between individuals and communities, frequently the sign of the contemporary stresses of urban decadence in contrast to the sturdy and redemptive values of rural Australia, 'the Bush'.

Later this simple moral opposition became complicated as Australia's escape from the Great Depression seemed to be tied to a move into a more modern, industrial and urban-centred economy. As it did so, the semiotics of jazz on screen also became more nuanced (see further Johnson 2009). Christopher Coady analyses the function of music in two Australian films from the 1990s to document this semiosis, the shift in meaning, of jazz-inflected music from the sound of the future to a mood of nostalgia, of retreat to more innocent times in personal relationships.

One of the issues in these relationships is gender politics, and again, jazz in Australia has always been implicated one way or another in these power dynamics. One of the recurring scenarios in Australian films of the 1920s was the moral and ethical dilemmas arising from a new range of possibilities in an era of post-war social emancipation, particularly in relation to gender politics. The 'modern woman' as portrayed in Australian film increasingly transgressed into and threatened sites of male power, and she did so to the sound of jazz, from as early as the 1919 film *Why Jesse Learned to Jazz* (see Pike and Cooper 1980: 118). An advertisement for the 1926 film *Should a Girl Propose?* proclaimed that 'The modern Girl jazzes, smokes, indulges in athletes [sic], enters law and politics, and, in short, does most things a man does, and in most things does better' (Pike and Cooper 1980: 170). In the 1920s, jazz was the music that embodied the glamour (in all senses) of urban modernity and the threat it presented to a bush-based *mythos* of Australian identity.

This antipathy was a staple of Australian films throughout the silent era as exemplified in Charles Chauvel's two films which present mirror images of precisely this tension—the city girl who goes to the country, the country girl who goes to the city (see further Johnson 2000: 69–76). In all the cases cited so far in this section, jazz was in significant ways a feminine principle implicated with the emasculating power of the modern city as opposed to the masculine values of 'the Bush'. The coding was strengthened by the number of women actually involved in various aspects of modern musical practices (see further Dreyfus 1999: passim). Jazz thus became the music of one of the major shifts that marked Western modernization: the emergence of the 'modern woman', often known as the Flapper, and often regarded as the cause of every modern social menace lamented by conservatives, from sexual license to international communism (see further Johnson 2000: 59–69). The stereotypical image of the 1920s, the 'Jazz Age', is the Flapper, in the extravagant and impudently inelegant posture of that most flamboyant of jazz dances, the Charleston. This gendered association is far more multi-faceted than we now generally appreciate in a period in which the meaning of jazz has since become fixed on (primarily) male instrumental performance.

While the band scene was dominated by men, women were nonetheless far more prominent as jazz and dance musicians than has ever been the case since the 1920s. Musical training had been traditionally a component of a genteel woman's education, ornamenting her role as wife; now the pool of such skills was available to challenge the limits of that role. Women were thus prominent in jazz performance, and were in the actual majority in the major public workshop for improvisational practice: musical accompaniment to silent movies (see Whiteoak 1999: 14, 61, 66). And as a Royal Commission of 1927 disclosed, movies themselves were predominantly a female recreation, providing women with images of the contemporary liberated lifestyle (Johnson 2000: 61–62). The gendering of jazz was still further strengthened when we remind ourselves of the opinion widely circulated in Australian print media that 'the jazz is a dance'. And dancing itself, like non-professional musical performance, was primarily imagined as a female recreation.

With the end of World War II and demobilization, however, post-war conservatism saw the strategic attempt to expel women from the public sphere in general and reinsert them into domestic spaces and roles. This process was also evident in the US, but on the evidence of popular music, this reaction appears to have been even stronger in Australia. The female orchestra, bandleader and solo instrumentalist largely disappeared from post-war jazz until the 1980s, and has never regained the presence she had in the 1920s. Jazz was imagined as an aggressively male domain, and even with the advent of gender-integrated tertiary jazz studies courses in the 1970s, the ratio of women to men has remained deeply incommensurate with the general population and employment demographics. There is a significant research area here, and a case study in the attempt to reopen space for women jazz musicians is provided in Louise Denson's review of the Melbourne International Women's Jazz Festival.

The proliferation of jazz festivals was one of the shifts in institutional support that can be seen as beginning in the 1970s with the establishment of tertiary jazz education programmes. The forms of support also extend to service organizations such as the various Jazz Action Societies which also began in Sydney in the 1970s, the government funded regional and national Jazz Co-ordination Associations throughout the late twentieth century, which provided touring and local performance circuits, CV services, arts lobbying activities, advice on career development, funding applications, and a national forum through its journal *Jazzchord*, which virtually brought into being an institutionalized professional jazz network. Also based on a collaboration between government and the jazz community is the Australian Jazz Archives hosted by the National Film and Sound Archive, and which, developing from initiatives in 1993, began formal operation in 1997 in conjunction with similar regional bodies, and activated a range of archival initiatives including synergies with local libraries, museums and exhibitions, gathering and generating materials through, for example filming, oral histories, and print and sound publications. Jazz has also become an increasingly standard component of arts festivals, with up to a hundred annual events in Australia by the turn of the century which are devoted entirely or in part to jazz. Brent Keogh surveys a sample of such festivals over the decade 2004–2014, providing a quantitative analysis of programming patterns, with some tentative extrapolations regarding the balance between local and imported musicians, gender balance, and the increasing *rapprochement* between jazz and the world music community. This constitutes a useful statistical database from which other scholars in the fields of jazz studies, and Australian cultural and music studies, may derive arguments, as well as providing useful comparative data for international researchers into the (jazz) festival phenomenon.

Musicians

In establishing a database for *The Oxford Companion to Australian Jazz* in the early 1980s, in addition to reading all the literature I could find—published, unpublished, ephemera and monographs—I canvassed scores of stakeholders in the music from every major metropolitan centre in Australia as to who should be considered for inclusion. The results were particularly interesting in revealing that a musician was often regarded as significant not for virtuosity or public visibility, but for embodying an aspect of the jazz profile that in some way represented the kinds of platform on which the Australian jazz community has been constructed. It might be as an informal mentor, the durable dedication of an amateur, administrative energy rather than musical prowess, or the regional band that becomes the nucleus of a local scene. If we want to assemble an inventory of some of the founding giants of Australian jazz as conventionally understood in the 'great man' model, then there are many names we would add apart from the Bells and Monsbourgh already mentioned, including the utterly *sui generis* John Sangster, whom I regard as among the most important performers/composers Australia has produced in any musical idiom. In addition to some of those covered in this collection, a great many Australian musicians have gained a high profile at an international level, including for example Frank Coughlan from the 1920s, and the members of the Australian Jazz Quartet/Quintet in the 1950s, Don Burrows, Bob Barnard, New Zealand-born Mike Nock and more recently James Morrison (on Australian jazz musicians abroad, see further Johnson 2000: 141–47). The section in this collection on 'Musicians', however, reflects the heterogeneity of the criteria that underpin impact and significance and should certainly not be taken to constitute a sample of 'the best' or the most famous, though some among those studied do arguably fall into those categories.

Karl Neuenfeldt's case study makes the point. Barely recalled even within the jazz community, Georgia Lee nonetheless achieved international recognition during her lifetime, but in ways that throw fascinating light on the convergence of gender and indigeneity in Australian culture in general and jazz in particular. The problems encountered by women in what became a disproportionately masculinized musical practice were, in Lee's case, rendered even more problematic and ambiguous by the fact that she was an Indigenous performer, one of the very few in Australian jazz. While 'blackness' has often been regarded internationally as a sign of authenticity in jazz performance, Australian aboriginality has been marginalized almost to invisibility. Neuenfeldt instructively tracks the confused lines of force that intersected Georgia Lee's career, in a country where, unlike the US, a local 'person-of-colour' had no extra jazz leverage.

The case of saxophonist Frank Smith also raises questions about the anomalies in the process of jazz canonization in Australian jazz—in particular, the relationship between public and professional profiles. Smith is a major, if publicly obscure, figure in the post-war modern movement. I mentioned earlier that in 1946, two streams of jazz suddenly burst the banks. One was the traditional/revivalist movement. According to contemporary accounts it was also in that year that the more formally progressive musicians were stunned by the arrival of the so-called '52nd Street' recordings, four tracks by young US boppers led by Dizzy Gillespie, recorded in February 1946. The modern jazz stream in Australia generally replicated the centralization of US models that was evident internationally, as institutionalized in the early tertiary jazz education programmes. The US-centric profile was so powerful that one of the early programme directors (imported from the US) informed me, on the record, that he actively discouraged any interest among the students in Australian jazz. In my view, this was deplorable for many reasons; apart from tending to alienate practitioners from their own culture, it obscured several developments in Australian progressive jazz that are locally distinctive.

Several of these are glimpsed in two of the studies in this section, the first by Ralph Whiteoak, as it relates to the highly influential work of Frank Smith. A casual listening to his relatively sparse commercially recorded output does little to disclose the fact that he arrived at his style not simply by the mechanical reproduction of the US source, but by a much more eclectic and independent assimilation of experimental models. As a mentor still recalled with reverence by his protégés—and now themselves influential mentors—Smith imparted musical models and attitudes that cannot be understood simply through the centre-margin relationship between the US and Australia. The same is true of the so-called 'modal jazz' movement as it unfolded in Australia, and again, largely because of the dominating influence of one independent jazz mind, Bryce Rohde. Generally, the understanding of George Russell's influence is refracted through the 1959 Miles Davis album *Kind Of Blue*. In an examination of what is probably the earliest example of music influenced by Russell's Lydian Concept outside of the USA, that of Australian pianist Bryce Rohde, Pierre-Emmanuel Seguin argues for an understanding of Russell's influence, which is more focused on an emerging chromatic approach to improvisation and composition. As in the case of Smith's protegés, Rohde's band members continued to develop Russell's concepts but with distinctive local inflections.

An emerging theme in these studies is that, however it might articulate itself and be articulated by commentators, the local voice remains a key in the understanding of Australian jazz. Saxophonist Sandy Evans brings her eminent practitioner's insight to bear in her study of three erstwhile Australian colleagues: Bernie McGann, Kim Sanders and Scottish-born Tony Gorman. Each exemplifies a different approach, assimilating different aspects of contemporary playing styles, and Evans explores the ways each reflects his cultural and personal history, drawing on and constructing a heterogeneous patchwork that has larger cautionary lessons against schematic essentializations of jazz practices based on simplistic canonical US-centric models. The final study reviews the approaches taken by the contemporary group The Necks, described by English critic John L. Walters as 'one of the most extraordinary groups on the planet' (*The Guardian*, 29 November 2002), 'a revolutionary consortium redefining music for the new century' (*The Guardian*, 6 December 2002). Drawing on musical analysis of their recorded output and interviews with the members, Lloyd Swanton, Tony Buck and Chris Abrahams, Jane Galbraith explores the musical attitudes and practices that help to identify what distinguishes the band. As in the case of the Bell coterie, something is going on in the work of Lee, Smith, Rohde, the trio of saxophonists and The Necks, which cannot be understood simply through a model of passive imitation of the source.

This collection gives further impetus to the growing interest in the jazz diaspora. They combine to tell us that diasporic jazz has lessons about the music that are unavailable to the old centre/margins jazz discourse that treated everything outside the US simply as derivative and diluted, and these in turn can provide a broader understanding of the diffusion of music and culture in a world globalized by the modern media. In particular, we learn something about what is distinctively Australian by attending to these lessons, and, more generally, we can similarly learn about regionalism in general. As a corollary, we should also regard the structural divisions of the collection as in instructive ways merely provisional. Like so many such collections on a theme, its content is largely determined by responses to a Call for Papers—in this case originally on Australian jazz. It is not difficult to review proposals and then construct a conceptual framework within which to arrange content. But it is specious to pretend that a CfP based project is conforming to premeditated detailed subdivisions within the general brief 'Australian jazz', and in fact it would be, I think, counterproductive to have predetermined those subdivisions. One of the instructive aspects of this process is to find out how a range of scholars of different generations and specialized interests interpret a Call for Papers on 'Australasian jazz', to find out the structure that emerges of itself. Speaking personally, if preparing a monograph rather than an anthology, I would have covered areas that are not covered here, but the collection speaks to me more eloquently for addressing issues and subjects that I as a sole author would not have thought of. The *ex post facto* structure within which I have arranged this volume has therefore been instructive to me, opening up my sense of the range that can be covered under the rubric 'Australasian jazz', providing an opportunity to form a revised perspective on the field.

References

Atkins, E. Taylor (2001) *Blue Nippon: Authenticating Jazz in Japan*. Durham and London: Duke University Press. http://dx.doi.org/10.1215/9780822380030

Atkins, E. Taylor, ed. (2003) *Jazz Planet: Transnational Studies of the "Sound of Surprise"*. Jackson: University Press of Mississippi.

Ballantine, Christopher (1993) *Marabi Nights: Early South African Jazz and Vaudeville*. Johannesburg: Ravan Press.

Bell, Graeme (1988) *Graeme Bell, Australian Jazzman: His Autobiography*. Frenchs Forest, NSW: Child & Associates.

Bisset, Andrew (1987) *Black Roots, White Flowers: A History of Jazz in Australia*. Revised ed. Sydney: ABC Enterprises [1979].

Boldiston, Bill (2007) *Sydney's Jazz and Other Joys of its Vintage Years*. Sydney: Bol d'Or Publishing.

Bourke, Chris (2010) *Blue Smoke: The Lost Dawn of New Zealand Popular Music 1918–1964*. Auckland: Auckland University Press.

Carr, Ian, Digby Fairweather and Brian Priestley (1987) *Jazz: The Essential Companion*. London: Grafton Books.

Clare, John, aka Gail Brennan (1995) *Bodgie Dada and the Cult of Cool*. Sydney: University of New South Wales Press.

Clunies-Ross, Bruce (1979) 'An Australian Sound: Jazz in Melbourne and Adelaide 1941-51'. In *Australian Popular Culture*, ed. P. Spearritt and D. Walker, 62–80. North Sydney: George Allen & Unwin.

—(1983) 'Dave Dallwitz and Australian Jazz'. *Jazz: The Australasian Contemporary Music Magazine* (May/June): 6–8.

Dean, Roger T. (2005) *Sounds from the Corner: Australian Contemporary Jazz on CD*. Sydney: Australian Music Centre.

Dreyfus, Kay (1999) *Sweethearts of Rhythm: The Story of Australia's All-girl Bands and Orchestras to the End of the Second World War.* Sydney: Currency Press.
Godbolt, Jim (1984) *A History of Jazz in Britain 1919–1950.* London, Melbourne and New York: Quartet Books.
Goddard, Chris (1979) *Jazz Away from Home.* New York and London: Paddington Press.
Haavisto, Jukka (1996) *Seven Decades of Finnish Jazz: Jazz in Finland 1919–1969*, trans. Roger Freundlich. Helsinki: Finnish Music Information.
Hall, Richard (1997) 'White Australia's Darkest Days'. *Sydney Morning Herald Good Weekend*, 15 March: [17]–22.
Hardie, Richard, and Allan Thomas, eds. (2009) *Jazz Aotearoa: Notes towards a New Zealand History.* Wellington: Steele Roberts.
Hayes, Mileham, Ray Scribner and Peter Magee (1976) *The Encyclopedia of Australian Jazz.* Brisbane.
Hopgood, Don, and Mel Hopgood (2014) *Jazz Voices: Hot Music in the City of Churches. The story of Jazz in South Australia 1918–2000.* Adelaide: SA Jazz Archive Inc.
James, David (2014) *World's Best Jazz Club: The Story of Bennetts Lane.* Melbourne: University of Melbourne/Victorian College of the Arts/K2.
Johnson, Bruce (1981) 'Is there an Australian Jazz'. *Jazz: The Australasian Contemporary Music Magazine* (December): 6–8.
—(1982a) 'Is there an Australian Jazz Part II'. *Jazz: The Australasian Contemporary Music Magazine* (February): 20–23.
—(1982b) 'Traditional Jazz in Adelaide: Dave Dallwitz and the Southern Jazz Group'. *Jazz: The Australasian Contemporary Music Magazine*, Part 1, (March/April): 10–13; Part 2 (May/June): 10–13; Part 3 (August): 10–13.
—(1982c) 'Traditional Jazz in Australia'. *Jazz: The Australasian Contemporary Music Magazine* (November/December): 4–6.
—(1987) *The Oxford Companion to Australian Jazz.* Melbourne: Oxford University Press.
—(2000) *The Inaudible Music: Jazz, Gender and Australian Modernity.* Sydney: Currency Press.
—(2002a) 'The Jazz Diaspora'. In *The Cambridge Companion to Jazz*, ed. Mervyn Cooke and David Horn, 33–54. Cambridge: Cambridge University Press.
—(2002b) 'Jazz as Cultural Practice'. In *The Cambridge Companion to Jazz*, ed. Mervyn Cooke and David Horn, 96–113. Cambridge: Cambridge University Press.
—(2008) 'Australian Jazz: An Overview'. In *Sounds of then, Sounds of Now: Popular Music in Australia*, ed. Tony Mitchell and Shane Homan, 113–29. Sydney: University of New South Wales Press.
—(2009) 'Jazz and Nation in Australian Cinema: From Silents to Sound'. National Film and Sound Archive's *NFSA Journal* 5/1: 1–12.
—(2010) 'Deportation Blues: Black Jazz and White Australia in the 1920s'. *IASPM Journal: Journal of the International Association for the Study of Popular Music* 1/1. http://www.iaspmjournal.net/index.php/IASPM_Journal/article/viewFile/297/502
—(forthcoming) 'Jazz Outside the U.S.'. In *Encyclopedia of Popular Music of the World*, ed. John Shepherd *et al.*
Kater, Michael H. (1992) *Different Drummers: Jazz in the Culture of Nazi Germany.* New York and Oxford: Oxford University Press.

Linehan, Norm (1983) 'Dave Dallwitz: The Creation of a Myth'. *Jazz: The Australasian Contemporary Music Magazine* (January/February): 20–21.
Mitchell, Jack (1988) *Australian Jazz on Record 1925–80*. Canberra: Australian Government Publishing Service.
—(1998) *More Australian Jazz on Record*. Canberra: National Film and Sound Archive.
—(2002) *EMAJOR: Even More Australian Jazz on Record*. Melbourne: Victorian Jazz Archive Inc.
Nettelbeck, Colin (2004) *Dancing with De Beauvoir: Jazz and the French*. Melbourne: Melbourne University Press.
Newton, Peter J. F. (2009) *Hot Gold: Celebrating the Sydney Jazz Club's First 50 Years, 1953–2003*. Sydney: Sydney Jazz Club Co-operative Ltd/PNIN Press.
Parsonage, Catherine (2005) *The Evolution of Jazz in Britain 1880–1935*. Aldershot: Ashgate.
Pike, Andrew, and Ross Cooper (1980) *Australian Film 1900–1977*. Oxford: Oxford University Press.
Potts, Donald, and Annette Potts (1985) *Yanks Downunder 1941–5: The American Impact on Australia*. Melbourne: Oxford University Press.
Rye, Howard (2014) 'Towards a Black British Jazz: Studies in Acculturation 1860–1935'. In *Black British Jazz: Routes, Ownership and Performance*, ed. Jason Toynbee, Catherine Tackley and Mark Doffman. Farnham: Ashgate.
Shand, John (2009) *Jazz: The Australian Accent*. Sydney: University of New South Wales Press.
Shapiro, Nat, and Nat Hentoff (1955) *Hear Me Talkin' to Ya*. London: Peter Davis.
Sharpe, John (2001) *Don't Worry Baby: They'll Swing their Arses off*. Canberra: Screensound Australia/Australian Jazz Archive.
—(2006) *A Cool Capital: The Canberra Jazz Scene 1925–2005*. Canberra: Canberra Publishing and Printing.
—(2008) *I Wanted to be a Jazz Musician*. Canberra: National Film and Sound Archive.
Starr, S. Frederick (1983) *Red and Hot: The Fate of Jazz in the Soviet Union 1917–1980*. New York and Oxford: Oxford University Press.
Sutcliffe, Mike (1997) 'Sonny Clay and the Coloured Idea'. *Australian Record and Music Review* 35 (October): 3–13.
Walser, Robert (1999) *Keeping Time: Readings in Jazz History*. New York and Oxford: Oxford University Press.
Ward, A. (2009) '"ANZAC, Hollywood and Home": Creating a New Zealand Jazz Culture'. In *Many Voices: Music and National Identity in Aotearoa/New Zealand*, ed. Henry Johnson, 93–102. Newcastle: Cambridge Scholars.
—(2013) 'Fascinating Rhythm: Australian and American Influences on Swing in New Zealand'. In *Shifting Sounds: Musical Flow. A Collection of Papers from the 2012 IASPM Australia/New Zealand Conference*, ed. Oli Wilson and Sarah Attfield, 187–97. Dunedin: IASPM Australia/New Zealand.
Whiteoak, John (1999) *Playing Ad Lib: Improvisatory Music in Australia 1836–1970*. Sydney: Currency Press.
—(2009) 'Across the Big Pond: Mapping Early "Jazz" Activity in New Zealand through Australian Jazz Historiography and Sources'. In *Jazz Aotearoa: Notes Towards a New Zealand History*, ed. Richard Hardie and Allan Thomas, 14–40. Wellington: Steele Roberts.
Williams, Mike (1981) *The Australian Jazz Explosion*. London: Angus & Robertson.

Cultural Contexts

1 Demons of discord down under

'Jump Jim Crow' and 'Australia's first jazz band'

John Whiteoak[*]

> He revels in the coarsest of jests; his language is vile, brutal, horrible; his cowardice is appalling... Possessing these [Sydney Larrikin] characteristics, one can imagine what a horror such a creature is when indulging in the negroic 'cake-walk' ('Our Sydney Letter', 1903[1]).

At 2.30pm on Saturday 22 June 1918, the audience at Ben Fuller's National Theatre in Sydney began to witness a vaudeville act billed as 'Australia's First Jazz Band':

> Belle Sylvia, who possesses a baritone voice of more than ordinary flexibility is accompanied by eccentric musicians, pianist, fiddler, trombonist, saxophonist, and drummer who 'jazzed' for the delight of a crowded house for the best part of half an hour.[2]

In his seminal introductory essay to *The Oxford Companion to Australian Jazz*, Bruce Johnson speculates that 'The knowledge that this was Negro music prepared the spectators for an ambiguous *frission*, a glimpse into a fascinating but disquieting darkness... It undermined morality' (Johnson 1987: 4). Other jazz historians (e.g. Bisset 1979: 9–11) have commented upon the historical significance of this act with the earliest suggesting in 1933 that its conceiver, Ben Fuller, might be considered 'the Founder of Jazz in Australia' (Sheldon 1933: 38). However, contemporary reports of this act, and later discourse concerning it, raise more questions than they answer.

---

[*] John Whiteoak is an Adjunct Professor at Sir Zelman Cowen School of Music, Monash University and writes extensively on Australian jazz-related and other popular music (and dance) topics, including Latin, brass bands, circus, cinema and stage music. His jazz studies PhD was published as *Playing Ad Lib: Improvisatory Music in Australia, 1836–1970* (1999) and he co-edited the *Currency Companion to Music and Dance in Australia* (2003).

1. *The Mercury* (Hobart), 2 May 1903: 7.
2. *The Newsletter: An Australian Paper for Australian People* (Sydney), 29 June 1918: 4.

In the article '"Jazzing" and Australia's First Jazz Band' (Whiteoak 1994: 279–95), I offered a musicological analysis of this act (henceforth as the 'Jazz Band') and its so-called 'jazzing'. I argued that its jazzing was largely the continuity of vocal and instrumental 'ragging' (ragtime improvisation) practice applied to ragtime hits in the context of an imaginative burlesque of the new American craze, 'jazz', with the main novelty aspect of jazzing being clever and extroverted novelty noise-making (especially by the drummer) accompanied by comedic rhythmic body movements and gestures. Yet many of Johnson's writings on jazz in Australia remind us that 'jazz' is both musical performance and culture. 'Until we have a rich jazz cultural historiography, Australian jazz is likely to be regarded and taught as some kind of second-rate and inauthentic copy of something else, rather than an "authentic" organic expression of who we are and where we came from' (Johnson 2004: 15). Moreover, both Johnson and Andrew Bisset have described the early performance and public consumption of so-called 'jazz' in Australia in terms of social action linked to high/low-class social dynamics, morality, and white Australian attitudes to race (Bisset 1974: 48–74; Johnson 2010: 12). A central theme in Johnson's polemic is how the character, development and history of 'jazz' in Australia have been shaped by social, cultural, regional and other influences and events specific to their Australian contexts, including Australian responses to American Jazz Age (ca. 1917–28) popular modernity, and even including residual class dynamics from a convict-era stained past or 'foundational criminality' (Johnson 2000: 10–13; 2004: 8–9).

The specific purpose of this chapter is to revisit Johnson's proposal that the 'spirit' of Australian jazz has its deepest roots in a convict-era stained past, and to argue further that a continuum of African-American-inflected popular entertainment and its performance practices from early colonial blackface minstrelsy to the Australian Jazz Age (ca. 1918–28) functioned as the 'medium' for a type of 'larrikin' (colonial ruffian) spirit that was oppositional to the morality, decorum, aesthetics and other values cherished by the ruling classes and protectors of such values (Bellanta 2012). A continuity of jazz-related African-American inflection in popular entertainment over this period was detailed from a musicological perspective in my PhD study of what I define as 'improvisatory music' in nineteenth- and twentieth-century Australia (Whiteoak 1993), later published as *Playing Ad Lib: Improvisatory Music in Australia, 1836–1970* (Whiteoak 1999). While there is no intention of re-presenting that research for the present study, two concepts developed for that work, 'improvisatory music' and 'imitation ecstatic' performance behaviour, are essential to understanding the musicological significance of the relationship between African-American inflection in performance practice and performance behaviour in pre-jazz Australia and the 'jazzing' of Australia's Jazz Age.

The concept of 'improvisatory music' (music or musical practice *pertaining* to what is widely but imprecisely perceived to be 'improvisation') reverses the contentious notion that 'real' improvisation can somehow be defined by select criteria by inviting the question: what categories of music or music-making are *not* 'improvisatory' in one way or another? More specifically, it embraces a continuum of musical practices ranging from Charles Keil's so-called 'participatory discrepancies' to the most spontaneous, indeterminate or 'open' forms of music-making imaginable (Whiteoak 1999: xii–xiii). Participatory discrepancies include barely perceptible but expressive surface embellishments, ornamentations, timbral variegations, rhythmic displacements and 'grooves' and other unscored alterations or creative 'noise'-making that are the musical signatures of individual performers, ensembles or acts (Keil 1994: 104). Spirited jazz, blues or rock performances, for example, are saturated with participatory discrepancies. Expressive or spirited interpolations or alterations in the performance of African-American inflected popular music and dance idioms became known as 'ragging' before the Jazz Age, as either 'ragging' or 'jazzing' for several years into Australia's Jazz Age, and thereon to the late 1920s as 'jazzing' (Whiteoak 1999: 111–239).

'Imitation-ecstatic' performance behaviour is performance that delineates qualities perceived to be associated with authentically ecstatic (and therefore improvisatory) performance behaviour, such as, say, black gospel singing or fervent traditional West African dancing or drumming (Whiteoak 1999: xiv). 'Imitation-ecstatic' particularly applies to blackface (white) minstrels delineating African-Americans as 'happy darkies', later urban-raised black (African-American) minstrels delineating the 'cakewalking' of plantation slaves or, for that matter, the 'jazzing' of the 1918 Jazz Band, and even later jazzing. Imitation-ecstatic performance behaviour is a traditional aspect of stagecraft and therefore presents in many other staged forms, such as wild 'Gypsy' campfire or Jewish wedding dance scenes. However, even as stagecraft, it can be both imitation-ecstatic and improvisatory. 'Imitation-ecstatic', moreover, does not preclude some interpolation of performance behaviour that might, in fact, relate to the socio-cultural history of the performer and is therefore not imitative.

Closely related to 'imitation-ecstatic' is the notion of 'grotesque' performance which is frequently encountered in Australian and other pre-jazz sources in relation to blackface and black minstrelsy. This had two related meanings: what was perceived to be the essentially primal nature of black slave-plantation performance behaviour and the more general meanings of comic distortion, parody or burlesque (Whiteoak 1999: 88). A prime example is the now infamous 'Jump Jim Crow' minstrel song and dance act which contributed to characterizing the African-American's future role in entertainment as typically 'grotesque, shuffling, peculiar, eccentric, jumping, loose-limbed, awkward, funny and, of course, rhythmic' (Emery 1988: 185).

Jump Jim Crow

The main nineteenth-century manifestation of African-American inflection in the popular entertainment of the English-speaking world was blackface minstrelsy by white artists in burnt-cork makeup, and its immense popularity enabled many African-Americans to contribute creatively to the genre after the American Civil War. As a theatrical genre, minstrelsy is widely, if inaccurately, perceived to have its origins in a solo blackface stage-song and dance act called 'Jump Jim Crow', invented and first performed in America around 1830 (the exact date is disputed) by Thomas Dartmouth ('Daddy') Rice (Lhamon 2003: 33).

Figure 1: Cover of 'Jump Jim Crow', published by Firth & Hall, New York (n.d.). Courtesy of the Lester S. Levy Collection of Sheet Music, The Sheridan Libraries, The Johns Hopkins University.

The act was supposedly based on the vernacular speech and afflicted body movements of a deformed and shabbily dressed African-American stable-hand whom Rice had observed singing a catchy quatrain with the couplet, 'Wheel about and turn about and do jis so, An eb'ry time I wheel about I jump Jim Crow', and dancing in a most peculiar way with an eccentric 'jump' at the end of each repetition of the couplet (see Figure 1). Whatever the truth of the provenance of his act (or that of the contemporaneous appeal of something so abhorrent to present-day sensibilities), the fame of Rice and his 'Jump Jim Crow' quickly spread around the globe. It was being reported in colonial Australia by 1833[3] and frequently performed there from 1838[4] as a song and dance act and bright and lively instrumental and dance tune, seemingly too lively for some circumstances:

> Captain Angerstein...desired a man [be] placed on the dickey [seat] with his key bugle to strike up the air of 'Jim Crow', ...but had not played many notes when the animals...started off at a tremendous rate...[and] dashed the carriage with fearful [and fatal] violence against a lamp-post...[5]

The influence of Rice's 'Jump Jim Crow' reached the Australian colonies mostly via Britain, where he toured with phenomenal success in 1836 and later. The craze was such that Prince Albert was reported in Australia as having purchased a parrot that sings the 'first verse of "Jim Crow" and afterwards whistles and jumps in a most ludicrous manner'.[6] 'Jump Jim Crowism' and 'twistification' entered Australian colonial vernacular to depict the action of politicians or others turning back on their word, and Jim Crow hats, pipes, statuettes and other 'Jim Crow' items were widely advertised in the colonial press. The astonishing global spread in popularity of this minstrel action-song was probably not equalled proportionally until the 1910s' introduction of Irving Berlin's 'Alexander's Ragtime Band' triggered its own global popular music revolution, as discussed below. The *Boston Post* reported on 25 May 1840 that 'The two most popular characters in the world at the present time are Victoria and Jim Crow' (cited in Cockrell 1997: 66). Russell Sanjek suggests that Rice 'enjoyed a fame not unlike Elvis Presley in the late 1950s' (Sanjek 1988: 164–65).

The success of blackface minstrelsy as entertaining stagecraft was largely dependent on the cleverness of delineation, humorous parody or burlesque

3. *Sydney Gazette and New South Wales Advertiser*, 5 October 1833: 3.
4. *Colonial Times* (Hobart), 9 January 1838: 2.
5. *Colonial Times*, 24 December 1839: 6.
6. *Southern Australian*, 23 July 1841: 4.

based on white perceptions of slave-plantation or urban black culture. Rice and the most talented of his colleagues were appreciated as brilliant delineators and humourists. However, African-American minstrels who later entered the field were often seen as just playing their African-American selves on stage, making for example 'the music of nature untrammeled by art or any degree of affectation' (an 1865 quote in Toll 1974: 202). Australia's first blackface minstrels were basically multi-talented immigrant or ex-convict British actors cleverly engaging with a profitable aspect of African-American inflected American popular modernity, just as professional Australian theatre and dance musicians would do in Australia's Jazz Age and had done previously with cakewalk music and other ragtime craze subgenres (Whiteoak 1999: 111–67).

Australia's Jim Crow era: 1838–49

Seemingly, the first of many subsequent colonial 'Jump Jim Crow' performances was presented at the Theatre Royal, Hobart, in January 1838 and colonial theatres with socially homogeneous audiences remained the most common forum for blackface minstrelsy until the 1850s.[7] In early 1839, a 'celebrated drama' popularized by Rice in England called 'Jim Crow, or Flight to America' was presented at the Victoria Theatre, Sydney, with a 'Chorus of Negros' and the 'Jump Jim Crow' act.[8] Minstrel songs, dances and blackface characters like Jim Crow or Zip Coon were often worked into colonial productions. However, the first decade of blackface minstrelsy in Australia mainly comprised solo variety song (or song and dance) acts such as 'Jump Jim Crow', 'Sich a Gettin up Stairs', 'Jim Along Josey', 'Coal Black Rose' or 'Gumbo Chaff', many of which had been popularized by Rice, along with solo dance acts including 'The Grapevine Twist' and 'Juba Dance'.

'[Negro] glees' were sometimes presented and a locally written melodrama called *The Negro's Vengeance: A Tale of the Barbadoes* [sic] was staged in Maitland during 1845,[9] but the earliest resemblance to the structured minstrel shows that later toured Australia was probably the minstrelsy-based shows presented by the famous colonial actor, fiddler, dancer, comedian, theatrical entrepreneur and blackface minstrel, George Coppin, at his Sydney entertainment 'saloon' during 1844.[10] This was only fifteen months after the Virginia Minstrels premiered at the Chatham Theatre, New York, and precipi-

7. *Colonial Times*, 9 January 1838: 2.
8. *The Australian* (Sydney), 9 April 1839: 3.
9. *Maitland Mercury and Hunter River General Advertiser* (NSW), 2 August 1845: 3.
10. *Sydney Morning Herald*, 8 June 1844: 1.

tated a global 'minstrel show' craze with immense implications for African-American inflected musical entertainment. Small minstrel companies began to arrive from overseas and assemble locally from 1849, but previous colonial minstrelsy had been largely dominated by the influence of Rice and acts were sometimes claimed to have been performed as Rice performed them, or even better: '"Clare the Kitchen" was sung [by Mr Phillips] in the real [Negro] style. Rice, the celebrated Jim Crow, is outrivaled.'[11]

Demons of disorder
What, then, are some conceivable connections or analogies between this 'Jim Crow era' of colonial minstrelsy and early 'jazz' in Australia? Here, it is possible to point to cultural and social themes addressed by the work of Bisset and, especially, Johnson: namely, class dynamics, engagement with popular modernity, and Australian racism. Social historian, Bisset, whose work was influenced by the Marxist intellectual, Humphrey McQueen, states that 'jazz bubbled up from the lower classes' (Bisset 1979: 39) and claims that colonial era 'labouring classes' had a 'mania for [Negro] minstrelsy' (Bisset 1974: 3). He also discusses the association of early jazz in Australia with borderline criminality and cultural elements perceived by the conservative classes as immoral, tasteless and even 'evil' (Bisset 1974: 45–62). Johnson takes this argument further with his suggestion that early 'jazz' in Australia was an example of an 'oppositional subculture' that led back to our foundational criminality and 'took over the spirit of convict and treason songs' (Johnson 2004: 9).

There is, in fact, some primary source evidence that ninety years or so years before the 1918 Jazz Band the 'Negro' music and dance of the Jim Crow era were perceived to be associated with lowbrow taste, criminality, antisocial behaviour, disdain for authority and the undermining of morality. 'English Extracts' in the colonial newspapers colourfully reinforced these perceptions. 'Music and Gin' describes a seedy London 'gin palace' where Jim Crow, played by a mechanical instrument, is accompanied by old women. It concludes that 'None but an eye-witness can imagine the effect of the music on the motley group assembled in this [place]'.[12] Another report describes the hanging of a murderer who, instead of repenting, rebelliously went to the gallows 'jumping, dancing, and singing "Turn about and wheel about, and do just so, everytime I turns about I jumps Jim Crow."'[13] A more light-hearted extract relates to the street arrest of a man 'with his face blackened and a negro cap upon his head, singing "Jim Crow" as loud as his lungs would enable him. [And]

11. *Sydney Gazette and New South Wales Advertiser*, 27 January 1842: 2.
12. *Hobart Town Courier*, 13 April 1838: 4.
13. *Sydney Monitor and Commercial Advertiser*, 24 November 1841: 4.

throwing himself into the most grotesque attitudes.' On being locked up, he defiantly 'indulged for the greater part of the night in singing "Jim Crow" and "Yankee Doodle", and nothing could stop him'.[14]

Local reports also sometimes link 'Jim Crow' and 'Negro' minstrelsy to defiance of authority, anti-social activity, and lowlife venues probably on a par with the legendary New Orleans brothels where some claim that jazz was born. Immediately below a 1838 Sydney report of a convict sentenced to two months 'working the treadmill' is that of police entering a low dive 'assailed by horrible fiddling and drumming' where they encountered 'a little shop-boy dressed as Jim Crow, looking very much like a dirty chimney sweep on a Mayday, who was immediately bundled into custody...'[15] An 1839 article, 'Life in Pitt Street [Sydney]' complains about how 'young strangers, *Bacchipleni*, were amusing the out-of-door theatricals with *Jim Crow* in all its characteristics of ragged coat and roofless hat... [a] thoughtless display of depravity and mischief'.[16] A later letter contributed by a long-suffering resident of Pitt Street, Sydney complains of police inability to suppress loud and 'horrid' piano-playing and 'musical [Negro]' songs, such as 'Jim Crow', emanating from a nearby grog shop, along with the 'howlings of the lost, their blasphemies and wailings [and]...the realities of shrieks, obscenity, and brutal outrages'.[17]

Further complaints about minstrelsy were concerned with the 'vulgar' nature of Jim Crow lyrics which presumably were perceived to somehow undermine the morality or aesthetics of 'decent people', for example: 'A mass of vulgar buffoonery and impiety called "Jim Crow", has been sung several times, but we trust the managers will not allow the ears of decent people to be annoyed by it any more',[18] or 'we must say that the contemptible and witless "[Negro] scene" which followed should never have been produced, even if it does gratify the worthless taste of the dirty ragamuffins'.[19]

Jim Crow-era Australia was a geographically fragmented frontier society founded on criminality, enforcement of good behaviour and deep ruling-class fear of disorder, sedition, rebellion and rampant depravity. Ruling-class fear of plebeian rebellion, for example, proved to be well-founded at the American-influenced Eureka rebellion, an event still deeply seared into the Australian psyche. In early colonial society that included many serving or emancipated penal 'slaves' and struggling immigrants and exhibited much crime, despera-

14. *The Australian* (Sydney), 7 September 1838: 4.
15. *Sydney Herald*, 28 January 1839: 2.
16. *The Colonist* (Sydney), 28 August 1839: 3.
17. *Sydney Morning Herald*, 6 March 1848: 3.
18. *Sydney Herald*, 12 September 1838: 2.
19. *Australasian Chronicle* (Sydney), 2 April 1842: 2.

tion, immorality and drunkenness, Jim Crow depicted a ragged cripple from the lowest stratum or 'underbelly' of pre-Civil War American society. Verse lyrics vary greatly between published versions of 'Jump Jim Crow' and, as Cockrell suggests in *Demons of Disorder*, portray Crow as an absurdly boastful, fighting, drinking, womanizing, black criminal lowlife:

> In summary, there was considerable overlap between Jim Crow and his audience. He can be tied (somewhat obliquely to be sure) to a culture of fisticuffs, riotous drinking, gambling, general rowdiness, and (perhaps) cohabitation without need or benefit of legal or religious sanction (Cockrell 1997: 70).

Another important factor is that this 'Negro music' was also improvisatory. It was a vehicle for spontaneous, partly pre-conceived or pre-conceived verses in (supposedly) Negro dialect on topical subjects (Cockrell 1997: 71) in a colonial era when playscripts required approval from the colonial authorities to ensure the absence of seditious or immoral content. Furthermore, 'gagging', the spontaneous interpolation of dialogue (or puns), was an essential art for early colonial actors because of rapidly changing programmes with minimal rehearsals. Topical 'extemporized song' was already a feature of the colonial stage even before 'Jump Jim Crow' was introduced.[20] Therefore, topical illusions interpolated in 'Negro dialect' as 'additional verses'[21] could be presented as playful humour or ridicule that subverted the authority, moral prescriptions and even the aesthetics of the ruling classes. In fact, a satirical version of 'Jump Jim Crow' with political references was contributed to a Sydney newspaper even before the act was performed there.[22] Other popular minstrel songs of this era, such as 'Zip Coon' or 'Sich a Gettin Up Stairs', had a similar verse-refrain structure that invited topical gagging.

Demons of dissonance
'Jump Jim Crow' and various other minstrel songs of the era were performed in ways that were comparable to both ecstatic and 'imitation-ecstatic' jazz performance in terms of their 'hot' surface characteristics or 'discrepancies' and therefore flew in the face of classical music aesthetics. The songs are, for example, sometimes billed as screeched forth, not sung,[23] as in the following colonial advertisement: 'MR. HOWARD will appear in that mirth-provoking, care dispelling, laughing, joking, tough yarn telling, screaming, roaring, jump-

20. *Sydney Herald*, 18 September 1834: 1.
21. *Sydney Monitor and Commercial Advertiser*, 1 October 1840: 3.
22. *Sydney Herald*, 31 August 1837: 6.
23. *Sydney Morning Herald*, 8 June 1844: 1.

ing, soaring, yelling, screeching, quelling, preaching, [Negro] Melody, "Sittin' on a Rail".[24] The rhythmic interpolation of nonsense or broken syllables that became a feature of vocal ragging and later 'scat singing' in jazz are present in one of the earliest and most popular blackface songs and jig tunes to be published, 'Zip Coon', better known as 'Turkey in the Straw'. Cockrell suggests that 'its infectious melody and sharply accented rhythms bespeak motion, dancing, perhaps sex, and a "good time" generally...it might have been that "Zip Coon" was [like jazz] associated with brothel life from the first' (Cockrell 1997: 94).

As instrumental music, and therefore devoid of 'vulgar' lyrics, this 'Negro music' was probably often enjoyed across social divides. For example, a journalist attending an 1838 Sydney Regatta commented that 'Decidedly the most amusing performance of the day in the musical way, was that of..."Jim Crow", by the Brass Band; it was received...with unbounded applause...'[25] One wonders how the music was played to make it 'amusing', unless it was 'jazzed-up' in some way. Another report evokes what could almost be an early black jazz marching-band scenario but, instead, with colonial military 'slave masters' employing 'Negro' music as extroverted musical gestures of vulgar impropriety and subversion of authority:

> Colonel Wodehouse refused to allow the Band of the 50th Regt. to play in the Barrack Square on Sunday afternoons, from a supposed desire to keep sacred that day. So far good. On Sunday last however, when the congregation was about leaving St. Phillips Church, the band and soldiers of the above regiment came out, and after forming, marched off to the enlivening tune of 'Jumping Jim Crow'.[26]

Johnson points out that 'In both idea and practice, jazz came into being through negotiation with the vehicles of its dissemination and with the conditions it encountered in any given location... Each diasporic site presented its own distinctive conditioning features' (Johnson 2002: 39). If it can be accepted that the historically deepest roots of the 'idea and practice' of jazz in Australia drew cultural and musicological sustenance from the specific 'conditions' and contingencies of the Jim Crow era, then Johnson's contention of 'jazz' in Australia as an 'oppositional subculture' leading back to 'foundational criminality' and 'the spirit of convict and treason songs' is, so far, supported by the above examination of early 'Negro' minstrelsy of the penal colonies era.

24. *Geelong Advertiser*, 21 July 1849: 3.
25. *Sydney Monitor and Commercial Advertiser*, 21 December 1838: 1.
26. *Sydney Monitor*, 2 May 1838: 2.

This 'early era' more or less ended in early 1850 when the Blythe Waterland Minstrels from England opened at the Royal Hotel, Sydney, and precipitated a colonial minstrel-show craze.[27] The Waterlands' own perceptions of the new 'Negro' minstrelsy correspond fascinatingly to later perceptions of the sweeping 1910s introduction of Irving Berlin-style ragtime and Jazz-Age white 'jazz'; namely, that superior new styles innovated by white figures such as Berlin, Art Hickman or Paul Whiteman eliminated crude and vulgar 'Negro' elements and 'polished' their music to white perfection:

> Rice's performances were, to the English, novel, quaint and humorous; their very absurdity helped to make them palatable for anything is excusable in a [Negro]; they were, however, vulgar. Since that time, fresh aspirants—artistes in black—have come among us, somewhat reducing the rude vulgarity of the American slaves' characteristic singing and dancing, and humorously introducing fresh and 'scientific' peculiarities. Several individuals, disdaining to be 'Jim Crows', struck out for themselves more refined characters, with vocal and instrumental performances, with dancing to boot, quite above the more rough, and boisterous, and uncouth feats of Rice... the original personifier of the drollery of the clown of colour. But it remained for the Ethiopian Serenaders to bring '[Negro] music' to perfection.[28]

Near the beginning of the Jazz Age, *Graphic of Australia* explained that 'the crude plantation Negro jazz idea was taken by men of musical learning... Jazz [was] brightened, polished up, and brought to perfection'.[29]

The early minstrel show era: 'demons' who harmonized

> The history of jazz...does not begin with ragtime, Negro spirituals, or the songs of early popular theatre, but with a few dozen [blackface minstrel] banjo tunes which have the flavour of the plantation (Nathan 1962: 213).

The 1850s brought an entirely new era of minstrelsy to the colonies in which an unfamiliar and unorthodox form of 'Negro music' ensemble suddenly entered colonial popular entertainment, just as the Jazz Band did in 1918. The fiddle, the bone-castanets and the tambourine supposedly represent-

27. *Sydney Morning Herald*, 6 April 1850: 1.
28. *Bell's Life in Sydney and Sporting Reviewer*, 27 April 1850: 3.
29. 'The Music World', *Graphic of Australia*, 23 March 1922: 11.

ing instruments played in slave plantation ensembles were already familiar to 1850s colonial audiences, just as the core instruments of the 1918 Jazz Band were familiar to its audiences. The minstrel banjo was however a brand new musical novelty and the improvisatory way that the banjo and the percussion instruments in particular were combined in minstrel show performance to portray or parody 'primitive' or 'grotesque' slave plantation music (Whiteoak 1999: 86–108) was unfamiliar, entertaining, amusing, bright, uplifting and immensely popular. In mid-1850, Melbourne's *The Argus* declared 'the whole town alive with the notes of the banjo and the rattle of the bones; and leading us in our astonishment as [to] the extent of the sable invasion'.[30]

THE ETHIOPIAN SERENADERS.

Figure 2: A blackface minstrel orchestra in 'imitation-ecstatic' mode. *The Illustrated London News*, 24 January 1846: 61. State Library of Victoria Newspaper Collection.

Illustrations of early minstrel show orchestras depicted in imitation-ecstatic musical flight often bear a striking resemblance to various illustrations and posed photographs of early Australian 'jazz bands' (see Figure 2). The sound of the small unorthodox minstrel 'orchestra' was saturated with participatory discrepancies, especially in the noisy, colourful (but not loud) minstrel 'overture' that opened the show and the noisy banjo, bones and tambourine driven finale of many colonial minstrel shows, called the 'Railway

30. *The Argus* (Melbourne), 17 July 1850: 2. Sadly and ironically, the white 'invasion' had already decimated Victoria's black population.

Overture'.[31] An 1845 playbill description of this finale brings to mind the 'hot' final chorus in jazz: '[it is the] imitation of the slocomotive bullgine, dat at de fust ob de beginning is very moderate, den as de steam rises, de power of de circumvolution exaggerates itself into a can'tstopimization, and runs clar ob de track [and explodes]' (Winans 1984: 90).

What appealed most to colonial audiences about the minstrel orchestra instruments and how they were played solo, in various combinations, and in song and dance accompaniment was not so much what was perceived as the 'primitive' nature of these 'plantation' instruments as the cleverness of the white artists in being able to extract very entertaining and even virtuosic music from them: 'Mr Knight really brings music out of that primitive instrument, the banjo, and does it too with a lightness and swiftness of touch, absolutely astonishing.'[32] What further fascinated their audiences was the sheer incongruity of opposing musical elements in the minstrel show: 'each instrument differed. The overture or other introductory music, mingling the soft and harsh of such heterogeneous instruments, pleased as much by the unanticipated effect.'[33] The irreverence of such juxtaposition is seen in the popular minstrel show genre, opera burlesque (opera sung straight and then in plantation dialect),[34] which might also be thought of as a precursor to vocal ragging, or even 'ragging the classics' (Whiteoak 1999: 90–91).

British Christy-style minstrelsy, with its emphasis on exquisitely tuneful minstrel part-singing, opera burlesque and dazzling musicianship, became dominant in the 1860s. A resurgence of American influence in the 1870s brought back some of the earlier emphasis on plantation material but it was increasingly watered down and displaced by variety acts and other entertainments or retained as 'old-time' minstrelsy segments of speciality company programmes (Waterhouse 1990: 40–44). Nevertheless, the blackface minstrel show as a concept and dynamic improvisatory format for entertainment remained a popular anachronism until, and well beyond, the Jazz Age, especially as an amateur minstrel-club activity.

'Georgia' or 'colored' minstrelsy

Medium to large black American so-called 'Georgia' or 'coloured' minstrel companies began to tour Australia from the late 1870s (Waterhouse 1990: 64–95). These included Corbyn's Original Georgia Minstrels (1886–89), Hicks'

---

31. *Sydney Morning Herald*, 16 October 1851: 1.
32. *Geelong Advertiser*, 10 July 1850: 2.
33. *The Courier*, 19 March 1851: 3.
34. *The Empire* (Sydney), 30 March 1863: 4.

Original Georgia Minstrels (1887–89), Mastodon Minstrels (1889–93) and Hicks-Sawyer Minstrels (1888–91) as well as ongoing tours of black jubilee singing companies claiming association with the world-famous Fisk Jubilee Singers. Mid-1899 brought the almost simultaneous arrival of two large black companies, McAdoo's Genuine Georgia Minstrels and Alabama Cake Walkers and Curtis's Grand African-American Carnival featuring cakewalk dancing and music, syncopated 'coon-song' (early ragtime song) and 'rag-time opera' (Whiteoak 1993: 275–90).

Far more than just a re-injection of plantation delineation onto the Australian popular stage, the black minstrels were initially promoted as 'former slaves' or from the 'slave states'—living exhibits of plantation life, customs and culture. Corbyn's, the first company to arrive, was billed as 'REAL COLORED MEN From the Slave States of America, [who] will Appear in an ENTERTAINMENT, Portraying the peculiarities of Negro Life on the Plantation'.[35] Hicks, the following company, claimed to have many former slaves and therefore was 'enabled to present the most truthful picture of slavery days'.[36]

Visual and sonic imaginings of the first black minstrels to appear on the colonial popular stage might bring to mind Johnson's speculation regarding the Jazz Band as 'a glimpse into a fascinating but disquieting darkness'. Instead, however, there were complaints that, unlike the uniform blackness of blackface minstrels, the Corbyn cast was 'piebald' (an ongoing complaint with black minstrelsy) with some being near-white and others blacked-up with burnt cork. There were also complaints that the 'orchestra' of fiddle, banjo, bones, tambourine and piano was inadequate and 'spoiled' the vocal items[37] and that the 'witticisms' were too derivative of burnt-cork minstrelsy.[38] One critic went further: 'I prefer artificial minstrels, as being both more amusing and more musical. I do not think I have heard anything as discordant as the Georgia's choruses since I listened to the excruciating agony of a Japanese fiddle'.[39] Not all reviews were this negative since they were perceived as possessing the attribute of being the 'real thing': '[the company's] speciality being its realistic nature, and freedom from the mere burlesque which usually characterises such performances'.[40]

35. *Newcastle Morning Herald and Miners' Advocate*, 15 December 1876: 3.
36. *The Argus* (Melbourne), 8 June 1878: 12.
37. *The Goulburn Herald and Chronicle*, 14 March 1877: 2.
38. *The Argus*, 5 June 1877: 6.
39. *The Australasian* (Melbourne), 9 June 1877: 19.
40. *Illustrated Sydney News and New South Wales Agriculturalist and Grazier*, 6 January 1877: 14.

Of the later (initially) more successful Hicks troupe, it was observed that 'Their movements are very fantastic, and they bound from their seats and play their bones and tambourines in attitudes that none but india rubber men or marionnettes could imitate'.[41] Another form of grotesque self-distortion that greatly amused colonial audiences played upon the cruel and enduring stereotype of African-Americans as having grotesquely large mouths: 'mouths that we have seen painted on signboards or caricatured in comic prints, but such as we have never before seen in the flesh'.[42]

Black 'rag-time' minstrelsy
The two large black companies, McAdoo's Genuine Georgia Minstrels and Alabama Cake Walkers, and Curtis's Grand African-American Carnival, who both arrived in mid-1899 brought the very latest in early ragtime-era popular entertainment (Whiteoak 1999: 131–34). It also included the already famous 'coon-song' artists Billy McClain and Ernest Hogan, pioneer of vocal ragging and composer of the immensely popular but controversial coon-song, 'All Coons Look Alike to Me' (1896) which references black female promiscuity. Coon-song lyrics and music cover illustrations increasingly depicted postbellum African-Americans as flashy, gluttonous, gambling-addicted, grotesquely ugly, razor-wielding, dangerously oversexed and 'rhythmic': the so-called 'hot coon' stereotype (Whitcomb 1987: 100).

Critics do not refer to anything immoral or otherwise offensive about either companies' programmes and even the suggestiveness of Hogan's 'rag-time opera' character, 'Rastus Hotbone the Interloper', escaped scrutiny (Whiteoak 1999: 123). The black visitors were however subsequently blamed for the evils perceived to be associated with the introduction of 'the abomination known as the "cake walk", introduced to Sydney by negro entertainers. The thing is dreadful enough in the low-class dance-rooms.'[43] Members of the next and final large-scale black minstrel company to tour Australia, Hugo's Colored Minstrels, were, at one point of their tour, refused accommodation on colour 'taboo' grounds[44] and had earlier been bashed by racist thugs and accused of miscegenation by the gutter press in headlines such as 'Black Bucks and White Wantons'.[45] Yet white Australian perceptions of black American artists were far more varied, shifting and nuanced than these extremely racist events suggest.

41. *South Australian Chronicle and Weekly Mail* (Adelaide), 13 October 1877: 15.
42. *South Australian Chronicle and Weekly Mail*, 13 October 1877: 15.
43. *The Mercury* (Hobart), 2 May 1903: 7.
44. *Albury Banner and Wodonga Express* (NSW), 6 December 1912: 20.
45. *The Truth* (Melbourne), 23 November 1912: 5.

Racism and racial stereotyping

American blackface and black minstrelsy has been well researched from musicological, theatre studies and cultural and sociological perspectives and, in particular, deeply and imaginatively theorized specifically from racial stereotyping perspectives by, for example, Lott (1993), Cockrell (1997) and Lhamon (2003). Racial stereotyping in British minstrelsy is exhaustively theorized by Michael Pickering, who argues that the belief in British superiority over 'benighted savages but also over other Europeans' was a key element in the ideology of late nineteenth-century British 'conscious imperialism' which hardened attitudes towards the 'lower races' and therefore produced harsher stereotyping of black artists in British minstrelsy (Pickering 2007: 112–20).

While Australia was a collection of British colonies until 1901, its social, cultural and political history was, however, significantly different to Britain, including its national birth in convictism, its strong trajectory towards a more egalitarian society, racial anxieties that were focused upon the Asia-Pacific region (see Scott-Maxwell in this issue) as well as its own black Australian population,[46] plus a theatrical entertainments culture that was far more profoundly inflected by American popular culture, especially via the Pacific entertainment circuit.

These differences no doubt mediated British-Australian reception of British and American minstrelsy racial stereotypes in various ways and, while there were shocking individual examples of Australian racism towards black American artists, there were also ample examples of the reverse, such as public adoration of black minstrels who remained on the Australian stage after their companies departed; intermarriage (Waterhouse 1990: 147–49); and the curious example of the combined white Australian and black American touring troupe formed in late 1913 as Hugo's New Minstrels after the financial collapse of Hugo's Colored Minstrels.[47] Waterhouse summarizes that, while white Australians perceived themselves to belong to a superior race, they were 'willing to allow black Americans greater freedom of action and experience

---

46. Very few Australian references equate minstrel stereotyping with Indigenous Australians. One oblique example is an 1843 minstrel advertisement mentioning that 'The "Juber Dance" is a characteristic of the "Long Island [Negros]" of America as the corroboree is of the native blacks of this colony' (*Sydney Morning Herald*, 6 July 1844: 3). However, Richard Waterhouse cites several examples in Australian literature in which Aborigines speak in minstrel dialect and he concludes 'that to some extent, at least, the prism through which Australians viewed Aborigines was one which was cut by the minstrels' (Waterhouse 1990: 100). There is also evidence of Indigenous Australians, themselves, identifying with the lyrics of coon-songs. See Breen (1989: 22–28).

47. *Cobram Courier* (Victoria), 8 January 1914: 4.

than was possible for Negroes in the United States' (Waterhouse 1990: 149). Pickering's summary of racial stereotyping in British blackface minstrelsy is, however, also valid for both Australia and America: 'blackface clowning must finally be seen as supporting rather than subverting the racialized values that underpinned the whole process of blacking-up... Blackface then operated as nothing other than comic racial mocking' (Pickering 2007: 158).

Demonic 'negroid' influences before jazz

One 1918 Melbourne reviewer described the music of the Jazz Band as 'full of devilment'[48] but there was no suggestion that its jazzing represented any moral danger for the Australian public. Yet the notion that jazz, as Johnson puts it, 'undermined morality' rapidly became an issue for Australian society, albeit primarily in relation to dancing (also called 'jazzing') to Jazz-Age dance music. Johnson has exhaustively explored the nexus between Jazz-Age 'jazz', 'jazzing' as dancing and morality (Johnson 2000: 69–76) and the remainder of this chapter reflects upon how some comparable issues were addressed in earlier Australian engagements with African-American inflected music and dance culture.

This chapter commenced with discussion of what Cockrell describes in *Demons of Disorder* as the 'anti-music' of Jim Crow-era minstrelsy: 'They heard the musics of the blackface and they proclaimed it was noise' (Cockrell 1997: 168). But while this 'noise' was often perceived to be of low origins and associated with crudity, degradation, indecorum, indecency and immorality, it became, like jazz, immensely popular. Moreover, just as early 'jazz' was as much about dance as music, the language of minstrelsy was equally about the semiotics of minstrel dance as (supposed) delineation or burlesque of genuinely ecstatic Negro dance: Rice's 'world...was of the movement and the body—not at all like that of the middle class or elite classes, with their cerebral fixation on delayed gratification, restraint, and discipline' (Cockrell 1997: 70).

The mostly absent American Negro male, as such, obviously posed no direct moral or other threat to Jim Crow-era colonial society, but he was often projected as a figure of ridicule and mirth in the colonial press even before the first colonial Jim Crow appeared, especially through parody of plantation vernacular which was, for whatever reason, considered hilarious.[49] The vernacular of black Australians was similarly ridiculed in later literature and in the captions of racist cartoons in magazines such as *The Bulletin* or *Smith's Weekly*. Waterhouse mentions how the popularity of *Uncle Tom's Cabin* as a novel and

---

48. *Daily Herald* (Adelaide), 19 August 1918: 5.
49. See, for example, 'Sambo's Servant', *Hobart Town Courier*, 28 June 1828: 3.

stage productions later evoked some colonial empathy for the plight of African-Americans (Waterhouse 1990: 72). The tours of jubilee singers as docile, fine-looking and talented black Christians also counterbalanced some of the fear and loathing of the 'coloured races' that spawned literature such as the *Yellow Wave* (McKay 1895), the shamefully racist 1928 film, *The Birth of White Australia*[50] and, the same year, the expulsion of the first black American jazz band to reach Australia, Sonny Clay's Plantation Orchestra, supposedly over accusations of miscegenation and drugs (Johnson 2010).

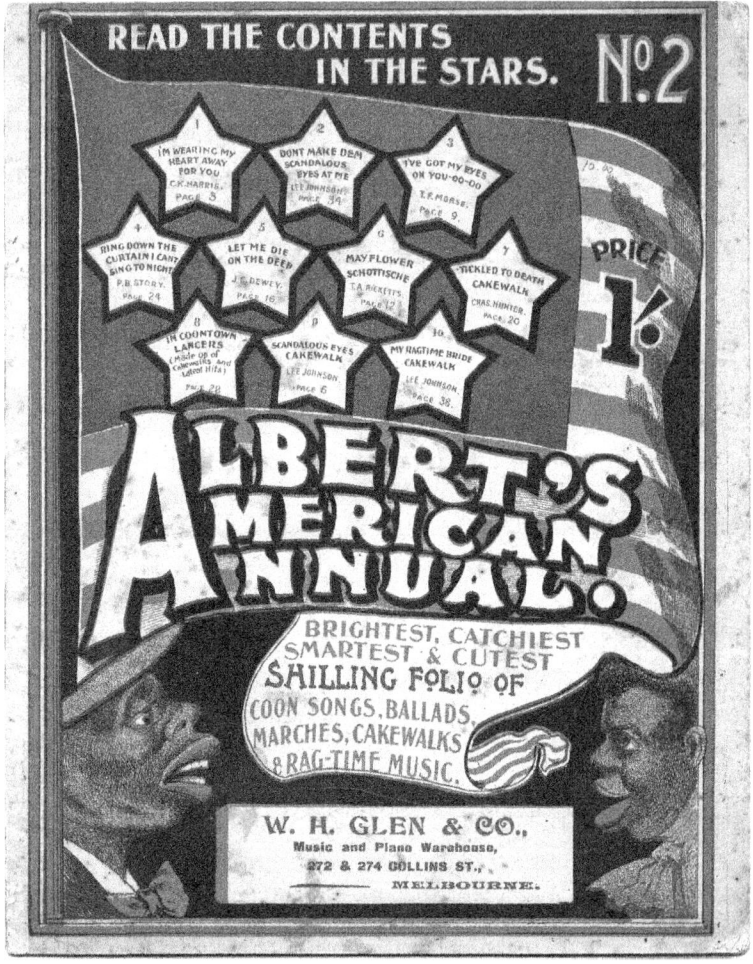

Figure 3: Cover of *Albert's American Annual* no. 2, 1905. Published by Albert & Son, Sydney (Author's Australiana sheet music collection).

50. Dir. Phil K. Walsh, Dominion Films, Australia.

However, the introduction of coon-songs from the 1880s and, with it, the increasing depiction of African-Americans as ugly, violent, compulsive, immoral and so forth was a counter influence to accrued empathy or respect. It is hard to gauge the exact extent to which Australians were influenced by the negative 'coon' stereotypes but there is ample evidence that they were, for example, in the cover illustrations (see Figure 3), titles and lyrics of locally-composed or arranged coon-songs and the linking of the cakewalk to immoral or degenerate behaviour in language reminiscent of Jim Crow-era complaints, especially with regards to cakewalk dancing:

> We talk of a white Australia; but a great many of our people 'cotton' to the dark-skinned ladies and gentlemen who hail from the American States, imitating them as much as possible, singing their coon songs, dancing their 'cake-walks', talking their 'twang', and, in fact playing the musical darkey to the life. No wonder these dusky folks like Sydney. They hear everywhere the music of the cake-walks; they see the young girls of a certain type going through the senseless 'steps' on the pavement, and being brought before the magistrates for making themselves an abominable nuisance. The young men and boys whistle the dreadful 'tunes' in the streets until sensitive musical people are driven nearly mad.[51]

As a ballroom dance, the cakewalk and its liberating practice of creating improvisatory whole-body movements and gestures to rhythm, as opposed to following a sequence of steps, represented a pivotal shift in Australian social dance development that opened the way for the freely expressive ragtime and jazz dancing or 'jazzing' (Whiteoak 1999: 122–24, 150–53). Cakewalking and later forms of ragtime dancing, so-called 'freak' dancing, were perceived to seriously 'undermine morality'. A 1904 Melbourne report, 'Half-Naked Women for Obscene Observation: The Carnal Cake Walk', suggested that:

> All the lynching of blacks in America are punishments for bestiality, and some of the [Negro] bestiality manifests itself in the cakewalk which respectable Australian mothers allow their daughters to learn and perform... Every movement in the 'Cake Walk' has an indecent meaning and is a representation, from beginning to end, of a couple who are working out with frenzy a licentious sexual scheme.[52]

From 1911, the new Irving Berlin-style 'ragtime' rapidly de-emphasized African-American inflection in ragtime (for example, eschewing burnt-cork

---

51. *The Mercury*, 7 February 1903: 8.
52. *The Truth*, 16 January 1904: 5.

makeup and black vernacular in themes and lyrics) and became the musical metaphor for (white) American modernity—modern American 'hustle' music.[53] The Australian press noted in early 1912 that a million copies of *Alexander's Ragtime Band* had sold within months of publication and that it was already being performed here.[54] By this time, the cakewalk was no longer fashionable and a confusing array of ragtime or 'freak' dances, with names such as Turkey Trot, Bunny Hug and Grizzly Bear,[55] were gaining popularity with younger, less-conformist dancers, somewhat to the concern of dance teachers and guardians of morality. The murmur of opposition to cakewalk dancing became the roar of moral panic about freak dancing in the 1910s. One important reason was that the tango, which reached Australia at the same time as the Irving Berlin-style ragtime craze, was widely perceived to be ragtime dancing and music, thereby superimposing salacious perceptions of the tango and its brothel origins on ragtime dancing (Whiteoak 2014: 45–46). In Melbourne, the Reverend James White declared the tango dance to be immoral.

> It is a spider's web, put by the devil to entrap weak women... The negroes danced it, but not as an innocent pleasure dance. It does not reflect much credit on our civilisation that any should be found emulating these ignorant savages.[56]

In 1914, Albert & Son's music house in Sydney commissioned a dance instructor to provide Australians with codified versions of ragtime and tango dancing that would 'defy local touches'. The author adds that 'one cannot refrain from noticing that an immoral element can easily put their own construction on a dance' (Salinger 1914: 31). The author of another local dance instructor explained that ragtime dancing is

> indeed as if some mischievously disposed persons were to add offensive detail to a chaste piece of classic sculpture, and thereby cause the statue to appear indecent... Can anyone explain how it is that ordinary inoffensive young Australians, when they dance, suddenly develop the spasmodic automatism of the coloured coon (Roberts 1912: 3).

---

53. *The Times* (London), 8 February 1913: 11. This detailed musical and social analysis of the new American so-called 'hustle music' was reprinted in many Australian newspapers the same year.
54. *Geelong Advertiser*, 15 February 1912: 5.
55. *Sydney Morning Herald*, 10 April 1912: 5.
56. *Clarence and Richmond Examiner*, 14 February 1914: 2.

Such reactions to ragtime-era dancing and to the, then, latest in modern rhythmic music, differ only marginally from Jazz-Age moral objections to Australian dancers jazzing to jazz band music.

> 'I instantly became, at a callow 16, an avid fan of the real American ragtime... When those Hedges boys let loose with their eccentric hand gestures and torso gymnastics I had to be physically restrained by ushers, so excited I had become.'[57]

The growth of what might have developed into some sort of Australian youth counterculture centred on American popular culture and ragtime dancing and music was halted by the War, the danger of sea travel for ragtime artists, and also public disappointment that America did not support the Allies until April 1917. Australian left-wing historian, Les Barnes, who was a Melbourne teenager with a keen ragtime dancing brother in the 1910s, explained that ragtime and ragtime dancing became somewhat emblematic of youthful pacifism before the Americans finally entered the war.[58] The notion of the 'flapper' as a promiscuous, social convention-defying young woman, so strongly identified with the Jazz Age, had already substantially evolved here during the Berlin-style ragtime era,[59] alongside a vogue for 'American bars', 'American barbers', 'American tailors' and the 'inordinate' demand for ragtime.[60]

The influence of Gene Greene, 'Emperor of Ragtime', an extraordinarily talented American 'ragger', who gave vocal ragging lessons to budding Australian raggers and established ragtime contests in the capital cities during his very successful 1913–14 tour, provides a tiny glimpse of how the attraction of a vogue that drew much of its creative vitality from African-American influence could capture the admiration of an urban generation when brilliantly delineated, interpreted or burlesqued by a white artist (as with Elvis Presley forty years on). This was despite any 1910s establishment misgivings about the 'Negroid' provenance of Greene's performance behaviour or its potential for further undermining the aesthetic, social and moral values already perceived as being eroded by freak dancing.

Former blackface coon-song artist, Greene, was, in a sense, both a Thomas Rice and an Elvis Presley, with his idiosyncratic manner of dressing, his rhythmic body contortions, steps and gestures to 'Negro' rhythm and, especially,

---

57. Recollections of a British ragtime fan cited in Whitcomb (1987: 157).
58. Interview with author, 1 April 1988.
59. See, for example, 'Slang in Language', *Bendigo Advertiser*, 29 June 1912: 8 or 'Fitzroy Flapper's Frailty', *The Truth*, 3 July 1915: 6.
60. *Australian Variety*, 12 August 1914: 8.

his ability to spontaneously rag any song requested to create something brand new, excitingly rhythmic and 'participatory discrepancy'-laden (Whiteoak 1999: 155–57, 159). Enthusiastic responses to Greene ragging 'at the will' of Australian audiences[61] could almost be mistaken for those of later rock stars:

> crowded audiences at both matinee and evening performances called him back more than half a dozen times…in the convulsive movements which accompany his singing of ragtime and, in fact, everything he sings and does, Gene Greene shows himself to be a thorough artist.[62]

The same reviewer noted wryly a few weeks later that 'Whether Mr. Greene is doing a kind thing to Australia in encouraging its youth to develop the ragtime habit must be left to his conscience'.[63]

There was nothing particularly uncouth in the published lyrics of the songs ragged by Greene, but the physical and sonic freedom of expression available to blackface and black minstrels and 1910s ragtime singers represents an especially important continuity between Jim Crow and the Jazz Band, and thereon to the post Jazz-Age crooning and scatting discussed by Johnson (2000: 81–135). This included the freedom to convey humorous vulgarity, such as Greene's possibly double-entendre articulation of 'goblin' on his Pathé recording of 'The Ragtime Goblin Man' (Pathé 538) or the humorous suggestiveness in the 1917 Tivoli performances of the ragtime-era flapper song, 'There's a Little Bit of Bad in Every Good Little Girl', where the female artist 'makes out a telling case for the bad girl'.[64] It was also the freedom to convey sensuality and seductiveness, as in this disturbingly essentialized 1914 Melbourne description of the ragtime singer, Josephine Gassman:

> her rendering made it a very different song to the hackneyed air to which we are all familiar. The expression of primal passion and burning desire put into it was a marvellous demonstration of savage feelings, and it fascinated the civilised white audience, that looked and listened spellbound.[65]

61. *The Age*, 10 November 1913: 10.
62. *The Argus*, 17 November 1913: 11.
63. *The Argus*, 15 December 1913: 11.
64. *Referee* (Sydney), 14 February 1917: 14.
65. *The Argus*, 29 June 1914: 6.

Jazz-age 'demons' of dissonance

While Gassman's performance was definitely a pre-Jazz-Age glimpse into a 'fascinating but disquieting darkness' (Johnson 1987: 4), the closest to direct acknowledgment that the Jazz Band was playing 'Negro music' were references to the similarity of the band's performance behaviour to 'the "darktown bands" of some of the old-time [white] companies of Christy minstrels',[66] or the observation that 'The band reminded one of the old-time minstrel bands. For the most part the members made more noise than music—simply "jazzed" away for all they were worth.'[67] At Melbourne's Bijou Theatre, where the Jazz Band was performing, the programme was temporarily changed to present an 'old-time' blackface minstrel show with the Jazz Band (presumably in burnt-cork) adding 'the coontown touch to the show' and providing the incidental music.[68] An association between the new American craze, 'jazz bands' and old-time minstrel bands continued to be reflected in blackface minstrelsy itself. The Jazz Band had only just departed Melbourne for Adelaide when the amateur Maldon Coons of Maldon in northern Victoria presented a minstrel show, including:

> the Jazz Band (under the direction of Mr. Hartley as conductor). Peal after peal of laughter rang through the building at the eccentricities of the conductor, and the music (!) resulting from the various instruments forming a heterogeneous collection.[69]

Even before the Jazz Band left Sydney, St. Benedict's Old Boys' Minstrel Company featured 'Everyone Loves a Jazz Band' as a chorus song on their programme.[70] However, the main conceptual link between burnt-cork minstrelsy and 'jazz bands' was the association between collective novelty noise-making and jazzing.

Minstrel clubs continued to feature 'jazz bands' throughout the 1920s[71] and there are various photos and reports of blackface 'jazz bands' with bizarre combinations of sound-makers, Jazz-Age dance bands in blackface, and even Aboriginal gumleaf and kangaroo-skin drum 'jazz bands'. As late as the 1940s, the famous 'traditional' jazz band led by Graeme Bell was photographed in blackface as 'Coons on Parade' (Bell 1988: 53).

---

66. *The Argus*, 22 July 1918: 7.
67. *The Advertiser* (Adelaide), 19 August 1918: 7.
68. *Punch* (Melbourne), 8 August 1918: 36.
69. *Maldon News*, 27 August 1918: 3.
70. *The Catholic Press* (NSW), 1 August 1918: 13.
71. For example: *Brisbane Courier*, 14 April 1924: 17; *Newcastle Morning Herald & Miners' Advocate*, 10 February 1926: 8.

Figure 4: Advert for the kazoo, the 'jazziest of jazz instruments', in *Australian Band and Orchestra News*, 26 November 1925: 20 (Author's Australiana music journals collection).

However, a more socially, culturally and musically profound outcome of the perceived association between 'jazz' and ecstatic, or imitation-ecstatic, noise-making was the understanding, or misunderstanding, that a dance band could evolve into a 'jazz band' simply by employing a drummer with novelty 'jazz' percussion instruments (which were collectively marketed as 'jazz') and that 'jazz' was riotously joyful noise-making. Therefore guests at the numerous post-World War I victory balls or so-called 'jazz frivols' were given noise-makers, such as kazoos, to create the desired 'jazz' atmosphere (see Figure 4). Johnson, who clearly identified the significance of novelty noise-making in his seminal introductory essay to *The Oxford Companion to Australian Jazz*, states that 'Almost anything capable of producing a curious sound was seen as a jazz instrument' (Johnson 1987: 6). One example was an 'impromptu jazz band, arranged by Mrs. Allardice—which included bottles, whistles, tins and gongs...greatly enjoyed by the dancers' at a society Christmas house-party ball in early 1920.[72] This perception of jazz as happy, clown band-like noise-mak-

---

72. *Table Talk*, 8 January 1920: 31.

ing persisted into the Jazz Age even as accurate models of white American jazz orchestra music became familiar to Australian ballroom dancers, theatregoers, record purchasers and, by the mid-1920s, radio listeners. It also reinforced negative criticisms that 'jazz' was noisy, degenerate musical nonsense or clowning for the lower classes (Johnson 1987: 6–10).

The 'spirit' of Australian jazz

In his deeply insightful article, 'An Australian Sound' (1979), cultural historian Bruce Clunies-Ross identifies a distinctly 'Australian accent' in the early (1940s) traditional jazz of the Bell Brothers and others as 'a freer, creative style' that, he argues, was the unique product of the Australian social, political and cultural context of its development. This included oppositional (radical left) politics, a (then) iconoclastic art movement with a bohemian or 'alternative living' social milieu, mischievously irreverent 'characters' (larrikins/demons?), a spirit of collectivism and also the egalitarianism and masculine Australian 'mateship' that left-wing historian Russell Ward traces back to what he calls the 'The Founding Fathers' (convicts) and 'bushmen' in his much-debated *The Australian Legend* (Ward 1958: 15–45, 71–11).[73]

Johnson, Bisset and various others agree with Clunies-Ross about a uniquely 'Australian accent' in this jazz and even the astute modernists, Tony Gould and Bruce Clarke, state, respectively, 'for all its rawness and crudeness, that was probably the only original sound that's been in Australian jazz' and that it was 'a bad but unique sound' (Breen 1987: 111). Bisset refers to the 'spirited, uninhibited, uncontrived guileless excitement' of Frank Johnson's Fabulous Dixielanders as defining its uniquely Australian sound (Bisset 1979: 124), while Johnson speaks of the 'breezy swaggering indifference' and 'aggressive egalitarianism' of the Bell band and points out that its jazz was perceived to be so unique overseas that it altered the course of British and Czechoslovakian jazz history (Johnson 2010: 149–57, 162). Tracing the oppositional spirit that generated this uniquely Australian jazz as music and culture back to the demimonde that was Australia's low-life foundational criminality presents difficulties, such as the need for this spirit to have inhabited the two decades of dance orchestra 'jazz' music and culture that came between the Jazz Band and the beginning of the traditional jazz movement.

This chapter has, nevertheless, presented some primary source evidence that supports the idea that a jazz-related oppositional spirit can be traced back

---

73. Ward's 'typical Australian' features, along with fierce independence, egalitarianism, inventiveness and mateship, Jim Crow-like irreverence for authority and blokey gambling, drinking and fighting tendencies.

from Australia's Jazz Age to its penal colony era. It proposes that Australian jazz history should not be perceived as commencing in 1918 Sydney with the Jazz Band but, instead, in the grim penal settlement of Hobart in January 1838, when actor-manager John Meredith introduced the 'far-famed song of Jump Jim Crow' into a melodrama subtitled *Thirty Years of a Gambler's Life*.[74] I have argued that African-American inflected music and dance both channelled the improvisatory antecedents of Australia's earliest 'jazz' and 'jazzing' and were also the channel for a breezy, swaggering, indifferent, oppositional and sometimes uncouth spirit that drew nourishment from the freedom of expression available in minstrelsy and ragtime. This was the freedom to make sonic or social dissonance, or 'noise', that was nevertheless popular, or even audaciously invent and present what appears to have been a hastily contrived and mischievous musical joke to the 1918 public as 'Australia's First Jazz Band'. This spirit was, I suggest, the 'down-under mateship' of two 'demons': the melding of American notions of egalitarianism, irreverence, independence, racism, 'boosterism' and 'breeziness'[75] inherent in Jim Crow with a type of Australian 'larrikinism' that was no doubt influenced by our foundational criminality.

References

Bell, Graeme (1988) *Graeme Bell Australian Jazzman: His Autobiography*. Frenchs Forrest, NSW: Child & Associates.
Bellanta, Melissa (2012) *Larrikins: A History*. St Lucia, Queensland: University of Queensland Press.
Bisset, Andrew (1974) 'The First Ten Years of Jazz in Australia'. 4th Year thesis. Canberra: National University of Australia.
—(1979) *Black Roots, White Flowers: A History of Jazz in Australia*. Sydney: Golden Press.
Breen, Marcus (1987) 'Bruce Clarke'. In *Missing in Action: Australian Popular Music in Perspective, vol. 1*, ed. Marcus Breen, 107–112. Kensington, Victoria: Verbal Graphics.
Breen, Marcus, ed. (1989) *Our Place Our Music: Aboriginal Music in Perspective Volume 2*. Canberra: Aboriginal Studies Press.
Clunies-Ross, Bruce (1979) 'An Australian Sound: Jazz in Melbourne and Adelaide 1941–51'. In *Australian Popular Culture*, ed. P. Spearritt and D. Walker, 62–80. Sydney: Allen & Unwin.
Cockrell, Dale (1997) *Demons of Disorder, Early Blackface Minstrels and their World*. Cambridge: Cambridge University Press.
Emery, Lynne Fauley (1988) *Black Dance from 1619 to Today*, 2nd revised ed. Princeton, NJ: Princeton Book Company.

---

74. *Colonial Times*, 9 January 1838: 2.
75. For example, *The Age* (Melbourne) reported on how 'well Mabel Morgan's ragging fit[s] in with the general American breeziness of the Jazzers' (22 July 1918: 8).

Johnson, Bruce (1987) *The Oxford Companion to Australian Jazz*. Melbourne: Oxford University Press.
—(2000) *The Inaudible Music: Jazz Gender and Australian Modernity*. Sydney: Currency Press.
—(2002) 'The Jazz Diaspora'. In *The Cambridge Companion to Jazz*, ed. Mervyn Cooke and David Horn, 33–54. Cambridge: Cambridge University Press.
—(2004) 'Tools of Our Own Making: Shaping Australian Jazz History'. In *The History and Future of Jazz in the Asia Pacific Region: Refereed Proceeding of the Inaugural Asia-Pacific Jazz Conference* (September 12th–14th 2003), ed. Philip Hayward and Glen Hodges, 6–15. McKay: Central Queensland Conservatorium of Music.
—(2010) 'Deportation Blues: Black Jazz and White Australia in the 1920s'. *Journal for the International Society for the Study of Popular Music* 1/1: 1–13, http://eprints.gla.ac.uk/84896/7/84896.pdf (accessed 7 June 2014).
Keil, Charles (1994) 'Participatory Discrepancies and the Power of Music'. In *Music Grooves: Essays and Dialogues*, ed. Charles Keil and Steven Feld, 96–108. Chicago: University of Chicago Press.
Lhamon, William (2003) *Jump Jim Crow: Lost Plays, Lyrics, and Street Prose of the First Atlantic Popular Culture*. Cambridge, MA: Harvard University Press.
Lott, Eric (1993) *Love and Theft: Blackface Minstrelsy and the American Working Class*. New York: Oxford University Press.
McKay, Kenneth (1895) *The Yellow Wave: A Romance of the Asiatic Invasion of Australia*. London: Richard Bentley & Son.
Nathan, Hans (1962) *Dan Emmett and the Rise of Early Negro Minstrelsy*. Norman, OK: Oklahoma University Press.
Pickering, Michael (2007) *Blackface Minstrelsy in Britain*. Aldershot, Hampshire: Ashgate.
Roberts, Henry (1912) *Robert's Manual of Fashionable Dancing*. Sydney: Albert & Son.
Salinger, George (1914) *How to Learn the Turkey Trot, Hesitation Waltz and Tango*. Sydney: Albert & Son.
Sanjek, Russell (1988) *American Popular Music and its Business: The First Four Hundred Years: From 1790–1909*. New York: Oxford University Press.
Sheldon, Eric (1933) 'Where Will it All End? Dance Music in Retrospect from Jazz to…?'. *Australian Music Maker and Dance Band News*, 1 December: 14–15, 25.
Toll, Robert (1974) *Blacking Up: The Minstrel Show in Nineteenth-Century America*. New York: Oxford University Press.
Ward, Russell (1958) *The Australian Legend*. Melbourne: Oxford University Press.
Waterhouse, Richard (1990) *From Minstrel Show to Vaudeville: The Australian Popular Stage 1788–1914*. Kensington, NSW: New South Wales University Press.
Whitcomb, Ian (1987) *Irving Berlin and Ragtime America*. London: Century Hutchinson.
Whiteoak, John (1993) 'Australian Approaches to Improvisatory Musical Practice, 1836–1970: A Melbourne Perspective'. PhD thesis. Bundoora, Victoria: Department of Music, La Trobe University.
—(1994) '"Jazzing" and Australia's First Jazz Band'. *Popular Music* 13/3: 279–95. http://dx.doi.org/10.1017/S0261143000007200
—(1999) *Playing Ad Lib: Improvisatory Music in Australia, 1836–1970*. Sydney: Currency Press.

—(2014) 'The Tango in Australia as Popular Entertainment and Music of "Place" before 1970s Latin-American Immigration'. In *Communities, Places, Ecologies Proceedings of the 2013 IASPM-ANZ Conference* (Dunedin), ed. Jadey O'Regan and Toby Wren, 39–55. Brisbane: IASPM Australia/New Zealand.

Winans, Robert (1984) 'Early Minstrel Show Music, 1843–1852'. In *Musical Theatre in America: Papers and Proceedings of the Conference on the Musical Theatre in America*, ed. Glen Lonney, 71–97. Westport, CN: Greenwood Press.

2 Early jazz in Australia as oriental exotica

Aline Scott-Maxwell[*]

'Oriental' exotica permeated popular culture in Australia from the mid-nineteenth century. Therefore, by the onset of Australia's Jazz Age (1918–28), Australians already had a long familiarity with so-called 'oriental' sounds through musical representations of the 'Orient' in popular stage and other entertainments as well as direct exposure to the music of touring and local performers from Asia, especially China. The 'jazz' that was imported to and adopted and adapted in Australia often incorporated or referenced 'oriental' elements in diverse ways.[1] Conversely, the 'strange', exotic sounds of Chinese music sometimes came to be confused with 'jazz' since, as jazz historian Andrew Bisset puts it, Australians in the 1920s had only 'hazy notions of what jazz was' (1979: 18). The conflation of oriental exotica and early jazz in Australia is mostly evident in superficial convergences, but it was especially exemplified in the successful 1927 Australian tour of Sun Moon Lee's Chinese jazz act, which was described in one review as both 'the real thing in jazz' and 'the real thing in Chinese'.[2]

This chapter examines both the tenuous and the more substantial connections and convergences between oriental exotica and early 'jazz' of the 1920s, the Australian Jazz Age, with reference to the broader historical tradition of oriental exoticism in Australian entertainment and the particular social and cultural conditions that informed it. It adds to the discourse on early jazz in the

---

[*] Aline Scott-Maxwell is an ethnomusicologist and popular music studies scholar with teaching and research specializations in Asian and Australian musical cultures. Her current research focuses on Australia's musical engagement with Asia and the music of Australian migration, especially popular music of the Indonesian, Italian and Jewish communities, and she has published extensively in these areas. She is an Adjunct Senior Research Fellow in the Sir Zelman Cowen School of Music at Monash University.

1. The quotation marks around 'jazz' acknowledge the fact that much of the music that was perceived to be jazz in the Jazz Age would not necessarily be classed as jazz from a present-day perspective.

2. *Brisbane Courier*, 3 May 1927: 18.

Australian context by arguing that diverse notions of jazz as exotica contributed to how 'jazz' was presented and perceived. Further, in presenting a jazz-centred perspective on the phenomenon and meanings of oriental exotica in Australian popular entertainment history, it demonstrates how the tropes and signifiers of oriental exotica were readily transferable into new musical contexts.

Discussion of the relationship of oriental exotica and early jazz necessarily embraces music created overseas and marketed, consumed and performed in Australia along with, albeit much rarer, examples conceived and created in Australia. Australia was firmly connected into the international cultural flows (especially from Great Britain and America) that fed Asia-Pacific entertainment circuits, but it was very remote from the models and social and cultural contexts that shaped the musical trends and products popularized in Australia. What is distinguishable with regards to connections between early 'jazz' and oriental exotica in Australia lay less in audible musical characteristics or performance practices than in the way that certain aspects of the Australian context, such as decontextualization from source models or previous experience of Chinese immigration, inflected local reception and enabled slippages in meaning and the creation of new meanings. It must be emphasized however that the most important primary sources on the presentation and reception of live popular entertainment, the entertainment columns of Australian newspapers, are for the most part brief, formulaic, repetitive and frustratingly lacking in insightful social observations and technical descriptions. This particularly limits the extent to which questions regarding performance practice and public reception can be answered.

Imaginings of the Orient in Australian popular culture were partly the product of transplanted nineteenth-century European and American constructions of and preoccupations with a remote and highly exoticized 'Orient' and therefore belong to a wider Orientalist othering of 'oriental' locales, in particular, the Middle East and 'Far East' but also, somewhat later, the Pacific. With Australia's post-settlement history positioning it as a British colonial outpost, Edward Said's proposition that Orientalism is 'a Western style of dominating, restructuring and having authority over the Orient' (1978: 2–3) is undoubtedly important to understanding Australian fascination with an imagined China and other oriental settings. By extension, the substantial body of northern hemisphere-focused scholarship about music and Orientalism, or exoticism, including Locke (2009), Scott (2003), Bellman (1998) and Born and Hesmondhalgh (2000), amongst others, is also broadly relevant to understanding the repertoires and musical and cultural processes that fed this fascination.[3]

---

3. Note, however, that critical perspectives taken on Orientalism within this body of literature vary significantly, as argued incisively by Bellman (2011).

However, Australia's adoption of European Orientalist strategies had some significant local inflections since, from a geographical perspective, the so-called Orient was not the far-away place for Australians that it was for Europeans or Americans. Therefore, imaginings and representations of the Orient cannot be read simply as a transplanted European or American phenomenon, since British-Australian perceptions of the Orient were also contextualized and coloured by localized circumstances, which included a significant—and, for many, menacing—Chinese presence in Australia from the mid-nineteenth century. As Clayton and Zon have argued, consideration of the role played by encounters with the 'real' Orient—in the Australian case, on-shore encounters—has been significantly missing from some Saidian-based critical interpretations (2007: 2–3). Some scholars of Australian cultural history have noted, for example, that 'Australia has had its own unique brand of orientalism, which, although British derived, developed its own characteristics through colonial displacement' that involved 'a simultaneous external and internal process of "othering"' (Jensen 2005: 103).[4]

There are other reasons to qualify the relevance of critical thinking about Orientalism based on the European situation. For example, a recent article by Hsu-Ming Teo (drawing on the work of Leach [1993], Edwards [2000] and Nance [2009]) presents the post-Saidian argument that American engagement with the Orient through popular culture was, rather than simply a derivative of European Orientalism, substantially a response to the rise of consumerist culture and a corresponding 'lack' in American culture that could be filled by the 'extravagant fantasy' of the East and its 'new colours, textures, sensuousness...and exoticism with a touch of the "impermissible"' (Teo 2014: 7). Given Australia's particularly significant historical engagement with American popular culture—the immense popularity of blackface minstrelsy, circus, vaudeville and American cinema, for example—this argument can be applied to the exoticization of early jazz in Australia. Especially in the absence of precise understandings about what jazz was, the familiar, largely fantasy world of oriental exotica provided an existing framework for, and could effectively connect into, jazz's primitivist, modernist expression of newness, its breaking-out from behavioural conventions and its predilection for noise, colour and movement.

---

4. The notion of an Australian Orientalism has been taken further by Australian theatre historian Veronica Kelly, who states that: 'since colonials were themselves constructed as, and resentfully mis/recognized themselves as being, an Other within imperial hierarchies, there exists an available reading position of identification with Orientalist spectacles as in some sense legitimating, even providing, imagery of their own alterised reality' (1993: 33).

Early jazzing as oriental exotica

Various historians of Australia's earliest 'jazz' have noted how profoundly it was perceived to be associated with loud, 'weird' or 'novelty' noise-making (Bisset 1979: 9; Johnson 1987: 4–7; Whiteoak 1999: 177–80). Reviews of the mid-1918 vaudeville act called 'Australia's First Jazz Band' (see Whiteoak in this issue) describe its so-called 'jazzing' as novelty noise-making that included farmyard and jungle sounds and, in particular, loud percussion-playing featuring a zany array of novelty sound-effect 'traps', amongst them, cow bells, pistol shots, whistles, kitchen utensils and 'thunder' effects (Johnson 1987: 4). This notion of jazz or 'jazzing' as weird noise-making continued to influence the perception and production of jazz until the late 1920s. Novelty noise produced by a diverse array of timbrally-varied sound effects was such a defining feature of early jazz that drummers' traps were advertised and described simply as 'jazz'.[5] The Jazz-Age concept of 'jazzing'—called 'ragging' before the Jazz Age—is that of altering, filling-out and embellishing popular music in performance (or through arranging) to 'jazz it up'. Jazzing functioned to make Jazz-Age popular music more colourful, evocative and rhythmically exciting or 'hot', as discussed extensively in relation to Australia's Jazz Age by Whiteoak (1999: 168–230).

A significant aspect of Jazz-Age jazzing as novelty noise was the use of 'oriental' effects, especially Chinese percussion. Drummers' traps in early jazz drum sets invariably included Chinese or supposedly Chinese instruments. The most common of these were woodblocks, one or more 'tack-head' tom-tom drums and Chinese cymbals,[6] but many drum kits also had sets of Chinese wooden temple bells and some are likely to have included a Chinese gong (tam-tam) on a stand.[7] A 1925 *Australian Band and Orchestra News* advertisement for Leedy Drummers' Traps provides a comprehensive illustrated list with prices of the traps that were available in all Allan's music stores. Amongst these are 'Chinese tom-tom', 'Chinese crash cymbals', woodblocks and, interestingly, 'Chinese musette' (see Figure 1).[8] The illustration of the latter clearly depicts a Chinese suona, a very loud double-reed (oboe-type) wind instrument that would have been an extremely effective novelty-noise maker. The

---

5. See advertisement in *Australasian Band and Orchestra News*, 26 July 1928: 32.
6. By the late 1930s, the tom-tom drums and Chinese cymbals were replaced by commercially-produced tensioned tom-toms and Turkish cymbals.
7. Some Australian accounts of early jazz bands refer to the clashing of a gong but some of these may be mistaken references to cymbals. See, for example, *The Age*, 10 April 1920: 10. For photographs and informed commentary on 1920s drum kits, see www.polarityrecords.com/vintage-drum-kits-1920s-and-30s.html (accessed 10 October 2014).
8. *Australian Band and Orchestra News*, 26 November 1925: iii. 'Rooster calls' sold by Leedy include a Shanghai rooster.

exotically oriental flavour of early jazz drum kits was enhanced by their visual impact, notably, the red and gold-lacquered temple blocks, which usually retained their traditional fish shape, and the invariably bright-red painted tom-tom with its colourful dragon or phoenix design on the drum-head. The illustration in the Leedy's advertisement also shows large Chinese characters painted on the crash cymbal.

Figure 1: An advertisement for jazz drummers' 'traps', including Chinese percussion and other instruments. Australian Band and Orchestra News, 26 November 1925: iii.

The association of jazz with what was modern, popular and fashionable in Australia's Jazz Age (Johnson 2000: 59–62) meant that Jazz-Age Tin Pan Alley-style songs were widely marketed and perceived as 'jazz' in Australia. These songs were vehicles for improvisatory jazzing, such as the interpolation of 'hot', 'blues' or 'novelty jazz' breaks learnt from recordings or locally marketed 'hot breaks' or jazzing tutors. 'Oriental' sounds and themes were incorporated into this jazz via Tin Pan Alley song genres such as so-called 'oriental fox-trots', Hawaiian waltzes or Hawaiian blues.[9] These were part of a shifting panorama of dance-song genres that came in and out of fashion through the 1910s to the 1930s. The oriental-style dance-song craze reached a peak of popularity in the early 1920s with songs that were mostly themed around or set in China (or Chinatown), an exoticized Middle East ('Araby'), or else—in what can perhaps be considered a parallel genre—Hawaii or an island Pacific. Oriental-themed songs were featured by Australian jazz, theatre and cinema orchestras and large quantities of them were also sold as song and piano sheets and, to a much lesser extent, discs and piano rolls, testifying to the persistent local popularity of the genre.

All aspects of this music—their titles, subject matter, lyrics, music and sheet music cover art—were highly conventionalized via stereotypical motifs that ranged from their exotic locations, such as desert caravan trains, palm-fringed lagoons, or Chinatown; their orientalist scenarios featuring romantic moonlit interludes with 'dark-eyed' or 'almond-eyed maidens'; to recurring musical devices, or 'orientalisms', designed to contribute colour and an exotic effect. Songs with a 'Chinese' theme, such as 'China Girl' or 'Down in Chinatown', exhibit gapped pentatonic scales, parallel fourths and fifths, and repeated stilted 'click clack'-sounding rhythms. Songs in the 'Araby' category make conspicuous use of chromatically altered scales, drone-like sustained notes and simple rhythmic representations (long-short-short) of 'tom-tom' drumming, galloping horses, or the loping gait of a camel, as in 'Kismet' or 'The Sheik of Araby'. Hawaiian-style songs are peppered with chromaticisms and arpeggiations representing the gliding sound of the Hawaiian steel guitar or the strum of the ukulele. However, these various musical devices were often applied indiscriminately in 'oriental'-style songs with little regard for consistency of representation.

The majority of the song sheets sold in Australia were American compositions, but they were re-published under licence by Australian local music houses and 'plugged' by local (or visiting) artists or inserted into revues and

---

9. The 'oriental' genre of Tin Pan Alley-style popular song in Australia is discussed more fully in Scott-Maxwell (1997).

pantomimes, as the photographs of the artists or promotional information about the shows on the music covers testify. Oriental-style songs were also written by Australian composers and lyricists in this period, for example, 'My Chinee Girl' by Vince Courtney (1917); 'Somewhere South of Shanghai' (1925) by Jack Lumsdaine; 'In Dreamy Araby' (1921) by Jack O'Hagan; 'Arabia Land' (1920) by Andrew MacCunn and Jack Haskell; 'Dreamy Honolulu' (1922) by Russ Johnston and Billy Edwards; and 'Sleepy Seas' (1921) by Reg Stoneham. While still relentlessly formulaic, they tend to be more diluted than their American counterparts: the stereotypes are somewhat less strongly drawn, the musical orientalisms less pervasive and exaggerated and the lyrics more benign and less specific in their subject matter. This subtle transformation of the American Tin Pan Alley model in Australian-composed songs highlights the somewhat different taste of the British-Australian public. There was even some naturalization of the genre. For example, Vince Courtney's 'My Chinee Girl' was included in the home-grown Australian musical, *The Bunyip* (the name of a mythical Australian monster) and sung by the composer as the Chinese cook character, Ah Fat. Featured alongside identifiably Australian-marked songs, amongst them, 'Corroboree Rag', 'Mother Waratah' and 'Nulla-Nulla', as well as characters such as Princess Wattleblossom and Ned Kelly, the Chinese elements become almost another element of the Australian landscape, as it were, rather than exotically 'other'.

Performative aspects further enhanced these songs' 'oriental' character, whether in a playful or grossly parodic way. Only a tiny fraction of the oriental-themed Jazz-Age popular music heard in Australia was recorded here in the 1920s and none before 1925. However, pre-1925 American recordings give some sense of how this music is likely to have been performed locally. For example, recordings of 'Hi Lee Hi Lo' (Victor 18242-A, 1923), sung by Billy Murray, and 'From Here to Shanghai' (Victor 18242A, 1917), sung by Gene Greene (who influentially toured Australia in 1913–14), both demonstrate use of an exaggeratedly sing-song vocal style, nasal vocal timbre and other forms of vocal distortion, imitation 'Chinese-accented' lyrics, and Chinese and other 'novelty' instruments, such as gong, woodblocks and swanee whistle. Australian dance and theatre orchestra backings to these songs would no doubt have been heavily 'jazzed' with Chinese or other 'oriental' effects available to percussionists—perhaps even including the 'Chinese musette'. Although recordings on disc were not made in Australia until 1925, early Australian jazz can be heard on a previous recording format, the piano roll (Whiteoak 1999: 149, 198, 205). Amongst the many Australian-produced rolls are 'Ching Chong' and 'Ching Chong Jazz Arrangement', both performed around 1924 by the Australian duo piano-roll performers, Laurel and Edith Pardey, and 'When China Boy Meets China Girl', performed by Edith Pardey (as Edith Murn). These recordings feature their notions of 'Chinese' inflections, and the deluge of 'oriental' jazzing effects at cadence points indicates that rolls were further embellished or 'jazzed' in the post-performance editing process.

The most persistent and therefore significant mode of exotica to intersect with early jazz, however, was not that evoking the so-called Orient but Hawaiian-inflected musical exoticism. A remarkably pervasive three-decade craze for Hawaiian-style music began in 1917–18 with the Australian tour of the immensely popular American musical, *Bird of Paradise*, which corresponded with the appearance of 'Australia's First Jazz Band'. The musical's troupe of Hawaiian musicians included the very accomplished steel guitar and ukulele player, Henry Peelua Bishaw, who stayed in Australia as a leading ambassador for this popular and lucrative craze (Coyle and Coyle 2003: 314). Ukulele tablature was subsequently incorporated into many Tin Pan Alley-style 'oriental' song sheets and the improvisatory sliding tones of Hawaiian steel-guitar playing—or musical representations of it—were perceived to be a form of jazzing (Whiteoak 1995: 115–17).[10]

A converse expression of Australian 'othering' of early jazz as not just exotically different but more menacing and explicitly racially charged was encapsulated in the response to the first black jazz band to visit Australia, Sonny Clay's Plantation Orchestra, in 1928. The band's tour was cut short when they were forced to depart Australia, purportedly due to pressure from the Musicians' Union, but principally because of the moral panic ensuing from allegations that the musicians were consorting with local white women and engaging in drug use (Sutcliffe 1997: 3–13). African-American minstrel shows and jubilee singers had toured Australia since the 1870s and had sometimes encountered comparable racism but, as Whiteoak points out in his chapter in this volume, the fact that black minstrels had to adopt and adapt the mocking and racial stereotypes of blackface minstrelsy, which colonial Australians had been familiar with for decades, diminished both their ability to exploit the exoticism of being black and, to some extent, the impact of difference and otherness that they might otherwise have had for their Australian audiences.

'Oriental sounds' and Chinese music in pre-jazz Australia

Chinese and other so-called 'oriental' sounds were, as already mentioned, not as novel and exotic to the Australian Jazz-Age public as might be imagined.

---

10. The association of the 'hapa haole' (half-white) style of Hawaiian music with ragtime and the use of the Hawaiian steel guitar in blues and jazz is documented in Cundle (2014: 36–37, 108–11).

Large numbers of Chinese came to Australia in the 1850s to seek their fortunes on the goldfields and Cantonese opera was a regular feature of mid-nineteenth-century goldfields entertainment. As recounted in Love (1985), Wang (1997), Wang and Doggett (2007) and Doggett (2008), many Australians became familiar with the sound of the music that is intrinsic to Chinese opera, especially the very loud and insistent percussion of gong, cymbals and drum—whether they chose to attend these performances (as some did) or were simply within earshot. The 'tremendous din of the orchestra' attracted frequent complaints with, for example, the *Mount Alexander Mail* reporting that 'those who visited the Italian Opera had to run the gauntlet of the hideous discords and caterwaulings of the Oriental one' and that 'residents were kept awake for an hour and a half after midnight by the horrid sounds'.[11] Many others witnessed Chinese music performances in street festivals or elsewhere, or else they read about them in the many, generally uncomplimentary, reports and comments about the music that appeared in colonial newspapers. Notably, the exact same adjectives that were used to describe Chinese music in these reports, such as noisy, discordant, hideous, cacophony, din, and so on, were applied over half a century later to early jazz.[12]

From the mid-nineteenth century to the early twentieth century, Australians were also exposed to the musical and visual representations of an exoticized and largely imagined Orient that saturated early popular stage entertainments via diverse music-theatre genres such as melodrama, pantomime, opera and operetta, musicals and variety acts—as well as silent and, later, sound cinema. The 'Orient' depicted on the popular stage, either in locally-produced or imported productions, mostly referenced China or an Arabian Nights-style Middle East, but sometimes conflated the two as, for example, in the massively successful 'oriental extravaganza', *Chu Chin Chow: A Musical Tale from the East*, that toured Australia from 1920 and again in 1922. The action in pantomime, melodrama, burlesque and other nineteenth-century popular stage genres was always underpinned by music, as demonstrated in a review of a notable locally-created Japan-themed production of the pre-Federation period, *Djin Djin the Japanese Bogie Man*: 'a liberal use [was] made of the shrill chromatics of the piccolo, the harsh clang of the gong, the roll of the drums, and the blare of brass instruments, which give a strikingly realistic effect to

---

11. *Mount Alexander Mail*, 11 November 1861 and 5 January 1859 (cited in Love 1985: 51).

12. For example, 'The Jazz', *The Mercury* (Hobart), 10 May 1919: 10; *Goomalling-Dowerin Mail* (Western Australia), 26 August 1921: 4. Numerous troupes of Japanese acrobats, performing to the accompaniment of the three-stringed plucked lute, the shamisen, also toured Australia after 1867.

the many weird and remarkable scenes presented'.[13] Comedic or burlesqued stage forms in particular gave great scope for bizarre 'oriental' musical effects.

By the Jazz Age, silent film was the preeminent form of theatrical entertainment in Australia, providing a major forum for the mass public consumption of so-called 'oriental music' and the assimilation of its musical language and representations. Cinema orchestras and silent-movie pianists employed 'oriental'-style music to create appropriate moods for scenes depicting oriental locations or characters, whether using improvised oriental-sounding moods, bridges and effects based on musical orientalisms familiar from other contexts, or published repertoire. 'Oriental music' was a major category in the film music catalogues of this period and was drawn or arranged from classical or popular repertoire, or comprised specially composed 'moods'. Parts and scores were made available to Australian cinema orchestras through major lending collections, such as that of the former Sydney State Theatre (now held in the National Library of Australia), which includes a large quantity of scores in the Chinese 'oriental' category.[14]

As noted above, however, there were factors that gave orientalism a particular inflection in Australia. Although the 'oriental' music and musical effects that were deployed in popular theatre and silent film undoubtedly owed much to modes of representation originating elsewhere, there is some evidence that local musical and other representations of China were also informed by Australians' direct experiences and perceptions of Chinese theatre and music. As described in more detail elsewhere (Scott-Maxwell 2011), direct or mediated exposure to Chinese music not only influenced how it was creatively represented on the popular stage but also how it was received, since audiences were able to compare and evaluate the cleverness of the representations or the sharpness of the parodies against what they knew about Chinese music. The following excerpt from a review of a visiting blackface troupe makes this clear:

> Mr C. Harvey played a couple of solos on a single-stringed Chinese fiddle [a Western novelty one-string fiddle], and the melody he managed to evolve out of the instrument would hardly be conceivable by those who have only listened to the Celestial making night hideous with his outrages on sound.[15]

---

13. *Adelaide Observer*, 28 November 1896: 45.
14. See Scott-Maxwell (2013) for a partial list of these and Scott-Maxwell (1997: 47–49) regarding the typology of 'oriental music' in film music manuals from the period.
15. *The West Australian*, 26 April 1890: 3.

Further, the sheer magnitude of Chinese immigration to Australia from the mid-nineteenth century and resentment of their success in finding gold and competitiveness in commerce and other areas, along with unwelcome cultural differences, engendered considerable anti-Chinese sentiment—alongside curiosity and, occasionally, admiration. With the rise of Australian nationalism from the 1880s, this sentiment evolved into a more generalized fear of 'invasion' of Australia's empty land by the 'yellow hordes' to the north and, immediately following Federation, was formalized in the 1901 Immigration Restriction Act (known as the White Australia Policy). The introduction of immigration exclusion laws and the subsequent gradual diminution of the permanent Chinese population in Australia reduced opportunities for Australians to witness first-hand Chinese music and theatre performed primarily for local Chinese consumption or at major public civic events. But, by this time, individual Chinese performers had also begun to represent themselves musically and theatrically on the popular stage as professional variety artists.

The rise of vaudeville brought visiting Chinese performers, acrobats and magicians on to mainstream Australian popular stage circuits, such as the Tivoli, in acts with 'appropriate' on-stage or accompaniment music and sound effects. Reports suggest that these Chinese performers often self-orientalized, playing to audience expectations of what Chinese performance and music constituted and reinforcing notions of a strange and mysteriously exotic 'Orient'. Chinese artists did not confine themselves to Chinese-referenced acts, however, thereby subverting stereotypes and audience expectations. For instance, Chinese-American comedian, Ben Nee One, began his Melbourne act with a song in Irish dialect and closed it with a Chinese song.[16]

'Chinese jazz'

An explicit Chinese/jazz association that emerged from the late ragtime era both as a fanciful parodied concept as well as on the live vaudeville stage was that of 'Chinese jazz'. An early example of this association is evident in a 1918 Australian promotion for New Jazz Word Rolls, which overlays a stylized piano roll with a line drawing of a prancing Chinese man in stereotyped traditional dress,[17] while the lyrics of some Chinese-themed 'oriental'-style Tin Pan Alley songs from the late ragtime and early jazz era, such as 'Pan Yan (and his Chinese Jazz Band)', 'Jazzie Jazz in Chinaland', 'Ching A Ling's Jazz Bazaar' and 'Hi Lee Hi Lo', explicitly reference Chinese playing, enjoying or dancing jazz.

---

16. *The Argus*, 2 March 1926: 12. See Moon for discussion of Ben Nee One and other Chinese vaudeville artists in relation to the American stage (2005: 112–62).

17. *Australian Musical News*, 1 April 1918: 278.

Through racialized (and highly derogatory) imitations of Chinese speech in the lyrics and music, these songs also play with an association between the perceived bizarre sound of Chinese language and music and jazzing.[18] The exaggeratedly parodic imitations of Chinese speech that often feature in these songs seem to have lent themselves particularly to the improvisatory practice of ragging or jazzing song lyrics, which involved, amongst other things, 'fills' comprising repeated broken syllables, as can be heard in Mack and Miller's recording of 'Ching A Ling's Jazz Bazaar'.[19]

The ways that jazz is referenced in these songs reinforces the notion of early jazz as primarily about zany sonic mayhem. It is therefore perhaps not entirely surprising to find an Australian newspaper report of what seems to have been a traditional Chinese ensemble being referred to as a 'Chinese jazz band':

> Mr Henry Foo's Chinese jazz band, which has been playing at broadcasting station 2BL, Sydney, comprises six performers, who play a three-string violin, a two-string banjo, another two-string instrument, a trumpet (or something like it) a cymbal and a drum.[20]

Chinese jazz as such was not just an imaginary of Tin Pan Alley songwriters, however. By the early 1920s in China there was already an established cafe and restaurant jazz scene (Field 2010: 38) and, from the mid-1920s, a fan base for jazz developed with the onset of radio broadcasting which, according to Australian reports, included jazz programming.[21] By 1928, Shanghai had become a mecca for Jazz-Age nightlife and entertainment (Field 2010: 53ff.) and Australian newspapers reported a 'jazz craze' and the opening of more than thirty Chinese-controlled dance halls and cabarets patronized mainly by Chinese.[22]

Bands in these cabarets appear to have been formed principally of American or European musicians and a specifically Chinese-inflected jazz culture did not emerge until the mid-1930s (Jones 2001). However, Chinese jazz bands were circulating outside China well before this, as there are reports of at least two such bands performing as stage jazz acts in Australia in the 1920s, both of them featured alongside more usual Chinese vaudeville fare such as juggling,

---

18. Songwriters also found other bizarre Chinese/jazz connections, for example, in 'Pan Yan (and his Chinese Jazz Band)' an association is made between the ivory of chopsticks and the ivories of the piano ('Chopsticks will do some queer tricks like Paderewski on the ivories').
19. www.youtube.com/watch?v=elbYWFrtkk8 (accessed 10 October 2014).
20. *The Canberra Times*, 28 October 1926: 12.
21. For example, 'Chinese Crystal Fans', *The Register* (Adelaide), 26 December 1925: 7.
22. For example, 'Jazz Craze', *Queensland Times*, 11 March 1929: 8.

acrobatics, magic, and so forth. Very little information is available about the first of these, which was advertised as taking part in a Sydney Chinese community charity event together with world-famous visiting Chinese-American acrobat, magician and performer, Long Tack Sam, and his troupe 'by permission of the Tivoli Theatre' in December 1923. The novelty of the event was underlined in the ad: 'Have you heard THE CHINESE JAZZ BAND?'[23] Long Tack Sam toured the Australian Tivoli circuit numerous times with his two daughters, who astounded audiences with their violin-playing and toe dancing. One review describes the act as 'a mixture of Oriental mystery and Western jazz' and mentions a 'Chinese flapper [who] played the violin and [tap] danced'.[24] Long Tack Sam also appeared on double bills with, variously, a Sydney jazz stage band of repute led by Billy Romaine, former leader of 'Australia's First Jazz Band', and another, then famous Australian comedic vaudeville jazz act, Lyn Smith's Royal Jazz Band.[25]

An extant Melbourne programme, a poster and many newspaper advertisements and reviews provide a much better picture of the other Chinese jazz band, which formed part of a visiting act by 'Sun Moon Lee and his Chinese jazz band with 14 oriental stars' that toured Australia in 1927. The conflation of jazz and exotica is explicitly referenced in a promotional blurb titled 'Jazz' (by Sun Moon Lee) contained in the programme brochure for the act's appearance at the Westgarth Theatre, Melbourne, which equates 'the blare of jazz' with 'the mystery of magic'. The act itself was reported to commence with a young girl emerging out of a descending carpet roll to dance 'a typical jazz number'.[26]

Yet jazz appears to have been central to the act, as the Westgarth Theatre brochure also states that 'the Jazz Band doesn't rely on the novelty of its nationality to interest—it seeks success in jazz—and attains it'. A Victorian newspaper review of the band seems to confirm that it was comparable to the 1920s 'Jazz-Age' jazz bands that the Australian public was familiar with:

> the greatest interest is evinced in the efforts of the jazz band—eight members with the typical instruments and mannerisms of similar combinations. Wisely they feature melodies of the light variety… the cornetist receives particular commendation, his handling of the cornet being quite in keeping with the best of his confreres.[27]

23. *Sydney Morning Herald*, 12 December 1923: 3.
24. *The Advertiser* (Adelaide), 4 December 1928: 17. See also *The Argus*, 30 October 1928: 16, and Tivoli Theatre Programme, 'Celebrity Vaudeville 1931'.
25. *Sunday Times* (Sydney), 21 October 1923: 7.
26. *Gippsland Times*, 18 August 1927: 4.
27. *Gippsland Times*, 18 August 1927: 4.

Another review refers to 'a merry succession of jazz and popular melodies, and dancing was interwoven with the music'.[28] The only specific indication I have found of what these melodies might have comprised is an Australian-published song sheet of 'Hong Kong Dream Girl', which advertises on its cover that it was 'specially featured by the Sun Moon Lee troupe during their Australian tour'.[29] While Sun Moon Lee was probably paid to 'plug' the song by the publisher, this nevertheless suggests the tantalizing possibility that Chinese jazz bands exploited the popularity of the oriental popular song genre for their own ends in a self-orientalizing fashion as well as engaging (perhaps in playful self-parody) with and simultaneously challenging the way that Chinese were represented in these songs.

However, whatever the tunes that Sun Moon Lee's band played, they were probably performed with Chinese inflections since, again according to the Westgarth Theatre brochure, 'To all the regular—and irregular—instruments played in Jazz, it has added those of China, with a result unusual and striking'. Another review states that:

> Jazz music may now be said to be universal. It has spread all over the globe, each country importing it, however, to tack on more or less to its own musical idiom... This was illustrated yesterday when Sun Moon Lee and his company of jazz artists took the stage at the Wintergarden Theatre.[30]

The advertisement in the *Brisbane Courier* for Sun Moon Lee's 'exotic six days' season' at the Wintergarden Theatre consists of a fascinatingly detailed cartoon-like line drawing depicting various parts of Sun Moon Lee's act.[31] Arrayed below the juggler and a ladder-balancer are the members of the jazz band in Chinese costumes with their instruments (see Figure 2). These include—besides a number of more-or-less recognizable Chinese instruments—some fantastic variants on jazz instruments, such as a horn with three bells, another with a dragon-shaped bell and a serpent-shaped instrument. The latter are clearly imaginary instruments that epitomize the playful, fantastic exotic world that both early jazz and Chinese jazz evoked.

Yet this was not a world that spoke just to Anglo-Australian audiences. Sydney's Chinese community provided a formal welcome to Sun Moon Lee's troupe on their 1927 visit, while on Long Tack Sam's earlier 1923 visit, he and his troupe were greeted on arrival in Sydney by the president of the New South

28. *Newcastle Morning Herald and Miners' Advocate*, 7 June 1927: 6.
29. Sydney: J. Albert & Son, c. 1924.
30. *The Brisbane Courier*, 3 May 1927: 18.
31. *The Brisbane Courier*, 2 May 1927: 2.

Figure 2: Advertisement for 'Sun Moon Lee and his Chinese Jazz Band with 14 Oriental Stars' at the Wintergarden Theatre, Brisbane. Text at the top of the advertisement reads: 'You heard Santrey's band—but you haven't heard jazz with the real oriental sway and rhythm until you hear Sun Moon Lee's oriental artists. It's wonderfully intoxicating—it will stampede your feet into action.' *The Brisbane Courier*, 2 May 1927: 2.

Wales Chinese Chamber of Commerce ahead of their fund-raising performance in a 'Chinese carnival' for the Royal Prince Alfred Hospital.[32] Moreover, there are Australian newspaper reports through the 1920s of various Chinese

32. *Sunday Times* (NSW), 3 April 1927: 25; *Sydney Morning Herald*, 15 December 1923: 18.

community events that involved dancing and jazz. Two local Chinese-Australian dance band musicians, Alma and Lorna Quon, played widely for dances and other public engagements, including (at the end of the Jazz Age) as members of the all-women dance band, the Merry Makers (Ryan 2003: 141; Dreyfus 1999: 82ff.). Sun Moon Lee himself claimed to have been born in Sydney before being sent as a teenager to China to acquire a Chinese education.[33]

By the time of Sun Moon Lee's visit in 1927, however, the novelty noise era of early jazz was drawing to a close and, with it, the use of 'oriental effects' in jazz. As one local newspaper article put it: 'a temple bell in a foxtrot "dates" it fatally now; so does a Chinese lilt. The public has had Chinese and Indian jazz effects and is sick of them.'[34] Moreover, from 1923 visiting white American or American-led jazz orchestras provided models for jazz performance that made it clear to Australian musicians and their public that jazz and jazzing were much more than adding loud and weird novelty noise to dance music (Bisset 1979: 11–27).

In parallel with evolving understandings of white jazz-orchestra jazz and jazzing, there was also growing awareness of a culturally modernizing China, and other forms of musical and non-musical engagement with China were beginning to emerge. The coalescence of early jazz and oriental exotica represented a time when the newness, apparent freedom and residual mysteriousness, even 'otherness', of jazz—as perceived in culturally decontextualized Australia—made it at least as interestingly alien or weird as 'oriental' music and therefore easily hybridized (or seen to hybridize) with it. Conversely, the exotic, colourful and mysterious soundscape of the 'Orient' embraced Chinese traditional bands, Chinese vaudeville performers of jazz, oriental musical and visual impressions on stage and screen and even the still mysterious and exotic sounds of jazz. Just before the close of the Australian Jazz Age and the onset of the Great Depression, 'Chinese jazz' brought these different worlds together in Australia in a wonderful and unrepeatable confluence of 'oriental' magic, acrobatics, aural extravaganza and jazz, as epitomized by the *Brisbane Courier*'s fanciful advertisement for Sun Moon Lee.

References

Bellman, Jonathan (2011) 'Musical Voyages and their Baggage: Orientalism in Music and Critical Musicology'. *Musical Quarterly* 94/3: 417–38. http://dx.doi.org/10.1093/musqtl/gdr014

Bellman, Jonathan, ed. (1998) *The Exotic in Western Music*. Boston: Northeastern University Press.

33. *Gippsland Times*, 18 August 1927: 4.
34. *Townsville Daily Bulletin*, 4 December 1928: 5.

Bisset, Andrew (1979) *Black Roots, White Flowers: A History of Jazz in Australia*. Sydney: Golden Press.

Born, Georgina, and David Hesmondhalgh, eds. (2000) *Western Music and its Others: Difference, Representation, and Appropriation in Music*. Berkeley: University of California Press.

Clayton, Martin, and Bennett Zon, eds. (2007) *Music and Orientalism in the British Empire, 1780s–1940s: Portrayal of the East*. Hampshire: Ashgate.

Coyle, Jackey, and Rebecca Coyle (2003) 'Hawaiian-style Music'. In *Currency Companion to Music and Dance in Australia*, ed. John Whiteoak and Aline Scott-Maxwell, 314–15. Sydney: Currency House.

Cundle, Guy (2014) 'Across the Pacific: The Transformation of the Steel Guitar from Hawaiian Folk Instrument to Popular Music Mainstay'. M.Phil. thesis. University of Adelaide, Elder Conservatorium of Music.

Doggett, Anne (2008) '"Strains from flowery land": Responses to Chinese Musical Activity in Mid-Nineteenth-Century Ballarat'. *Context: Journal of Music Research* 33: 107–120.

Dreyfus, Kay (1999) *Sweethearts of Rhythm: the Story of Australia's All-Girl Bands and Orchestras to the End of the Second World War*. Sydney: Currency Press.

Edwards, Holly, ed. (2000) *Noble Dreams Wicked Pleasures: Orientalism in America 1870–1930*. Princeton, NJ: Princeton University Press.

Field, Andrew David (2010) *Shanghai's Dancing World: Cabaret Culture and Urban Politics, 1919–1954*. Hong Kong: Chinese University Press.

Jensen, Lars (2005) *Unsettling Australia: Readings in Australian Cultural History*. New Delhi: Atlantic.

Johnson, Bruce (1987) *The Oxford Companion to Australian Jazz*. Oxford: Oxford University Press.

—(2000) *The Inaudible Music: Jazz, Gender and Australian Modernity*. Sydney: Currency Press.

Jones, Andrew F. (2001) *Yellow Music: Media, Culture and Colonial Modernity in the Chinese Jazz Age*. Durham, NC: Duke University Press. http://dx.doi.org/10.1215/9780822380436

Kelly, Veronica (1993) 'Orientalism in Early Australian Theatre'. *New Literatures Review* 26: 32–45.

Leach, William (1993) *Land of Desire: Merchants, Power, and the Rise of a New American Culture*. New York: Pantheon Books.

Locke, Ralph (2009) *Musical Exoticism: Images and Reflections*. Cambridge: Cambridge University Press.

Love, Harold (1985) 'Chinese Theatre on the Victorian Goldfields, 1858–1870'. *Australasian Drama Studies* 3/2: 45–86.

Moon, Krystyn R. (2005) *Yellowface: Creating the Chinese in American Popular Music and Performance, 1850s–1920s*. New Brunswick, NJ: Rutgers University Press.

Nance, Susan (2009) *How the Arabian Nights Inspired the American Dream, 1790–1935*. Chapel Hill, NC: University of North Carolina Press. http://dx.doi.org/10.5149/9780807894057_nance

Ryan, Jan (2003) *Chinese Women and the Global Village: An Australian Site*. St Lucia, Qld: University of Queensland Press.

Said, Edward (1978) *Orientalism: Western Conceptions of the Orient*. London: Penguin.

Scott, Derek, B. (2003) 'Orientalism in Musical Style'. In Scott, *From the Erotic to the Demonic: On Critical Musicology*, 155–78. Oxford: Oxford University Press.

Scott-Maxwell, Aline (1997) 'Oriental Exoticism in 1920s Australian Popular Music'. *Perfect Beat: The Pacific Journal of Research into Contemporary Music and Popular Culture* 3/3: 28–57.

—(2011) 'Representation and Authenticity Intertwined: Early Australian Constructions of "China" through Popular Music and the Popular Stage'. In *Instruments of Change: Selected Proceedings of the IASPM-ANZ 2010 Annual Conference*, ed. Jen Cattermole, Shane Homan and Graeme Smith, 117–24. Melbourne: School of English, Communications and Performance Studies & School of Music-Conservatorium, Monash University.

—(2013) 'Australian Encounters with an Imagined China in Early Musical Entertainment'. In *Encounters: Musical Meetings between Australia and China*, ed. Nicholas Ng, 20–35. Toowong, Qld: Australian Academic Press.

Sutcliffe, Mike (1997) 'Sonny Clay and the Colored Idea'. *Australian Record and Music Review* 35: 3–13.

Teo Hsu-Ming (2014) 'American Popular Culture through the Lens of Saidian and Post-Saidian Orientalist Critiques'. *Critical Race and Whiteness Studies* 10/1: 1–17.

Wang Zheng-Ting (1997) *Chinese Music in Australia—Victoria: 1850s to Mid 1990s*. Melbourne: Australia Asia Foundation.

Wang Zheng-Ting, and Anne Doggett (2007) 'Chinese Music on the Victorian Goldfields'. *Victorian Historical Journal* 78/2: 170–86.

Whiteoak, John (1995) 'Hawaiian Music and Jazzing'. *Perfect Beat: The Pacific Journal of Research into Contemporary Music and Popular Culture* 2/3: 115–17.

—(1999) *Playing Ad Lib: Improvisatory Music in Australia 1836–1970*. Sydney: Currency Press.

3 Got a little rhythm?

The Australian influence on swing in New Zealand during the 1930s and 1940s

Aleisha Ward[*]

Introduction

In the first half of the twentieth century the Australian dance music/jazz scene was inextricably entwined with the New Zealand scene. Musicians from each country regularly performed and resided in the other, creating close connections between both scenes to the point that during the 1930s and 1940s there was almost an overarching trans-Tasman jazz/dance music scene (see Whiteoak 2009). In this chapter I examine one specific instance of these connections by investigating the Australian influence on the New Zealand swing scene during the 1930s and 1940s.

The performance of swing music in New Zealand was strongly influenced by Australian bands, but two particularly stand out: Theo Walters' Personality Band, and Tut Coltman's Swingstars. Both bands held long-term residencies at prestigious cabarets, toured New Zealand and made regular radio broadcasts. These activities served to familiarize New Zealanders with the visitor's styles of swing, and both bandleaders hired New Zealand musicians and arrangers thereby influencing the style and performance of swing among New Zealand bands.

This chapter examines the activities of the Coltman and Walters' bands in Australia and New Zealand. I investigate the mobility of musicians and music between the two countries, and how these Australian bands helped to shape

[*] Aleisha Ward holds a PhD in music from the University of Auckland where her thesis was on jazz in New Zealand 1920–1955. She is currently a freelance writer, editor, lecturer and tutor in music history, and also works in a library. Aleisha writes about jazz in New Zealand for audioculture.co.nz, *New Zealand Musician*, on nzjazz.wordpress.com, and on Twitter as @nzjazzhistory. She writes about other topics on jazzhistorianafterhours.wordpress.com, and about jazz flute for flutejournal.com.

the New Zealand swing scene. Additionally I examine how the New Zealand tours had a lasting effect on Coltman and Walters' careers.

Tut Coltman and Theo Walters were considered superstars of Australian jazz/dance music when they came to New Zealand, but who were they on the Australian scene? Neither is mentioned in detail in the histories of Australian jazz that cover this period (Bisset 1987; Johnson 1987; Whiteoak 1999, 2009). In the following sections I will briefly outline each bandleader's career and their tours to New Zealand before considering their effects on the New Zealand jazz scene, and how their New Zealand sojourns affected their Australian careers. As it is impossible to fully detail the events discussed here within the constraints of this publication I direct the reader to my previous writings on Coltman and Walters (Ward 2012, 2013b). For cultural context about the New Zealand jazz scene during this same period I direct the reader to my previous writings on jazz in New Zealand (Ward 2010, 2012, 2013a, 2013b) and also to nzjazz.wordpress.com/got-a-little-rhythm/ for supplementary material.

Swing

In the 1930s swing music in Australia and New Zealand was a concept around which there was a great deal of confusion. As Bruce Johnson has so eloquently put it: 'While it was clear that "swing was the thing", there was very little agreement about *what* the thing was' (Johnson 1987: 18). This confusion marked the development of swing in both countries as well as the terminology used to describe the music. In Australia the terms 'hot music', 'hot rhythm', 'modern rhythm' or 'modern rhythmic dance music' (Johnson 1987: 15–16, 18; Whiteoak 1999: 221–22; 2009: 26) were popular synonyms for 'swing' in Australia during the 1930s. In New Zealand the equivalent terms were 'swing tempo', 'modern rhythm' and 'modern dance music' (EPW 1936: 21, col. 6; NZRR 1936a: 20).

What this variety of terminology meant in musical practice was equally disputed. The repertoire of Australian and New Zealand swing musicians spanned light classical, opera, the latest in novelty and popular music to what we now consider standard jazz repertoire (Johnson 1987: 18; Whiteoak 1999: 222–23, 239; 2009: 28–30; Ward 2012: 92–97, 135–38; 2013b: 189–92). Because of this it would appear that swing was a performance practice rather than a genre to Australasian musicians. There were various aspects to this performance practice, some of which will be discussed in this chapter because they were fundamental to the impact and influence of Australian musicians on the development of jazz in New Zealand. However, there are two important aspects of what denoted swing that I will mention here. First was the practice of 'swinging' music. At its broadest conceptualization this meant musicians would create swing rhythm through intensifying rhythmic accents and the displacement of what John Whiteoak describes as 'attack points': delaying or anticipating the beat (Whiteoak 1999: 223). The second aspect is the use of improvisation. Although jazz musicians used forms of improvisation throughout the 1920s and early 1930s the conceptualization moved away from the seemingly chaotic approach of 1920s style jazz (especially in New Zealand—see Ward 2012: 112, 117–21), to a more sophisticated melodic extemporization that began to conform more closely to American ideals of jazz improvisation (Whiteoak 1999: 235–38).

It should also be noted that the definition of swing in Australia and New Zealand changed over the course of the period under investigation here. Swing developed from a set of performance practices that were applied to any type of music to a more formalized genre. Swing bands began to adhere to certain groupings of instrumentation; the repertoire (although still loose) began to conform to what American swing bands would play, and the performance practices became codified to resemble the types of practices used by American bands (Bourke 2010: 92–93; Ward 2010: 97; 2012: 137–38).

Tut Coltman

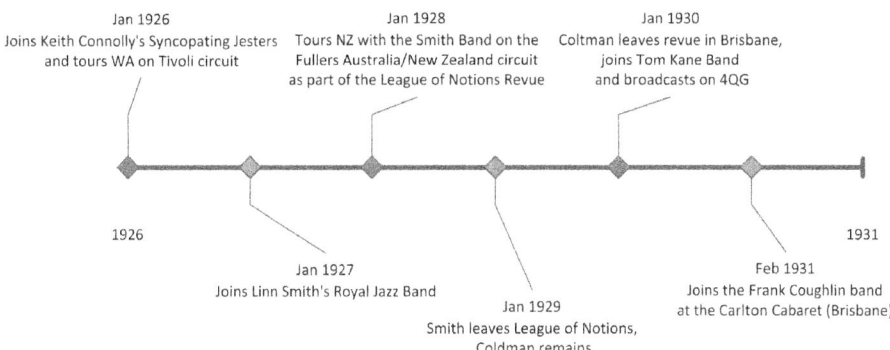

Figure 1: Tut Coltman's early career activities

Trumpeter/saxophonist W. Stan 'Tut' Coltman began his performing career in Sydney after leaving high school. His first known engagement began in early 1926 with Keith Connolly's Syncopating Jesters touring West Australia on the Tivoli Vaudeville circuit (see Figure 1) (DNP 1926: 7, col. 2), and followed this by joining Linn Smith's Royal Jazz Band in 1927 (AMM 1937e: 13). During the 1920s the Smith band was considered one of the hottest jazz bands in Australia, frequently outdoing American bands at playing 'the real thing...stimulating, seductive jazz' (Bourke 2010: 21 [citing *Fuller News*, 14 March 1925: 2]).

As a vaudevillian stage jazz band, it is hard, by today's standards, to consider a band such as the Linn Smith Band a 'seductive' jazz band despite their promotional material. However, by the standards of 1920s Australian (and New Zealand) musicians and audiences they were as hot a jazz band as anything that was heard via local radio or on the vaudeville circuits (Whiteoak 1999: 182–83) (for more see nzjazz.wordpress.com/got-a-little-rhythm/). During this period the Smith outfit worked on the Fullers Vaudeville circuit around Australia and New Zealand, and Coltman's first New Zealand visit with Smith was in 1928 (EPW 1928: 4, col. 6). The period with the Smith organization introduced Coltman to many Australian and New Zealand musicians that he would regularly work with after leaving Smith, including banjoist Cluny McPherson, saxophonists Jimmy Coates and Tommy Stratton, and trombonist Frank Coughlan. His time with Smith was something of an apprenticeship period for Coltman, teaching him many musical and stage skills. By the time the band was performing in the *League of Notions* revue (1929) Coltman was a featured soloist, and was being noticed in the press independently of the band (AA 1929: 8, col. 3).

Coltman left the revue in Brisbane in 1930 (BC 1930: 15, col. 2), remaining there for the rest of the year, playing with bands in cabarets and on the radio. It is unknown whether he led any bands while he was in Brisbane, however. Additionally, it is also unknown how deliberate a choice Coltman made in leading a band (whether this was the next logical step in his career, or whether it was the right opportunity at the right time), but his first known experience was to occur not in Australia, but in New Zealand.

On Easter weekend 1931 Coltman began a residency at Wellington's Adelphi Cabaret (see nzjazz.wordpress.com/got-a-little-rhythm/ for information on venues) with a band he had brought with him from Australia (see Table 1 below) (AMM 1937e: 13). The residency lasted eighteen months (see Figure 2) during which time some of the original musicians were replaced by locals, including Syd French and his former Smith band mate Tommy Stratton on saxophones, and Alan Brown on drums. In addition to their residency at the Adelphi the band regularly performed at other venues for balls, and as part of theatrical entertainment (EPW 1931: 3, col. 2).

After the residency ended in November 1932 Coltman took the band on a tour of the lower North Island (as far north as New Plymouth on the west coast and Napier on the east) giving the provinces (see nzjazz.wordpress.com/got-a-little-rhythm/) a taste of the latest jazz that they would usually only hear on the radio (ADBN 1932: 22). The band returned to Wellington for the Christmas season before returning to Australia early in 1933 (AMM 1937e: 13). On his return to Australia Coltman settled in Sydney and was employed by his former sideman Jimmy Coates for a residency at the Empress Ballroom and he would remain with the Coates band until 1937 (AMM 1937e: 13). In early 1937 Coltman toured New Zealand with Coates, and it is likely he set up his next tour of New Zealand during that tour (AMM 1937c: 7).

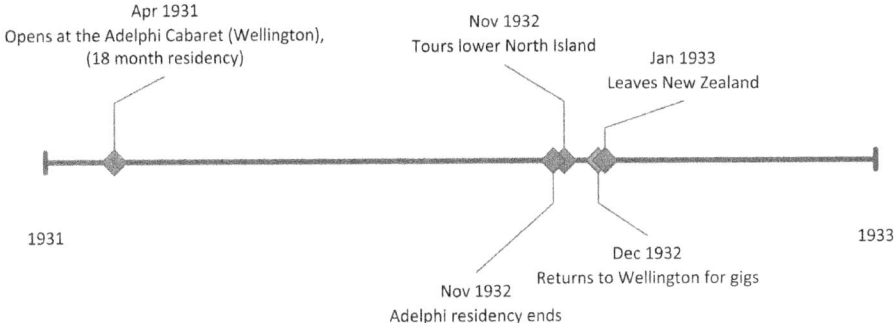

Figure 2: Tut Coltman's first New Zealand tour

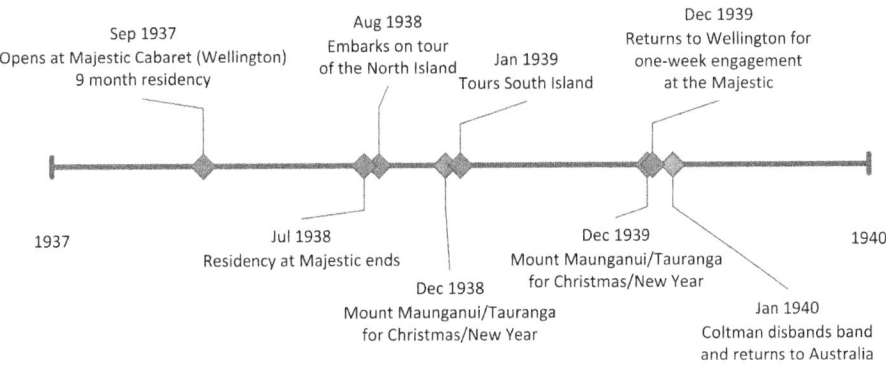

Figure 3: Tut Coltman's second New Zealand tour

In September 1937 Tut Coltman returned to New Zealand with his new band the Swingstars (see Table 1 below). As noted in Figure 3, the band resided at the Majestic Cabaret in Wellington from 30 September 1937 to July 1938 (EPW 1937a: 4, col. 8; 1938: 5, col. 4), regularly broadcasting from the cabaret via relay on station 2YA and in-studio for the light entertainment programme *Revudeville and Rhythm* on 2YD (EPW 1937b: 4, col. 6).

The Swingstars were popular among dancers and musicians in Wellington, and Coltman was noted for encouraging the arranging abilities of his musicians (AMM 1938a: 53). By the end of their residence at the Majestic in 1938 the Coltman band featured a number of Wellington jazz musicians, including saxophonist Bob Girvan (also one of the band's arrangers), pianist Noel Fields and drummer Allan Brown (AMM 1938d: 54).

In August 1938 the Swingstars embarked on a national tour. The band toured North Island provincial towns throughout the rest of 1938 (Bourke 2010: 86), and in 1939 Coltman toured the South Island before taking a residency at Frascati's Cabaret, Christchurch (see nzjazz.wordpress.com/got-a-little-rhythm/), in mid-1939 (AMM 1939c: 45; 1939d: 50). The Swingstars remained in Christchurch until late 1939 when they returned to the North Island for summer engagements in the Bay of Plenty, remaining there until Coltman decided to return to Australia in early 1940 (AMM 1940a: 13).

After returning to Australia Coltman resettled in Sydney (AMM 1940a: 13) and was soon leading a band on the Hoyts theatre circuit, which included saxophonist Jim Buckley and pianist Lou Lewis (AMM 1940d: 12). Coltman continued to lead bands around Sydney (in theatres, clubs and on the radio) until mid-1942 when he joined the Australian Army and its Antiaircraft Training Regiment Dance Band (AMM 1943: 18). Coltman was based in New South Wales during the latter part of his service performing with, and leading, bands there in 1944 while still attached to the military. Billed as 'The King of Swing' (SA 1944: 3, col. 6; DC 1944: 3, col. 3), Coltman traded on both his military service (doing his 'bit') and his reputation that was built on his New Zealand and Australian activities.

Although not as prolific as many other swing musicians after the war, Coltman continued to trade on his past tours and activities to carve himself a niche in the Sydney and broader New South Wales dance music scene. He continued to broadcast and perform on a regular basis, and although advertising and press notice diminished over the 1940s, he appears to have continued to have a steady career.

Theo Walters

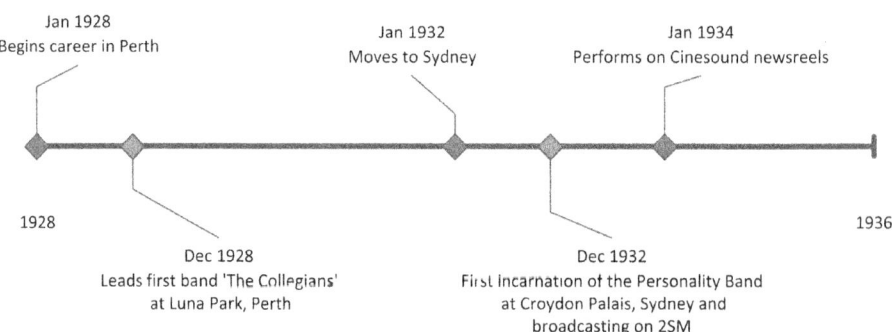

Figure 4: Theo Walters' early career activities

Saxophonist Theo Walters began his performing career in Perth circa 1928 in dance and variety bands, playing mostly in cabarets and for charity shows (STP 1928: 35, col. 7; WAP 1928: 7, col. 4). By late 1928 Walters was leading a band at Perth's Luna Park's Palais de Danse (see Figure 4) (DNP 1928: 12, col. 3). Walters moved to Sydney in 1932 and began leading the first incarnation of his Personality Band at the Croydon Palais (see Table 1 below) (ASy 1932a: 31, col. 1). This band gained significant local media attention with sellout crowds (ASy 1932b: 27, col. 4), and by early 1933 Walters had come to the notice of *Australian Dance Band News* who profiled him, noting that he had the only ten-piece band in Sydney at that time, which was proving a hit with dancers, as much for their showmanship as for their music (ADBN 1933: 5).

Walters was very forward thinking about how to gain the best exposure for his bands. In addition to the performances in cabarets, for private parties and for charity concerts, the Walters band regularly broadcast on radio (ASy 1932b: 27, col. 4), and also regularly performed on film shorts and newsreel entertainment (NS 1934: 9, col. 1).

The Theo Walters Personality Band (see Table 1 below) debuted at the Majestic Cabaret, Wellington (see nzjazz.wordpress.com/got-a-little-rhythm/ for more information), in September 1936 and quickly became popular with Wellington dancers and musicians (NZRR 1936b: 17). In early 1937 the Walters band departed Wellington for a residence at the Peter Pan Cabaret in Auckland (see Figure 5). Billed as 'Australia's Greatest Showman' Walters had expanded the band to include New Zealand musicians such as Baden Brown (saxophone) and George Campbell (bass) (see Table 1). The Walters Band debuted at the Peter Pan Cabaret on 23 January 1937 for a three-month residency (AMM 1937a: 5).

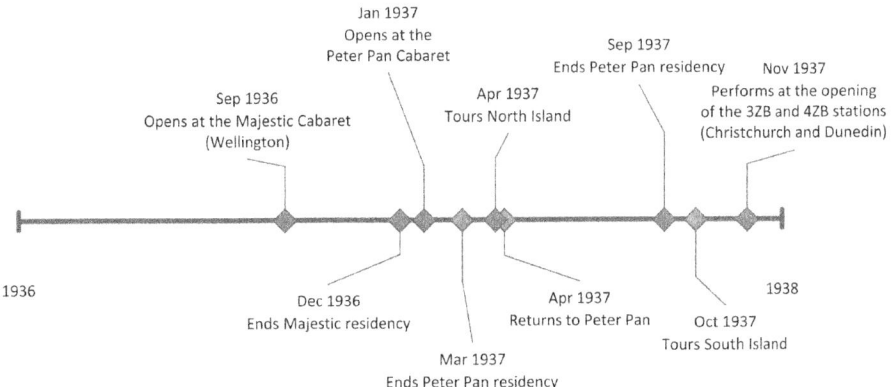

Figure 5: Theo Walters' first New Zealand tour

The Auckland correspondent for *Australian Music Maker and Dance Band News* noted that the Walters band was of great 'educational value' for the local jazz scene (AMM 1937b: 25). The band was known for their instrumental versatility, their emulation of Benny Goodman's swing style and, importantly, for their showmanship. This last was dramatically different from many New Zealand bands in this period, which according to reports was virtually non-existent (AMM 1937b: 25; 1937f: 45; 1938b: 53). Reports in *Music Maker* indicate that the Walters band impressed Auckland musicians and dancing audiences with their musical and comedic presentations between dance sets. Reports in newspaper women's columns also indicate that the columnists were extremely impressed by the band, calling them 'masters of syncopated rhythm' and praising their swing arrangements and musical versatility (AS 1937a: 11, col. 4; 1937b: 10, col. 6).

In March 1937 Walters took the band on a two-week tour of the North Island (see Figure 5), returning to the Peter Pan for another residency from 10 April (AMM 1937d: 26; AS 1937c: 22, col. 3). This lasted until September when Walters took the band on a larger tour, including the South Island, allowing their now extensive fan base outside of Auckland and Wellington to see the band before Walters and the Australian contingent returned to Australia at the end of 1937.

Returning to Australia Walters was soon engaged at the Oriental (formerly the Ginger Jar) in Sydney (see Figure 6) with a band that was almost identical to the personnel of his original New Zealand tour Personality Band (AMM 1938c: 6). The Walters band re-established themselves on the Sydney scene and, in addition to their cabaret/club work, they began broadcasting on station 2GB (TWNS 1938: 45, col. 1).

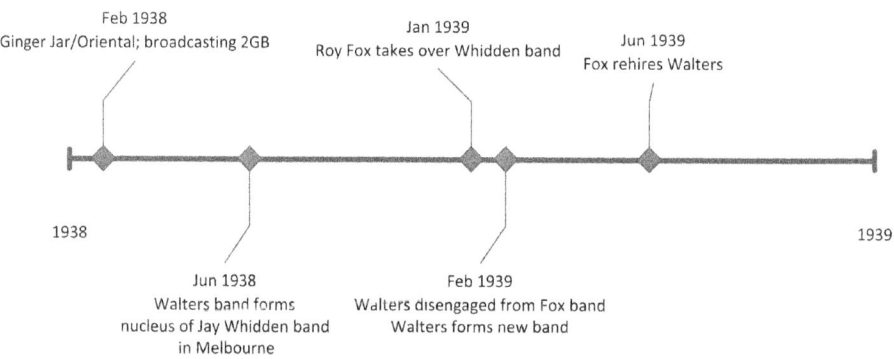

Figure 6: Theo Walters' Australian return activities

By the middle of 1938 Walters and his Personality Band formed the nucleus of American bandleader Jay Whidden's band and were performing in Melbourne (AM 1938: 22, col. 4; AMM 1940e: 20). Initial reports indicated that Walters and his men were to return to the United States with Whidden (AM 1939: 7, col. 4); however in 1939 the Whidden band was taken over by American-British bandleader Roy Fox (CC 1939: 2, col. 4).

Walters and his sidemen remained with Fox until February 1939 when Fox suddenly fired Walters. While Walters' now former sidemen remained with Fox, Walters organized a new band and engagements on the Hoyts Theatre circuit (AMM 1939a: 20). However, Fox soon re-employed Walters as a vocalist (TNA 1939: 2, col. 2) and it was rumoured that Walters was to follow him to the United States (AS 1939: 9, col. 5; AMM 1939e: 3). Unexpectedly, however, Theo Walters (sans band) returned to New Zealand in November 1939 (see Figure 7) leading the house band at the Peter Pan Cabaret. Soon he was splitting this band's time between the Peter Pan, and theatre and radio engagements.

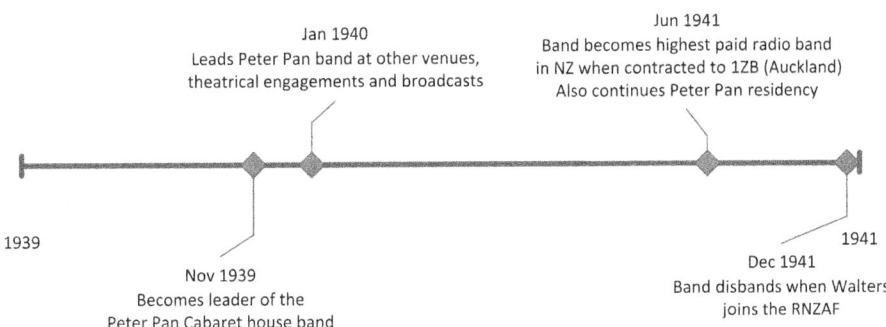

Figure 7: Theo Walters' second New Zealand tour

In mid-1941 Walters negotiated a contract with station 1ZB (Auckland) for his band to become their house band (AMM 1941: 39). The contract terms were very generous by the standards of the New Zealand Commercial Broadcasting Service with each side musician earning nine pounds per week (for details see nzjazz.wordpress.com/got-a-little-rhythm/). The Walters band (see Table 1 below) now became the most prominent swing band in New Zealand. The band's primary programme, *Band Waggon*, was touted as a half-hour showcase, and they provided music for a number of other programmes during the course of the week (*Tempo* 1941: 10; NZL 1941a: 11; 1941b: 41). This engagement was short, however, as the band disbanded in late 1941 when Walters enlisted in the Royal New Zealand Air Force (RNZAF) Band (Bourke 2010: 113–14).

Walters remained with the RNZAF throughout the war, becoming the leader of their swing band, The Swing Wing in 1944. He was released from military service in early 1945 and returned to Australia. By April 1945 Walters was leading a band at the Cocoanut Grove in Brisbane. As Coltman had, Walters traded on his New Zealand activities and his military service, especially as leader of the RNZAF Swing Wing, to promote himself (SM 1945: 6, col. 8). In late 1945 Walters transferred his talents to radio (AWW 1945: 23), remaining based in radio as a musical comedian for the rest of his career, with band work becoming secondary (WAP 1948: 8, col. 5).

Influences on New Zealand swing

As I have noted elsewhere (Ward 2009; 2012; 2013a), outside musico-cultural influences via live performance, radio and recordings were vital to the development of jazz as both music and culture in New Zealand, *especially* in the first half of the twentieth century. Both Coltman and Walters epitomize the type of influences on musicians and audiences that helped that development.

As I noted in the introduction, both Coltman and Walters were considered superstars of Australian jazz when they arrived in New Zealand. This was due, at least in part, to their publicity, which made much of their status in Australia (see, for example, NZRR 1936b: 17). This status was enhanced by their holding residencies at prestigious cabarets, particularly the Peter Pan Cabaret and the Majestic Cabaret, from which they would regularly broadcast to the rest of the country. These factors, and the enthusiastic reception from the local media and contributors to *Australian Music Maker*, placed the Coltman and Walters' bands at the top of the New Zealand jazz scene hierarchy above the existing local top bands on the scene.

Because of their status both bandleaders were in a position to influence the evolution of the New Zealand swing scene in a variety of ways. Both bands were known for their showmanship and the press frequently focused on their flair and style. Their approaches to showmanship influenced local perceptions about swing performance practices, and importantly making the band the central attraction for the audience (AMM 1938a: 53; 1938b: 53).

Musically, showmanship was demonstrated by an increase in tailored arrangements for bands as Coltman and Walters encouraged their musicians to compose and arrange specifically for their bands (AS 1937a: 11, col. 4; 1937b: 10, col. 6; AMM 1938a: 53; 1938b: 53). The tailored arrangements were not necessarily more complex, but rather they highlighted the best features of the bands and of individual musicians. This led to other New Zealand bands using more tailored arrangements, or composing for specific combinations (Warren, interview with author, 21 September 2008).

Coltman and Walters' influence on swing performance practices was demonstrated through musical and extra-musical practices. Extra-musical influences were frequently demonstrated through aspects such as choreography for sectional solos. Musically, swing performance practice was manifested through rhythm and sound/timbre. While mentions of sound/timbre in the press were vague and focused on quality and volume (the comment 'excellent sound' was common), rhythm was an aspect that even the non-musical press could understand. Press reports frequently discussed how crisp the rhythms of these two bands were. The idea that the rhythm was 'crisp' spans several different aspects. From the perspective of the women's columnists (and the dancing audience), 'crisp' rhythm included tempo, how well the band executed rhythmic ideas and how well it suited dancing (AS 1937a: 11, col. 4). To the *Music Maker* columnists 'crisp' rhythm was influenced by a variety of factors ranging from the purpose of the arrangement (dancing or floorshow), to performance practices (including precision of technique) and broadcasting techniques (AMM 1938a: 53; 1938b: 53; 1939c: 45).

An important aspect of the influence of Coltman and Walters on the New Zealand swing scene was the inclusion of New Zealand musicians. These bands became educational forums in technique, performance practices, arranging and composition, and general musicianship. For musicians outside of these bands, Coltman and Walters provided models that they could emulate in terms of sound, showmanship, stage behaviour, improvisation and other performance practices. Walters was particularly noted for finding new talent, including trumpeter Jim Warren and singer Winsome Walsh. For both Warren and Walsh this was their first job with a swing band of this calibre and taught them everything from sight-reading skills to improvisation and showmanship (Warren, interview with author, 21 September 2008; AMM 1940b: 34; 1940c: 39).

Both bands strongly influenced the popularity of swing in New Zealand. Through their tours and radio broadcasts Coltman and Walters quickly spread and popularized swing to general audiences. This could not have been accomplished in the same time frame by New Zealand bands that rarely toured; while they broadcast regularly they were not given the same press exposure as touring bands. *Music Maker* praised both bands for their 'education' of the audience (AMM 1938a: 53; 1940b: 34), but singled out Coltman for touring the provinces: taking the time to introduce swing to the locals and making it accessible to a wider audience, rather than just to jazz fans (AMM 1939b: 44).

The Walters and Coltman bands were vital to establishing swing as the newest form of jazz/dance music in New Zealand. Their strong presence physically, in the press and on radio became the backbone of the New Zealand swing scene, boosting the incipient swing scene and providing much-needed competition for established jazz bands to improve their performance. Additionally they contributed to the development of professional skills that musicians could utilize in the practice of jazz/dance music both in live performance and radio broadcast.

Influences on Coltman's and Walters' Australian careers

Despite the publicity in New Zealand (prior to touring) about their popularity and prowess, neither Coltman nor Walters were very well known in Australia outside of their scenes. Walters was better known than Coltman due to his radio work and the Cinesound films, but neither had the same stature as trumpeter/bandleader Frank Coughlan or drummer/bandleader Jim Davidson (Johnson 1987: 133–35, 139–40). However, Walters and Coltman's New Zealand activities affected their stature on the Australian jazz scene. Because of their popularity in New Zealand the *Music Maker* correspondents made frequent mentions of them in their columns during their tours. These mentions had a trickle-down effect, doubtless helping to keep Walters and Coltman in the minds of their fellow musicians and the Australian fans and people in the industry (venue/station managers etc.).

When Walters and Coltman returned to Australia both traded on this publicity. It is clear that Walters was business-oriented, and made a point of mentioning his success in New Zealand in his advertising. Coltman, conversely, did not trade as much on his New Zealand reputation, which might partly account for his lesser popularity.

Interestingly, I discovered in the course of researching this chapter that the people who benefited the most from Walters and Coltman's activities were their sidemen (see Table 1 below). George Dobson and Geoff 'Dutchy' Turner, for example, went on to prominence and had regular columns in *Australian Music Maker* (Whiteoak 2009: 29), a publication that was very influential on New Zealand musicians. Jimmy Coates led a prominent band, and hired his former bandleader, Coltman. Nor were the other Australian sidemen impeded by their association with Coltman or Walters. All of the New Zealand sidemen benefited greatly, becoming sought-after arrangers, sidemen and leaders (Bourke 2010: 80, 86–87; Ward 2012). A number of them would 'cross the ditch' or 'cross the big pond', a New Zealander/Australian phrase meaning to succeed on the Australian scene (for more information see nzjazz.wordpress.com/got-a-little-rhythm/).

The Tasman jazz world

In the first half of the twentieth century New Zealand and Australia were isolated from the rest of the jazz world. Knowledge of developments in jazz from the United States was primarily through recordings, radio and film rather than live performances. As researchers have argued (see Bisset 1987; Johnson 1987; Ward 2009, 2012, and Whiteoak 1999, 2009) this had important repercussions on the development of jazz in both Australia and New Zealand. It affected how musicians and audiences perceived jazz, how they approached it, played it and received it. Thus, close connections between New Zealand and Australia became significant in the development of jazz as music and culture, and vital to the development of the scenes and industry of both countries.

The concept of a Tasman world is one that resonates through cultural and musical histories of New Zealand. Researchers Philippa Mein Smith, Peter Hempenstall and Shaun Goldfinch (Mein Smith *et al.* 2008) and others have argued that Australia and New Zealand have alternately ignored and embraced each other from the earliest colonies and have surrounded themselves with myths about the other, each claiming a distinctiveness that sets them apart and above (see, for example, Belich 2001 and Rickard 1996 [1988]). Despite these myths New Zealand and Australia were closely entwined in myriad ways during the interwar period, and this was particularly true of the jazz scenes.

While it is certainly possible to examine each country's jazz scene in isolation, there were inextricable links between the two countries through the mobility and flow of musicians, the ability of each country to hear the radio broadcasts of the other (when the weather was fine), and the centrality of music publishing and recording in Australia (primarily Sydney) (see Ward 2012). Being the smaller country and scene, such connections were more important to New Zealanders than to Australians, but Australians benefited greatly from these connections as well.

In New Zealand, Australian jazz musicians were automatically perceived as being better than New Zealanders at jazz because they came from a larger, supposedly more sophisticated and certainly more extensive scene (Bourke 2010: 6–7, 21–22, 80; Ward 2010: 95–101; 2012: 72–75, 93–96, 142–43; 2013b: 187–88). New Zealand musicians had certain ideas about the Australian jazz scene, how good the musicians were and how much more 'authentic' Australian musicians were at playing jazz (Bourke 2010: 80; Meehan 2010: 37–45; Ward 2010: 97–100). These perceptions meant that in the 1930s and 1940s any Australian jazz band visiting New Zealand was automatically considered 'better' than any New Zealand jazz band, and pre-tour publicity from Australian bands played on this. The fact that both Walters and Coltman were little known outside of their individual scenes did not hamper their identity as superstars to New Zealanders: their popularity traded on where they came from. However, this does not detract from the fact that, by all accounts, they were very good and were extremely influential to the New Zealand jazz scene. They *were* more experienced than most of the musicians they encountered in New Zealand and (as demonstrated above) it showed!

The influence of the Coltman and Walters bands on the New Zealand jazz scene also led many New Zealand musicians to move to Australia and try their luck there (Whiteoak 2009: 30–31; Bourke 2010: 51–53, 80). During the late 1930s, especially, New Zealand musicians would move to Australia for work—seemingly undaunted by the Australian Musicians Union strict rule of one-year residence before being allowed to join the Union and legally perform; far stricter than the New Zealand Musicians Union rules (see also nzjazz.wordpress.com/got-a-little-rhythm/)—to gain broader experiences than they could in New Zealand, particularly in broadcasting and recording. A number of musicians from this period (including the abovementioned Syd French and Tommy Stratton) would actually spend nearly equal periods in both countries for a number of years, while others such as reeds player Charlie Munro (Johnson 1987: 215) would settle in Australia permanently in the late 1930s and 1940s.

Conclusion

The Coltman and Walters' bands were highly influential in the development of swing in New Zealand. Their presence in the 1930s and early 1940s helped them essentially to become the base of the New Zealand swing scene. Both Walters and Coltman's bands gave the New Zealand scene a boost by providing competition and examples of excellent musicianship and showmanship. Through their use of New Zealand musicians Coltman and Walters provided educational forums, especially in arranging and composition, and performance practices such as improvisation. This flow of knowledge confirmed their status as superstars in New Zealand musicians' eyes and further boosted Coltman and Walters' reputations. These activities (as well as socializing with musicians and fans) led to more industry attention via the New Zealand Notes columns in *Australian Music Maker* and a broader reputation that would have enhanced their résumés on their return to Australia.

Once returning to Australia, both Coltman and Walters used their New Zealand reputations to differing degrees, with differing levels of success in the post-war period. Although Tut Coltman and Theo Walters were never known as important figures in Australian jazz, it was on the New Zealand jazz scene that they truly made their mark by influencing an entire generation of jazz musicians and helping to create a localized swing scene.

Table 1: Band personnel charts

Tut Coltman Bands

1931	Late 1931	1932
Tut Coltman Trumpet/saxophone	Tut Coltman Trumpet/saxophone	Tut Coltman Trumpet/saxophone
Jimmy Coates Saxophone	Cluny MacPherson Banjo	Cluny MacPherson Banjo
Cluny MacPherson Banjo	Tommy Stratton Saxophone	Claude Bennett Piano
Frank Chapple Rhythm section	Jerry Connolly Drums	Syd French Saxophone
Jim Downes Rhythm section	Pianist and bassist unknown	Allan Brown Drums
Bill Thompson Rhythm section		Bassist unknown

Tut Coltman Bands

1937	Late 1938	1939
Tut Coltman Trumpet/saxophone	Tut Coltman Trumpet/saxophone	Tut Coltman Trumpet/saxophone
Wal Johnson Tenor sax, clarinet, trumpet, vocalist	Bob Girvan Alto sax	Bob Girvan Alto sax
Jim Creary Alto sax, clarinet, vocals	Tiny McMahon Tenor sax	Jim Gower Bass, trumpet
Jack Stiles Trombone, arranger	Noel Fields Piano	Allan Brown Drums
Emil Kewe Piano, arranger	Claude Bennett Piano	Jim Creary Alto sax
Len Mehden Bass, arranger	Jim Gower Bass	Jackie Roberts Piano
Allan Brown Drums, effects	Allan Brown Drums	
	Mel Naylor Vocals	

Theo Walters

1932/33 Personality band	1936 NZ Tour Majestic Cabaret band	1937 Peter Pan band
Theo Walters Saxophone	Theo Walters Saxophone	Theo Walters Saxophone
Archie Robinson Tenor sax	Geoff 'Dutchy' Turner Saxophone	Bernie Duggan Piano
Kev. Egan Saxophone	George Dobson Trumpet	Sal Martin Drums
Reg Orrell Trumpet	Bernie Duggan Piano	Baden Brown Saxophone
Jerry Coughlin Trumpet	Sal Martin Drums	Jimmy Watters Saxophone
Roy Simpson Trombone		Vern Wilson Trumpet
Harry Bloom Guitar		Phil Campbell Trumpet
Tom King Piano		Max Roberts Bass
Orm Wills Bass		George Campbell Bass
Rube Gilday Drums		

Theo Walters

1938 Ginger Jar/Oriental band	1941 1ZB band
Theo Walters Saxophone	Theo Walters Saxophone, leader
George Dobson Trumpet	Norm Egerton, Jimmy Watters, Pat Watters, Gordon Lanigan Saxophone
Geoff 'Dutchy' Turner Trombone	Phil Campbell, Billy Pritchard, Allan Hills, Brian Marston, Harry Unwin Brass
Bernie Duggan Piano, accordion	Len Hawkins Piano
George Watson Drums	Fred Gedson Drums

Abbreviations

AA	*Advertiser*, Adelaide
ADBN	*Australian Dance Band News*
AM	*Argus*, Melbourne
AMM	*Australian Music Maker and Dance Band News*
AS	*Auckland Star*
ASy	*Arrow*, Sydney
AWW	*Australian Women's Weekly*
BC	*Brisbane Courier*
CC	*Camperdown Chronicle*
DC	*Dungog Chronicle and Gloucester Advertiser*, NSW
DNP	*Daily News*, Perth
EPW	*Evening Post*, Wellington
NS	*Northern Star*
NZL	*New Zealand Listener*
NZRR	*New Zealand Radio Record and Electric Home Journal*
SA	*Singleton Argus*, New South Wales
SM	*Sunday Mail*, Brisbane
STP	*Sunday Times*, Perth
TNA	*The News*, Adelaide
TWNS	*The World's News*, Sydney
WAP	*West Australian*, Perth

References

Advertiser (Adelaide) (1929) 'Majestic Theatre: "League of Notions" Revue'. 27 August: 8, col. 3.
Argus (Melbourne) (1938) 'To Play in U.S.A.'. 14 September: 22, col. 4.
—(1939) 'Welcome to Famous Band Leader'. 18 January: 7, col. 4.
Arrow (Sydney) (1932a) 'Croydon Palais' [Advertisement]. 16 December: 31, col. 1.
—(1932b) 'Doing Dances'. 23 December: 27, col. 4.
Auckland Star (1937a) 'Topics for Women: Peter Pan'. 1 February: 11, col. 4.
—(1937b) 'Topics for Women: Peter Pan'. 8 February: 10, col. 6.
—(1937c) 'Peter Pan' [Advertisement]. 7 April: 22, col. 3.
—(1939) 'Music Personality'. 21 November: 9, col. 5.
Australian Dance Band News (1932) 'New Zealand Notes'. November: 22.
—(1933) 'Walters' Success'. February: 5.
Australian Music Maker and Dance Band News (1937a) 'Theo Walters & Co. Move into Peter Pan, Auckland'. February: 5.

—(1937b) 'From all the States: Auckland N.Z.'. February: 25.
—(1937c) 'Jimmy Coates Returns to Empress'. April: 7.
—(1937d) 'From all the States: Auckland N.Z.'. April: 26.
—(1937e) 'The Bandland Reporter'. October: 13.
—(1937f) 'From all the States: Auckland N.Z.'. October: 45.
—(1938a) 'Tut Coltman in N.Z.'. January: 53.
—(1938b) 'From all the States: Auckland N.Z.'. January: 53.
—(1938c) 'The Oriental (Late Ginger Jar) Changes Band: Theo Walters Takes Over'. February: 6.
—(1938d) 'New Zealand Notes: Wellington N.Z.'. May: 54.
—(1939a) 'Theo Walters'. April: 20.
—(1939b) 'From all the States: Opotiki'. April: 44.
—(1939c) 'From all the States: Dunedin N.Z.'. April: 45.
—(1939d) 'From all the States: Dunedin N.Z.'. June: 50.
—(1939e) 'Theo Walters at Peter Pan Cabaret'. December: 3.
—(1940a) 'Chatter'. March: 13.
—(1940b) 'From all the States: Auckland N.Z.'. March: 34.
—(1940c) 'From all the States: Auckland N.Z.'. 30 April: 39.
—(1940d) 'Swinging in Sydney'. May: 12.
—(1940e) 'Bernie Duggan'. March: 20–21.
—(1941) 'New Combination has Highest-paid Contract in N.Z.'. August: 39.
—(1943) 'Many Familiar Names in Army Dance Band'. June: 18.
Australian Women's Weekly (1945) 'New Time for Joke Session'. 1 December: 23.
Belich, James (2001) *Paradise Reforged: A History of the New Zealanders from the 1880s to the Year 2000*. Auckland: Penguin.
Bisset, A. (1987) *Black Roots, White Flowers: A History of Jazz in Australia*. Sydney: ABC Enterprises.
Bourke, C. (2010) *Blue Smoke: The Lost Dawn of New Zealand Popular Music 1918–1964*. Auckland: Auckland University Press.
Brisbane Courier (1930) 'League of Notions Revue'. 5 May: 15, col. 2.
Camperdown Chronicle (Victoria) (1939) 'Roy Fox's Band'. 10 June: 2, col. 4.
Daily News (Perth) (1926) '"Syncopating Jesters": Keith Connolly's Success'. 26 February: 7, col. 2.
—(1928) 'Luna Park'. 6 December: 12, col. 3.
Dungog Chronicle and Gloucester Advertiser (1944) 'Tillegra: Bright Ball'. 29 August: 3, col. 3.
Evening Post (Wellington) (1928) 'His Majesty's Theatre' [Advertisement]. 19 May: 4, col. 6.
—(1931) 'Majestic Theatre'. 24 December: 3, col. 2.
—(1936) 'Song Hit'. 26 March: 21, col. 6.
—(1937a) 'Pleasure Cruise' [Majestic Cabaret advertisement]. 30 September: 4, col. 8.
—(1937b) 'Broadcasting'. 22 November: 4, col. 6.
—(1938) 'Dancing Tonight' [Majestic Cabaret advertisement]. 14 July: 5, col. 4.
Johnson, B. (1987) *Oxford Companion to Australian Jazz*. Melbourne: Oxford University Press.
Meehan, Norman (2010) *Serious Fun: The Life and Music of Mike Nock*. Wellington: Victoria University Press.

Mein Smith, Philippa, Peter Hempenstall and Shaun Goldfinch (2008) *Remaking the Tasman World.* Christchurch: Canterbury University Press.

New Zealand Listener (1941a) 'On Opening Day...' 17 October: 11.

—(1941b) '1ZB' [Listings 24 October]. 17 October: 41.

New Zealand Radio Record and Electric Home Journal (1936a) 'Among New Releases'. 3 April: 20.

—(1936b) 'N.Z. Grabs One of Australia's Ace Melody Makers'. 2 October: 17.

News, The (Adelaide) (1939) 'Palais Royal' [Advertisement]. 13 June: 2, col. 2.

Northern Star (1934) 'Entertainments: Cinesound Review'. 29 December: 9, col. 1.

Rickard, John (1996 [1988]) *Australia: A Cultural History.* 2nd edn. New York: Longman.

Singleton Argus (1944) 'South Singleton Church of England Ball' [Advertisement]. 30 June: 3, col. 6.

Sunday Mail (Brisbane) (1945) 'Cocoanut Grove' [Advertisement]. 8 April: 6, col. 8.

Sunday Times (Perth) (1928) 'Coming of Age Party'. 4 March: 35, col. 7.

Tempo (1941) 'Theo Walters Stars in New Zealand with First Class Band'. November–December: 10.

Ward, A. (2010) '"ANZAC, Hollywood and Home": Creating a New Zealand Jazz Culture'. In *Many Voices: Music and National Identity in Aotearoa/New Zealand*, ed. Henry Johnson, 93–102. Newcastle: Cambridge Scholars.

—(2012) '"Any rags, any jazz, any boppers today?" Jazz in New Zealand 1920–1955'. PhD thesis, University of Auckland.

—(2013a) 'Artie Shaw in New Zealand 1943'. *Current Research in Jazz Online* 5. http://www.crj-online.org/v5/CRJ-ShawNewZealand.php

—(2013b) 'Fascinating Rhythm: Australian and American Influences on Swing in New Zealand'. In *Shifting Sounds: Musical Flow. A Collection of Papers from the 2012 IASPM Australia/New Zealand Conference*, ed. Oli Wilson and Sarah Attfield, 187–97. Dunedin: IASPM Australia/New Zealand.

West Australian (Perth) (1928) 'Concert for Charity'. 5 December: 7, col. 4.

—(1948) 'Radio Stars Help Surf Contest'. 2 February: 8, col. 5.

Whiteoak, J. (1999) *Playing Ad Lib: Improvisatory Music in Australia 1836–1970.* Sydney: Currency.

—(2009) 'Across the Big Pond: Mapping Early "Jazz" Activity in New Zealand through Australian Jazz Historiography and Sources'. In *Jazz Aotearoa: Notes Towards a New Zealand History*, ed. Richard Hardie and Allan Thomas, 14–40. Wellington: Steele Roberts.

World's News, The (Sydney) (1938) '2GB' [Advertisement]. 23 February: 45, col. 1.

4 The reception of jazz in Adelaide and Melbourne and the creation of an Australian sound in the *Angry Penguins* decade

Bruce Clunies Ross[*]

> So blowing this lily as a trumpet with my lips
> I assert my original glory in the dark eclipse.
>
> Ern Malley

'An Australian Sound', published in 1979 in *Australian Popular Culture*, edited by Peter Spearritt and David Walker, was an attempt to show that some of the jazz being played in Melbourne and Adelaide in the 1940s had a distinctive local style. The essay was the outcome of unfinished conversations with Leon Atkinson (1930–85),[1] historian, clarinettist and leader of the West Side Jazz Band in Adelaide, but the idea was current among other musicians and jazz lovers, for whom it may have seemed natural to extend the distinctions among styles of jazz where it evolved, in New Orleans, Chicago, Kansas City and New York, to the local scene. It also provoked some scepticism and did not pass unchallenged.

Since its publication, jazz education and research have spread globally, and the circulation of teaching materials and methods encourages an international style, performed by musicians who are likely to have academic qualifications. As jazz has become international, local distinctions have diminished,

---

[*] Bruce Clunies Ross was enchanted by jazz at school in Adelaide in the 1940s, and listened compulsively to the music discussed in his article. After a ratbag decade he resumed his education and moved to an Assistant Professorship in English at the University of Copenhagen, from which he retired in 2001. He continues to write about poetry and music. His latest essay is on the work of Les Murray.

1. This chapter could not have been written without the inspiration of my late friend Leon Atkinson and the continuing generous assistance of my old school friend Jim Smith.

and the idea that in Melbourne and Adelaide in the 1940s there was, briefly, a local style, hardly seems relevant to Australian jazz musicians, or their audience, in the second decade of the twenty-first century, when jazz is generally accepted as an art, detached from the culture in which it evolved. An entirely different perception of jazz prevailed up to the 1940s, and traces of this persisted into the seventies, when the essay was written.

Jazz spread rapidly around the world in the decade following the First World War, mainly as a result of its influence on popular songs and dance music, but at the time there were no settled ideas about what jazz actually was. Its sources in Afro-American culture might be generally acknowledged, but the term 'jazz' was often loosely applied to any lively popular music. The jazz craze faded with the stock market crash and the world-wide depression which ensued, and it was around this time that the aspiring musicians who were to give jazz in Australia a distinctive sound first discovered it. There were already a few gifted jazz musicians in Australia, but the primary sources of inspiration for these young jazzmen were the 78 rpm recordings available in the early thirties, most of them made in the previous decade, before the rise to popularity of the big swing bands. To ears first attuned to jazz around that time, there was a categorical difference between swing music and jazz. This did not always entail a rejection of swing, but to a few listeners the jazz records had a compelling attraction. The music on them was mainly improvised by small ensembles associated with New Orleans and Chicago, and, with perhaps the addition of early recordings of the Duke Ellington orchestras and one or two larger African American bands, this formed the whole of jazz, as opposed to swing, at the beginning of the thirties. In retrospect, the musicians who gave jazz distinctive Australian sounds are sequestered in the category of 'traditional jazz', but there was no such thing when Graeme Bell, his brother Roger, Ade Monsbourgh and a few friends began to play in Melbourne. It was just jazz; an improvised, unwritten music, to be learned aurally, by trial and error, practice, and listening to records intently and repeatedly. This naturally inspired creative experiments, rather than emulation and preservation. It was not until the following decade that the revival of traditional jazz, and the controversies associated with it, caught up with the Graeme Bell band.

Recordings became a predominant medium for jazz, but they removed it from the culture in which it was being created, or, to put this positively, they exposed jazz to an international audience. However, they captured only a fragment of the jazz performed in the predominantly, but not exclusively, African-American culture in which it came into existence. Listening to these recordings was nothing like listening to a band. The technology of recording and sound reproduction, though it improved during the early decades of jazz recording, left much to the imagination. Occasionally, a jazz lover might be discovered with his head stuck into the horn of a gramophone, or the speaker of a radiogram at full volume. What he was trying to achieve was the imaginative amplification which 78 rpm records inspired. In other respects, 78 rpm recordings called for a kind of listening unlike that to which we are now accustomed. They were fragile, awkward to transport, not good enough technically to support muzak and therefore circulated in a time of intermittent silence, before recorded music became ubiquitous. Record collecting was not a widespread practice and jazz records were comparatively rare. This fostered intensely focused listening, in contrast to the extended impression obtained from CDs or long-playing records, which are easily overheard, rather than heard. The appreciation of a particular band or instrumentalist might be based on one or two three-minute sides, but aspiring jazz musicians would generally know every audible note and chord on the important sides, and immediately recognize deviations in new or imitative performances.

It is not unusual for jazz lovers to identify the moment when they were 'hooked' by a certain recording. At the beginning the thirties, Kym Bonython in Adelaide was 'only dabbling in the waters of jazz' until his friend Dean Hay introduced him to some new Duke Ellington recordings, including 'It Don't Mean a Thing if it Ain't Got That Swing'. 'I could have taken that as a motto from then on. I became an instant addict' (Bonython 1979: 116). A world away, at Stow school in Buckinghamshire, after the outbreak of war, a friend played George Melly 'Eccentric', a recent recording by Muggsy Spanier and his Ragtime Band. They listened to it over and over again, and George Melly 'walked across Cobham Court to my dormitory a convert' (Melly 1965: 11). Back in Adelaide, at the university jazz lover's club in 1946, Tas Brown, a young clarinettist with a love of classical music, heard the famous chorus of 'High Society' on a recording by Sharkey Bonano and his Kings of Dixieland and remembered it for the rest of his life (Brown n.d.). Around the same time, at Vermont on the way to the Dandenong Mountains in Victoria, John Sangster heard the trumpet of Bix Beiderbeck, on the Frankie Trumbauer recording of 'Riverboat Shuffle', played on a wind-up gramophone, and was inspired to steal, from his father's wallet, the money to buy 'a lovely little silver Boosey and Hawkes cornet, which became the love of my life for the next many years' (Sangster 1988: 2). At school in Melbourne, early in the thirties, Roger Bell, Ade Monsbourgh and 'Spadge' Davies may have experienced similar epiphanies, without being enticed into crime, but Graeme Bell was not instantly converted by the recordings his brother played him. He had to 're-examine the jazz business and open up [his] ears' before he 'joined the club of those who were hooked on this music' (Bell 1988: 29).

When they began playing together in the early thirties, the Bell brothers and their friends were not the first jazz musicians in Australia, and around the same time there were, no doubt, similar awakenings and beginnings elsewhere, not only in Australia. In Adelaide, still comparatively isolated from Melbourne, Kym Bonython and a few friends had also begun to play jazz (Bonython 1979: 115–17). The significance of these beginnings is that at the time they occurred, in the early thirties, the obvious, indeed only, course for musicians inspired to play jazz by listening to records was to follow the example of the bands whose recordings had ostensibly defined an idea of jazz by the end of the twenties. Big band swing, comparatively new, exciting and fashionable, did not offer the same scope for free expression, and the small, improvising, riffing ensembles associated with the big bands had hardly begun to record, though Kym Bonython was soon in touch with some of them, through the fan letters he was writing to American musicians.

At the turn of the twenties into the thirties, Australian jazz in its home territories continued to develop in various ways, but recordings tend to fix developments, and by the end of the twenties a body of recorded jazz existed which has quite justly assumed classic status, even though it represents only a fraction (and in some respects a misleading one) of jazz as it was actually performed. These recordings became the references for the serious attempts to define jazz and describe its origins, around the time the Bell brothers and their friends were acquiring the art. Some of the earliest books were by Europeans who knew jazz primarily, or solely, from records, although Paul Bernhard's very early *Jazz: Eine Musikalische Zeitfrage* (1927) is perhaps more inspired by the craze for modern dancing in the Weimar Republic, and the musical ensembles in clubs and bars that catered for it. Like Robert Goffin's first jazz book, *Aux Frontières du Jazz* (1932) it has apparently never been completely translated,[2] possibly because its speculations seem inconsistent with jazz scholarship. Both books present translation problems, as they employ passages of evocative prose to present jazz as a sensuous, physical experience, and they are valuable as evidence of jazz as something felt, which needs to be taken into account when considering its acquisition by aspiring jazz musicians, including the Bell brothers and their friends. The nearest equivalent in English to these books is Cedric Pearce's *trumpet in the night*, discussed below. Graeme Bell mentions that he, and his fellow musicians, read everything about jazz they could find, but he does not refer to anything specific, and the possibilities at the time were limited.[3] They were also scouring second-hand shops

---

2. An article by Bernhard, which was incorporated in his book, appeared in the *Frankurter Zeitung* in 1926 and was translated as 'The German Side of Jazz' in *The Living Age*, New York, 11 September 1926: 580–85.

3. Some idea of the writings on jazz available in Australia in the thirties and forties can be gleaned from the catalogue of William V. Holyoak's library, cited below.

for records, which were doubtless their primary source of knowledge about jazz, and at first, probably, their only one. Jazz records were scarce in Australia, which restricted the delights available to jazz-lovers, but encouraged local inventiveness, to the point of filling the gap with an impressive body of Australian jazz recorded in the 1940s.

The Bell brothers supplemented the thin trickle of jazz records available in Melbourne by importing records from the Commodore Music Shop in New York. In Adelaide, the young drummer, Kym Bonython, a scion of one of its grandest families, was assembling a collection in the same way. Both Australian cities also had notable collectors with extensive collections of imported recordings, and these had a formative influence on the local development of jazz. William V. Holyoak, in Adelaide, was one of Australia's pioneering experts on jazz, with an extensive record collection, largely made up of imports, supplemented by an excellent library of jazz books and periodicals.[4] His counterpart in Melbourne, William H. Miller, already had an interest in jazz when he arrived in Oxford in 1933; he built up a collection from the wide range of jazz records in England, and returned to Melbourne with it in 1938. The two collectors were at the centre of early jazz lovers' societies in the two cities, their collections formed the foundation of the first serious jazz radio programmes, and they were responsible for recording local jazz in the forties on their independent labels: Miller's 'Ampersand' and Holyoak's 'Memphis'. Miller wrote about jazz in publications such as his *Australian Jazz Quarterly*, whereas Holyoak spread his knowledge and ideas in dialogues with the presenter of his late Tuesday night radio programme *The Real Swing* on 5AD. Miller's writings strongly suggest that he was a traditionalist with a deep knowledge of early jazz, and appreciation of collective improvisation in small ensembles. Holyoak had similar inclinations, but also exposed his audience to swing, early bop, cool jazz and the music of Stan Kenton, amongst other heresies. He encouraged an open-minded approach and kept in touch with new developments, but his programmes were predominantly an education in the traditions of jazz. This was valuable at a time when his listeners had limited access to the classic recordings.

The influence of Miller and Holyoak is apparent in the slightly different developments of early jazz in the two cities. Melbourne became, and remained, the major Australian locale for traditional jazz, with an impressive array of bands in the wake of the Graeme Bell ensemble. In Adelaide, Dave Dallwitz aimed to develop the traditional style, working with groups in the standard seven- or eight-piece format for collectively improvised jazz. His inspiration

---

4. His jazz library, kept together as named collection, is now in the State Library of South Australia; the catalogue is online at http://www.catalog.slsa.sa.gov.au/search~S1?/gHolyoake/gholyoake/-3,0,0,B/exact&FF=gholyoak+collection&1,160/indexsort=-

was Jelly Roll Morton, whose classic recordings from the twenties already show the style being developed, and Duke Ellington, from whom he derived the art of foregrounding the distinctive sounds of individual instrumentalists, and orchestrating them harmonically, to create atmospheric jazz. Throughout the brilliant chapter on Jelly Roll Morton in *Early Jazz*, Gunther Schuller draws comparisons between Morton and Ellington, the distinctive jazz composers in its first decade, who ignored each other (Schuller 1968: 143). Dave Dallwitz's music gives us an idea of what cross-fertilization might have produced, though it derives more from Morton than Ellington. However, Dallwitz did not copy Morton; his records gave him an idea of how jazz might be developed, with respect for its stylistic conventions. This was not always appreciated by traditionalists, in the controversies stirring among jazz enthusiasts.

These derive from attempts to define jazz, which led to debates which developed simultaneously with the emergence of distinctive sounds in Australian jazz.[5] They were provoked first by the growing popularity of big swing bands, which had absorbed a number of creative jazz musicians, and then, about a decade later, by the emergence of bop. At one level, the debates were between jazz lovers who did not regard these as authentic developments of jazz, and those who kept an open mind about them, but on another level there was a narrower debate about the nature of 'authentic' or 'real' jazz,[6] and stylistic variants, such as 'New Orleans', 'Chicago' and 'Dixieland'. It was in the context of this debate that some of the pieces that were introducing distinctive sounds into Australian jazz were criticized. Graeme Bell's 'Chicken and Almonds' was an example, though otherwise the original numbers by the Bell brothers and Ade Monsbourgh generally had approval. The criticism was mainly directed at the music of Dallwitz, who did not work with a stable group of like-minded musicians, similar to those who formed the core of the Graeme Bell band. From the perspective of the twenty-first century and the academic reception of jazz, these and subsequent developments can be appreciated as parts of a coherent, if complex, phenomenon, but the early writings, which defined jazz more narrowly, as collectively improvised music, following traditions established by the recordings of the twenties, should not be discounted as misguided or insufficiently informed. There was a moment when the idea that jazz might follow alternative developments was tenable, and this was part of the ferment in which Australian jazz was created.[7]

---

5. There was contention wherever jazz was taken seriously. In England, it was apparent from Constant Lambert's elaborate refusal to define it in a broadcast talk on the BBC on 15 April 1936 (Lloyd 2014: 507).
6. Cf. the title of Hugues Panassié's second treatise, *The Real Jazz* (1942).
7. See Tom Pickering's theory, discussed below.

In Melbourne and Adelaide, controversies about jazz were enveloped in a larger one: the struggle for the modern in Australia. Up to the eve of the Second World War, the radical innovations in the arts, which were later collectively identified as modernism, had not made much impact in Australia, not only because of its isolation but also because influential cultural conservatives wanted to preserve it from the infection. One of these was Robert (later Sir Robert) Menzies, who proposed an Australian Academy of the Arts, with a Royal Charter, for the 'great purpose [of] raising the standards of public taste [and] directing attention to good work'.[8] It was made clear that art showing the degenerate traces of modernism would not be admitted, and the resistance to it was evident in a number of public scandals: the newly knighted Sir Lionel Lindsay's attack on modernist art, which he dismissed as largely a Jewish conspiracy, the book *Addled Art*, published in 1942, and widely recommended by cultural conservatives; the damaging, but ultimately unsuccessful, attempt to deprive William Dobell of the Archibald Prize for portraiture by legal action, in 1944, on the ground that his winning painting was not fine art, but something more like caricature, and the outraged reaction in Adelaide to the award of the Melrose Prize to Russell Drysdale's great painting, *Woman in a Landscape*, in 1949.

The most significant of all was the elaborately successful Ern Malley hoax, in 1944, aimed at the magazine *Angry Penguins* and its editor, the poet Max Harris, followed by the absurdity of his prosecution when poems that the hoaxers had contrived to be nonsense were discovered by Detective Vogelsang, of the South Australian Police Force, to be indecent, immoral or obscene.[9] *Angry Penguins* had been started in Adelaide in 1940, as a journal of contemporary writing, art and ideas, by Harris and two other young poets, Donald Kerr and Paul Pfeiffer, who were killed serving in the air force during the war.[10] It was transferred to Melbourne, with the financial and editorial support of John Reed, in 1943, and expired in 1946, but not before it had flamboyantly proclaimed the arrival of 'modernism' in Australia.

John Reed's response to the idea of an Australian Academy was to form the Contemporary Art Society, from which the memorable paintings of the time, by Sidney Nolan, Arthur Boyd, Albert Tucker, Joy Hester, John Perceval and others, emerged. Nolan's first, great Ned Kelly series, now in the National Gallery of Australia, was painted at Heide, the house where John Reed lived with his wife Sunday. It was a haven for young artists, writers and intellectuals

---

8. Quoted in Haese 1981: 43.
9. There are many accounts of this famous hoax, the most comprehensive being Heyward 1993.
10. See Miles 2000 for a full account.

from the stifling cultural conservatism of the time, and also the scene of sessions by the Graeme Bell band (Haese 1981: 238).

The association between the artists creating Australian modes of modernist painting, and jazz musicians, is not surprising. The artists were, in various ways, expressionists, interested in how art might access deep levels of consciousness; jazz, which was improvised and spontaneous, leading to moments when performers and audience were 'gone', in the parlance of the time, or 'seeing the rafters', as Johnny Sangster put it (Sangster 1988), seemed a way of doing this. A few artists, such as the sculptor Clem Meadmore, a keen washboard player, were practically involved in jazz, and several of the jazz musicians of the forties were active in the visual arts, including Dave Dallwitz, a painter and art teacher, Kym Bonython, a notable collector of modern painting, gallery owner and editor of books on modern Australian art, and Graeme Bell who studied painting with Max Meldrum for three years, before 'jazz took over' (Bell 1988: 36). He recalled that the most important event for the band in the early 1940s was a performance at the Contemporary Art Society exhibition of 310 works by modernist and social realist artists, including Sidney Nolan, Albert Tucker, Noel Counihan, James Gleeson, Yosl Bergner and Danila Vassilieff, in the Australia Hotel on 28 October 1941, which Richard Haese later described as 'a massive assault on all assumptions about art in Australia' (Haese 1981: 72). Graeme Bell's memoir recaptures something of the intellectual atmosphere of the time. 'During intermission and after the concert people mingled over drinks and food looking at the paintings and discussing jazz, a music that was new and exciting to many of them', and he quotes from the report in the Melbourne *Truth* (Bell 1988: 43–44):

> the show on Tuesday brought together the strangest combination seen in Melbourne for a long time. Long-haired intellectuals, swing fiends, hot mommas and truckin' jazz boys rubbed shoulders on friendly terms. While swingsters hollered 'Go to Town' and jitterbugged in the aisles, the intellectuals learnedly discussed differences between the rhythms of hot jazz and the pigment of Picasso.[11]

About six months later, intellectuals, artists and jazz fiends in Adelaide were meeting in the house of Dave and Joan Dallwitz, which the painter Jeffrey Smart remembered as 'an oasis in a conservative desert' where he and the artist Jacqueline Hick first heard Ellington's *Mood Indigo* and Stravinsky's *Symphony of Psalms*, and enjoyed parties where

---

11. The same passage from *Truth* is quoted by Richard Haese, who mentions that Don Banks also performed at the jazz evening (Haese 1981: 72).

> Dave would extemporise while Max Harris stood by the piano and sang 'The Cunt Song'.[12] It just consisted of saying the word over and over again with different expressions, very funny and sometimes tragic, occasionally desperate. Max would recite his poetry and we would all sing dirty songs (Smart 1996: 78–79).

The song may seem puerile from the enlightened perspective of the twenty-first century, but Jeffrey Smart's recollection, late in life, of his amusement at the time is a whiff of Bohemian Adelaide in the middle of the war, when Harris was about twenty and had not yet fallen for the Ern Malley hoax. The purpose of meeting was to form a South Australian branch of the Contemporary Art Society and it was led by young Max Harris (Haese 1981: 75; Hylton 1989: 16). Looking back, he claimed that Adelaide, in the decade between about 1935 and 1945, was the turbulent centre where, after the Jindyworobaks had invoked 'environmental values', Australian modernism began. Melburnians might disagree, but Harris pointed out that in Melbourne Robert Menzies 'ruled the Australian Academy of Art with a rod of iron' (Harris 1989: 9), though, as Harris surely knew, and his vocal efforts demonstrated, repression could be a provocative inspiration. There was certainly an impulse to scandalize the *bourgeoisie* in jazz circles, more apparent among fiends than musicians, and under control in the music of the Graeme Bell band and Dallwitz's Southern Jazz Group. It was also a consequence of the exposure of *Angry Penguins* to public attention as a result of the Ern Malley affair.

In the issue following the publication of Ern Malley's poems, *Angry Penguins* set up a jazz section headed 'A Riff in the Blue' which was intended to be a regular part of the magazine. It opened with four quotations from a surrealist rhapsody on 'the great Negro race which alone keeps American from falling apart' and some of its leading jazz musicians, from *The Colossus of Maroussi*, a recent book by Henry Miller. An unsigned introduction (which betrays the hand of Max Harris) announced 'The aim of this section is to assist jazzmen to become intellectually articulate, to develop a deeper level of jazz criticism, and to assist intellectuals and other artists to appreciate jazz by talking to them about it in adequate language' (unsigned article in *Angry Penguins* 8 [1945]: 110).[13] Among the jazzmen straining to become intellectually articulate in

12. A play on 'prick song'.
13. The tone suggests that Harris (if he wrote this) had not been chastened by the Ern Malley hoax. It passed in the tiny intellectual circles of Adelaide and Melbourne and reflects their sense of alienation in a country which at the time seemed predominantly Philistine, as depicted in Albert Tucker's cover design for this issue of the magazine, which is reproduced at http://pictify.com/514039/albert-tucker-cover-design-for-the-magazine-angry-penguins-1945

this issue of *Angry Penguins* were the Oxford educated lawyer, record collector and washboard virtuoso, William H. Miller and David Dallwitz, who had been associated with the magazine since one of his paintings had been the subject of critical appreciation in an early issue. Their contributions are arranged to reflect controversy about the nature of jazz, and both adopt a pedagogical tone, addressed to an uninformed reader; otherwise they are completely different. 'He That Hath An Ear', the significant title of Dallwitz's contribution, is largely devoted to a detailed discussion of a single three-minute record; Duke Ellington's 'Bakiff' (1941, composed by Ellington's Puerto Rican valve trombonist, Juan Tizol), an innovative orchestration, even for Ellington, around a long violin solo. Dallwitz assumes that readers who appreciate the music of Ravel, Debussy and Delius might be led by 'Bakiff' to 'the jazz language', and he concludes the piece with a clear explanation of the difference between Ellington's composed music and 'pure jazz', collectively improvised on a given theme and harmonic structure, with the reservation that the two 'cannot be entirely dissociated' (Dallwitz 1945: 110–11). Miller's 'Introduction to Jazz' (1945) is a more polemical argument which presents jazz as essentially an improvised form of music that can only be performed by a small band of, ideally, seven instruments, without the hindering intrusion of saxophone, vibraphone or violin, and he suggested that the listener's ear has to be trained to appreciate the intonation and tonal quality of jazz instrumentalists. For Dallwitz jazz is an art with expressive potential, related to other forms of music, whereas Miller claims it is essentially a separate art. This distinction was reflected in the different receptions of jazz in Adelaide and Melbourne at a time when they were still comparatively remote from each other:[14] the traditionalists were much stronger in Melbourne, and also in Hobart, where there was a talented group of jazz musicians playing in a distinctive style. One of them was Cedric Pearce, author of *trumpet in the night: a background to the enjoyment of jazz music*, published in 1945 by William H. Miller, which was anonymously reviewed in the jazz section of *Angry Penguins*. The short book, with an epigraph from Ezra Pound, is a monologue, apparently spontaneous, intimately addressed to the reader, perhaps an attempt to represent jazz improvisation. It ranges widely, but reveals an undogmatic preference for traditional jazz.

The next issue of *Angry Penguins*, in 1946, was the last, and it included a report by Inez Cavanaugh[15] on the 'American Jazz Scene: 1945', which locates controversy about jazz in the context of the crucial developments taking

---

14. Interstate travel was not permitted during the war, unless there were exceptional circumstances. Harris appears to have got around this somehow.

15. Her name is always spelt 'Cavanagh' in *Angry Penguins*, but Rosenkrantz spells 'Cavanaugh' and I assume that is correct.

place in New York just as the American recording ban was lifted and bop was emerging. Among the musicians active in New York at the time, she mentions Erroll Garner, Don Byas, Ben Webster, Illinois Jacquet, Charlie Ventura, and significantly, Dizzy Gillespie, whose influence, she claims, was as strong as Armstrong's once had been. From the point of view of jazz history as it is now understood, this was as up-to-date as it was possible to be, anywhere, at the time, and *Angry Penguins* deserves credit for it, but it was not well-received by a number of prominent Australian jazz lovers. Inez Cavanaugh was probably a mystery to them, but a clue to how she came to write for *Angry Penguins* was dropped in her next appearance, where she mentioned Harry Roskolenko, an American poet who had been in Australia during the war, published in the magazine, and become friendly with Max Harris. She was a journalist, one of the early African-Americans to write about jazz, a singer who recorded with Erroll Garner, and the life-long partner of Timme Rosenkrantz, sometimes known as the 'Jazz Baron', the aristocratic Danish collector whose passion for jazz had taken him to Harlem in 1934, where he met Inez in a bar opposite the Apollo Theatre (Rosenkrantz 1964: 80). Between 1938 and 1945 he made a number of recordings as nominal leader of pick-up bands comprising some of the leading musicians at the time, including some of those mentioned by Inez Cavanaugh in *Angry Penguins*, most of whom were disregarded by traditionalists in Australia.

The first Australian Jazz Convention was in 1946, and the programme was in the form of an *Angry Penguins Broadsheet*, with the bold headline, 'JAZZ: AUSTRALIA' over a picture of Roger Bell playing the blues with the Harlem trumpeter, Morris Goode, in an American Army uniform. It was the last trace of the magazine.[16] In addition to listing the events, it included an introduction by Graeme Bell, where he casually mentioned the strange absence of musicians from Sydney: 'which could not at that time boast of one single group who had bothered to find out what authentic New Orleans jazz was. The musicians of this city were more interested in the slick, flashy variety—the polished up product' (G. Bell 1947: 2);[17] something, perhaps, like the music promoted by Timme Rosenkrantz and Inez Cavanaugh. Her excellent description of a day with Duke Ellington,[18] illustrated with a photograph of him working at a kind of piano-

---

16. The front page is reproduced in Haese (1981: 119). An advertisement on p. 13 of the magazine announced that 'it has now reached the end of its financial resources'.

17. Sydney was later the base for a number of outstanding modern jazz musicians who created distinctive sounds, notably Bernie McGann, the 'Australian Bird, more kookaburra than nightingale', as Paul Grabowsky said in a note on their 2006 CD *Always*.

18. She reported the other side of the story about the occasion when the Duke Ellington orchestra performed in Percy Grainger's lecture series at NYU in 1932. Billy Strayhorn

desk, was included in this *Angry Penguins Broadsheet*, along with an article on orchestral jazz by the English writer Charles Fox. Significantly, though, there was a letter from Roger Bell, objecting to Inez Cavanaugh's first article in *Angry Penguins* and an interesting essay, 'The Pure Stream: A Theory of Jazz Development' by the Tasmanian clarinettist, Tom Pickering. He argues that as jazz was detached from its cultural sources through recording, which spread it around the world '[t]rue jazz will never again have a "public"... It has become an art, and like modern painting, poetry and prose, it will always be appreciated by the few' (Pickering 1946: 21). This leads him to suggest that the acquisition of jazz through listening to records is the third stage in its development, after New Orleans and Chicago jazz. It is implicitly a rejection of Inez Cavanaugh's account of developments in New York, though at least he mentioned some of the major African-American musicians who emerged in the thirties: 'Eldridge, Tatum, Wilson, Bailey, Webster etc.' but he dismisses them as 'susceptible to the white man's detrimental refining influence' and goes on to suggest that 'it looks as if the future of jazz depends more on the "whites" of integrity and discerning taste' (Pickering 1946: 25). From the perspective of jazz history almost seventy years later this is wrong-headed and implicitly, but no doubt unintentionally, racist, and even at the time it would have provoked disagreement in Australian jazz circles. However, it reflects the attempt of a thoughtful musician to discover a context for what he, and the other creators of Australian jazz, were doing, at a time when their sources were limited to the available 78 rpm recordings and a few writings. The effect of this was ambiguous. Leon Atkinson once suggested, privately, that 78s had a comparable influence on Australian jazz musicians as the post cards and reproductions through which the *Angry Penguins* painters acquired a knowledge of modern art: they were inspiring without being overwhelming and left space for development. Graeme Bell noticed, when he heard Claude Luter's band at the Hot Club of France during its European tour in 1947, that the French band's 'only fault was that they copied the old jazz, whereas we used it as our model from which to express our own music' (Bell 1988: 99).

Melbourne and Adelaide, in their remoteness from the sources, were ideal places in which to cultivate this approach to jazz, and its distinctive sounds were created at a moment when a combination of several factors made it possible, notably the constraints of its reception at a distance, and the intellectual and artistic ferment in the forties, the decade when jazz acquired an Australian sound. It remains a moot point if that is a correct description. Dave

told her that the Duke looked glum when Grainger suggested he must have been influenced by Delius; he had never heard of Delius, but he went out and bought all the Delius recordings he could find, and when he played them later to other listeners, he used to say 'That's my influence'.

Dallwitz once objected, privately, 'It's not an Australian sound, it's the Dallwitz sound', and Graeme Bell might have argued similarly, though he was intrigued when he discovered on its European tour in 1947 that the band was identified as having 'an Australian style'.

> [W]e were at first at a loss to see the distinction. We realized that it could well be that something different had evolved in our music because, after all, no American band had ever visited Australia and we had always drawn on our own resources (Bell 1988: 114).

Jim Godbolt recalls that the band's manager promoted it as 'Australian':

> There's something I've got to make clear to you, son. The billing is Graeme Bell and his *Australian* Jazz Band and in your publicity they're to be described as a *New Orleans* band, not Dixieland. You got that, son? (Godbolt 1984: 212).

It would not have seemed heretical to the Graeme Bell band, in Melbourne, or Dave Dallwitz, in Adelaide, to treat the style of New Orleans jazz as a musical language with expressive possibilities. The idea that it was something to be preserved and emulated, with the implication that its day was past, had not yet hardened. From the beginning, Graeme Bell and his band were after something different from the other jazz that was emerging in Melbourne:

> a collective sound, collective improvisation in the classic jazz mould. Solo playing constituted a small and unimportant role compared to our ensemble playing. There was no ego tripping. You would be lucky to get sixteen bars solo interspersed with ensembles and then the whole tune would be taken out with anything up to six full band choruses. To my knowledge, nobody had done this previously (Bell 1988: 42).

At the same time, they built up a repertoire of their own compositions, sometimes in the form of twelve-bar blues or sixteen-bar stomps, but Roger Bell's 'That Woodbourne Strut' and 'Old Man's Beard' (named after a Nolan painting of the plant) illustrated the possibilities of developing more complex forms, comprising several modulating strains, which enlarge the scope for collective improvisation and inhibit the degeneration of a performance into a string of solos. Polythematic forms, which derive from ragtime, were integral to New Orleans jazz, especially in the music of Jelly Roll Morton, but as jazz became increasingly a soloist's art they were displaced by simpler forms. Their recovery in Australia, where they were used extensively by Ade Monsbourgh and Dave Dallwitz, is a notable aspect of jazz with an Australian sound.

Ade Monsbourgh was described by Graeme Bell, in his introduction to the programme for the first convention, as 'one of the most—if not the most—outstanding jazz musicians in Australia'. He played most of the instruments in the band with equal skill, and had a precise sense of where each voice—trumpet, clarinet, valve trombone or saxophone—fitted into the ensemble. His solos were expressive and often beautifully laconic, except when he let go on the saxophone, and he was a brilliant ensemble player, with a gift for harmony and voice-leading that enabled him to shape collectively improvised music spontaneously, as it evolved. As an instrumentalist he was a true original, particularly when he picked up the saxophone, on which he cultivated a personal style adapted to the conventions of traditional jazz, at a time when purists despised the instrument. He contributed largely to the distinctive sound of the Bell band and his own ensembles, which recorded as Lazy Ade and His Late Hours Boys, in both of which his understated playing might be described as characteristically Australian. This matched his compositions such as 'Look Down the Road' or 'Tell the Boys You Saw Me' and notably his creation of a kind of lazy ragtime, which develops the polythematic forms on some of the classic recordings of the twenties in a distinctly personal style. There is nothing else quite like it, but it contributes perfectly to the formation of an Australian sound. A fine example is 'Clever Fellow' (the title refers to an Aboriginal Man of High Degree, and the piece might be considered Jindyworobak[19] jazz), recorded in 1950 by a group entitled Lazy Ade & His Late Hours Boys, but actually consisting of Ade Monsbourgh and members of the Southern Jazz Group with Dave Dallwitz on piano.[20]

Monsbourgh and Dallwitz often worked together, and there was an affinity between them that inspired some of the finest Australian jazz. The titles of many of their numbers (and of those by Graeme and Roger Bell) indicate that they deliberately aimed to embody or reflect aspects of Australia in their music. Dave Dallwitz was not primarily an instrumentalist (he played trombone in the first Southern Jazz Group and piano in the second) but a bandleader, composer and arranger, who worked with the individual 'voices' of jazz musicians, and their combined sounds in the ensemble. His major contribution to jazz is a repertoire of numbers with distinctive qualities, which made the music of his two Southern Jazz Groups, particularly the second, unlike any other jazz. When he took over the first Southern Jazz Group, as leader, in the

---

19. The Jindyworobaks, a group of South Australian poets that overlapped with the Angry Penguins, proclaimed 'environmental values', derived in part from what they understood of Aboriginal culture. See Clunies-Ross 1981.

20. There is a much later recording on the album *Nullabor*, 1972, by the Dallwitz-Monsbourgh Jazzmen.

mid-forties, he gave the band an obvious New Orleans sound, to which his own tailgate trombone contributed. Fundamental were the two springy off-beats of the insistently precise rhythm section, driven by the banjo and tuba. Bob Wright, the band's tuba (more precisely, sousaphone) player was a virtuoso, whose tone, attack and beautifully articulated base lines, even on the fastest numbers, was a major component in the overall sound of the band, and Dallwitz created a showcase for his artistry in an early composition, 'Ragtime Tuba'.[21]

While he was leading a band firmly in the New Orleans tradition, Dallwitz was writing the analysis of Ellington's experimental arrangement of Juan Tizol's 'Bakiff' (1941), with its long violin solo by Ray Nance, and unresolved coda, for the jazz issue of *Angry Penguins*. It is a clue to the development of his mature style. Like Monsbourgh, he used the polythematic form of ragtime extensively, but combined it with impressionistic effects, derived from the music of Duke Ellington. 'Passion Rag', recorded in 1949 for Jazzart, with the sounds of Ade Monsbourgh on trumpet and clarinet, and Tom Pickering on clarinet, added to the Southern Jazz Group, is an early example of how this combination might sound, but it came to fruition in Dallwitz's work, around 1950–51, with the second Southern Jazz Group. He retained the traditional instrumentation of the first band, and had one of the stars of jazz in Australia, Keith Hounslow, on trumpet. He was a naturally gifted instrumentalist who had informally apprenticed himself to the former Ellington cornetist, Rex Stewart, on his Australian tour in 1949. Hounslow's distinctive sound, inspired improvised playing and mastery of the half-valve and mute techniques he acquired from Stewart added an Ellingtonian 'voice' to the band, which Dallwitz used effectively in numbers such as 'Crocodile Creep' which combines polythematic form with impressionistic instrumentation. It was, Dallwitz said privately,[22] composed to rival Morton's 'Jungle Blues', though its sources are completely assimilated in a personal style with Australian associations.[23] The repertoire of the second Southern Jazz Group substantially comprised compositions by Australian composers, and in July 1951 the band recorded 45 of them for the ABC (Australian Broadcasting Commission). They represent the culmination of jazz with an Australian sound (but not of jazz in Australia), cre-

---

21. First recorded in Adelaide in 1948, and issued on Bill Holyoak's Memphis label.
22. In a conversation with the author, 20 November 1977.
23. In his chapter on Morton, previously referred to, Gunther Schuller identifies Ellingtonian attributes in some of Morton's compositions. 'Jungle Blues' is not explicitly mentioned, but it fits the description. Schuller's account of Morton is unwittingly illuminating about Dallwitz, whose compositions reveal a detailed appreciation of Morton's work, similar to that which emerged from Schuller's fine analysis, some years later.

ated in the decade following the first recordings of the Bell band in 1941, until Dallwitz resurfaced, after a long absence from jazz (but not music) to make the LP albums of the seventies. These include *Nullabor, Stompology, Melbourne Suite, Midnight Crawl, Illawarra Flame, Gold Fever, Ned Kelly Jazz Suite* and the *Ern Malley Suite*, a tribute to the laureate of the turbulent years when Graeme and Roger Bell, Ade Monsbourgh, Dave Dallwitz and a few fellow musicians created a jazz idiom akin to other artistic developments of the period: the 'environmental values' of Adelaide's Jindyworoback poets; the modernist experiments of the Angry Penguins, and the expressionistic imagination of the Melbourne painters who adopted their name, including Sidney Nolan, Albert Tucker, Joy Hester, Arthur Boyd and John Perceval. It is the most original of these late albums, all of which develop the conventions of jazz established by the classic recordings of the twenties, and it seems strangely apt that the spirit of Jelly Roll Morton should haunt the music inspired by Ern Malley. The nine sections of the suite—instrumental portraits of Ern Malley, Sid Nolan and Max Harris, and six settings of passages from Malley's *Darkening Ecliptic*—scored for a slightly enlarged ensemble, based on the banjo and tuba players from the first Southern Jazz Group, develop and refine the mode that Jelly created with larger bands in 1929. Dallwitz's achievement was finally crowned with a five-star review in the leading American music magazine, *Down Beat* (12 July 1979):

> The trad revival in Australia...has developed genuinely valuable insights into jazz of an earlier day. Trumpeter Roger Bell, vocalist Penny Eames, trumpeter/reedman Lazy Ade Monsbourgh and composer Dave Dallwitz are original artists of international stature: they and a few others simply have no equivalents on the imitative, joyless American and European trad scenes... Dallwitz's music begins with 1928–30 Ellington (and Ellington's sources); his compositions are episodic, multi-thematic, with evocative ambitions that are occasionally even fulfilled—his 1975 *Ern Malley Suite*, enclosed in one of the greatest of all record covers, is a brilliant, beautiful piece of eccentricity.

The record cover is a reproduction of Nolan's portrait of Ern Malley, used in the fine, limited edition of the *Darkening Ecliptic* which Nolan illustrated and published[24] around the same time as Dallwitz was composing the suite, and the two works are complementary. Another Nolan painting, one of the famous images of Ned Kelly, from the early series, adorned the cover of Dall-

---

24. The date of publication, by R. Alistair McAlpine, is not given, but the introduction is dated 1974.

witz's *Ned Kelly Jazz Suite*. The *Down Beat* reviewer[25] understandably identifies the distinctive qualities of jazz in Australia with the 'trad revival' but the creation of an Australian sound goes further back, to a time before the jazz recorded in the twenties had been categorized as 'traditional', when, rather than being a mode to emulate, it could be the foundation for further developments. It is significant that in the context of the 'trad revival' a late composition in this mode can be described as a 'a piece of eccentricity'; 'brilliant' and 'beautiful' it certainly is, but if it sounds eccentric, it is because Dallwitz found imaginative ways of extending the style artistically without breaking out of it. Whatever his wrong-headedness in other matters, Tom Pickering had a point when he claimed that recordings made jazz an art; that is how the handful of musicians who created an Australian sound adopted it. It was, as 'An Australian Sound' suggested, almost immediately swamped by the extensive revival of traditional jazz, and from the global perspective of contemporary jazz it is barely noticeable, yet in the wild season of *Angry Penguins*, from Melbourne and Adelaide (with input from Hobart) it gave Australia its music.

It may seem remarkable in retrospect that the jazz associated with an upsurge of modernism in the arts was in the 'traditional' mode, but this was the natural outcome of its reception in Melbourne and Adelaide, when jazz lovers and musicians still belonged to an esoteric circle. It included musicians alert to developments in modern jazz, including those who would later form the Australian Jazz Quintet, but stylistic apartheid had not taken root in the jazz milieu, and musicians of various persuasions sometimes played together, as a few early recordings reveal, notably the first Ampersand, recorded in Melbourne in 1943, with the early Chicago trumpeter, Max Kaminsky (then a member of Artie Shaw's Navy orchestra, on its wartime Pacific tour) and a group led by Roger Bell, which included the boppish Splinter Reeves and Charlie Blott, and the future eminent composer, Don Banks, with Ade Monsbourgh and Pixie Roberts. Modern jazz was evolving rapidly on its home territory during these years but there was no stable body of work which could have been exploited in the way the Bell brothers, Ade Monsbourgh and Dave Dallwitz used the conventions of classic jazz. An Australian sound in jazz was created in the frame of these conventions, but it need not remain fossilized there. It would be interesting to hear what an ensemble of modern jazz musicians, trained in conservatoria and music schools, could do with it.

---

25. Identified only by the name *litweiler*, presumably the jazz critic and sometime editor of *Down Beat*, John B. Litweiler, author of books on free jazz and Ornette Coleman.

References

Bell, Graeme (1947) 'Introduction: Jazz in Australia'. *Angry Penguins Broadsheet* 10: 2.
—(1988) *Graeme Bell: Australian Jazzman: His Autobiography*. Frenchs Forest, NSW: Child & Associates.
Bell, Roger (1947) 'Reply to Inez Cavanaugh'. *Angry Penguins Broadsheet* 10: 8.
Bernhard, Paul (1927) *Jazz: Eine Musikalische Zeitfrage*. München: Delphin Verlag.
Bonython, Kym (1979) *Ladies' Legs and Lemonade*. Adelaide: Rigby.
Brown, Tas (n.d.) 'Ludwig and the Duke: Musical Memoirs', unnumbered pages. Chapter 4 of unpublished memoir in typescript.
Cavanaugh, Inez (1946) 'The American Jazz Scene: 1945'. *Angry Penguins* 9: 110–11.
—(1947) 'A Day with the Duke'. *Angry Penguins Broadsheet* 10: 3–7.
Clunies-Ross, Bruce (1979) 'An Australian Sound: Jazz in Melbourne and Adelaide 1941–51'. In *Australian Popular Culture*, ed. Peter Spearritt and David Walker, 62–80. Sydney: George Allen & Unwin.
—(1981) 'Survival of the Jindyworobaks'. *Kunapipi* 3/1: 56–63.
—(1983) 'Dave Dallwitz and Australian Jazz'. *Jazz: The Australian Contemporary Music Magazine* (May/June): 6–8.
Dallwitz, David (1945) 'He That Hath An Ear'. *Angry Penguins* 8: 110–11.
Godbolt, Jim (1984) *A History of Jazz in Britain, 1919–1950*. London: Quartet Books.
Goffin, Robert (1932) *Aux Frontières du Jazz*. Paris: Editions du Sagittaire.
Haese, Richard (1981) *Rebels and Precursors: The Revolutionary Years of Australian Art*. Ringwood, Victoria: Allen Lane.
Harris, Max (1988) 'Introduction'. In *Angry Penguins and Realist Painting in Melbourne in the 1940s*, 13–25. London: South Bank Centre.
—(1989) 'Introduction'. In *Adelaide Angries*, 8–12. Adelaide: Art Gallery Board of South Australia.
Heyward, Michael (1993) *The Ern Malley Affair*. London: Faber & Faber.
Hylton, Jane (1989) *Adelaide Angries: South Australian Painting in the 1940s*. Adelaide: Art Gallery Board of South Australia.
Lloyd, Stephen (2014) *Constant Lambert: Beyond the Rio Grande*. Woodbridge, Suffolk: Boydell Press.
Melly, George (1965) *Owning Up*. London: Weidenfeld & Nicolson.
Miles, John (2000) *Lost Angry Penguins: D. B. Kerr & P. G. Pfeiffer: A Path to the Wind*. Adelaide: Crawford Publishing House.
Miller, William H. (1945) 'Introduction to Jazz'. *Angry Penguins* 8: 112–14.
Panassié, Hugues (1942) *The Real Jazz*, trans. Anne Sorelle Williams, adapted for American publication by Charles Edward Smith. New York: Smith & Durrell, Inc.
Pearce, Cedric (1945) *Trumpet in the Night: A Background to the Enjoyment of Jazz Music*. Melbourne: William H. Miller.
Pickering, Tom (1946) 'The Pure Stream: A Theory of Jazz Development'. *Angry Penguins Broadsheet* 10: 21–25.
Rosenkrantz, Timme (1964) *Dus Med Jazz: Mine Jazzmemoirer*. Copenhagen: Chr. Erichsens Forlag.
Sangster, John (1988) *Seeing the Rafters: The Life and Times of an Australian Jazz Musician*. Ringwood, Victoria: Penguin Books.

Schuller, Gunter (1968) *Early Jazz: Its Roots and Musical Development*. New York: Oxford University Press.
Smart, Jeffery (1996) *Not Quite Straight: A Memoir*. Melbourne: William Heinemann Australia.

5 Cuba Street parade

Identity, authenticity and self-expression in contemporary Australasian jazz scenes

Nick Tipping[*]

In the second decade of the twenty-first century, jazz is more or less a global music. Specialized studies of jazz scenes in Britain (Moore 2007), Japan (Atkins 2003), Ghana (Feld 2012) and South Africa (Ballantine 2012), for instance, attest to both the reach and the adaptability of jazz. Yet, by their very nature, these studies implicitly define themselves in contrast to the dominant discourse on jazz, which continues to frame jazz as an American art form. As a result, Australian and New Zealand jazz musicians must contend with the persistent message that they are somewhat on the margins of jazz culture. Publications addressing recent developments in jazz, including Ake, Garrett and Goldmark (2012) and Heble and Wallace (2013), ignore jazz outside North America, despite the rich possibilities that a broader investigation would provide: Ake, Garrett and Goldmark justify their position by referring to the US's 'continued position as arbiter of global jazz tastes' (2012: 6). Paul Berliner's landmark study, *Thinking in Jazz: The Infinite Art of Improvisation* (1994), is similarly constrained in its scope: while Berliner, in an effort to cover a broad base, purposefully included women and members of ethnic minority groups, none of the 52 artists interviewed was born outside the US, despite Berliner's description of his subjects as 'a representative sample of the professional artists and aspirants who make up the core of the jazz community' (Berliner 1994: 7). And, most recently, the definitive *Jazz* (DeVeaux and Giddins 2009) includes virtually no mention of jazz outside North America. Thus the implication is clear: even in the twenty-first century, and despite strong and dura-

---

[*] Nick Tipping is a PhD student, lecturer and bass player in Wellington, New Zealand. His dissertation focuses on the Wellington jazz scene, and issues of identity, both within the community and in relation to global jazz. Nick led the jazz programme at the New Zealand School of Music from 2007–2011, and has lectured in jazz studies and performance at Massey University, the NZSM and the University of Auckland.

ble scenes existing in many parts of the world, jazz continues to emanate from the US; jazz created elsewhere must be, at best, borrowed and, at worst, derivative.

Certainly, the traditions and history of jazz today remain firmly rooted in twentieth-century American culture. There is no debate over provenance; if there is a debate over ownership, it is dominated by the African American/European American question. Although Nicholson (2005) and many of the authors cited above examine the implications of jazz taking on new forms in different geo-cultural contexts over the course of its history, the persistently Americo-centric view within the discourse in general is exemplified by Travis Jackson:

> Studies of jazz outside the United States...act as supplements that mildly challenge the standard narratives without necessarily expanding the role of geography. Those narratives and regions are simply other places whose roles in jazz's development merit consideration. The master narrative itself, however, remains intact—at least in the United States—and isn't subject to modification or elaboration (Jackson 2012: 53).

An investigation into the provenance of jazz is outside the reach of this particular study, the purpose of which is to examine the implications of such perspectives. More germane is the fact that discussions over (African) Americanness in jazz in relation to other global and local jazz identities remain the province of that scholarship which particularly deals with those identities. In other words, 'jazz', unless additionally qualified (as *Australian* jazz, *Japanese* jazz, etc.), remains American by default.

Australia and New Zealand have participated in the global jazz scene since the birth of the music, and the other chapters in this volume illustrate the longevity and breadth of the Australasian scene. Scholars including Johnson (1987, 2000), Whiteoak (1996), Shand (2009), Ward (2012) and Hardie (2009: 41–55) have chronicled and examined elements of the development of Australasian jazz throughout the twentieth century. Musicians such as Mike Nock, Matt Penman, Tal Wilkenfeld and James Morrison have made a significant impact in global terms, and scenes have appeared and developed in most major cities, particularly Sydney, Brisbane and Melbourne in Australia, and Auckland, Wellington and Christchurch in New Zealand.

Yet Australian and New Zealand jazz remains a minor part of the global scene, comparatively isolated by virtue of travel time, distance and expense. Like other smaller global scenes, the various local scenes must negotiate their identity in relation to the dominant culture and tradition. The question of authenticity, which remains central to jazz discourse, is compounded in smaller Australasian scenes by consideration of what it means to be an Australian or a New Zealander who plays jazz. To what extent is it possible to adhere to the dominant (canonical) jazz 'tradition' and still play Australian music? Does jazz, through its capacity for improvisation and self-expression, allow New Zealanders enough room to present their own New Zealand voice? Have the various (and collective) Australian and New Zealand scenes developed traditions of their own? The different scenes around Australasia necessarily present varying answers to these questions. Differences in population size, geographical layout, the presence or lack of formalized jazz education and the individual makeup of each scene mean that generalized answers would not be representative. In order to examine these issues I am focusing on the scenes in Melbourne and Wellington: two strong, but different, centres of jazz in Australasia. My conclusions are presented in the spirit of generating discussion.

The scenes

Melbourne and Wellington present different sets of opportunities to jazz musicians. With a population of around four million, Melbourne is ten times the size of Wellington (in fact, the population of Melbourne is similar to that of the whole of New Zealand). Geographically, both cities are focused on a compact and walkable centre, but Melbourne boasts additional areas of cultural activity and nightlife such as Fitzroy, St Kilda and Brunswick, whereas Wellington's entertainment district is located in the Cuba Street and Courtenay Place areas within the city centre.

Both cities boast a number of venues which regularly host jazz. The Uptown Jazz Café, Paris Cat, and Bennett's Lane (sadly closed in June 2015) in Melbourne, and the Rogue and Vagabond, and to some extent Meow and Havana in Wellington, act as the centres of the scenes, but each city also contains a number of other venues which regularly present live jazz. Both scenes are active, with multiple jazz gigs on any given night. One crucial difference, however, is that while Melbourne's jazz clubs present daily performances to paying customers, who are expected to sit and listen, there is no venue in Wellington of this nature. With very rare exceptions, no jazz gig in Wellington has a cover charge. Bars and restaurants hosting jazz continue to function as eating and drinking establishments, and so the patrons present on any given occasion are by no means necessarily present to hear the music. Wellington musicians, as a result, often play to a room full of people, most of whom are conversing and paying little attention to the music.

Common among musicians I spoke to was the characterization of Melbourne as a larger, more fragmented scene than Wellington; particularly among those with experience of both. A number of people indicated that in Melbourne musicians tend to operate within set socio-musical groupings, and that the communities are demarcated along lines of style, creative approach or other factors. This contrasts strongly with Wellington, wherein the community of jazz musicians is, for the most part, a tightly cohesive whole, in which musicians who don't play together are nevertheless aware of and familiar with each other. Wellington is an 'overgrown village' (Cranson, interview with author, 2011), tightly connected by musical and personal relationships.

Any cursory glance at the activity in the Melbourne and Wellington jazz scenes will quickly reveal the constant breadth of activity: from the minimalist fusion of Tim Willis to the conventional approach of Bopstretch in Melbourne; and from the eclectic envelope-pushing of Wellington's The Troubles to classic New Orleans/Dixieland music, which has been fashionable in the city in the last few years. Clearly, jazz of all descriptions has transferred into these antipodean contexts, but it has changed in the process. Musicians in both cities have adopted jazz as a medium of self-expression, but in doing so they engage with its elements of creativity, authenticity and tradition in new ways. The mass-media dissemination of jazz, as Johnson (2002: 108) points out, allows multiple meanings to be created, both through personal mediation and also recontextualization. In the case of Wellington and Melbourne, jazz still exists as an alternative, borrowed music, in contrast to more commonly accepted native forms of music (such as the Wellington dub sound, or alternative pop/rock). Yet jazz musicians there feel strongly that the jazz they play is integral to the music scene overall, and given that self-expression is central to the music, it could be argued that jazz produced by Wellingtonians, for example, is by definition New Zealand music.

However, when it comes to a negotiation with the jazz tradition, approaches differ—as they do elsewhere. Atkins (2001: 19–43) writes of the crisis of authenticity faced by Japanese jazz musicians, who must find an identity for themselves within a strongly Americanized global jazz culture; and the same questions apply in Melbourne and Wellington. Jazz is many things: a creative art form, or a fixed set of practices; a canonized tradition, or a creative approach to music. Musicians in both cities personify and articulate these tensions, both through their creative practice and in conversation. In preparation for this chapter, I have spent time in both cities, attending and playing in jazz gigs, and interviewing key figures in the scene. Many of the issues faced by Melbourne and Wellington musicians have to do with authenticity. Authenticity is a term that needs some unpacking: for example, Kivy (1995: 7) proposes four authenticities, relating respectively to the composer's intention, the sound, the performer's expression and the audience's reception. Atkins (2001:

24–25) analyses authenticity in jazz as being significant on two levels. To be authentic as a jazz improviser, one must be true to oneself; one must authentically represent one's inner self (or, as Christopher Small [1998] might suggest, an idealized version thereof [134]). On the other hand, to be regarded as authentic in a jazz context, an improviser must be true to the tradition and the fundamental elements of jazz culture, which might differ from the culture of the improviser. The tension between the two authenticities, as illustrated by the concept of jazz musicians from one culture embracing a second, imported culture in order to express themselves, echoes Ralph Ellison's assessment of identity in jazz:

> each solo flight, or improvisation, represents...a definition of his identity; as individual, as member of the collectivity and as a link in the chain of tradition. Thus because jazz finds its very life in improvisation upon traditional materials, the jazz man must lose his identity even as he finds it (Ellison 1966: 234).

In a discussion on the jazz tradition, Travis Jackson (2004: 360) outlines the middle ground, in which successful personal expression in a jazz context is dependent on assimilating and building on the tradition. For the purposes of this discussion I take my cue from Atkins and Ellison, and theorize 'inward' authenticity, which relates most closely to Kivy's third type, and 'outward' authenticity, which relates to an adherence to the 'tradition', or accepted norms of jazz performance. In jazz practice both inside and outside the US, both outward and inward authenticity are privileged, but for different reasons. Both authenticities are viewed in relation to the contextual differences between the US and the other sites of jazz.

Outward authenticity

In Melbourne and Wellington, outward authenticity links musicians to the 'tradition', through ritual, myth and a canon of greats.[1] Musicians emulate performative practices, both sonic and stylistic, which allows them to align their musical identities with their heroes—but with the added twist of contextual difference, which lends a new layer of exoticism. These multiple layers allow musicians in contexts such as Australasia to engage with the tradition while demonstrably creating something new. That the music they create bears close stylistic resemblance to accepted forms of jazz remains a source of conten-

---

1. Christopher Small (1998) examines the use of ritual and myth in musical performance: following prescribed actions or ritualized formulae allows musicians to act out and connect with idealized myths, and to reinforce their relationships to them.

tion in both Wellington and Melbourne; charges of derivativism compete with claims that the improvisation within the music (inevitably informed by the clear contextual difference between present-day Melbourne and 1950s New York, say) imbues it with sufficiently different meanings to be regarded as new.

Among the musicians I spoke to in both cities, most were quick to emphasize the importance of the tradition in the development of a musician, and some are notable in their embrace of the canon throughout their careers. Singer Michelle Nicolle and guitarist James Sherlock (Melbourne), and trumpeter Lex French and trombonist and bandleader Rodger Fox (Wellington) all sought to highlight the importance of standard jazz repertoire and styles; most also play a significant amount of original music, but it remains stylistically close to the canon. Each chooses to engage with the tradition directly by emulating it: Nicolle's weekly residency at the Brunswick Green, or Sherlock's at the Uptown with Bopstretch (both of which feature almost exclusively standard repertoire), Fox's Wellington Jazz Orchestra (a big band that plays repertoire largely derived from the Woody Herman/Buddy Rich/Maynard Ferguson schools) or French's Richter City Rebels (a New Orleans-style marching band, known for parading down Cuba Street), all allow the musicians involved to identify themselves openly with the heritage of jazz:

> that band (the Richter City Rebels) is so good, because it's [in] a New Orleans tradition…we're addressing that—we're trying to do it, trying to pay homage to it as best we can, trying to be as deep with it as best we can (French, interview with author, 2013).

Familiarity with the canon of greats, and the ability to emulate canonical styles, is seen as an indication that a musician recognizes the importance of tradition, and positions themselves alongside it:

> I think with any art form, it's vital to understand what's gone before. So…from the get-go I think that's always been my thing, I've always wanted to know as much about the history of it as possible. To really steep myself in that (ibid.).

Positioning themselves in this manner allows musicians to align some elements of their identity with traditional figures, concepts and tropes, and in doing so to place themselves within a historical tradition. The broader the mastery of that tradition, in terms of style, the more respected the musician (at least by those who valorize outward authenticity), and the more their musical identity draws on the strength of the conventional jazz historical narrative. Almost all of the artists emulated in this way are American, and local traditions and canons are directly emulated to a far lesser degree.

The recent history of the Wellington Jazz Festival, for example, presents an instance in which local musicians reacted against a perceived lack of local representation among the artists; but not necessarily local material. When the format changed to allow greater involvement on the part of the Wellington jazz community, much of the resulting local participation involved Wellingtonians playing music from the canonical US tradition.[2] It is most unusual to hear a Wellington ensemble playing music written by a New Zealander, if that person is not a member of that ensemble.

In Melbourne, James Sherlock and Michelle Nicolle both expressed the commonly held opinion that a sound knowledge of the conventional styles was vital for musicians seeking to become a part of the scene. Just as the jazz tradition (in its most conventionally constructed sense, DeVeaux [1991] and others notwithstanding) can be traced through the development of various styles, so many musicians contend that a sound knowledge of those styles is vital in order for the groundwork to be laid for a career in jazz. In practice, this is as much an economic argument as a pedagogical one.

> I think people ditch [playing standards] too early in their own experience. And I nearly did too you know. You think, oh yeah I've got that, got that. What's next, what's next. But I still think there's enough general work for people to see that you do need to have some sort of connection to some sort of history to be able to successfully play gigs (Sherlock, interview with author, 2014).

A common thread throughout many interviews in Melbourne and Wellington was the importance of jazz as a universal language, in that knowledge and aptitude both confer respectability and open up opportunities for collaboration and the increased potential for paid work. This is particularly so in Wellington, where competence in a variety of styles, genres and ensembles is celebrated, and opportunities can come from any direction at any time. The small size of the scene, and the range of musical activity it nevertheless contains, mean that in order to work with any frequency a musician must be prepared to accept a range of opportunities, encompassing a variety of contexts and styles. Most musicians I spoke to in Wellington pursue multifaceted playing careers: Lucien Johnson, Nick Granville, Reuben Bradley and Lauren Ellis

2.   The highest-profile local concert series in the 2014 festival involved recreations of classic albums including *Kind Of Blue*, *Headhunters*, *Heavy Weather*, *Bitches Brew* and *The Thelonious Monk Orchestra Live at Town Hall*. Other popular gigs included 'Monk meets Mars Volta', the Rodger Fox Big Band of New Zealand, and the Wellington Mingus Ensemble. Original NZ music was certainly performed, however, by bands such as The Jac, Dog (from Auckland), and the Justin Firefly Quartet.

all work in popular music as well as jazz, and many of Wellington's most successful bands are populated by musicians who are also respected jazz players.

The value placed on competence is often conflated with the notion of respect. Authentic reproductions or re-presentations of the canon are often justified as an illustration of the esteem musicians hold for the music (or musicians) being reproduced. In an antipodean context, this means that any local Australian or New Zealand identity that might be conveyed through the performance is at risk of being outweighed by a broader, US-based jazz identity: outward authenticity trumping inward authenticity. Of course the extent to which this happens varies from performance to performance, and context to context: the Richter City Rebels, parading in New Orleans costume through Cuba Street in the heart of Wellington's entertainment district create new meanings for their versions of New Orleans classic repertoire by virtue of the contextual change they embody, whereas bop revival bands such as Melbourne's Bopstretch or Wellington's Boptet more directly channel 'traditional' practices, and it is harder to discern any particularly Australian or New Zealand traits. This is, of course, not to call into question the credentials of any ensemble or musician that chooses to make music (or to musick[3]) in this way: I myself often choose to play jazz that falls into this category, and find it a fulfilling and valid form of self-expression.

Inward authenticity

However, some musicians I interviewed spoke strongly about the need for originality in Australian and New Zealand jazz. Tony Gould, a pianist who has been heavily involved in Australian jazz education, has been active in encouraging young Australian musicians to find inspiration in the world around them. To Gould, knowledge of historical styles of jazz is a good thing, but for present-day Australians, emulation of those styles is inauthentic:

> [Students would] sing Ella Fitzgerald... I'd say to the singers, 'Why are you doing that? She's dead. You're not black. Write your own music. Learn from it by all means, but don't do it in front of me please. Unless you're totally brilliant and you're an impersonator, you're going to sound third rate.'

> We assessed a very fine pianist the other day, beautiful pianist. He played a whole bunch of bebop in a technical exercise. I said 'try not to play that in front of people, the bebop era's over' (Gould, interview with author, 2014).

3. Small 1998.

While Gould admitted to being deliberately provocative, his attitude is reflected in the Melbourne scene. Pianist and composer Andrea Keller cited Gould, as well as influential musicians and educators Brian Brown, Allan Browne and Vince Jones, as musicians whose approach encouraged her to move away from the canonical (US) tradition in order to find her own authentic voice. Classically trained, Keller came to jazz relatively late, but was encouraged early on to play *her* way:

> I was thinking I didn't feel legitimate playing this music, but then when I thought about it from a different angle, and thought about actually why Allan [Browne] kept calling me to do the gig, I realized it wasn't because of my legitimate knowledge of the jazz tradition, it was about something else. It was about the spirit in the music and all these other things that made me *me*, and made me different to other people, and that's actually what he wanted, and then I realized that that's actually legitimacy. If I play it the way I hear it then I'm being legitimate (Keller 2014).

To Keller and Gould, inward authenticity is consonant with the jazz tradition, in that it draws on the creativity inherent in jazz. Yet, in doing so, it necessarily involves actively discarding elements that are not consonant with a musician's own experience, and treating jazz purely as a creative process. Keller, citing Australian pianist Paul Grabowsky's (2007) description of jazz as an adverb, told me:

> it's a way of doing things, it's a process. Some people think it's a noun, it's a pre-1950s style of music, but actually, if you approach it as a way of doing things and a process, then it is all about something else (Keller 2014).

Thus, rejecting a somewhat ossified canon, which predominantly derives from the US of several decades ago, in favour of a process-based approach, which involves searching for authenticity in one's own context, provides those Australian and New Zealand artists who do so with the opportunity to acknowledge the jazz tradition without compromising their own identity. All of the artists I spoke to in both cities emphasized the importance of knowing the tradition, but musicians such as Gould, Keller and Tim Willis in Melbourne and John Rae, Lucien Johnson and Jeff Henderson in Wellington have demonstrated a conscious disregard for convention, resulting in a variety of new approaches to jazz.

Jazz education

It is important not to underestimate the influence of jazz education on the scene of both cities. The two scenes are largely populated by graduates of the local jazz education institutions; and to a certain extent the values of the scenes necessarily reflect, and are reflected by, the schools. The younger musicians in Melbourne tended to cite the staff and curriculum of the Victoria College of the Arts (VCA) and Monash University as having influenced their creative direction, by encouraging them to broaden their horizons and look beyond traditional sources for inspiration; at the VCA, for example, students are actively encouraged to look beyond the canon, and even beyond jazz, in order to find their own voice: the playing of standards is only compulsory in the first year. While Nicolle and Sherlock (as above) cautioned that canonical knowledge is important from an economic perspective, to a greater or lesser extent all the musicians I interviewed in Melbourne alluded to the importance of finding new, individual modes of expression, whether or not they are closely tied to mainstream jazz. While James Sherlock told me 'I think one thing that's particular to Melbourne is that everyone does their time in some sort of traditional band', other Melbourne musicians described traditional, canon-based playing as just one of a number of creative options open to musicians in the scene.

Wellington jazz education presents a different approach. The curriculum at the local jazz institution, the New Zealand School of Music (NZSM), is firmly based on the canonical tradition. Students learn the traditional styles and a prescribed list of standards, and must demonstrate technical facility over standard chord progressions. This is in large part tied to the particular economic context that obtains in Wellington, described above; musicians are almost always playing to the general public, and so must consequently tailor their performances for accessibility. Says former NZSM Associate Professor Norman Meehan:

> Musicians are trying to make a living from it and they necessarily have to compromise, they have to have something that they can sell. There are very few people who have enough of a reputation for their audience to trust them to do anything (Meehan, interview with author, 2011).

A university department with roots as a polytechnic course, the NZSM jazz programme takes greater account of economic and industry-based necessities than its counterparts in Melbourne, with the result that, at undergraduate level at least, it focuses more on traditional, mainstream, skills-based approaches, and less on boundary-pushing, context-dependent expression. Senior Lecturer Rodger Fox told me: 'Everything we do is mirrored off what we've heard. You don't come to school and learn NZ jazz...you are listening to the masters who are American primarily' (Fox, interview with author, 2013).

Of course, each scene's relationship with the tradition is complex: there are healthy traditionalist and experimentalist jazz populations in both Melbourne and Wellington. But jazz is a contextual music: with every individual performance dependent on a myriad of environmental factors, antipodean responses to the question of tradition are far from uniform. Emulation and re-creation of canonical styles imply respect for the greats; yet that respect is largely musical. Social or other contextual factors receive less attention. Discussing the relationship of jazz to the fractured history of race relations in the US, one musician told me: 'It's important to remember that, but more important to put that in the past…the music should continue as far as we are concerned' (Henderson, personal communication, 2013). Playing standards, or utilizing standard musical techniques, is an assertion of identity; in aligning her/himself with a tangible tradition, a jazz musician assimilates elements of that tradition into his/her identity, and claims a place in the global scene. The recontextualization works both ways: musicians may thus import jazz into an antipodean context, while also claiming a broader, global context for their own creative endeavours. For musicians playing a minority music in a geographically isolated scene, this is an important connection. Jazz is assimilated into an Australasian context, and then the resulting music (and musical identity) may then be re-exported: Mike Nock presents perhaps the most compelling example.

Unique approaches?

It is difficult to tell whether specific Australian and New Zealand (or more local) tendencies exist in jazz, much less whether such tendencies have coalesced into anything resembling a localized tradition. Traditions may be constructed genealogically: players may trace their lineage back through generations of teachers and mentors. Senior figures exist in both the Melbourne and Wellington contexts, who have had a profound influence on their respective scenes: Vince Jones, Brian Brown and Tony Gould in Melbourne, for instance, or Colin Hemmingsen, Paul Dyne and Roger Sellers in Wellington. But measuring or assessing their impact is difficult, as it is likely that it would relate more to an attitude towards the music rather than any discernible sonic or stylistic attribute. It is also interesting that no player I spoke to for this project or my larger investigation traced their own lineage back any further than one generation; the concept of a recognizable tradition has not yet developed, at least in Melbourne and Wellington.

However, it is possible that a cohesive approach has developed organically, without attracting attention. Douglas Lilburn, in calling for other New Zealand composers to consider their own national identity, noted that this had already happened in the field of literature, quite by accident:

> it hasn't happened as a result of groups of people self-consciously setting out to produce a national literature. These people have been working independently of each other, getting to grips imaginatively with things about them, and when Sargeson or Curnow collects the best of this work together we find that a literature with some distinctive trends has already emerged (Lilburn 2011: 28).

Much of the limited discourse addressing the issue of locally evolved 'sounds' in Australasian jazz alludes to a certain rough-and-ready approach present in both New Zealand and Australia. Norman Meehan (2010: 104) describes the DIY (do-it-yourself), 'makeshift' element in the playing of Mike Nock, a New Zealander who has had a profound effect on the jazz of both countries. Discussions I have had with successive seminar classes have come to the same conclusion: that New Zealand jazz often has a low-fi, DIY quality. However, that may be in part due to the familiarity local listeners have with local players, combined with a certain 'cultural cringe',[4] which might predispose New Zealanders to look at local jazz as somehow less highly professional or polished than jazz from elsewhere. Tony Gould alluded strongly to what he termed the 'gothic mode' in Australian culture: 'look too close, and it'll appear to be rough... [You have to] see the beauty in the roughness' (Gould, interview with author, 2014). To Gould, Australian jazz shares this quality—a roughness that could be dismissed (unfairly) as 'carelessness or disregard for the music', but which is simply influenced by the same pioneering, frontier, DIY mentality to which Meehan refers.[5]

Yet the valorizing of outward authenticity makes it much more difficult to establish any locally specific jazz tendencies, or a local jazz tradition. Steve Garden, the Auckland-based manager of jazz and contemporary music label Rattle, commented on the cost of the quest for outward authenticity:

> I don't think we have [a unique sound] yet, but I think it is coming... So long as musicians and composers stay within the tradition, then the music we make here will always sound like traditional jazz, it will always sound like an imported culture. It will only become something unique to New Zealand when we find our own voice within that tradition (Garden 2010, in Burns 2010: 19).

Garden's assessment of jazz musicians in this part of the world embracing an 'imported culture' at the expense of local tradition echoes Ralph Ellison's

---

4. 'Cultural cringe' is the belief that one's own culture (often a national culture) is inferior to other culture(s).
5. See Shand (2009) for a further examination of this question.

observation, quoted earlier: to Garden, a musician, expressing him/herself through a medium derived from a culture different to their own, runs the risk of losing central elements of their identity.

Jazz musicians in both cities assert their identity every time they improvise or compose. At times that identity is derived from the juxtaposition of mainstream jazz culture, based in the US, with a contemporary urban Australian or New Zealand context. Yet in other instances their embracing of the concept of 'jazz as adverb' allows musicians to apply the creative, hybridizing quality of the jazz tradition to create new identities; these sit in opposition to the mainstream, and assert uniquely local characteristics through their assimilation of contextual factors. The search for authenticity leads Melbourne and Wellington jazz musicians in a number of directions; the varied contexts presented by the two cities allow musicians to explore a range of authenticities, which combine to form the rich scenes enjoyed by both cities.

References

Ake, David, Charles Hiroshi Garrett and Daniel Goldmark, eds. (2012) *Jazz / Not Jazz: The Music and its Boundaries.* Berkeley: University of California Press. http://dx.doi.org/10.1525/california/9780520271036.001.0001

Atkins, E. Taylor (2001) *Blue Nippon: Authenticating Jazz in Japan.* Durham, NC: Duke University Press. http://dx.doi.org/10.1215/9780822380030

Atkins, E. Taylor, ed. (2003) *Jazz Planet.* Jackson, MS: University Press of Mississippi.

Ballantine, Christopher (2012) *Marabi Nights: Jazz, 'Race' and Society in Early Apartheid South Africa.* Scottsdale: University of KwaZulu-Natal Press.

Berliner, Paul (1994) *Thinking in Jazz: The Infinite Art of Improvisation.* Chicago: University of Chicago Press. http://dx.doi.org/10.7208/chicago/9780226044521.001.0001

Burns, Lori (2010) *Challenges to the Wellington Jazz Community from a Business Perspective.* MBA thesis. Wellington: Victoria University.

DeVeaux, Scott (1991) 'Constructing the Jazz Tradition: Jazz Historiography'. *Black American Literature Forum* 25/3: 525–60. http://dx.doi.org/10.2307/3041812

DeVeaux, Scott, and Gary Giddins (2009) *Jazz.* New York: W. W. Norton.

Ellison, Ralph (1966) *Shadow and Act.* New York: New American Library.

Feld, Steven (2012) *Jazz Cosmopolitanism in Accra: Five Musical Years in Ghana.* Durham, NC: Duke University Press. http://dx.doi.org/10.1215/9780822394969

Grabowsky, Paul (2007) 'Introducing... Paul Grabowsky'. *State Library of Queensland*, 13 June, http://www.slq.qld.gov.au/__data/assets/pdf_file/0004/65587/SLQ-Paul_Grabowsky_transcript-9_Jun_07.pdf (accessed 8 October 2014).

Hardie, Richard (2009) 'Jazz on a Summer's Night'. In *Jazz Aotearoa: Notes Towards a New Zealand History*, ed. Richard Hardie and Allan Thomas, 41–55. Wellington: Steele Roberts.

Heble, Ajay, and Rob Wallace (2013) 'People Get Ready: The Future of Jazz is Now'. In *People Get Ready: The Future of Jazz is Now!*, ed. Ajay Heble and Rob Wallace, 1–28. Durham, NC: Duke University Press. http://dx.doi.org/10.1215/9780822399728-001

Jackson, Travis (2004) '"Always New and Centuries Old": Jazz, Poetry, and Tradition as Creative Adaptation'. In *Uptown Conversation: The New Jazz Studies*, by R. O'Meally, B. H. Edwards and F. J Griffin, 357–73. New York: Columbia.
—(2012) *Blowin' the Blues Away: Performance and Meaning on the New York Jazz Scene*. Berkeley: University of California Press. http://dx.doi.org/10.1525/california/9780520270442.001.0001
Johnson, Bruce (1987) *The Oxford Companion to Australian Jazz*. Melbourne: Oxford University Press.
—(2000) *The Inaudible Music: Jazz, Gender and Australian Modernity*. Sydney: Currency Press.
—(2002) 'Jazz as Cultural Practice'. In *The Cambridge Companion to Jazz*, ed. Mervyn Cooke and David Horn, 96–113. Cambridge: Cambridge University Press.
Kivy, Peter (1995) *Authenticities: Philosophical Reflections on Musical Performance*. New York: Cornell University Press.
Lilburn, Douglas (2011) *A Search for Tradition and a Search for a Language*. Wellington: Lilburn Residence Trust in association with Victoria University Press.
Meehan, Norman (2010) 'Mike Nock: A NZ Voice in Jazz'. In *Many Voices: Music and National Identity in Aotearoa/New Zealand*, ed. Henry Johnson, 103–10. Newcastle: Cambridge Scholars.
Moore, Hilary (2007) *Inside British Jazz: Crossing Borders of Race, Nation and Class*. Aldershot: Ashgate.
Nicholson, Stuart (2005) *Is Jazz Dead? (Or has it Moved to a New Address)*. New York: Routledge.
Shand, John (2009) *Jazz: The Australian Accent*. Sydney: University of NSW.
Small, Christopher (1998) *Musicking: The Meanings of Performing and Listening*. Middletown, CT: Wesleyan University Press.
Ward, Aleisha (2012) 'Any Rags, Any Jazz, Any Boppers Today?: Jazz in New Zealand 1920–1955'. PhD dissertation, University of Auckland.
Whiteoak, John (1996) '"Jazzing" and Australia's First Jazz Band'. *Popular Music* 13/3: 279–95. http://dx.doi.org/10.1017/S0261143000007200

Interviews with author
Cranson, Rick (2011) Interview with author. 8 September.
Fox, Rodger (2013) Interview with author. 9 July.
French, Lex (2013) Interview with author. 6 May.
Gould, Tony (2014) Interview with author. 24 June.
Henderson, Robert (2013) Personal communication. 16 October.
Keller, Andrea (2014) Interview with author. 24 June.
Meehan, Norman (2011) Interview with author. 4 October.
Nicolle, Michelle (2004) Interview with author. 20 June.
Sherlock, James (2014) Interview with author. 23 June.

6 The lost history of jazz on early Australian popular music television

Liz Giuffre[*]

Introduction

The existing historical narrative of early popular music television in Australia is relatively narrow in scope. Rock and pop programming dominates these narratives almost exclusively, and what little work there is on Australian music television's development has been re-circulated many times and seldom questioned (Stockbridge 1989, 1992a, 1992b). My own work on Australian music television has also had a primary rock and pop focus (Giuffre 2009, 2012, 2013), as a result of working backwards from contemporary industry practices to look for similar patterns from the past. This chapter seeks to move beyond these patterns, showing that rock and pop were important parts of the development of music television, but were not the only players. Upon gaining access to production documents for one of Australia's first popular music programmes, *Six O'Clock Rock* (ABC TV 1959–1962), I discovered that for a short time jazz was just as much of a presence as pop and rock in early music television programming. Here I seek to disclose jazz's pioneering role in the broadcast form, and examine why the genre was displaced. I also acknowledge that jazz's omission in existing histories has contributed to the pop/rock centricism of current music television scholarship (including my own). I present this chapter as a step towards the development of a more diversified research in the future.

Frith's arguments for the connection between music television and rock/pop (2002) remain influential for popular music historians and contemporary practice scholars. His emphasis is on the popular uptake of both the genre and the medium around the same time in the 1950s and 60s, a focus

---

[*] Dr Liz Giuffre is a Lecturer in Communication at the University of Technology Sydney.

that implies that new forms of popular music were the only sounds to feature in this type of broadcasting. However, as Wald argued in *How The Beatles Destroyed Rock and Roll* (2009), the persuasiveness of such dominant narratives tempts researchers away from continuing to explore the field, and, in doing so, it is easy to oversimplify cultural histories. To illustrate: The Beatles' performance on *The Ed Sullivan Show* is an iconic interaction between popular music and television that Wald argues can be seen as either 'liberating or limiting' (2009: 247) depending on whether the narrator wants to write an origin story of genre and medium, or if they are seeking to explore a broader chronological and musical timeline. The Beatles' influence on popular music discourse in subsequent decades has come to frame this interaction as a success; however, it doesn't take into account what other forms of music were displaced as a result of that success. One of many examples Wald gives is the impact that this televisual event had on artists who built audiences through live performance primarily, saying, 'when The Beatles appeared on *The Ed Sullivan Show*, it was the last time a live performance changed the course of American music' (ibid.).

Of course rock and pop music and its performance have featured heavily throughout the international development of music television. There is also no doubt that a strong connection between the genre and the medium has been maintained since the formative years of both, evidenced most obviously with the near-exclusive conflation of music television as a form with MTV and its offshoots (Goodwin 1992: 24; Allan 2002: 220; Austerliz 2007: 30). However, a focus on rock and pop overlooks the fact that when television started, particularly in Australia, jazz was also a popular form with audiences, and, as such, it also featured heavily in early popular music television programming. The material to follow demonstrates jazz's presence on early music television, drawing on written archives of ABC television as they are now housed in the National Archives repository in Chester Hill in Sydney. The files have been largely untouched for decades, and took over eighteen months to access because of their status as 'unclassified' (meaning either 'sensitive', or, simply, 'not previously requested, therefore not a priority for classification'). Like most programmes of this era, very few audiovisual copies of broadcast editions remain; however, the existing written archives provide useful insight into how and why broadcast decisions were made. These documents also help to explain how much jazz was present during this time, and why and when this type of music was taken off the air. Rock and pop eventually came to dominate, but denying jazz's presence in the beginnings of music television obscures the nuances of the cultural industries at the time.

Paving the way for popular music television on the Australian National Broadcaster

Six O'Clock Rock was the first locally produced popular music television programme broadcast on the ABC, the then sole public service broadcaster in Australia.[1] The show has been widely enshrined as a launching pad for Australian rock and roll, not least of all because of its famous compere, Johnny O'Keefe. O'Keefe's title as 'King of Australian rock and roll' is one that was fostered during his career and subsequently. But notwithstanding the way the early episodes of *Six O'Clock Rock* are now recalled, they show that O'Keefe in fact had a significant jazz pedigree that has been subsequently written out of cultural histories. The explicit generic link in the programme's name, *Six O'Clock Rock*, present from the beginning, was not an indication of the programme's sole music focus.

ABC television was launched in November 1956, two years before *Six O'Clock Rock* was aired. Following an overseas visit in 1957, controller of programmes Keith Barry submitted a report on international developments in 'Light Entertainment: Television—BBC and ITV' (Barry 1957: 1) where the seeds for local music television production were sown. Dated 16 November 1957, Barry recalled a meeting in London at which music television was discussed with 'Ronnie Waldman, the BBC Head of Light Entertainment, Television, and his two [unnamed] Chief Assistants'. In this report Barry doesn't name specific programmes, but discusses the development of local versions of 'some of [the BBC's] TV light entertainment shows'. Interestingly, the report begins by emphasizing the financial implications, rather than content, audience or other types of resources required, of making this type of television. As Barry notes in his first main paragraph:

> These are the half-hour ones [programmes] which feature the big stars, and about the first thing which hits one about them is the fee which has to be paid. The point is that the star has to give up almost the full week to rehearsals, and can accept very little other work—even programmes on Sound;[2] this helps to explain why Jimmy

---

1. The ABC, the Australian Broadcasting Company, and later Australian Broadcasting Corporation, was established in 1932, starting with capital city radio broadcasts and gradually developing its network across the country and across media to include television in 1957. It was joined by a second public service broadcaster, SBS (the Special Broadcasting Service), in 1980.

2. In these communications Sound is typed using a capital 'S' throughout; it is not clear if it is a reference to a particular audio-only programme, or the name of a branch of BBC production more generally. However, the point remains that light entertainment television is here evolving as something that presents new and distinct challenges.

> Edwards, Hancock and others get fees in the vicinity of the £750 mark. An interesting sideline is that this television work is more exhausting than Sound, and while staff and artists in Sound sometimes work a 7-day week, the Television people feel they must have a spell each week. Jimmy Edwards, for instance, who is well known for his ability and perhaps desire to make money, now wants to go down to his farm when the week-end comes (Barry 1957: 1).

Later in the document Barry outlines the cost for other types of performers in British productions, noting '[t]here is no house orchestra or variety band for I.T.V.' (ibid.). He also notes that 'an arrangement is made with [presenter] Eric Robinson to have the use of a combination he provides on a certain number of occasions over a given period' (ibid.), most likely a cost-saving measure. Barry continues to explain the details of each television production period including rehearsals where 'the minimum rate which can be paid for a musician is £6 for a 5-hour call' and refers to required meal breaks and subsequent subsidies. Barry also notes differences in types of payments to be made for musicians with more experience, reporting that 'an orchestral or dance band player can earn £10. The top men, of course, want more than the minimum fee' (1957: 1).

In the next section of the report Barry discusses the logistics of putting together an Australian music show similar to the existing BBC productions. He outlines his concerns about budget capacity, and also raises concerns about the Australian popular music industry itself, saying 'the trouble about the television variety show is that a desperate search must be made for new talent each week' (Barry 1957: 2). Given this comment, it would be easy to assume the ABC had commissioned the local show in order to showcase and develop local talent (and no doubt this did help the broadcaster meet its requirements in annual reports at the time); however, Barry's communication suggests that the prohibitive price of syndicating a BBC programme also significantly contributed to the eventual format and style of *Six O'Clock Rock*. The need to stick to a strict budget is one that continued to plague the national broadcaster during this time, and, arguably, is one that continues to significantly influence programming decisions.

Following Barry's 1957 communication, solid planning for local Australian popular music programming finally began. The launch of *Six O'Clock Rock* on 28 February 1959 was announced by ABC Deputy General Manager Clement Semmler in a report titled 'TV Light Entertainment Programme: Six O'Clock Rock', dated 21 January 1959. Semmler's address appears to be speaking directly back to concerns raised in Barry's overseas communication in 1957. It begins by citing notes on costings and talent recruitment from the 'DLE' (Director of Light Entertainment), and, interestingly, includes specific details of musicians drawn from jazz as well as the then emerging pop and rock genres. The report also makes a clear comparison between the proposed new show and the BBC's *Six-Five Special*:[3]

> The proposed costing of this show [*Six O'Clock Rock*] is shown hereunder, and you will note that two bands are involved. In order to forestall accusations of extravagance, may I refer to the fact that 'Six-Five Special' never has less than three bands, occasionally four, in addition to skiffle groups, etc. Here, we are booking Johnny O'Keefe and his Band, and pairing it with Freddie Logan's All-Stars to provide straight jazz and vocal accompaniments: in the latter case, not less than five special arrangements will be required from the leader (DLE in Semmler 1959: 1).

Following the comparison to the BBC's programme and its format (noting that the ABC will be hiring fewer bands overall), Semmler, again quoting the DLE, defends what he sees as an anticipated backlash about costs. Semmler argues 'the two bands make this programme [*Six O'Clock Rock*] seem expensive at first glance, but we in the department are convinced that they are needed' (ibid.), a reference, likely, to Barry's 1957 report about the pressures in securing enough local talent to sustain a music programme.

Under Semmler's leadership the ABC seemed determined to create popular music television that could be distinctive in the Australian media landscape as well as comparable to internationally renowned productions like the BBC's music television programming. In the same announcement of *Six O'Clock Rock*'s launch he wrote:

> the time was opportune for us to present a similar type of programme related to the Australian conditions in a late Saturday afternoon period where I feel we have a first-class opportunity to capitalize on a programme of this type (ibid.).

Semmler does not specify what the 'Australian conditions' are initially, although it is reasonable to assume this is a reference to the types of popular music being produced in Australia at the time. His emphasis earlier on the 'very needed' two bands, one playing 'straight jazz' and the other led by Johnny O'Keefe, suggests that at the time of writing the Australian popular music landscape was indeed inclusive of both these older and emerging genre forms. Interestingly, Semmler doesn't note whether or not O'Keefe and the

---

3. The connection between *Six O'Clock Rock* and *Six-Five Special* has also been made by several scholars since, notably Stockbridge (1989: 74).

jazz performers would be playing together, also implying that there may be some genre crossover.

Semmler's report also outlines the broader broadcast context for the proposed local popular music production, saying there is 'little real competition from the commercials at this point' (Semmler 1959: 1). He qualifies this argument by noting that one commercial station has been populating its Saturday afternoon schedule with recycled (and likely international) programming, 'a repeat of various film series' (ibid.), while the another 'has a disc jockey programme ending at 6.10pm which is followed by "Superman" repeats' (Semmler 1959: 1). It is important that the ABC leader should lament the lack of exposure of local artists in the commercial broadcast space at this time. This further emphasizes the contribution that *Six O'Clock Rock* would make to the Australian cultural landscape. Semmler identifies difference in terms of the programme's target audience as well, as he describes the proposed *Six O'Clock Rock* as 'a well mounted variety programme...especially angled for teenagers', noting how it could be 'certainly more attractive' than 'the rather tired sort of programme presented at the moment by Roy Hampson under the title "Vincents [sic] Rhythm Roundup" at 5.40pm on Channel 7'.[4] He notes that the Channel 7 show was made up of 'mainly teletranscriptions', the type of international rerecorded programme that Barry's 1957 report showed to be financially out of reach for the ABC. As a result of this desire to be distinctive in the market, and meet budget, Semmler argues that 'we [the ABC] will be breaking new ground with a live programme of top class rhythm and skiffle artists' (ibid.).

Six O'Clock Rock and Six O'Clock Jazz

As Semmler planned, *Six O'Clock Rock* did go ahead on air in 1959 with a substantial jazz presence. While most of the audiovisual records from the

---

4. Semmler provides no other detail about *Vincents Rhythm Roundup* on Channel 7, and like much early Australian and international television, its details have been lost, not yet apparently archived at the National Film and Sound Archive (NSFA) or on Trove. The only other details about the programme still readily available appear to be a television guide listing from the *Sydney Morning Herald*, 1 December 1958, which gives no detail of the musical content of the show, but does note that it was 'presented by Roy Hampson with the "Poster Girl" Competition' (SMH 1958: 14), and later that night the station also played a cigarette-sponsored music programme 'Astor Showcase—variety programme with [presumably local] ATN orchestra', while on the same day Channel 9 was showing *Bandstand* at 3pm, listed with no other details apart from naming host Brian Henderson (ibid.). I searched both the catalogues of the NSFA and Trove using 'Vincents Rhythm Roundup' and 'Vincent's Rhythm Roundup', in case the ABC communication had a spelling mistake, with no results found, on 18 October 2014.

programme have been lost, the National Archives paper collection has a comprehensive listing of the artists who appeared on individual episodes including, importantly, the song and artist lists for the shows in the programme's opening season. According to these records the programme's debut on 28 February 1959 featured Johnny O'Keefe and/or his band The Dee Jays in five musical numbers, with another five musical appearances allocated to the high-profile jazz group The Australian All Stars (either by themselves or accompanying a vocalist). The second show's list for 7 March 1959 features O'Keefe and the Dee Jays slightly more often (six for the All Stars, eight for O'Keefe); the All Stars remained prominent with appearances including solo features. This pattern of rock/jazz alternating features appears to have continued in subsequent episodes (14 March 1959); however, after this date the paper archives appear to be incomplete. Regardless of the missing data, what remains is evidence of the broadcaster's commitment to a mixed jazz and pop/rock set during the formative period of building the programme's audience and profile in the television landscape of the time.

Popular press reports from the time also acknowledge the appearance of both jazz and rock in early *Six O'Clock Rock*. In her 'Television Parade' column for the *Australian Women's Weekly* Nan Musgrove reported on the opening episodes of the programme, saying it was made up of 'Johnny O'Keefe's band, a jazz group, and 120 enthusiastic teenagers who turned the first show into one of those bouncy but dedicated occasions that is a rock-n-roll festival' (Musgrove 1959: 74). Interestingly, here, both jazz and O'Keefe are mentioned together as part of the fare, that is, both seen as contributing to the appeal of the show even if descriptions of 'rock-n-roll' dominated. Later in the piece she notes the importance of the dance segments in the programme, and while she doesn't name the All Stars, a review of the early run sheets identifies them as the band who provided accompaniment to these (in particular for dancers Milton Mitchell and Lee Neilson on the 28 February programme, and for Anita Ardell and Joe Jenkins on 14 March). Interestingly, in the intervening programme on 7 March O'Keefe and the Dee Jays are listed as accompanying unnamed dancers for a feature performance of 'Rebel Rouser', suggesting again that jazz and rock were being intermixed quite seamlessly during this time.

While it is beyond the scope of this publication to give more details of the diversity of these early episodes, even a brief analysis of the National Archives paper holdings for the show invites contemporary researchers and cultural historians to reconsider how we have thought about Australian popular music television previously. In addition to episode lists and booking guides, the National Archives' *Six O'Clock Rock* paper collections also include undated publicity stills of jazz musicians clearly staged for television performance. For example, the image labelled 'Vocalist Patti Monroe singing with Gus Merzi's Sextet in *Six O'Clock Rock* from Channel 2 – ABN' shows a TV camera framing the singing woman while standing on the steps of a studio riser, with musicians positioned behind her in a clear sextet configuration including trumpet, sax, trombone, double bass, piano and accordion; three images of the NSW Police Choir shot firstly by themselves with a conductor, then framed by the ABC camera, then with Johnny O'Keefe; and a headshot of household jazz name Graeme Bell with no notation other than his name written in pencil on the back of the image. Also included is an image labelled the 'Freddie Logan Quintet', with players in matching striped shirts displaying bongos, sax and shaker, and an unnamed, unlabelled image of a five-piece group showing their instruments: a piano accordion, clarinet, double bass, drum and guitar. While the details of when and what these musicians performed on screen (and, sometimes, even who they were) has been lost, the inclusion of these images in the archive tends to confirm that there was much more to the *Six O'Clock Rock* sound and image than rock and pop.

So why has the jazz featured on *Six O'Clock Rock* been forgotten?

Jazz bands were phased out of the *Six O'Clock Rock* regular schedule by the end of the programme's first year on air, and, put simply, it seems that jazz just became too expensive to commission. Despite claims prior to the debut in February 1959 that the budget would normally be around £250, the remaining correspondence seems to suggest that subsequent episodes during 1959 regularly exceeded this. As a result, it appears cost-cutting measures were ordered by ABC management—measures that would have necessarily changed what the show's producers could commission for the viewing audience. Less money meant simply that fewer people could be employed—adding further to the conflation of Johnny O'Keefe with *Six O'Clock Rock*, as he remained on the roster while others were removed. A memo from the Director of Light Entertainment, David Porter, dated 4 August 1959, stated: 'As from this week we intend to drop the second band in the above programme [*Six O'Clock Rock*]' (1959a: 1). Here the second band is not named but later files show it to have been the straight jazz of the Australian All Stars.

When *Six O'Clock Rock* was first conceived it was expected that both rock and jazz musicians would supply accompaniment for singers and dancing (specifically The All Stars and The Dee Jays). However, it seems that with budgetary pressure such diversity came to be considered overkill rather than variety. The choice was made to continue on with O'Keefe's band as both a feature and sole accompanying group. As Porter detailed in the rest of the 1959 memo, the arrangement would require some reordering of funds, but would still be more cost effective than keeping both the rock and jazz bands on the books:

> the O'Keefe group will [now] have to play six or seven additional numbers and they have requested an increase in their fee to cover arrangements. I consider this request fully justified and will be grateful if you would approve the payment to them of £110 per show. This covers Johnny O'Keefe's singing and work as compere, payment to the musicians for playing, and payment to the pianist/arranger for some nine or ten items per programme. This, I am sure you will agree, is a fair deal for the ABC, and it means that the programme will cost some £50 per week less expensive (Porter 1959b: 1).

Porter's summary of the individual costs of the show make clearer the reasons for cutting costs, and how such budget restraints were met. Although there is nothing from O'Keefe in the National Archives files to provide further insight into why his band should be chosen over the All Stars, it is likely that O'Keefe insisted that he would only stay as compere if his band remained employed with him. Interestingly, however, Porter does add a coda to his communication suggesting some hesitation about moving from a multi to mono genre style of programming—'I should like to add that experience may result in our re-introducing a second band; the O'Keefe group may become too monotonous on its own' (Porter 1959a: 1). Porter's memo was confirmed and approved a few days later by ABC manager Keith Barry in another correspondence on 7 August 1959. Here Barry wrote, 'I am pleased to know that some £50 per week will be saved in this way and agree that the matter can be re-considered at any time if the re-introduction of a second band should be considered advisable' (Barry 1959: 1). Again, this is confirmation that the loss of the jazz component of the programme was not necessarily a choice that was intended to be final, and, perhaps, one that the broadcaster felt might upset the existing audience.

Although it now seemed that jazz would be lost from *Six O'Clock Rock*, the ABC did seem interested in maintaining the music as part of its music television schedule in other ways. On 10 August 1959 David Porter sent an inter-office memo regarding the *Six O'Clock Rock* changes and the light entertainment bill more broadly, providing further insight into the organization's wish to spread musical content across its programming. Porter proposed four points for TV light entertainment for consideration during August/September, sparked partly by the success of *Six O'Clock Rock* to date but also in response to the poor performance of other programmes such as *Rooftop Rendezvous*, a programme that was 'partly designed' around British performer Edwin Styles and something that had become 'a definite failure' (Porter 1959b: 1). Porter argued for the development of the programme *Make Ours Music* and its use of the All Australian All Stars as feature artists (ibid.). While Porter did not made an explicit connection between the band's dismissal from *Six O'Clock Rock* and this new potential appointment, the memo shows that the ABC remained, at this time, committed to trying to find a way to continue to feature jazz on television.

Porter's memo also includes his aspiration to 'start a fortnightly series of old-time music hall programmes…including an elderly top-liner as guest', as well as a return to 'Café Continental' which 'proved a success in the past and it is evidence that many people would like to see it back' (1959b: 1). In the final section Porter writes about what he believes to be the possible fate of *Six O'Clock Rock*, noting, importantly, that he did not expect the show's success to last. Following the strategies for diversifying its other music output and audience reach, Porter wrote:

> 'Six O'Clock Rock', which is probably the most successful live programme produced by the ABC, should continue until the ratings start to fail. This, in my opinion, is bound to happen sooner or later, particularly in view of the intensity with which the teen-age angle is being exploited by other channels and the press: it seems it must wear itself out very quickly (1959b: 1).

When combined with the costings memo from 4 August 1959, it appears here that Porter was not against televised jazz, or necessarily *for* televised rock and pop. Rather, he appeared simply concerned with diversifying the light entertainment department's outputs and reach. His expectation that the 'teen-age angle…must wear itself out very quickly' proved to be premature, and, indeed, the connection between young adults and popular music only increased for television. What did change was the type of popular music that was kept on screen. As a telex sent from the Sydney to Melbourne ABC offices on 12 August 1959 confirms, a couple of weeks later jazz was removed, and instead: 'SIX O'CLOCK NEW FORMAT ALMOST EXCLUSIVELY ROCK AND ROLL' (Porter 1959c: 1).

Financial pressure continued during the programme's run into 1960 and 1961. A memo sent by Bruce Webber, Associate Director of Light Entertainment, on 10 May 1960, noted the need for *Six O'Clock Rock* to honour new Equity award conditions for its performers,[5] and in the memo several 'means of reducing cost' under the new conditions were proposed (Webber 1960: 1). These included 'us[ing] each singing in four numbers rather than employing

---

5. Equity was the trade union for musicians and performers at the time, now encompassed within the contemporary Media, Entertainment and Arts Alliance.

four singers in one number each'; however, Webber argued he felt 'this would be undesirable from the programme point of view if the viewer was to see a handful of performers returning on four occasions within the hour' (ibid.). While it's unclear from this communication, or others prior, if all performers were required to be Equity members when employed by the ABC, Webber does acknowledge the need to find some type of compromise. He concludes by suggesting a reduction of the hour of broadcast time back 'to the "Rock's" old duration of 45 minutes', which he claims would only cost £17.16.0 rather than the 'full rate of £21.6.9' quoted earlier in the memo (ibid.). Cost aside, shorter time on air would have also significantly affected the ability for the show to broadcast jazz—a form that tends to work in longer form than rock and pop.

Secondary commentaries of the ABC's 1950s music television have acknowledged the broadcaster's ambitions to a point, but as with The Beatles' dominance over rock and roll, here narratives of *Six O'Clock Rock*'s connection to Johnny O'Keefe have taken over. For example, Bryden-Brown's (1982) biography of O'Keefe recalls:

> One of David Porter's ambitions was to produce a teenage programme, and he discussed the project with ABC producer, Peter Page... To start with, they wanted a permanent group to star in the show and decided that it would be one of the top groups in Australia at that time—Johnny O'Keefe and the Dee Jays, or Cole Joye and the Joy Boys... After a lot of consideration, it was decided to compromise on a rock and jazz combination (1982: 57–58).

The 'compromise' in Bryden-Brown's account is unclear about what was being relinquished. He could be referring to the compromise of musical genre form, compromise on booking available talent, compromise on audience reach or simply compromising on the stretch of limited ABC budget. Either way, the development of *Six O'Clock Rock* into a more homogeneous type of popular music production appears to have been a deliberate choice based on financial pressure. The mainstream popular music industry's preference for different genre types has of course changed over time (as it has continued to do since the 1950s); however, these documents have shown that jazz was taken off popular music television for practical reasons rather than merely for an apparent change in audience and artistic taste.

The memory of JOK takes over from the reality of *Six O'Clock Rock*'s original lineup

In light of the materials that I have presented from the National Archives, it seems that histories of *Six O'Clock Rock*'s development are clearly romanticized in relation to the narrative of rock's all-conquering arrival, which overstates its dominance in youth music television. The aim of these histories is the glowing recollection of the programme's radical achievements—a noble aim but one that misleadingly overlooks the contributions of musicians who were not rock and pop performers. For example, former performer turned chronicler, Lonnie Lee, wrote in a popular history of the programme:

> Unlike today where money is the motivator, the music industry was born and nurtured under the loving parental guidance of the 'love of music' and 'love of performance'. This was a poor family with very little money to be made, but a lot of fun to be had. The love and comradeship amongst its siblings would broadcast the thrill of the new Rock 'n' Roll across the sleepy Australian continent and in doing so, create the country's first pop music stars (Lee 2007: 1).

Lee's idealized account unfortunately underestimates the role of budgetary considerations in the 1950s music industry. As I have shown in the earlier section, money was a clear driver of musical choice for *Six O'Clock Rock*, and ultimately it was cost that pushed the programme towards an exclusive pop/rock focus. Lee's emphasis is not necessarily negligent, since access to such internal communication would not have been easy (if at all) when his piece was being produced. Having said that, I feel it is naïve to assume that a sudden changing of the bill (jazz disappeared swiftly all within the show's first year of broadcast) would go un-noted and unquestioned altogether, with the only passing reference to it made during a note in the book's introduction: 'The first shows were 50% Jazz and 50% the new Rock'n'Roll until the viewers demanded the latter. There were two bands per show, one Jazz, the other Rock'n'Roll' (Lee 2007: 2). As shown above, the suggestion that overwhelming 'viewer demand' under the irresistible pressure of a new musical vogue was all that moved jazz off the bill can now be considered suspect.

A similarly selective account of the programme came via broadcaster Bob Rogers's description of *Six O'Clock Rock* and its relation to its audience. Rogers argued that the programme was important in how it excluded older viewers, arguing that artists on the show were performing with a relative rawness, 'penetrating a lot of alien living rooms through ABC television allow[ing] thousands of Mums and Dads at least to define the "enemy"' (Rogers and O'Brien 1975: 74). Such accounts may have been true of O'Keefe's vocals and compere skills, but certainly not of outfits such as the Australian All Stars. Unlike these accounts of a show framed by rocker O'Keefe's apparently rough and ready spontaneous, unprepared appearances, the All Stars and their contemporaries come across in the remaining audiovisual footage of the show as

6 The lost history of jazz on early Australian popular music television 129

composed and tightly rehearsed. Such careful preparation is also reflected in various documents from the ABC archive which outline extensive rehearsal periods and rehearsal notes often passed interstate prior to performances—a necessary preparation for this and other jazz bands who were used on the show as accompaniment for guest vocalists as well as feature acts in their own right. While jazz is a form that allows for (and expects) a significant amount of adaptability from its performers, the time allocated to preparation suggests that these televisual presentations were to be as carefully prepared as possible.

Rogers's account has been echoed by other former audience members such as Denise Young, who wrote, '*Six O'Clock Rock* burst onto the screen like fireworks, with skyrockets, Catherine wheels and double bungers [firecrackers] all going off at once. It was wild and raw, spontaneous and rough, and it was all our own' (2006: 25). Given the relative lack of experience in all television production, elements of the programme were surely unplanned. However, to suggest that the show was wholly a spontaneous rock party does not seem accurate on the basis of background documents, nor is it consistent with the small amount of footage of the programme that remains. It is also at odds with the type of show that *Six O'Clock Rock* was meant to be—modelled on the BBC's *Six-Five Special* which was aimed at teenagers but 'also meant to appeal to parents', so that the television context was able to present 'youth music [providing] a bit of a laugh for grown-ups' (Frith 2002: 283).

O'Keefe's charisma should not be denied, and this chapter does not seek to challenge his pioneering work in pop and rock music. His contribution to music television in Australia was not limited only to *Six O'Clock Rock*, and he continued as a television presenter with music programmes on Channel 7 (*The Johnny O'Keefe Show/Sing Sing Sing*) and 10 (*Where the Action Is*) during the 1960s, as well as live and recorded performances until his death. Indeed, I have been one of the academics to use O'Keefe as something of an Australian music television template for the form's developments. O'Keefe's persona and the branding appeal of a particular host is a formula that was developed during the 1970s and 1980s with *Countdown* (Giuffre 2013), while his emphasis on audience engagement with music in a domestic space could be seen with music quiz programmes such as *Spicks and Specks* and *RocKwiz* (Giuffre 2012), and his influence directly flowed into the continuing music video programme, *Rage*, which still features footage of O'Keefe in its opening credits (Giuffre 2009). There is validity in acknowledging O'Keefe's emphasis on locally produced rock music, which earned him titles like 'the antipodean Elvis' (Bowden 2006: 53). While such commentaries emphasize how 'O'Keefe (and *Six O'Clock Rock*) paved the way for Australian-made pop music' (Bowden

2006: 53), it is a misleading perpetuation of the 'rock as disruption' thesis to ignore the significance of other genres that began on the programme but that have not also been acknowledged. However, it seems that memories of the show, and that time in music television, remain dominated by commentaries of O'Keefe as, by his own description in the 1958 single, a 'Wild One'. Young's retrospective account of *Six O'Clock Rock* clearly framed O'Keefe's life in terms of showbiz drama and the briefly blazing rock legend; she called him Australia's 'first meteoric celebrity [who] suffered the burnout we've come to expect from such figures: depression, breakdown, drug abuse, a serious car accident. Dying young was also part of it: Johnny died at forty-three' (Young 2006: 27).

In this chapter I propose that jazz be reconsidered when the formative years of Australian popular music television broadcasting are recalled. This reassessment gives us a more historically accurate account of the context of both the popular music and broadcasting industries as they developed, but also reminds contemporary and future researchers to go beyond the model of total dominance that pop and rock came to enjoy. There have been some commentators who have sought to argue for jazz's place; however their work is itself yet to be foregrounded. One unsurprising advocate for jazz was the ABC's Semmler, who wrote about the significance of the genre in Australian broadcasting following his retirement from active work at the organization:

> it would be appropriate to mention the part played by the ABC in the establishing of a greater appreciation of jazz in Australia... This is because I have always believed that jazz must be recognized as an important element in twentieth-century popular culture (Semmler 1981: 149).

Semmler's assessment of jazz's place in the broader cultural landscape in Australia has clearly been influenced by his time working actively in broadcasting. His connection between the public service broadcaster and the broader context of 'twentieth-century popular culture' draws the reader to consider the station's role in representing the diversity of the Australian public taste. Other excellent histories of Australian jazz in its popular context do exist (notably Johnson 1987, 2000), and Semmler would also continue on to be an active advocate for the promotion of jazz in Australia (notably through his presentation of the Fifth Annual Bell Jazz Lecture in 1997). However, Semmler and Johnson have tended to focus on live performance and audio recordings rather than jazz on television, an omission perhaps based on the difficulty of accessing archives when both scholars were writing.

I have noted already that there are only a handful of recordings of *Six O'Clock Rock* still in existence in the National Archives/ABC collection; however, there seem to be more emerging on popular media like YouTube. For example, the video recordings available at the National Archives have dates but no additional running sheet materials listed with them, while the YouTube additions often have performer lists added by the YouTube user, but which are often incomplete.[6] As I continue to explore Australian broadcasting content and contexts from this time, I note the holdings of both official and amateur archives, following McKee's advice that contemporary researchers need to consider a variety of established and emerging archives (2011). This chapter has also been influenced by Baker and Huber's work into the voluntary community of Australian jazz archivists that are increasingly using this and other digital platforms to publish previously-believed lost materials (2012). Clearly, however, further information needs to be retrieved.

Jazz was removed from *Six O'Clock Rock* in 1959, but not from television altogether. There is yet to be a comprehensive history of the diversity of programming on television at this time in Australia and subsequently. This is partly because such research has been constrained by restricted and incomplete archives, but also because of the dominance of rock and roll narratives. A notable, but still limited, exception is Clarke (2003), although additional work on jazz in Australia is building momentum at the time of writing. In going through the remaining playlists for the early *Six O'Clock Rock* episodes, particularly those after O'Keefe left as compere, I have found glimpses of how much more there is to be learned about the musical and televisual landscape of the time. The presence of a regular female host, Tanya Halesworth, for example, is something that has been seldom noted, while the archives also suggest a diversity of age and ethnic groups present in the audience for these popular music programmes watching in the studio and at home. These small snippets again challenge the dominant existing narratives of popular music television as the exclusive domain of only a certain type of musician, presenter and audience.

Conclusion

Jazz was eventually dropped from the *Six O'Clock Rock* lineup; however, an examination of source materials at the time shows that financial and logistical production considerations informed this decision rather than a mere change

---

6. I refer here in particular to the segments uploaded by YouTube user 'Sallie6', who appears to be adding some additional reference materials but without verifiable links to check them. While this is not to say they are unreliable, it is difficult to prove that they are. The Sallie6 Channel is available at http://www.youtube.com/user/sallie6/featured (accessed 23 October 2014).

in the audience's and artists' genre preferences. There remains much more yet to be done to uncover the forgotten diversity of early music television; however, so far the dominance of stories about young rock and roll boys like Johnny O'Keefe has been allowed to prevail. In forgetting to even look to jazz, researchers have assumed that it was not present during this time—an omission that tells only a small part of the story. The remaining documents are incomplete, but they do indicate song choices (a mixture of traditional, folk, showtunes and apparently new compositions of the time), while images of unnamed or little-known performers also remain traces for future researchers to follow. While continuing to look for jazz where we didn't think it present, perhaps future researchers will also find a greater depth of gender, genre and ethnic diversity than previously thought.

Despite the dominance of narratives that connect early television to the development of rock and roll, an examination of source materials from the time demonstrates that this was not the only genre broadcast live and for a young audience. For a few formative months at least, rock and jazz were played interchangeably as part of the ABC's pioneering *Six O'Clock Rock*, a successful programme that sought to bring local talent to Australian lounge rooms and develop the existing scene. By re-examining some of the remaining archives of early Australian music television production, I have been able to show that the context for popular music and culture production and reception was more diverse and complex than scholars have previously acknowledged. Put simply, while rock and roll and Johnny O'Keefe were important pioneers, they were not all that was present at the time. I urge new researchers, as well as existing ones, to continue to place dominant narratives in broader context and to continue to explore new archival opportunities as they emerge.

References

Allan, B. (2002) 'Music Television'. In *Television: Critical Methods and Applications (Second Edition)*, ed. J. G. Butler, 219–52. London: Lawrence Erlbaum Associates.

Austerlitz, Saul (2007) *Money for Nothing: A History of Music Video from The Beatles to the White Stripes*. New York: Continuum.

Baker, Sarah, and Alison Huber (2012) '"Masters of our own destiny": Cultures of Preservation in the Victorian Jazz Archive in Melbourne, Australia'. *Popular Music History* 7/3: 263–82.

Barry, Keith (1957) 'Overseas Visit: Report from the Controller of Programmes—Dated 16th November 1957'. Report No. 48, unpublished internal ABC communication held in National Archives, Sydney, accessed May 2014.

—(1959) 'Six O'Clock Rock: 7 August 1959'. Unpublished internal ABC communication held in National Archives, Sydney, accessed May 2014.

Bowden, Tim (2006) *50 Years: Aunty's Jubilee*. Sydney: ABC Books.

Bryden-Brown, John (1982) *JO'K: The Official Johnny O'Keefe Story*. Sydney: Doubleday.
Clarke, Bruce (2003) 'Television'. In *Currency Companion to Music and Dance in Australia*, ed. J. Whiteoak and A. Scott-Maxwell, 645–48. Sydney: Currency Press.
Frith, S. (2002) 'Look! Hear! The Uneasy Relationship of Music and Television'. *Popular Music* 21/3: 277–90. http://dx.doi.org/10.1017/s0261143002002180
Giuffre, Liz (2009) 'Maintaining Rage: Counting Down without a Host for 20 Years'. *Perfect Beat* (special issue on Music and Television) 10/1: 39–57. http://dx.doi.org/10.1558/prbt.v10i1.39
—(2012) 'Trivial Pursuits: The Resurgence of Music Quiz Programmes on Australian Television'. *Metro Magazine* 166: 132–36.
—(2013) '*Countdown* and Cult Music Television Programmes: An Australian Case Study'. *Intensities: The Journal of Cult Media* 6 (Autumn/Winter): 31–56.
Goodwin, A. (1992) *Dancing in the Distraction Factory: Music Television and Popular Culture*. London: Routledge.
Johnson, Bruce (1987) *The Oxford Companion to Australian Jazz*. Melbourne: Oxford University Press.
—(2000) *The Inaudible Music: Jazz, Gender and Australian Modernity*. Sydney: Currency Press.
Lee, Lonnie (2007) *Six O'Clock Rock: The Facts*. 2nd ed. Liverpool, NSW: Starlite Publishing.
McKee, Alan (2011) 'YouTube versus the National Film and Sound Archive: Which is the More Useful Resource for Historians of Australian Television?' *Television and New Media* 12/2: 154–73. http://dx.doi.org/10.1177/1527476410365707
Musgrave, Nan (1959) 'Television Parade'. *Australian Women's Weekly*, 18 March: 74.
Porter, David (1959a) 'Six O'Clock Rock: 4 August, 1959'. Unpublished internal ABC communication held in National Archives, Sydney, accessed May 2014.
—(1959b) 'TV Light Entertainment Programmes August/September 1959: 10 August 1959'. Unpublished internal ABC communication held in National Archives, Sydney, accessed May 2014.
—(1959c) 'Adsyd to AdMelb Neil from Porter, 12/8/59'. Unpublished internal ABC communication held in National Archives, Sydney, accessed May 2014.
Rogers, Bob and O'Brien, Denis (1975): *Rock 'n' Roll Australia: The Australian Pop Scene 1954–1964*. Sydney: Cassell.
Semmler, Clement (1959) 'TV Light Entertainment Programme: "Six O'Clock Rock": 28 February, 1959'. Unpublished internal ABC communication held in National Archives, Sydney, accessed May 2014.
—(1981) *The ABC-Aunt Sally and Sacred Cow*. Melbourne: Melbourne University Press.
SMH (1958) 'Sydney Morning Herald's Guide to TV Programmes on All Channels'. *Sydney Morning Herald*, 1 December 1958: 14, accessed via Google News. http://news.google.com/newspapers?nid=lL5f5cZgq8MC&dat=19581201&printsec=frontpage&hl=en (accessed 18 October 2014).
Stockbridge, S. (1989) 'Rock 'n' Roll Television'. *Cultural Studies* 3/1: 73–88. http://dx.doi.org/10.1080/09502388900490051
—(1992a) 'From Bandstand and Six O'Clock Rock to MTV and Rage: Rock Music on Australian Television'. In *From Pop to Punk to Postmodernism: Popular Music and Australian Culture from the 1960s to the 1990s*, ed. P. Hayward, 68–85. Sydney: Allen & Unwin.

—(1992b) 'Rock 'n' Roll Television'. In *Stay Tuned: An Australian Broadcasting Reader*, ed. A. Moran, 135–42. Sydney: Allen and Unwin.

Wald, Elijah (2009): *How The Beatles Destroyed Rock and Roll: An Alternative History of American Popular Music*. Oxford: Oxford University Press.

Webber, Bruce (1960) 'Six O'Clock Rock: Equity Award, 10/3/60'. Unpublished internal ABC communication held in National Archives, Sydney, accessed May 2014.

Young, Denise (2006) 'Six O'Clock Rock'. *Meanjin* 65/3: 24–27.

7 Shotgun weddings and bohemian dreams

Jazz, family values and storytelling in Australian film

Christopher Coady[*]

Introduction

The idea that jazz is a musical genre capable of speaking at cross-purposes lies at the heart of what has come to be known as the 'New Jazz Studies'. Stemming from calls for a more historically precise and sociologically nuanced approach to the study of jazz emerging from Scott DeVeaux's 1991 essay 'Constructing the Jazz Tradition', the past twenty or so years of jazz research has increasingly focused on the heterogeneous nature of jazz 'meaning' both in the United States and across the globe. This critical turn has allowed us to revise some persistent (if not always agreed-upon) narratives about jazz, such as the supposedly 'revolutionary' nature of bebop (DeVeaux 1997), the idea that jazz produced outside the United States is more often than not marked by indigenization efforts (Atkins 2001) and the notion that appropriating Western art music effects into jazz tends to denote a purely assimilative act (Floyd 1995; Howland 2009)—to name but a few. Indeed, a shift in focus to how historical energies have shaped the music of individual practitioners has taught us a great deal about diversity within apparently unified scenes and movements. Such knowledge has, by extension, laid the foundation for thinking about jazz less as 'a knowable object' (to use Sherrie Tucker's words) and more as a medium through which the unique ideas of jazz practitioners are worked out or realized. This is the phenomenon Tucker is referring to when she writes of the paradoxical '"subjectless subject" of New Jazz Studies' (Tucker 2005: 35)—the fact that, overwhelmingly, practitioners of the New Jazz Studies

---

[*] Dr Christopher Coady is a Lecturer in Musicology at the Sydney Conservatorium of Music, University of Sydney. His research interests include cool jazz, Third Stream music and the use of jazz in film. He is author of *John Lewis and the Challenge of 'Real' Black Music*, forthcoming from University of Michigan Press.

approach tend to focus on the process of how meaning is made *through* jazz rather than what meanings might be ascribed, in an absolute sense, *to* jazz.

The spirit of such a methodological approach is in no way absent from jazz studies produced within the Australian context. Bruce Johnson's extensive work on jazz and national identity, for instance, has frequently positioned jazz practice at the centre of the story of how Australians have worked out their ideas about the types of modern citizens they hoped to become (Johnson 2000: xii; Johnson 2004: 9–11). John Whiteoak's *Playing Ad Lib: Improvisatory Music in Australia 1836–1970* (1999) in turn begins with a call to arms made in the rhetoric of the New Jazz Studies movement:

> Any study of Australian music that focuses only upon the composer or the score and fails to consider music as process, as cultural, social and political action, as a vehicle for artistic expression or exploration, tells only a small part of the story (Whiteoak 1999: xiii).

Through a series of particular case studies, Whiteoak demonstrates what taking such a position might mean for the way we interpret the music made by Australian jazz practitioners. His discussion of the music of Melbourne guitarist/composer Bruce Clarke is emblematic of this approach, teasing out how the 'pragmatic' values of the 'union based culture of...fully professional Melbourne dance/jazz musician[s]' inspired Clarke to reject the idea of 'art for art's sake' and pursue a particular brand of electronic experimental music equally suitable to 'commercial recording, jingles and teaching enterprises' (Whiteoak 1999: 277). Such an analysis goes beyond a discussion of the familiar commercial vs. authentic debate so often tied to 'pragmatic' music-making by shifting focus to Clarke's process, effectively demonstrating that, despite its sound, Clarke's commercial works were authentically conceived in alignment with the Melbourne scene's values. This exploration of a specific individual's interaction with a particular local culture helps illuminate the very real fact that, as Johnson has pointed out, 'Australian culture itself is not simplistically homogeneous' (Johnson 2004: 9) and that understanding this diversity can help us better interpret the significance of particular moments of Australian jazz production.

Such a philosophy can in turn be seen to underpin Johnson's (2009) recent study of jazz use in early Australian film. Drawing on the films *Tall Timber* (1926) and *The Squatter's Daughter* (1933), among several others, Johnson demonstrates how jazz was used in the late 1920s and early 1930s by opposing ideological camps as a means of denoting either impending threats to the provincial values of the bush or the political and social aim of '"bridging" rural and urban' cultures (Johnson 2009: 10). Central to this thesis is the idea that jazz was coded for many during this period as a symbol of 'USA-dominated... urbanised mass culture' (Johnson 2009: 2) and that filmmakers played with this coding in a variety of ways. In *Tall Timber*, for instance, the values of such a culture are rejected plainly and conservatism can be seen to prevail as the police are called in to break up a 'wild jazz party' (Johnson 2009: 4).[1] In *The Squatter's Daughter*, the urban symbolism of jazz is utilized to make a different point, underscoring a scene about bush modernization and the industriousness of the Australian spirit (Johnson 2009: 10). It is important to note here that identifying the shared ways in which jazz was heard during this historic period provides the platform for Johnson's analysis. His findings therefore serve as a useful reminder that as we pursue projects aimed at highlighting the different sentiments jazz has been used to express, we must not write out of existence the ways in which members of a society continue to hear in jazz familiar connotations and themes.

In this chapter, I aim to move the discussion of jazz semiotics and social commentary in Australian film to two films of more recent vintage: Paul Harmon's *Shotgun Wedding* (1993) and Gillian Armstrong's *The Last Days of Chez Nous* (1992). Through an examination of American and Australian film production during the 1980s and early 1990s, I will demonstrate how the coded nature of jazz in Australian film seems to have been affected in at least a few cases by jazz-scoring clichés developed in connection with what Ness (2008: 67) has referred to as the 'second cycle' of *noir* films produced in the United States. In parallel with Johnson's (2009) work, I then argue that these clichés function as gears in a complicated storytelling system in which the ideas they trigger are used to counterpoint and thereby enhance unique narrative strains. In particular, I argue that the coding of these clichés continues to aid the expression of opposing societal visions, a fact evident in the ways *Shotgun Wedding* scored by Alan Zavod and *The Last Days of Chez Nous* scored by Paul Grabowsky explore contemporary debates on family values through the use of *noir* musical tropes.

Studying the mechanics of this sort of storytelling in the Australian context clearly embraces the call of the New Jazz Studies movement to investigate how meaning is created through jazz. Yet it is an approach that simultaneously builds on calls in Australian Film Studies discourse to read film music as actively 'speak[ing] for notions of contemporary cultural identities' (Coyle 2005: 1). Rebecca Coyle elaborates on this concept in the introduction to her

---

1. Johnson's analysis is derived from the shooting script for the film held by the Australian National Film and Sound Archives. Neither Johnson nor I have been able to locate a copy of the film within the Archives.

seminal monograph on Australian film music, begging us to understand the heterogeneous nature of Australian film scores as a complex phenomenon 'at once centred on *shared* pleasures, memories and the familiar as well as on *unique* stories and idiosyncrasies' (Coyle 2005: 16; italics in original). Johnson's (2009) work demonstrates what can be learned about 'contemporary cultural identities' within a particular historical moment when we embrace such an approach—how various ideas about the most fruitful path towards a better society can be uncovered by analysing how 'familiar' jazz meanings are played with and developed in the context of 'unique stories'. By illuminating how two films from the early 1990s put forth both a conservative and a liberal vision of family values through the aid of their jazz scores, I aim to expand our understanding of the sorts of stories jazz might be called upon to support within the Australian context. In turn, by showing how 'familiar' jazz meanings shift over time, I highlight the importance of unpacking the use of jazz in film in relation to specific historic moments.

Sounding nostalgia through 'Bluesy Themes on Solo Horns'

There can be little doubt that jazz has been of historic use in achieving the aesthetic goals of Australian filmmakers working across a variety of different production contexts. As an illustration of this diversity, consider that from the spectrum of Australian films produced since 1950 that utilize jazz-inflected scoring one might draw, essentially at random: John Sangster's score to the aboriginal rock-art documentary *Images of Man* (1980), The Necks' score to the psychological thriller *The Boys* (1998), Don Banks's score to the animated educational short *The Paying Bay* (1958), Alan Zavod's score to the *noir*ish *Shotgun Wedding* or Paul Grabowsky's score to the family drama *The Last Days of Chez Nous*. The wide range of plots and themes in this collection of titles is undeniable, matched only by the spectrum of jazz styles that comprise their music tracks. The Necks' score for *The Boys*, for instance, draws on the group's well-known minimalist aesthetic rooted in drones and slow motivic development while Grabowsky's score for *The Last Days of Chez Nous* weaves together the sound of a jazz quartet with country western themes and Baroque inspired harpsichord solos.[2] Zavod's score to *Shotgun Wedding* in turn rewrites the Easybeats song 'Come and See Her' (1966) into a bluesy riff that serves as a unifying trope across the film while Sangster's *Images of Man* begins with a considerably funky bass solo replete with pitch-bends and flat-fifth sonorities.

---

2. For a discussion of the compositional processes utilized in *The Boys*, see Hill 2011. An exploration of the score's semiotics can in turn be found in Johnson and Poole 2005.

Acknowledging such diversity of course does not negate the way certain jazz sounds occasionally emerge in these films as clichéd symbols of particular thematic content. The first shot of ex-con Jimmy and his pregnant girlfriend Helen's Kings Cross apartment in *Shotgun Wedding*, for example, is underscored by a bluesy bass motif, bringing to mind the scoring conventions identified by Phil Ford as tropes of the 'urban demimonde' in his 2008 essay 'Jazz Exotica and the Naked City' (Ford 2008: 113). Jean-Pierre's tryst with his wife Beth's younger sister in *The Last Days of Chez Nous* is in turn underscored by a saxophone solo, drawing plainly on the sexualized coding of the instrument linked to decades of similar use in American film (Butler 2002: 168). Such familiar moments work to strengthen the connection between these films by highlighting the presence of shared musical codes amidst scores that otherwise differ dramatically in terms of instrumentation, form and the treatment of thematic material.

Current understanding of these codes holds that they solidified as tropes in film (in the American context at least) through their frequent use during the second cycle of film *noir* produced during the 1970s and 1980s (see Butler 2002; Ness 2008). David Butler (2002) has dismissed an actual connection between these sounds and the *noir* movement of the 1940s and 1950s, claiming that despite the fact that an 'association of jazz with film noir can be found in all manner of media today…it [jazz] is curiously not so prevalent in the actual original artefacts' (Butler 2002: 2). Yet, as Butler (2002) and Ness (2008) have pointed out, this historical truth does not detract from the fact that filmmakers during the 1970s and 1980s sought to trigger the memory of film *noir*, a landscape Richard Naremore described as the combination of 'low-key photography, images of wet city streets, pop Freudian characterizations and romantic fascination with femmes fatales' (Naremore 1998: 9) through the use of specific jazz-influenced scoring conventions.

Consider, for instance, Ness's (2008) discussion of the trope of the 'solo horn'. In reference to the scores for *Chinatown* (1974), *Klute* (1971), *Body Heat* (1981), *Taxi Driver* (1976), *Angel Heart* (1987) and *Romeo is Bleeding* (1993), Ness argues that film composers of the 1970s and 1980s frequently turned to bluesy solo horn melodies (whether trumpet, flugelhorn or saxophone) as a way of 'generat[ing] a feeling of the way audiences think *films noirs* sounded' despite the fact that 'one cannot find bluesy themes on solo horns in the *noir* films of the 1940s' (Ness 2008: 69). In other words, the fact that 'bluesy themes' are largely absent from the first wave of *noir* texts does not prevent them in later *noir* films from 'evok[ing] the erotic undercurrents of the genre and the character of the femme fatale' by way of an imagined association (Ness 2008:

55).³ Nor does it prevent them from triggering a sense of 'constructed nostalgia' uniquely tied to this false memory, a phenomenon Ness unpacks in relation to the work of cultural critic Dean MacCannell (Ness 2008: 69).⁴ Thus the erotic and the nostalgic are twinned in neo-*noir* films through the use of the solo horn, facilitating the telling of stories centered on both erotic intrigue as well as nostalgic preoccupations with the past (criteria almost all of the films on Ness's list easily meet).

Returning to an examination of the Australian context, the influence of American film conventions on 1980s Australian crime films is a phenomenon openly acknowledged in Australian film discourse yet so far unexplored in relation to music (Mayer 1993; Spicer 2013). For instance, in his discussion of the 1983 Australian film *Goodbye Paradise* (dir. Carl Schultz), Andrew Spicer focuses on how American narrative tropes derived from film *noir* were adapted into the Australian domain. Claiming that *Goodbye Paradise* 'works self-consciously with a concept, style, and mode of narration—film noir—derived from American popular culture', Spicer goes on to posit that the film uses this platform to 'explore critically preoccupations and issues that are distinctively Australian' (Spicer 2013: 2). To this end, the film *noir* trope of urban decay is re-imagined in *Goodbye Paradise* through an 'attack on the contemporary avaricious decadence of Surfer's Paradise…where the film is set' (Spicer 2013: 2).

Writing about 1980s Australian crime films twenty years earlier, Geoff Mayer made a series of similar observations. Comparing *Goodbye Paradise* to the *noir* films *The Big Sleep* (1946) and *Farewell, My Lovely* (1975), Mayer argues that the film enacted 'transformation[s] of recognizable conventions' linked to film *noir* 'situations, characterisations and setting' through references to 'distinctive Australian imagery' (Mayer 1993: 114). As an example, he points to the character of the corrupt doctor in *Farewell, My Lovely*, who is reincarnated in *Goodbye Paradise* as an opportunistic sleaze preying on Gold Coast retirees, a character trait made overt in the doctor's gleeful claim that 'this town [Surf-

---

3. There are of course some films from the 1950s that do rely on prominent bluesy horn lines, the most obvious being Miles Davis's score to Louis Malles's *Ascenseur Pour L'Echafaud* (1957). Ness's point here seems to be simply that these films are exceptions or outliers within the first wave of *noir* texts, rather than the rule.

4. MacCannell's work focuses on the trope of the imagined city of *noir* films—a setting recognizable more in relation to our fears about the urban than the reality of the urban. He writes: 'The city [in film *noir*] is not constituted through a simple nostalgic appeal to a universalizable "past" and a possible utopic future—as in *The Wonder Years*, say. Rather it figures as the guilty horizon of bourgeois comfort and detachment' (MacCannell 1993: 280).

er's Paradise] is what Australians have instead of an afterlife...they come like Christmas Beetles crawling down the wall to die within the smell of the sea' (quoted in Mayer 1993: 114). Mayer follows this line of argument into a discussion of Chris Thomson's film *The Empty Beach* (1985) in which a detective modelled on *The Big Sleep*'s Philip Marlowe investigates the disappearance of a wealthy real-estate developer against the backdrop of Sydney's eastern beaches. While Mayer finds *The Empty Beach* to be less successful than *Goodbye Paradise* in keeping its references to film *noir* overt, he nonetheless acknowledges its nods to certain *noir* staples, such as the 'right wing conspiracy' theme that underpins the film's narrative arch (Mayer 1993: 119).[5]

This practice of using film *noir* conventions as a means of exploring uniquely Australian stories extends into the musical scoring of both *Goodbye Paradise* and *The Empty Beach* as well. In particular Ness's solo horn trope rises clearly to the fore as a trigger of eroticism and nostalgia. In *Goodbye Paradise*, former Deputy Police Commissioner Michael Stacey (played by Ray Barrett) stumbles upon a plot to enact a military coup in Queensland while investigating the disappearance of a wealthy friend's daughter—a storyline not subtly linked to Queensland Premier Joh Bjelke-Petersen's allusions to secession made during the late 1970s (Lunn 1978: 214). Throughout the film, composer Peter Best draws on the solo trumpet as a means of distinguishing between the morality of old-school Australian 'battlers' (embodied in the perpetually honest and persistently drunk Stacey) and the new world order of greedy land developers and power-hungry politicians. Stacey's 'theme'—a scoring cue of piano chords utilizing pendular thirds and solo trumpet—underpins the vast majority of his reflective voice-overs in the film, observations that consistently frame the ex-Commissioner as both down to earth and morally superior to his peers despite his failure to keep up with the Gold Coast wealthy elite. Such intent is evident, for instance, in the voice-over delivered as he travels to meet Senator McCredie, his old school friend, towards the start of the film. While en route to the Senator's house via the Senator's speedboat, Stacey reflects in tandem with the trumpet melody: 'It'd be nice to say he hadn't changed a bit, but he had. A lot of it was the Labor Party Caucus; you couldn't blame him for that. And part of it was his new wife, a social climbing airhostess with designs on Buckingham Palace' (14:08).

In a later scene, the erotic and Stacey's traditional values are brought together against a scoring cue of synthesized chords and solo saxophone. Having brought a drug-addled young women back to his room thinking she is

---

5. *The Empty Beach* is a film adaptation of Australian crime writer Peter Corris's 1983 novel of the same name.

the Senator's daughter, Stacey is propositioned with sex while the saxophone plays a series of riffs against undulating minor chords (44:24). Stacey kindly rejects the advance and begins to tell the girl a children's story as the modality shifts to major and the saxophone continues to play. Stacey's genuineness is undoubtedly positioned in this scene against what Spicer refers to as the 'avaricious decadence of Surfer's Paradise' (manifest in the mental state of the drug-addled teenager), and these themes are neatly tied together through the coded nature of the saxophone melody, at first a marker of the scene's erotic undercurrents but then quickly a symbol of Stacey's maturity and old-school values.

Martin Armiger and Red Symons's score for *The Empty Beach* in turn draws frequently on improvised solo horn melodies (both trumpet and saxophone) as symbols of reflection and loss. The investigation undertaken by the film's protagonist, Cliff Hardy (played by Bryan Brown), leads to the death of two innocent characters: investigative journalist Bruce Henneberry (played by Nick Tate) and homeless informant Leon (played by Harry Lawrence). Hardy's burgeoning friendship with Henneberry is conveyed to the audience as Hardy arrives early for a meeting with the journalist and sits on the shore laughing admiringly at Henneberry's surfing skills while a reggae groove and funky trumpet improvisation work to underscore the scene (27:35). The music then grows ominous as Henneberry is tackled by a fellow surfer and washes up dead on the beach. A mournful improvised trumpet melody is subsequently heard as Hardy pulls Henneberry's body from the surf and faces for the first time the possibility that his investigation is causing collateral damage. In a later scene, Hardy is once again left to ponder his role in the murder of an innocent after his informant Leon is killed (39:37). Again, a solo horn improvisation is heard, this time played by the saxophone, as Hardy reflectively paces against the backdrop of the Sydney skyline considering the loss of yet another friend.

There are of course more complicated jazz semiotics at play in *The Empty Beach*. The compound-time funk grooves that permeate the score and the frequent use of improvisation against more positive narrative strains make it impossible to argue that jazz symbolizes just one thing in the film. Yet such plurality of meaning does not change the fact that specific moments of jazz-imbued scoring continue to signify memories of the past (both good and bad) in a manner reminiscent of second-cycle *noir* films from the US. In the following discussion of *Shotgun Wedding* and *The Last Days of Chez Nous*, I will show how such coding was used both inside and outside the film *noir* genre to facilitate storytelling in Australian film focused on an entirely different set of themes related to Australian family values.[6]

---

6. It is important to note I am not arguing that the scores for *Goodbye Paradise* and *The Empty Beach* necessarily be read as emblematic of the sound of Australian *noir* films. I

A brief overview of Australian family values debates during the 1990s

Before presenting such an analysis, however, it is necessary to briefly outline the parameters of the cultural debate on Australian family values upon which both films draw. Judith Brett's (2003) analysis of Liberal Party leader John Howard's social conservatism, articulated in his 1988 policy document *Future Directions*, provides a useful starting point for this discussion by illuminating the emergence of a style of social thinking in Australian politics that sought to defend 'the traditional home against other sorts of homes, [such as those] inhabited by gay couples, single mothers or blended families... [homes] fragile and threatened by family breakdown, crime and social decay' (Brett 2003: 185). Brett argues that the roots of this sort of thinking lay in the Liberal Party's perception that the political gains of demographics associated with 'sexual tolerance' and 'gender equity' movements of the 1970s were increasingly working to marginalize 'mainstream' Australians (Brett 2003: 186–87). Those who had championed sexual tolerance and gender equity during the 1970s of course felt differently, arguing, as Brett surmises, that 'differences in gender, sexuality, race and ethnic background created inequalities of power, resources and life chances and were [therefore] amendable to reform by state action' (Brett 2003: 186). As debates on the role and extent of state support for individuals progressed throughout the 1980s and 1990s, these competing conceptions of state responsibility gradually solidified into ideological cornerstones on which competing political arguments would become increasingly reliant.

One particularly contentious aspect of debate to arise during the early 1990s was the extent to which 'special interest' groups should be catered for when designing legislation pertaining to Australian family interests. Throughout the 1980s, academic discourse in Australia had increasingly argued for government policies to be more inclusive of family difference (Edgar 1980; Russell, James and Watson 1988; Winchester 1990), and in 1992, Prime Minister Paul Keating would echo such sentiments to the National Family Summit, stating:

> When we talk about Australian families today, we have to include families of all sorts and sizes. Families with children where both parents are present. Families with children headed by sole parents—women or men. Families that include several generations living

simply wish to point out that they appear to be two cases in which American musical conventions have been adopted. Indeed, an examination of the music tracks for other Australian crime films from the 1970s and 1980s reveal quite an array of approaches to the form. See, for instance, the 1978 film *Money Movers* (dir. Bruce Beresford) with a soundtrack derived largely from Bartok's 'Music for Strings, Percussion and Celesta' or Cameron Allan's ethereal synthesized score for the 1982 film *Heatwave* (dir. Phillip Noyce).

> under the same roof. Families where one member cares for another who is frail aged, chronically ill, disabled or suffering from HIV/AIDS. And let's not forget all the other combinations, the single people, the childless, the once- or never-married who live alone, the 'empty-nesters' and all the others who are equally entitled to be included when we speak of the great family of our nation (Keating 1992: 2–3).

Such an expansive view of the Australian family worked to erode traditional gender roles and made room for more dynamic family trajectories in the realm of public policy. Yet, at the same time, it was a vision that unnerved social conservatives such as then Liberal Party leader John Hewson who believed there were already 'enough forces working to divide families' in Australian society (Peake 1992: 3).

Hewson could of course not deny the economic imperative of bringing women into the workforce during the 1990s recession and his 1991 policy document *Fightback!* included initiatives aimed at facilitating this objective. Along these lines, the *Fightback!* policy document argued for means-tested cash or tax rebates for childcare (Liberal and National Parties of Australia 1991: 181–82), an economically conservative twist on the same sort of benefits Labor would in turn seek to deliver as part of their policy package. Yet the vision of childcare's intended effect between the political parties differed dramatically. Indeed, where Labor's policies were marketed along the lines of increasing the independence and agency of women and addressing the needs of changing family structure in Australia (see Jupp and Sawer 1994: 16), the Liberal-National policy was sold as an initiative aimed at strengthening the nuclear family. Such a position is evident in comments Hewson would make regarding the ways in which economic distress was effecting nuclear families by leading to 'health problems, marriage breakdowns, and suicide' (Uhlmann 1993: 1), and the assertion that while current 'economic and social realities dictate that governments now give due recognition to child care policies', the Coalition continued to feel that 'the most ideal form of childcare is in the home' (Liberal and National Parties of Australia 1991: 181). Such statements failed to engage with the theme of societal transformation that underpinned Labor's vision of the family in the early 1990s and instead worked to frame women's participation in the workforce as something only temporarily necessary in the ongoing struggle to ensure the stability of traditional family structure.

Tension between these two visions of the family was of course felt outside the political realm as well during the late 1980s and early 1990s. Lizzie Francke (1993), for instance, points to Ann Turner's *Celia* (1988) and Jane Campion's *Sweetie* (1989) as examples of films produced during the period that put forth 'skewed visions of the world', particularly in relation 'to the traditional female occupations of family and friends' (Francke 1993: 18). Tim Winton's 1991 novel *Cloudstreet*, on the other hand, worked to reinforce the idea that personal redemption and spiritual fulfilment lay intrinsically in the institution of marriage and the miracle of childbirth. Helen Garner's interrogation of the 1992 sexual harassment scandal at Ormond College documented in *The First Stone* (1995) would in turn engage—at least peripherally—with questions regarding the relationship between women and the institution of family, including whether or not 'family is inimical to the feminist cause' and whether or not 'motherhood exploits women' (Garner 1995: 76), while the conservative American non-profit organization Focus on the Family—which aims to help 'families navigate a troubled world from a Christ-centered foundation' (Focus on the Family Australia: n.d.)—would launch its Australian branch in 1993.

The marshalling of such evidence is not meant to suggest that the early 1990s were a historic period particularly charged with debates about the future of the Australian family unit. Indeed, as Brett (2003) and others have pointed out, a true reckoning of cultural visions would not be witnessed in the public sphere until the 1996 federal election in which John Howard and the Liberal Party would run their now famous (or infamous, depending on one's political leanings) values-based campaign (see Brett 2003: 188; Hutchison 2009: 122; Kelly 2009: 329). The overview of the period presented here is simply meant to make clear that the salient themes of the 1996 election are plainly visible in the social and political discourse of the preceding decade. It is therefore against this backdrop that references to the family in the films *Shotgun Wedding* and *The Last Days of Chez Nous* might be best read.

Shotgun Wedding
Paul Harmon's *Shotgun Wedding* picks up on the themes of traditional gender roles, the sanctity of marriage and individual responsibility to one's family as it explores a young couple's struggle to stay together during an encounter with a corrupt police force. The film is set during the late 1960s and opens with the character Jimmy Becker (played by Aden Young) being released from prison on car-theft charges and returning to Sydney's Kings Cross in order to reunite with his pregnant girlfriend Helen (played by Zoë Carides). In a bid to start a new life away from the temptations of the city, the expectant parents move to a dilapidated farmhouse in Sydney's south-west but are soon set upon by two corrupt cops associated with Jimmy's previous car racket bent on shutting Jimmy up for good. Helen accidentally discharges a shotgun as the cops attempt to break down the farmhouse door and Jimmy pretends to hold Helen hostage in the hope that the corrupt cops will disperse. Yet the gun-

shot triggers the attention of the neighbours and the fake hostage situation quickly escalates with police reinforcements being called in and a large contingent of newspaper and television reporters descending on the farm. Helen then goes into labour and a police nurse is recruited to deliver the baby. Following the birth of their son, Jimmy and Helen decide that they must get married and the police commissioner arranges for a ceremony to take place inside the farmhouse. Following the wedding, control of the police operation eventually slides back into the hands of the corrupt officers and the police tactics become more aggressive, forcing Jimmy to give himself up in order to ensure the safety of his young wife and family.[7]

The music track for *Shotgun Wedding* plays a central role in articulating the unfairness of the situation Jimmy finds himself in and the threat posed to his family in relation to his impending arrest. The composed score, written by Alan Zavod, is largely structured around various settings of a four-note motive that echoes the opening guitar riff of the Easybeats song 'Come and See Her'. The 1966 recording of 'Come and See Her' is in turn used throughout the film and switching between the Easybeats song and the motivic score is used as a means of separating out scenes related to the growing public interest in the hostage crisis from scenes related to Jimmy and Helen's personal crisis. Throughout the composed score, references to jazz abound, extending from the frequent use of a musical cue involving a bluesy bass figure to the use of an improvised saxophone solo played by Jeremy Cole over an instrumental version of 'Come and See Her' as Jimmy, Helen and a crowd of onlookers prepare for the wedding.

Yet of primary interest to the discussion of jazz semiotics under examination here is Zavod's use of the bluesy solo horn trope, delivered most prominently in moments when the saxophone plays Zavod's four-note motive. This particular scoring cue occurs four times throughout the film and is used as a reminder of the danger Jimmy's past poses to his family. The first of these moments occurs shortly after Helen goes into labour. Despite asking the police for a doctor, no help seems forthcoming and Jimmy is faced with the decision of giving himself up and returning to jail or allowing his wife and unborn son to die. The saxophone delivers the solo call employing both flat-seventh and minor-third blues sonorities as Jimmy acquiesces to the need to give himself up and to the reality that he may never be able to meet his son (34:56). The

---

7. The film opens with a text statement suggesting that it is loosely based on the 1968 Glenfield siege in which a gunman named Wally Mellish held his ex-girlfriend and her infant son hostage while demanding a reconciliation and that the police perform a marriage (neither Glenfield nor Mellish are mentioned directly in the text but many references correlate).

Police Commissioner's last-minute decision to supply a nurse before Jimmy can leave the farmhouse extends the inevitable, and Jimmy is able to remain with his wife while his son is born.

Jimmy's eventual arrest is of course increasingly assured as the siege continues, and Zavod foreshadows this by pairing the saxophone cue with scenes of father/son bonding. In the first of these scenes, the young family falls asleep together in the same bed and the saxophone cue is heard before the camera cuts to a panning sweep of the police officers stationed en masse outside the farmhouse (46:19). In the second, Jimmy explores the shapes of objects in the house with his son following his marriage to Helen (1:06:00). Jimmy has already agreed with the police to give himself up and there is an impending sense in this moment that the clock is well and truly running out for the new father. Indeed, in the penultimate scene of the film, the solo horn trope is used a final time to announce the ultimate destruction of the family as Helen and Jimmy's son are whisked away by police and Jimmy is placed under arrest (1:24:21).

By first foreshadowing and then announcing the struggle Helen and Jimmy's son will face once Jimmy's past has finally caught up with him, the use of the bluesy solo horn trope in *Shotgun Wedding* brings into relief a conservative valuation of traditional family structure. In other words, the trope helps tell the story of an impending fracturing of family life by referencing the looming presence of unfinished business. The broad goal of the film might therefore be best read as an attempt to document the tragedy of a family unfairly torn apart—a tragedy not at all dissimilar to that feared by conservative politicians and pundits in the face of the early 1990s economic recession. Indeed, while it is likely a stretch to argue the filmmakers of *Shotgun Wedding* purposefully pursued such political affinity with the Liberal/National coalition, the story put forth in the film undoubtedly endorses a particular vision of family structure held by political conservatives during the time of its production.

The Last Days of Chez Nous
Gillian Armstrong's *The Last Days of Chez Nous* uses the nostalgic symbolism of the solo horn to tell a different story about family relationships. The film charts the return of Vicky (played by Kerry Fox) to her older sister Beth's Sydney terrace house following a period of living abroad. Beth (played by Lisa Harrow) and her French husband Jean-Pierre (played by Bruno Ganz) have built a life based on Bohemian values, which includes the presence of multiple lovers, a marriage of convenience to assure Jean-Pierre's residency and the incorporation of boarders into the day-to-day life of the family. Vicky's return coincides with Beth's desire to pursue a more conservative vision for her life, including

the demand that Jean-Pierre stop having affairs and that her father takes a more active interest in her. As Beth pursues the latter by taking her father on a three-week road trip through rural New South Wales, Vicky and Jean-Pierre fall in love and begin a romantic relationship. Upon Beth's return, Jean-Pierre initially holds out hope that the three might live together in a polyamorous relationship but is soon confronted by Beth's newfound conservatism, which eventually leads to the disintegration of their marriage and Beth's estrangement from her sister.

Throughout the film, there is the sense that Beth's 'mania for resolution' (as Jean-Pierre puts it [21:03]) will ultimately serve to undo her against the messiness of the real world. Paul Grabowsky's score for the film works with this idea by using the solo horn trope as a marker of the Bohemian ideals Jean-Pierre and Beth once shared, first in reflective moments between the couple and then increasingly in connection with the romantic relationship that grows between Jean-Pierre and Vicky. In other words, the trope's storytelling function lies in its ability to signal a more complicated but simultaneously more fulfilling lifestyle once shared between Jean-Pierre and Beth before working to demonstrate Beth's current distance from the Bohemian mindset.

The first scene to use the solo horn in this way finds Jean-Pierre and Beth in bed together shortly after Vicky's arrival. Jean-Pierre reflects on the banality of their present lives and Beth asks: 'Do you think we'll ever make love again?' a question to which Jean-Pierre responds 'Why do you say this? It's not the right question' (8:53). The twinned erotic/nostalgic coding of the saxophone cue works to remind us of the absence of sex in this scene, or rather the presence of sex when the life of the couple was less domestic. The cue is similarly deployed during a lunch Jean-Pierre and Beth share with two friends and their newborn baby. As Jean-Pierre holds the baby, Beth discusses the terms of their marriage of convenience and the fact that both of them were opposed to the idea of marriage on principle (33:16). Jean-Pierre and Beth's recent arguments about fidelity are positioned against the past in this moment, both through Beth's comments and through the sound of the bluesy horn that serves as underscore.

As the film progresses, this Bohemian vision is increasingly transplanted onto Jean-Pierre and Vicky's burgeoning relationship. During their first night together, Jean-Pierre assures Vicky that their behaviour is compatible with the values upon which his relationship with Beth is built. The sound of a jazz quartet with saxophone-led melody underpins his remarks in post-coital bliss that 'There's no worry, we can work it out' (1:00:50), and upon Beth's return, Jean-Pierre attempts to do so, telling Beth in tandem with the sound of the bluesy horn that: 'If I had another wife, I could love you better' (1:08:02). The saxophone then continues to emerge in moments when Jean-Pierre and Vicky kiss (1:11:54 and 1:13:38) while Beth's frustration is underpinned by a variety of alternate scoring cues, including an elaborate harpsichord solo that accompanies her destruction of a bathroom upon learning for certain that Jean-Pierre and Vicky have fallen in love (1:16:08).

The closing scene of the film in which Beth and Jean-Pierre (who has recently moved in with Vicky) discuss the messiness of life while reconciling on the Sydney harbour foreshore drives home the film's message regarding the futility of attempting to predict or control the direction of the human heart. Beth is in a sense liberated in this moment from the need to construct an impossibly perfect marriage while Jean-Pierre is forgiven the taboo of pursuing a romantic relationship with his wife's sister. Unlike *Shotgun Wedding*, the happiness of the characters in *The Last Days of Chez Nous* can be seen to have necessitated the fracturing of their domestic life and the acceptance that there were other ways to live in connection to each other without necessarily adhering to traditional family norms. The film can therefore be read as putting forth a vision of contemporary relationships that seems to echo Keating's call for acceptance and celebration of family difference while in turn embracing calls on the left that questioned the potentially oppressive nature of the traditional family model.[8]

Conclusions

The discussion of *Shotgun Wedding* and *The Last Days of Chez Nous* above demonstrates clearly how contemporary debates about Australian families were explored in early 1990s Australian film through the aid of jazz-scoring conventions. The nostalgic coding of the solo horn trope—a trope grown out of *noir* films in both the United States and the Australian context during the 1970s and 1980s—plays a particularly strong role in this exploration, conjuring the notion of a looming past in narratives focused on emotional struggles taking place in the present. Certainly such use of jazz stands in contrast to the deployment of the genre as the sound of impending modernity charted out in Johnson's (2009) study. Yet, both the early period of jazz use in Australian film surveyed by Johnson and the contemporary period under examination here can be understood as engaging jazz scoring towards similar rhetorical ends. That is to say, use of jazz scoring in both contexts makes present tensions not easily depicted through film dialogue or action alone. In *Shotgun Wedding* this

---

8. The fact that similar themes are explored in *The First Stone* and *The Last Days of Chez Nous* is of course unsurprising given the fact that Helen Garner served as screenwriter for the latter.

is apparent in how tension is built by positioning sonic references to Jimmy's inescapable past against his new life as a father. In *The Last Days of Chez Nous*, a similar phenomenon occurs as sonic references to an earlier, more fulfilling Bohemian way of life are juxtaposed against Beth's increasingly conservative demands.

Such an exploration of jazz semiotics holds relevance to the wider discussion of Australian jazz practice taking place across this collection of essays for two reasons. First, as I have shown in relation to film, while Australians have sought to create meaning through jazz in a variety of different ways and to a variety of different ends, such an endeavour tends to flow out of shared understandings regarding the encoded nature of particular jazz sounds. I do not mean to imply that these understandings are universally held across Australia, simply that they reside sufficiently in the imagination of enough Australians to make them useful communicative tools. At the same time, however, it is crucial to note that these understandings appear uniquely tied to historic moments. For instance, whereas the sound of jazz in general once represented the sound of the modern and was used to this end by filmmakers during the 1920s and 1930s, by the 1990s the sound of jazz—at least in terms of the trope of the bluesy solo horn—had come to represent a cry from the past.

As the study of jazz presence in Australian culture continues to grow, it is worth keeping the dynamic nature of these semiotics in mind. The heterogeneous nature of jazz produced within Australia and the diverse ways in which jazz has been used as an expressive device in association with other media in the Australian context cannot be united through singular taxonomies of jazz 'meaning'. Yet, simultaneously, the communication of ideas through jazz necessitates a level of shared understanding related to the sounds employed by jazz practitioners. Therefore, as we continue to study what is communicated in moments of Australian jazz production, we must as a matter of course consider the ways in which the familiar is drawn upon and how what is familiar in turn changes over time. Only by engaging with these sorts of questions can we begin to piece together the web of interrelated yet simultaneously unique visions expressed through jazz taking place across the Australian context.

Acknowledgements

The author wishes to thank Philip Emery of the University of Western Sydney along with Simon Drake and Kathryn McLeod of the National Film and Sound Archive of Australia for their assistance in the preparation of this chapter.

References

Atkins, E. T. (2001) *Blue Nippon: Authenticating Jazz in Japan*. Durham, NC: Duke University Press. http://dx.doi.org/10.1215/9780822380030

Brett, J. (2003) *Australian Liberals and the Moral Middle Class*. Cambridge: Cambridge University Press. http://dx.doi.org/10.1017/CBO9780511481642

Butler, D. (2002) *Jazz Noir: Listening to Music from Phantom Lady to The Last Seduction*. Connecticut: Praeger.

Corris, P. (1983) *The Empty Beach*. Sydney: Allen and Unwin.

Coyle, R., ed. (2005) *Reel Tracks: Australian Feature Film Music and Cultural Identity*. Sydney: John Libbey Publications.

DeVeaux, S. (1991) 'Constructing the Jazz Tradition: Jazz Historiography'. *Black American Literature Forum* 25/3: 525–60. http://dx.doi.org/10.2307/3041812

—(1997) *The Birth of Bebop*. Berkley: University of California Press.

Edgar, D. (1980) *Possible Directions for an Australian Family Policy*. Melbourne: Institute of Family Studies.

Floyd, S. (1995) *The Power of Black Music: Interpreting Its History from Africa to the United States*. New York: Oxford University Press.

Focus on the Family Australia (n.d.) 'The Focus Logo'. http://www.families.org.au/default.aspx?cat=5 (accessed 30 January 2015).

Ford, P. (2008) 'Jazz Exotica and the Naked City'. *Journal of Musicological Research* 27/2: 113–33. http://dx.doi.org/10.1080/01411890801989596

Francke, L. (1993) 'Dark Side: Alison Maclean, the Director of the Unsettling *Crush*, Talks with Lizzie Francke'. *Sight and Sound* 3/4: 18–19.

Garner, H. (1995) *The First Stone: Some Questions about Sex and Power*. Sydney: Pan Macmillan Australia.

Hill, M. (2011) 'Beneath Clouds and The Boys: Jazz Artists Making Film Music'. *Screensound: The Australasian Journal of Soundtrack Studies* 2: 27–47.

Howland, J. (2009) *Ellington Uptown: Duke Ellington, James P. Johnson, and the Birth of Concert Jazz*. Michigan: University of Michigan Press.

Hutchison, H. (2009) 'Family Values'. In *The Culture Wars: Australian and American Politics in the 21st Century*, ed. Jim George and Kim Huynh, 110–26. South Yarra: Palgrave Macmillan Australia.

Johnson, B. (2000) *The Inaudible Music: Jazz, Gender and Australian Modernity*. Sydney: Currency Press.

—(2004) 'Tools Not of Our Making: Shaping Australian Jazz History'. In *The History and Future of Jazz in the Asia-Pacific Region*, ed. Philip Hayward and Glen Hodges, 6–17. Rockhampton: Central Queensland University Publishing Unit.

—(2009) 'Jazz and Nation in Australian Cinema: From Silents to Sound'. *Journal of the National Film and Sound Archive, Australia* 4/1: 1–12.

Johnson, B., and G. Poole (2005) 'Scoring: Sexuality and Australian Film Music, 1990–2003'. In *Reel Tracks: Australian Feature Film and Music and Cultural Identities*, ed. Rebecca Coyle, 97–121. Eastleigh: John Libbey Publishing.

Jupp, J., and M. Sawer (1994) 'Building Coalitions: The Australian Labor Party and the 1993 General Election'. *Australian Journal of Political Science* 29 (Special Issue): 10–27.

Keating, P. (1992) *Address to the National Family Summit, Parliament House, Canberra ACT, 11*

November 1992. http://pmtranscripts.dpmc.gov.au/browse.php?did=8719 (accessed 30 January 2015).
Kelly, P. (2009) *March of the Patriots: The Struggle for Modern Australia.* Carlton: University of Melbourne Press.
Liberal and National Parties of Australia (1991) *Fightback! Taxation and Expenditure Reform for Jobs and Growth.* Fyshwick: Pirie.
Lunn, H. (1978) *Joh: The Life and Political Adventures of Sir Johannes Bjelke-Petersen.* St. Lucia: University of Queensland Press.
MacCannell, D. (1993) 'Democracy's Turn: On Homeless Noir'. In *Shades of Noir: A Reader*, ed. Joan Copjec, 279–98. New York: Verso.
Mayer, G. (1993) 'A Hard-Boiled World: *Goodbye Paradise* and *The Empty Beach*'. *Literature/Film Quarterly* 21/2: 112–20.
Naremore, J. (1998) *More than Night: Film Noir in its Contexts.* Berkeley: University of California Press.
Ness, R. (2008) 'A Lotta Night Music: The Sound of Film Noir'. *Cinema Journal* 47/2: 52–73. http://dx.doi.org/10.1353/cj.2008.0011
Peake, R. (1992) 'Family to "Fight Back"'. *Canberra Times*, 13 November: 3.
Russell, G., D. James and J. Watson (1988) 'Work/Family Policies, the Changing Role of Fathers and the Presumption of Shared Responsibility for Parenting'. *Australian Journal of Social Issues* 23/4: 249–67.
Spicer, A. (2013) 'Introduction: The Problem of Film Noir'. In *A Companion to Film Noir*, ed. Andrew Spicer and Helen Hanson, 1–13. Sussex: Blackwell. http://dx.doi.org/10.1002/9781118523728.ch0
Tucker, S. (2005) 'Deconstructing the Jazz Tradition: The "Subjectless Subject" of New Jazz Studies'. *Jazz Research Journal* 2/1: 31–46. http://dx.doi.org/10.1558/source.v2i1.31
Uhlmann, C. (1993) 'AMA Plans Impress Hewson'. *Canberra Times*, 23 February: 1.
Whiteoak, J. (1999) *Playing Ad Lib: Improvisatory Music in Australia 1836–1970.* Sydney: Currency Press.
Winchester, H. (1990) 'Women and Children Last: The Poverty and Marginalization of One-Parent Families'. *Transactions of the Institute of British Geographers* 15/1: 70–86. http://dx.doi.org/10.2307/623094
Winton, T. (1991) *Cloudstreet.* Melbourne: McPhee Gribble.

Selected filmography
Goodbye Paradise (1983). DVD. Directed by Carl Shultz. Canberra, ACT: National Film and Sound Archive.
The Empty Beach (1985). VHS. Directed by Chris Thomson. Canberra, ACT: National Film and Sound Archive.
The Last Days of Chez Nous (1992). DVD. Directed by Gillian Armstrong. Kew, Victoria: Umbrella Entertainment.
Shotgun Wedding (1993). VHS. Directed by Paul Harmon. Canberra, ACT: National Film and Sound Archive.

Infrastructures

8 Perspectives on the Melbourne International Women's Jazz Festival

Louise Denson*

Introduction

Since the 1990s, women have become an increasingly significant force on the Australian jazz scene. Professional jazzwomen are no longer confined to the roles of vocalist or pianist as they may have been in the past. They play brass and wind instruments, drums, bass and guitar. They write and arrange their own music and are commissioned to write for other ensembles, including big bands. They lead and co-lead ensembles and play as sidewomen in other musicians' projects. They are being recognized nationally and internationally for their excellence and achievements. Nevertheless, there remains a significant gender disparity in terms of numbers of professional jazz musicians and their visibility on the local and national scenes. In 1997, an initiative was launched which sought to address the issues of low visibility and lack of access to performance opportunities faced by many women in jazz—the Melbourne Women's Jazz Festival (as of 2002, Melbourne Women's International Jazz Festival—MWIJF). It has taken place every year except 2008 and 2011, and has proven to be a significant event for women who have been featured in its programmes.

This chapter seeks to present the MWIJF within the historical context of women's participation in jazz in Australia and internationally. An initial overview of the history of women in Australian jazz will reveal periods of both activity and invisibility within a cultural tradition distinguished by its extreme masculinity. The commonality of experience with jazzwomen in other national

---

* Louise Denson is a Senior Lecturer in Jazz Studies at the Queensland Conservatorium, Brisbane. She is a pianist/composer whose musical interests span contemporary jazz and classical music, and the musics of South and Central America. She has issued four CDs of original music and has performed at Australian and North American jazz festivals with a variety of ensembles. Her primary research interests are gender issues in jazz, and jazz in the Australian context.

contexts will become evident through reference to the American and European jazz scenes. The latter part of the chapter focuses on the MWIJF and its promotion and support of contemporary women jazz musicians. Nine women were interviewed[1] about their experiences with the MWIJF as performers, composers and/or organizers, as was the founder of the festival, Martin Jackson. Their comments illuminate the role that the MWIJF has played in their own professional lives and within the Australian jazz scene.

Women's historical participation in Australian jazz

Research in the past twenty years has revealed that women have participated in Australian jazz to a much greater extent than is evident from conventional historiography. Whiteoak (1995: 21) says that women have suffered from 'extreme marginalization within Australian jazz subculture', which is to a large extent a reflection of the historical masculine dominance in Australian society. In 1900 there were still 10 per cent more men than women in Australia, a decrease from the highest ratio of 3:1 in the 1830s.[2] Werth (2011) argues that the 'male breadwinner' model has prevented women from taking up occupations constructed as 'masculine' throughout the twentieth century: professional music-making most certainly numbers among them.

Despite this marginalization, Johnson (2000: 67–68) asserts that '[a] surprising number [of women] were recognized as exponents of the new African-American musics' in the first two decades of the twentieth century, playing an important part in the dissemination of jazz as both performers and consumers. Whiteoak (1995: 23) makes the intriguing suggestion that the first Australian recordings of jazz improvisation may have been done by female pianists who were able to transform melodies 'through various forms of embellishment, or jazzing'. Music, piano-playing in particular, 'was part of a woman's education in gentility' (Johnson 2000: 68), which meant that many of them would have had the requisite skills to learn the new African-American popular music making its way to Australia. Whiteoak notes that women 'were also strongly identified with the teaching of improvisatory piano accompaniment practice or so-called "vamping"' (1995: 22), and that they were widely employed as accompanists for silent movies, a practice that necessitated highly developed improvisational skills. In other words, far from being excluded from the realm of popular music in early twentieth-century Australia, in which jazz was to play an increasingly important role, women were at the heart of it.

    1.   The interviews took place either in person, via Skype, telephone or email, between March and August 2014.
    2.   Australian Demographic Statistics, at http://adsri.anu.edu.au/demo-stats/aust

Placksin (1982: 42–43) says that African-American women played a similarly central role in the early years of jazz in the United States. Pianists with reading and improvising abilities were employed in cabarets, tent shows, pit orchestras, society bands and 'hot' combos. However, it was as vocalists that women made an indelible contribution to American jazz. Blues singers such as Bessie Smith, Mamie Smith, Ma Rainey and others dominated the African-American entertainment market in the 1920s, creating a 'new industry and employment option for young black women' (1982: 9) throughout the United States, and opening doors for some of the leading jazz musicians of the day by employing them as accompanists (1982: 9).

A detailed history of women in music as a profession in Australia in the first half of the twentieth century is recounted in *Sweethearts of Rhythm* (Dreyfus 1999). Family orchestras such as the Lightfoots and the Funstons (Dreyfus 1999: 14–17), and all-women ensembles such as The Magpies Ladies Orchestra, founded in 1913, gave young women the training and impetus 'to make careers as professional musicians' (1999: 27). They were engaged for every sort of public and private function (1999: 24), enabling them to make 'a transition from private, amateur music-making to public, professional performance' (1999: 27). The 1920s saw the emergence of a large-scale entertainment industry as social dancing became the leisure activity of choice for the modern masses. Large and elaborate dance palais were built in all major Australian cities, and dance orchestras were assembled to provide the music. The old social mores which had governed public activity and conduct were being replaced by a new modern social code. Central to this evolution was the changing status of women, who were emerging from the Edwardian domestic sphere and demanding greater social and personal freedoms. Johnson (2000: 64) suggests that jazz played a fundamental role in the modernization of Australian society: it was the 'soundtrack' of the modern age, becoming 'the pre-eminent musical expression of women's emancipation'. He points out that the word 'jazz' referred as much to the expressive dancing that accompanied the new 'hot' music as to the music itself (2000: 64). Thus, 'the image of the flapper embodied a convergence of jazz with the 1920s version of feminism' (Johnson 1987: 8). He theorizes that so great was the association between liberated young women and jazz at this time that the music itself became 'feminized'. He cites evidence from early Australian films which contrast the rugged, masculine, outback environment with the soft, feminized atmosphere of the city with its frivolous entertainments and pastimes such as live music and dancing (Johnson 2000: 66–76). Fornäs (2003) reports a similar dynamic in Sweden, where early jazz was viewed as emblematic of the invasion of dangerous American modernist ideas. Women were depicted in popular songs as neglecting their domestic duties and becoming 'addicted to excessive jazz dancing' (Fornäs 2003: 218), while men in the urban environment were at risk of drifting from 'macho androcentrism to androgynous feminization' (2003: 223).

Given the strong association between 'modern women' and 'jazz', it is ironic that just as hundreds of jobs came available in Australian cities to meet the growing demand for live entertainment, women found themselves virtually shut out of the mainstream of professional music-making. Modelled on American swing bands, the new dance palais orchestras required professional musicians in large numbers. Many players were drawn from the exclusively male world of the brass band, with some 'becoming saxophonists to meet the sudden demand for this instrument' (Whiteoak 2001). Dreyfus (1999: 44) observes that '[w]omen musicians participated along with the men in this boom, but not as equals. For if the "flapper" is always female, the "jazz hero", whether dance-band-leader or virtuoso soloist, is always male'.

Excluded from the most lucrative markets,[3] women continued to perform professionally in their own ensembles. All-women dance bands worked throughout the 1920s and '30s, despite the Depression causing a drastic reduction in the overall numbers of available jobs (Dreyfus 1999: 81). A few exceptional women were hired into all-male orchestras;[4] but the feeling that the inclusion of women in an orchestra's ranks would require men 'to modify the band room behavior they so enjoyed' (Whiteoak 2001: 38) ensured the continuation of gender segregation in these professional musical settings.[5]

A period of unforeseen opportunity for all-women bands in Australia, the United States and the UK was during World War II. The ranks of all-male bands were decimated as musicians were conscripted and sent overseas. In Australia, men who remained at home found their evening activities restricted as manpower controls required them to work in essential occupations during the day (Bisset 1979: 77). As a result, women were given a chance to work in the prestigious big-city venues. An all-women orchestra led by bandleader Dick Freeman worked for two and a half years at Sydney's premier dance venue, the Trocadero, playing for American and Australian servicemen. The tenor saxophonist, Daphne Hubner, was later to become the only woman whose playing

---

3. Bisset (1979: 60) says, 'Perth had a number of bands led by women, which were regarded as equal to the bands led by men and they got their share of the best jobs'.
4. Grace Funston, who played nine instruments, toured to Ceylon with trumpeter Sammy Sharpe's orchestra (Dreyfus 1999: 89).
5. 'The men used to drink a lot. They didn't like doing these things with women' (drummer Alma Quon, cited in Dreyfus 1999: 118). For contemporary insight into this issue, see Stewart (2007: 273–74).

can be heard on record from the dance band era when she stayed on at the Trocadero with a band led by the jazz elder statesman, Abe Romain (Dreyfus 1999: 116).

In the UK, 'popular music seemed an ideal field for women's advances' (Baade 2008: 91) during World War II. Tenor saxophonist Ivy Benson and her Ladies' Dance Orchestra were engaged in 1942 as a house band by the BBC, generating a storm of controversy and misogynist comments from the nation's male musicians. Not surprisingly, regular national broadcasts brought success to the band including recording and touring opportunities, and 'opened possibilities for women dance musicians as a group' (Baade 2008: 113).

Sherrie Tucker's *Swing Shift: "All-Girl" Bands of the 1940s* (2000) describes the far-reaching success of several all-women dance bands in the United States during World War II. Her research has revealed that there were in fact hundreds of all-women bands in the 1920s, '30s and '40s, travelling the same regional and national tour circuits as the all-male bands. With the exception of the celebrated International Sweethearts of Rhythm, women's extensive participation in big band jazz has generally not been acknowledged in American jazz historiography. Many accounts state that the Swing Era ended at the outbreak of the war, which 'ensure[s] the continued invisibility of all-woman bands' (Tucker 2000: 16).

In Australia, by the end of World War II, according to Johnson (2008: 121), 'jazz had become so masculinized that it retrospectively obscured the role women had played. The female orchestra, bandleader and solo instrumentalist largely disappeared from postwar jazz until the 1980s'. Indeed, very few women instrumentalists were to be heard in the next several decades of jazz practice in Australia. Nonetheless, a significant female presence on the contemporary jazz scene in Sydney in the 1960s–70s was New Zealand-born pianist/composer Judy Bailey. An exceptional musician, she was a regular on gigs and jam sessions at El Rocco Jazz Cellar where she collaborated with the most progressive improvisers in the country. She has worked in television and radio as well as performing, touring and recording extensively: her website lists 15 CDs ranging from solo piano to big band, featuring Australia's most accomplished jazz musicians. Her compositions include works for classical ensembles as well as countless jazz tunes and arrangements. Bailey's exceptional musicianship is evidenced by the fact that she was one of the first lecturers hired by the Sydney Conservatorium when it launched its Jazz Studies degree in 1973. Given that even today the number of women occupying positions on jazz faculties around the world is miniscule, this remains a truly remarkable achievement. Bailey has been recognized for her unique contribution to Australian music, receiving a Medal of the Order of Australia (OAM) for her services to jazz music and education in 2004. In 2008, she also received an award for Distinguished Services to Australian Music at the Classical Music Awards, presented jointly by the Australasian Performing Right Association (APRA) and the Australian Music Centre (Bailey n.d.).

The next highly accomplished woman to achieve a major profile as an instrumentalist on the Australian jazz scene was saxophonist/composer Sandy Evans. Evans has played with many groundbreaking ensembles in her thirty-year career, starting with her own group, Women and Children First, in the 1980s. She has made significant contributions as a composer and player to such groups as Clarion Fracture Zone, Ten Part Invention, The catholics, Waratah, the Australian Art Orchestra and GEST8. Her compositional output includes the remarkable two-hour setting of a libretto by Pulitzer Prize-winning American poet Yusef Komunyakaa on the life of jazz legend Charlie Parker (Denson 2008: 108–10). Always seeking to expand her musical palette, her recent explorations have included an intensive study of South Indian Carnatic music, described elsewhere in this volume. Like Bailey, Evans has long been involved with mentoring the next generation of jazz players, young women in particular. In partnership with the Sydney Improvised Music Association (SIMA), in 2002 she established the annual Young Women's Jazz Workshops in order to create 'a supportive environment for aspiring female jazz musicians to explore their creativity and develop their skills' (SIMA n.d.). Like Bailey, she has been awarded a Medal of the Order of Australia for her services to music, as well as numerous other awards for musical excellence.

Johnson (1999: 70) has suggested that it was only in the 1990s that the numbers of women playing jazz in Australia began to approximate the numbers in the 1920s. By the 1990s, such noteworthy players such as bassist Nicki Parrott, saxophonists Gai Bryant and Lisa Parrott, and pianists Jann Rutherford and Cathy Harley had emerged (Sharpe 2008: 47). It is both appropriate and unsurprising, then, that the inaugural MWIJF took place in 1997, 19 years after the first Women's Jazz Festival was held in Kansas City, in 1978. Tucker (n.d.) writes that the 'women's liberation movement in the 1960s and 1970s brought new interest in women's status, history, and cultural expression, and thus, a new audience for…recordings and literature pertaining to historical women in jazz'. The Kansas City Festival had a 'women-only' policy, aiming to create a safe, supportive, women-only space in which they could undertake activities, discussion and identity development. Deemed a success and the first of many such events in the United States and elsewhere, the festival engendered a still unresolved debate about 'women's jazz' events: are women's jazz festivals 'a double-edged sword?', as multi-reed player Leigh Pilzer says (in Stokes 2000: 64). While such events are meant to celebrate and promote the accomplishments of women in jazz, do they in fact serve to reinforce the marginalization that women have always experienced in the jazz world? McMullen (2008: 144) argues that this marginalization is at least subliminally evident in the presentation of The Diet Coke Women in Jazz Festival by Jazz at Lincoln Centre in New York City. She says:

> it is hard to think of a single other product that bears its marked, attenuated, 'feminized' and shadow-self image more precisely than Diet Coke... Could there be a more masterful way to 'allow' women onto the jazz stage while simultaneously writing them off of it, or a better way to patently signify women-in-jazz as the continued margin of jazz? (2008: 144)

She goes on to say that because Jazz at Lincoln Centre is such a prestigious enterprise, women still aspire to play at the festival, because '[to forego] such a venue does assure an even more certain invisibility for women in the jazz master narrative' (2008: 146). There is no such ambiguity in the intentions of the organizers of the MWIJF; but as we shall see, any focus on gender rather than music and musicianship can be uncomfortable for the participants.

The Melbourne Women's International Jazz Festival

MWIJF takes place annually in early December. Centred on Bennetts Lane, Melbourne's best-known jazz venue, other venues also host performances when the budget allows for a more extensive programme. The festival has presented a wide stylistic range including straight-ahead jazz, big bands, free improvisation, performance installations and Latin, Brazilian, African and classical cross-genre projects. In addition to the featured performances, MWIJF provides the context for the presentation of the Jann Rutherford Memorial Award.[6] Jann Rutherford was a much-celebrated pianist/composer who migrated to Sydney from New Zealand in 1989 to attend the Sydney Conservatorium of Music. Described as a 'wonderful pianist... [with a] sensitive ear for harmonic nuance and warm expressiveness' (Nock 1999), she was a significant presence on the Australian scene until her untimely death from cancer in 2003. The award, established in 2005, is given annually to a meritorious young female musician from New South Wales. It comprises a recording at Australian Broadcasting Corporation (ABC) Radio National, assistance with promotional materials, and performances for the Sydney Improvised Music Association (SIMA), MWIJF and other organizations where possible. The

---

6. Jann Rutherford Memorial Award, http://jazz.org.au/jann-rutherford-award/ (accessed 12 September 2014).

winner is selected by a panel of prominent women jazz musicians, chaired by Sandy Evans. The award is jointly funded by private donations, MWIJF, SIMA and ABC Radio National. MWIJF has also offered activities aimed at nurturing the next generation of players. Improvisation workshops for girls and young women aged 10–16 took place from 2001–2008, in conjunction with the creative arts space ArtPlay at Federation Square. In 2004–2006, a 'superband' of female secondary school students rehearsed and performed as part of the festival. Significant emerging artists such as guitarist Stella Skinner, trombonist Louise Cuming, trumpeter Maddy Foley and pianists Sarah Mackenzie and Kate Kelsey Sugg were part of these projects.

The first MWIJF was presented by the Melbourne Jazz Co-op, an organization that has presented around 2,500 jazz concerts in Melbourne since its inception in 1983. The Co-op's CEO, Martin Jackson, recounts that after lobbying the Victorian Parliamentary Secretary for an increase in funding, the Co-op unexpectedly had some money in the second half of 1997. He 'thought that the money needed to be spent...so I went with the women's festival' (personal communication, 2014). He felt that a women's jazz festival was 'something natural to be doing', and he regarded the accomplished women musicians on the Melbourne jazz scene as an under-utilized resource: 'If you've got a resource...it's crazy that you're not using it. It'd be like having pineapples in Queensland and not using them...it just seemed to be logical that that was part of the scene' (ibid.). Logical and natural it may have been, but Jackson's role in establishing MWIJF as an important annual Australian jazz event should not be underestimated. He undertook to apply for and acquit grants for funding at federal, state and municipal levels, and mount the festival virtually on his own for the first seven years of its existence. As current MWIJF CEO and drummer Sonja Horbelt says, 'it's always a real struggle, you find that often you're just running on a shoestring and people's goodwill [to do] the running round and organizing...it's a total labour of love' (personal communication, 2014). Jackson also personally supported many of the women invited to perform in the festival. Pianist/composer Andrea Keller recalls that he 'was incredibly encouraging of me to play my music and...to present it at the festival' (interview with author, 2014). Saxophonist/composer Fiona Burnett mentioned his support for her application to the Australia Council in 2002 for funding to compose her second work for jazz trio and string quartet, 'Four Corners of a Circle'. Although Jackson stepped back from involvement in the festival as of 2004, his support for the event and the women involved in it has been unflagging. Keller says: 'Martin in particular was fantastic at creating pathways for young musicians to develop as artists and to develop...original stuff, he's really put an incredible amount of energy into that, and it made an enormous difference to me' (ibid.).

Jackson's organizational role in MWIJF was taken over by the Alliance of Melbourne Women Improvising Musicians, a committee consisting of festival participants such as Keller, Burnett, bassist Anita Hustas and saxophonist Martha Baartz. By 2003, Lynette Irwin, a principal force behind the promotion and presentation of jazz in Queensland, had emerged as co-director of the festival with Horbelt. This team has devoted incalculable time, energy and generosity to mounting the festival, which has run every year except 2008 and 2011 when the combination of lack of funding and other circumstances prevented it from going forward. Funding for the festival has come from all three levels of government—federal (Australia Council); state (Arts Victoria); and municipal (City of Melbourne). As with virtually all Australian jazz festivals, there is no ongoing source of funding, so grant applications must be submitted and acquitted annually; in any given year there is no guarantee that sufficient funding will be procured to mount the festival. Grant applications may target specific activities such as commissioning new works, staging workshops or inviting an international guest; or alternatively a larger amount might be requested for operational expenses such as artist wages, transport and accommodation, or publicity materials and advertising.

The aim of the MWIJF has always been, according to Artistic Director Lynette Irwin, to

> [foster] opportunities for female jazz and improvised music performers, composers, arrangers, bandleaders and instrumentalists. The festival celebrates women's growing participation in the jazz community and recognizes the important contribution and investment women make to the cultural capital of our nation (Irwin, personal communication, 2012).

The intention of the festival has never been to exclude men: featured ensembles are led by women and emphasize music written by women, rather than consisting exclusively of women. Horbelt says:

> We've never had a discussion about it being exclusively women—ever. And I think we all feel very strongly that that's not the point of the music... if it happens to be an all-female band then great...we work with men, all the time...they're also your friends and your colleagues, so in terms of musicality, I think it's not an issue... It's about the person (personal communication, 2014).

Jackson recalls that initially there weren't enough accomplished women jazz musicians in Melbourne to have imposed a 'women only' policy, even if it had been thought to be appropriate. Furthermore, he has always felt, as do the current organizers, that the quality of the performances should not be

> compromised by creating groups that [aren't] working groups... [It's important] to have working groups rather than thrown together all-star ensembles which...much as people like seeing those, generally the real innovations [in jazz] come about through working groups or...musicians that have long-standing histories (2014).

One featured event at MWIJF may seem to contradict this philosophical position, however. Since 2000, the closing night of the festival has featured the Festival Sextet, an all-women ensemble convened yearly for this one gig. This is the only group presented at the festival which is intentionally all-female, and some of the members of the Sextet are not altogether comfortable with this, as will be discussed below.

All the women interviewed for this study agreed that being involved with MWIJF has been significant in their musical lives. The primary importance for the majority has been the opportunity for creative development. Since the festival seeks to present women as both performers and composers, the creation and presentation of original work has always been a priority. The festival has commissioned many new works from musicians such as Keller, Baartz, bassists Belinda Moody and Anita Hustas, trombonist Shannon Barnett and composer Jenna Cave. With an invitation to perform at MWIJF, Fiona Burnett successfully secured a composition commission from the Australia Council under her own auspices. The festival has also facilitated the presentation of projects that would otherwise be difficult to stage: Moody's commissioned suite 'Epic Whispers' (2005) for jazz trio, string quartet and three vocalists is only one of many examples.

For some, such as Sandy Evans, trombonist Alex Silver and vocalist Ingrid James, the festival allows a 'Melbourne premiere' of work they have already presented in their home states. Others have used the festival as a platform to launch CDs: two examples among many are internationally acclaimed vocalist Kristin Berardi and guitarist James Sherlock, and the Lisa Young Quartet, both in 2006. That same year, Barnett's ensemble recorded a work commissioned by MWIJF as part of the performance series at La Mama. Many have valued the opportunity to hear and/or collaborate with international artists, such as trumpeter Felicity Provan or pianist Satoko Fujii. Several of the women interviewed suggested that playing in MWIJF is of more importance to young and emerging women jazz musicians than it is to more established professional players. Bassist Tamara Murphy described how nervous she was in her 'early days of leading things', when she was asked to introduce the tunes at a festival performance with guitarist Fran Swinn:

> I was more nervous about introducing the tunes than I was about performing...that was really good for me...just being put in that position where you're performing original stuff and having to rehearse it to get it up to standard by the time of the gig, and then performing to a fairly large audience, that was really great (personal communication, 2014).

Silver performed at MWIJF as the 2007 winner of the Jann Rutherford Memorial Award. She said that appearing at the festival 'was part of a package, the entire package was very important for me, because it was...the first time that I really stepped out as a leader, so I would definitely include it as being significant in that respect' (personal communication, 2014).

In addition to the opportunity for artistic development, women mentioned the importance of the festival in terms of career advancement. Horbelt says that one of the aims of the festival is to act as a stepping-stone towards further opportunities, such as invitations to play at the Melbourne International or Wangaratta Jazz Festivals, or to be recorded by the ABC. She says:

> the festival...is a launch pad for the artists to take [their] project... to the next step, be it on an international scale, where they start to apply for international festivals, or a local scale where it's...a young artist who wants to get a gig...somewhere else in Melbourne... maybe a month-long residency...or if it's a more established artist, if they want to...get the project into Wangaratta or the Melbourne Jazz Festival (personal communication, 2014).

One woman mentioned years of subsequent gigs at Bennetts Lane under her own name, and many collaborations with other musicians as direct results of her participation in MWIJF.

The festival has played a very significant role in the careers of two highly accomplished Australian jazz musicians, Fiona Burnett and Andrea Keller. Burnett has been described as a 'burning, intense, astoundingly virtuosic soprano saxophonist' (Clare 2002). She holds a Master's degree from the Victorian College of the Arts, and has released seven CDs under her own name. Her involvement with the MWIJF dates to its inaugural year, and she appeared annually until 2006, and again in 2009. She remarked that the festival has 'facilitated the launching of a number of different projects of mine' (personal communication, 2014). In 1999 she was invited by Jackson to present her suite, *Soaring at Dawn*, for trio (saxophone, bass, drums) and string quartet. It was then performed at the Melbourne International Jazz Festival in 2001, and recorded as Burnett's debut album on the ABC Jazz label. Burnett recalled, 'half [the night at MWIJF] was the *Soaring at Dawn* project and the other half was…the first gig of the trio, so that launched that project' (ibid.). Her trio with Ben Robertson (bass) and David Jones (drums) worked together until 2006, which indicates the importance of this initial event to her subsequent musical life. In 2002, she presented another trio and string quartet project, *Four Corners of a Circle*; and in 2005, her Electric Band was launched at the festival prior to recording their CD *Imagine* (ABC Jazz). Burnett has also been a frequent member of the Festival Sextet. Thus MWIJF has provided many opportunities for her to create new works, present her music to an informed public and attract attention from influential stakeholders in the industry.

Similarly, Andrea Keller has had a long and significant involvement with MWIJF. A multi-award-winning musician,[7] Keller said, 'I'm pretty sure that the festival has presented each project that I've done…there's always been this sense that if I have something exciting to present, they're willing to put it on and help make it happen' (personal communication, 2014). As with Burnett, presenting new works at MWIJF has been a precursor to further opportunities. Her first CD *Icedreaming* (Newmarket), with bassist Anita Hustas, followed on from their performance in 1997, shortly after she had finished her studies at the Victorian College of the Arts. Her quintet debuted in 1999, then performed at the Wangaratta Jazz Festival, recorded for the ABC Jazz Track radio programme, and issued the award-winning CD *Thirteen Sketches* (Newmarket). Keller's *Mikrokosmos: The Bartók Project* (ABC Jazz) was presented in 2002, while an Australia Council commission, initiated by Jackson, for an extended work to commemorate the life of Jann Rutherford resulted in the CD *Angels and Rascals* (ABC). Keller has appeared in many settings over the years and, like Burnett, has also been a key member of the Festival Sextet.

Vocalist Ingrid James, from Brisbane, offered another perspective on the importance of the MWIJF for out-of-state musicians. Both of her appearances at the festival have involved collaborations with Melbourne-based musicians. She said, 'working with a different pool of musicians [is] great from a creative point of view', adding that 'a forum like the MWIJF gives [an] opportunity for artists to work towards another concept…materials that they don't… or aren't…able to present to a general audience' (personal communication, 2014). Coming from a smaller and more conservative jazz scene in Queensland, James said that performing at MWIJF had made her aware of 'how many artists are working towards finding their own sound…working towards originality' (ibid.). On a more practical level, James noted that an invitation from

---

7. Keller has been the recipient of three Aria Awards, an Art Music Award (co-sponsored by APRA and the Australian Music Centre), three Australian Jazz 'Bell' Awards, an MCA/Freedman Foundation Jazz Fellowship and an Australia Council Fellowship.

a festival can facilitate travel which would otherwise be difficult to undertake because of the great distances and expense: 'When a festival like this takes care of your airfares and accommodation, that is a great relief and I think that's extremely, extremely helpful' (ibid.).

As a significant annual jazz event, MWIJF has been able to attract attention from the media—to the extent that any jazz activity in Australia is able to do so. Several women mentioned the importance of the exposure to new audiences and industry stakeholders made possible by their performances and surrounding publicity. The festival promotes the artists via ABC radio programmes such as *Daily Planet* and *Jazz Track*, and jazz programmes on community stations. Advertisements are placed in the large-circulation dailies *The Age* and the *Herald Sun*, and articles and interviews appear in local papers. The MWIJF, Jazz Australia and state jazz organization websites all feature programme information, articles and links. Reporter Jessica Nicholas of *The Age* has been an unflagging supporter of MWIJF, publishing annual reviews of the Sextet and featured artists, as well as previews and summaries of the week's performances. The benefits of having such attention drawn to one's work are self-evident, especially when jazz as an art form is itself chronically under-reported, if not categorically ignored, in the Australian media. One participant in this study suggested that women suffer in particular from this neglect, and that their accomplishments are 'relatively discarded by some with competitive attitudes'.

The interviewees generally agreed that the Australian jazz scene is a more women-friendly and egalitarian place than it has been in the past, and that women jazz players are more visible than ever before. But they all remarked that an extreme gender imbalance in overall numbers of players still exists. For this reason they also agreed, almost unanimously, that there is a continuing need for the MWIJF or similar women-focused jazz events[8] to take place in Australia. This comment is representative of the overall feeling: 'There is not enough women's participation in jazz in Australia. It is an insecure industry for women, even though…female sensibility and emotivity/creativity and expression lends itself perfectly to it' (Baartz, personal communication, 2014).

In addition to providing women with opportunities for artistic and career development, MWIJF was seen by every woman interviewed as an important showcase for female role models for young women interested in pursuing a career in jazz. People are still surprised to see women playing certain instruments. Horbelt can tell many stories of encounters with incredulous members of the public when they see her playing drums (Jackson, personal communi-

---

8. The Sydney International Women's Jazz Festival is establishing itself as an annual event, having been launched in 2012.

cation, 2002). Burnett says she often needs to prove herself to her secondary school-age students who 'still have no idea that women can play...every teacher they've had previously has been a man, and they...look at me and go, who are you? And what do you do?' (personal communication, 2014). Baartz cites modelling for the next generation as a primary reason for her involvement with the festival:

> The prime reason I invested so much importance and energy into this festival is so that young women would be encouraged to follow this path. It is a very unbalanced scene, especially on certain instruments. Young women need role models, otherwise they are battling all sorts of insecurities (personal communication, 2014).

All the women interviewed were pleased to accept their invitations from MWIJF and acknowledged the benefits that have flowed from their participation in it; and Horbelt states that no one has ever declined to participate on political grounds (personal communication, 2014). But the question: 'How do you feel about participating in an event that is explicitly branded as a "women's jazz" event?' elicited a variety of responses. Evans stressed that the motivation behind such an event is an important determining factor:

> I think for me...if it's purely done for economic reasons, or marketing, or...some kind of more what you might consider cynical reasons, then I think it is marginalizing. But if it's done from a genuine... desire to celebrate and affirm women's creativity, then I think it's an absolutely wonderful thing (personal communication, 2014).

She added that MWIJF organizers have always demonstrated this sort of commitment, and that she places 'a huge value on it' (ibid.). Baartz expressed similar feelings:

> I am proud [to participate]... The festival is very careful to keep the standard of the highest level possible, making sure to invite international guest artists who deserve an audience. It is an event to make women proud, and to show support to women in an industry that is mostly male (personal communication, 2014).

Two of the younger interviewees had some reservations, however. It is worth quoting the thoughts of one of them at length:

> It does [make me] a little bit [uncomfortable]. I've always shied away from being associated as a female jazz musician solely, because I think that kind of defeats the purpose. If you can't succeed and be recognized just as a jazz musician—I think the fact that you're

> female should be irrelevant. So I'm sort of in two minds about the whole female jazz festival thing... I think it's really good for young musicians to be able to see other females out there doing it...but at the same time... I don't want to just be thought of as a female musician, I want to be thought of as a musician, so it's sort of a double-edged sword, it depends what day you get me on how I feel about it.

These sentiments are echoed throughout literature on women in music across genres and around the globe.[9]

An equally serious concern was voiced by one interviewee: that women-focused events are potentially detrimental for women jazz musicians:

> I think having a place where women can play music together and celebrate and understand each other is fantastic, but when it becomes a public event, it unfortunately draws criticism and ridicule from some (primarily) male jazz musicians, which in turn makes our mission to help women flourish in the scene more difficult. The festival and other initiatives are seen by them to be a sign of weakness, and we are still weak, in number only—but to them that translates as not good enough to be a significant part of the scene.

To my knowledge, no research has been done in Australia into how male jazz musicians view women-focused jazz events, but this anecdotal assertion suggests that such a study could be very informative and useful.

These concerns coalesce in particular around the Festival Sextet, with opinion again divided about whether it should be a featured MWIJF event. Evans fully supports it, as she does all initiatives that create opportunities for women to develop their musical skills. She recalled that when she was younger she was ambivalent about playing in all-women bands, so her participation in the first Festival Sextet was a revelation:

> I found the experience to be incredibly powerful and affirming. To be part of a social group that was so...creatively strong [and] also women was very significant for me... I had such a great experience that I've always jumped at the chance to do it again (Evans, personal communication, 2014).

Other women, however, remain ambivalent. While they acknowledged the powerful message about women in jazz that such a high-level group can deliver, they voiced concerns on musical grounds. Keller says: 'I think the ques-

---

9. See, for example, Placksin (1982), Gourse (1995), Enstice and Stockhouse (2004) and Stokes (2000).

tion comes up every year, should the Sextet really still be there, because it's not a working band...it's just this throw-together thing that happens once a year' (personal communication, 2014). Murphy also used the descriptor 'thrown-together', since all the women involved are very busy with their own projects and are unable to devote time to the Sextet until the festival is imminent: it 'often ends up being a bit thrown together at the last minute... I feel like it isn't the best representation of what we do...it just doesn't really have a band sound, necessarily' (personal communication, 2014). Her next comments illustrate beautifully how women musicians—or perhaps all musicians—feel when they find themselves playing together for non-musical reasons:

> We're all such different musicians...we get along really well...but just musically though, we didn't really necessarily have heaps of stuff in common...it's just that it was a bit forced being together...we just felt like it didn't really do us a favour as women jazz musicians... every year we'd be doing it and all of us sitting there going oh, this doesn't feel quite right... It's great, but it's not, you know? It's frustrating (ibid.).

She added that the ideal would be for 'the sextet to be a very strong group artistically, to simultaneously take the focus off the fact that it is an all-female group, but coincidentally, it happens to be an awesome ensemble, comprised solely of women' (ibid.). It may be that the Festival Sextet is an idea whose time has come and gone, but, for now, the positives seem to still outweigh the negatives for the women involved.

Conclusion

Current research cited in this chapter has shown that although women's participation in Australian jazz has been greater than a casual reading of the history might indicate, it has been sporadic, and women have always been greatly outnumbered by men. Their early involvement, or even leadership, was followed by a sudden exclusion from the lucrative positions in professional dance bands in the 1930s. Despite a brief window of opportunity for all-women bands during World War II, with the demise of the big bands after the war female jazz musicians found themselves unemployed and out of step with changing musical tastes. While every national context is unique, many aspects of women's experiences within the Australian jazz subculture are reflected in women's experiences in the American and European jazz contexts.

The post-World War II era of contemporary and experimental jazz was heavily male-dominated. Judy Bailey was virtually alone as a female instrumentalist at the heart of the scene in the 1960s and 1970s. By the 1980s, Sandy

Evans also most frequently found herself to be the lone woman among male colleagues. Both these women have been pioneering role models for successive generations of young women through their activities as practitioners and teachers. Despite a steady increase in numbers and growing acceptance within the scene, women still represent only a small percentage of the total number of professional jazz musicians in Australia. Initiatives such as the MWIJF are vital in bringing attention to the quality and quantity of their accomplishments. Through commissioning and presenting new work, showcasing performers at various stages of their careers, and sponsoring developmental activities for young women, the MWIJF has played a significant role in the musical lives of many Australian jazzwomen. The extreme gender disparity in the profession suggests that there is a continuing need for women's participation to be encouraged and celebrated through women-focused jazz events such as the MWIJF.

References

Baade, C. (2008) '"The Battle of the Saxes": Gender, Dance Bands, and British Nationalism in the Second World War'. In *Big Ears: Listening for Gender in Jazz Studies*, ed. Nichole T. Rustin and Sherrie Tucker, 90–128. Durham, NC: Duke University Press.

Bailey, Judy (n.d.) http://judybailey.jazz-planet.com/bio.html (accessed 14 September 2014).

Bisset, A. (1979) *Black Roots, White Flowers: A History of Jazz in Australia.* Sydney: Golden Press.

Clare, J. (2002) 'Slater Takes Jazz into the Digital Age'. *Sydney Morning Herald*, 16 July 16. http://www.smh.com.au/articles/2002/07/15/1026185159998.html (accessed 14 September 2014).

Denson, M. L. (2008) 'Jane Bunnett and Sandy Evans: One World, Worlds Apart'. In *Post-Colonial Distances: The Study of Pop Music in Canada and Australia*, ed. Bev Diamond, Denis Crowdy and Daniel Downes, 105–18. Newcastle upon Tyne: Cambridge Scholars.

Dreyfus, K. (1999) *Sweethearts of Rhythm: The Story of Australia's All-Girl Bands and Orchestras to the End of the Second World War.* Sydney: Currency Press.

Enstice, W. and J. Stockhouse (2004) *Jazzwomen*. Bloomington, IN: Indiana Press.

Fornäs, J. (2003) 'Swinging Differences: Reconstructed Identities in the Early Swedish Jazz Age'. In *Jazz Planet*, ed. E. Taylor Atkins, 207–24. Jackson, MS: University Press of Mississippi.

Gourse, L. (1995) *Madame Jazz*. New York: Oxford University Press.

Jackson, A. (2002) 'Beating the Odds to Maintain the Beat'. *The Age*, 29 November: 3. http://newsstore.theage.com.au/apps/viewDocument.ac?page=1&sy=age&kw=%22Beating+the+odds%22&pb=age&dt=selectRange&dr=entire&so=relevance&sf=headline&rc=10&rm=200&sp=nrm&clsPage=1&docID=AGE021129HJUFS2K78MU (accessed 15 May 2015).

Johnson, B. (1987) *The Oxford Companion to Australian Jazz.* Melbourne: Oxford University Press.

—(1999) 'The Ambiguous Flapper'. In *Musical Visions: Selected Conference Proceedings from 6th National Australian/New Zealand IASPM and Inaugural Arnhem Land Performance Conference*, 70–73. Kent Town, SA: Wakefield Press.
—(2000) *The Inaudible Music: Jazz, Gender and Australian Modernity*. Surrey Hills, NSW: Currency Press.
—(2008) 'Australian Jazz: An Overview'. In *Sounds of Then, Sounds of Now: Popular Music in Australia*, ed. Shane Homan and Tony Mitchell, 113–29. Hobart: ACYS Publishing.
McMullen, T. (2008) 'Identity for Sale: Glenn Miller, Wynton Marsalis and Cultural Replay in Music'. In *Big Ears: Listening for Gender in Jazz Studies*, ed. Nichole T. Rustin and Sherrie Tucker, 129–54. Durham, NC: Duke University Press.
Nock, M. (1999) Liner notes to *Jann Rutherford: Discovery*. Tall Poppies.
Placksin, S. (1982) *Jazzwomen: 1900 to the Present*. London: Pluto Press.
Sharpe, J. (2008) *I Wanted to be a Jazz Musician*. Canberra: National Film and Sound Archive.
SIMA (Sydney Improvised Music Association) (n.d.) http://www.sima.org.au/22014Young WomensJazzWorkshops/945/n/3/0/0/ (accessed 14 September 2014).
Stewart, A. (2007) *Making the Scene: Contemporary New York City Big Band Jazz*. Berkeley: University of California Press. http://dx.doi.org/10.1525/california/9780520249530.001.0001
Stokes, W. R. (2000) *Living the Jazz Life: Conversations with Forty Musicians about their Careers in Jazz*. Oxford: Oxford University Press.
Tucker, S. (n.d.) 'Women in Jazz'. http://www.pbs.org/jazz/time/time_women.htm (accessed 14 September 2014).
—(2000) *Swing Shift: "All-Girl" Bands of the 1940s*. Durham, NC: Duke University Press. http://dx.doi.org/10.1215/9780822380900
Werth, S. (2011) 'Survival of the Male Breadwinner'. *Hecate* 37/1: 145–56.
Whiteoak, J. (1995) 'Australian Women in Performance-Time Composition: 1880–1925'. In *Repercussions: Australian Composing Women's Festival and Conference, 1994*, ed. Thérèse Radic, 21–24. Clayton, VIC: National Centre for Australian Studies, Monash University.
—(2001) 'Popular Music, Militarism, Women and the Early "Brass Band" in Australia'. *Australasian Music Research* 6: 27–48.

Personal communications with author

Baartz, Martha (2014) Personal communication, 18 September.
Burnett, Fiona (2014) Personal communication, 28 July.
Evans, Sandy (2014) Personal communication, 28 July.
Horbelt, Sonja (2014) Personal communication, 2 August.
Irwin, Lynette (2012) Personal communication, 6 August.
Jackson, M. (2014) Personal communication, 18 July.
James, Ingrid (2014) Personal communication, 18 July.
Keller, Andrea (2014) Personal communication, 18 July.
Murphy, Tamara (2014) Personal communication, 17 July.
Silver, A. (2014) Personal communication, 1 August.

9 'A tale of five festivals'

Exploring the cultural intermediary function of Australian jazz festivals

Brent Keogh*

Introduction

Music festivals have been broadly defined as 'a series of performances, of a generally celebratory nature, given by large numbers of individuals and groups over a limited period of time' (Kernfield 1988: 360). Music festivals have become a significant subject of analysis in the study of popular music, particularly since the 1990s (Gibson 2007: 65). The attraction of studying festivals most probably arises from the increased number of festivals from this period, but also from the ways in which festivals transform spaces, contribute to local economies and have become focal points in the musical and cultural fabric of communities across the globe (Curtis 2010: 102; Gibson and Connell 2012: 4). Music festivals have also proven to be interesting case studies of 'neo-tribalism', which employ Maffesoli's (1995) theoretical framework to describe and study festivals as informal networks that provide spaces for solidarity and belonging, proximity, hedonism and a politics of survival (Riley *et al.* 2010: 348; see also Bennett 1999). Festivals also provide new forms (albeit rather fleeting) of sociality through shared consumption patterns, commodities and branding (Cummings 2007: 2).

Reflecting global trends, music festivals in Australia have become increasingly important sites of cultural expression, characterized by the complex interrelation of sounds, space, economies, power structures, producers, consumers and cultural intermediaries. The significance of music festivals in Australia is evidenced by Graeme Smith's (2005: 67) argument that music

---

* Brent Keogh is a musician and academic, specializing in the areas of popular music studies and ethnomusicology. His doctoral studies examined the discourse of world music in Australia. He has published in the areas of arts policy, musical sustainability, music ecology, and music festivals. He currently teaches at Macquarie University and UTS in the areas of popular music, media studies, cultural studies, and international communications.

festivals have become 'the most important public activity' in Australian folk music from the 1990s onwards. More specifically in regards to jazz festivals, Australia is historically significant as it is possibly one of the first places to hold jazz festivals in the world (Johnson 2003: 276). Jazz festivals are particularly significant to studies of music festivals in Australia, not only because of the significance of jazz generally in the shaping of national identity (Johnson 2010: 54), but also because jazz festivals represent the second largest number of music festivals in the country (17.4% of all music festivals in 2006–2007) behind country music (Gibson 2007: 70).

Jazz festivals became widespread throughout Australia from the 1960s, and a boom in jazz festivals in the 1990s corresponds to broader trends in Australian festivals (Gibson 2007: 65; Johnson 2003: 276). A number of reasons have been given to explain the rise in these festivals. Gibson (2007: 71) argues that one of the reasons for the rise in the popularity of jazz festivals in Australia is the creation of a network of 'inland heritage tourism', and the ways in which festivals particularly contribute to the local economies of rural towns in Australia. Curtis (2010: 106) has made a similar argument in her study of Wangaratta Festival of Jazz and Blues (hereafter Wangaratta), where the residents of Wangaratta were pleased about the cultural and economic benefits to the town through 'musical tourism' rather than the actual merits of the music per se.

In this chapter I will be considering the role of jazz festivals in Australia as cultural intermediaries and providers of patronage for musicians. I use the term 'cultural intermediaries' in similar fashion to Bourdieu's original use, referring to the 'occupations involving presentation and representation', and those 'institutions providing symbolic goods and services' (Bourdieu 1984: 359). In this passage he particularly highlights sales, marketing, advertising, public relations, fashion and decoration as examples of the work and occupations of cultural intermediaries. Some of these roles are directly relevant to the function played by festival organizational staff, particularly those of marketing, advertising and promotion, and the importance of these roles in bridging the distance (or perhaps reproducing that distance) between the processes of production and consumption (Negus 2002: 504, 511).

Providing symbolic goods and services, however, is not the only role of these cultural intermediaries at music festivals. I agree with Negus when he describes the role of cultural intermediaries as consisting of intervening between production and consumption, playing an active role in the construction of cultural goods, as well as controlling access to cultural production (Negus 2002: 511–12). However, where Negus is a little more hesitant with the term 'gatekeeper' (Negus 2002: 512), I believe this term is also relevant to the role festivals play as co-producers, tastemakers and selectors (Foster *et al.* 2011: 248). Here I would like to incorporate and foreground the 'search and selection' function of the 'gatekeeper' as outlined in the work of Foster *et al.* (2011). Incorporating the 'search and selection' function of the gatekeeper into the discourse of cultural intermediaries provides a more accurate description of the roles festivals play as providers of symbolic goods and services. The work of festival organizers thus involves the gate-keeping functions of co-producers, tastemakers and selectors, in addition to the cultural intermediary roles of advertising, marketing and promotion. For simplicity, the term cultural intermediary (insofar as festivals are concerned) will be understood to incorporate all of these roles. In this chapter, I will draw particular attention to the 'search and select' function as a key role of the cultural intermediary bringing together producers and consumers of jazz music in Australia.

It is because festivals play such an important role as cultural intermediaries that it is significant to study their programming patterns. This study of jazz festivals in Australia provides an insight into the role of cultural intermediaries at festivals, especially with regards to the selection process. Understood in this way, jazz festivals as cultural intermediaries play a significant part in constructing the environments that allow jazz in Australia to come into being; they are significant sites of jazz discourse and construct highly visible spaces whereby sounds connect with audiences primarily (though not exclusively) through live performance (Johnson 2008: 126).

While the case studies presented here are Australian, the subject has significance for the wider field of jazz studies (particularly diasporic jazz), music festivals and contemporary Australian popular music. I adopt a slightly different approach from previous studies of jazz festivals in Australia, especially in terms of the scope of the analysis, and the research questions driving the study. Here I consider the artistic programming of five Australian jazz festivals, drawn from 41 festivals from the period of 2004–2014. My purpose in doing so is to provide an insight into the complex role of festivals as cultural intermediaries in current Australian jazz scenes and detect some trends by way of data analysis.

Research questions

Origins
The collation and analysis of data in this study are guided by some core research questions. Firstly, I wish to explore the role of festivals as cultural intermediaries in selecting local and international acts. Throughout this chapter, the term 'origin' does not refer to the place of birth or citizenship of the artist(s); rather I use it to identify whether the bands/ensembles/groups that

were booked had to be flown in from overseas, or, conversely, whether these artists were based in Australia. My interest in the place of origin of a particular artist stems from previous work on world music festivals in Australia. A significant theme that arose in this research for festivals such as WOMADelaide was the preference given to overseas bands/ensembles/groups over local artists (Keogh 2014: 118–19). I have argued that this is partly explained by the need to represent 'the global' (see Isar 2012) at a 'world' music festival (Keogh 2014: 242–45). The preference towards international groups is also partly explained due to the complex logistics involved in booking artists from remote parts of the world, and the relative distance of Australia in comparison to the festivals of Europe and North America (Alter and Keogh 2013: 8). Here I wish to highlight this role of the festival as cultural intermediary in searching for and selecting artists to perform at a given festival. This highlights the role that festivals play in providing patronage to Australian and overseas-based acts, as well as contributing to the complex intertwining of jazz and Australian identity, discourses of genre, and the dialectic of global and local.

Frequency

The second research question concerns the frequency with which artists are programmed at festivals. My purpose here is to explore the role festivals play in providing repeated patronage for certain artists. The 'search and selection' function of the cultural intermediary, by repeatedly programming the same or similar artists, helps to further ingrain the meanings of symbolic material. Negus comments on this role (here speaking of the gatekeeper) where '"symbolic goods and services" may be conducted through the adherence to standardized occupational formulas and generic conventions, and operating within rather than across the boundaries of organizations' (Negus 2002: 513). Whether it is due to pragmatic or sub-conscious reasons, cultural intermediaries tend to reinforce what Negus refers to as 'established routines' (Negus 2002: 512). This could be understood as contributing to established notions of genre and identity. Regarding artist patronage, these 'established routines' could also contribute to a sense of stability for the performers (knowing that you are likely to get a gig at a particular festival), and stability for the festival organizers (knowing that this artist is reliable, is 'good' and will please the patrons).

Gender

The third research question explores the 'search and selection' function of cultural intermediaries as it pertains to issues of gender. Historically, jazz in Australia was symbolically encoded as a symbol of female liberation; however, this encoding has since morphed into what Johnson describes as the 'subsequent masculinisation of jazz performance' (Johnson 2000: 64). Certainly, the perception of male dominance in Australian jazz continues in the present (see, for example, Evans 2008: 25 and Dunn 2013). In this study I have highlighted the distribution of the sexes in terms of the leaders of bands/ensembles/groups, as well as the sex of the people featured on the programme in order to provide an insight into the selection patterns of festival programmers regarding gender.

Borders of jazz and world music
The fourth research question focuses more acutely on the 'search and selection' function of the cultural intermediary, as it pertains to the crossover between artists associated with world music and jazz. This reflects my previous research into world music in Australia, but also responds to the literature which suggests there has been increasing artist crossover between the genre boundaries of jazz and world music in Australia, particularly in the latter part of the twentieth century to the present. For example, in a study of Australian folk festivals, Smith (2005: 71) has observed that jazz performers have been increasingly programmed at festivals such as Woodford. Johnson (2008: 126) has also argued that the 'world music phenomenon' has contributed to the increasing eclecticism in Australian jazz and the proliferation of styles. In this study, therefore, I have sought to identify where possible those bands/ensembles/groups that have used 'world music' (or who have been labelled as such in the programme) to describe their act in order to highlight crossover acts between the jazz and world music scenes in Australia. In doing so, I wish to add further to the research I have conducted in collaboration with Andrew Alter (Alter and Keogh 2013), as well as my own doctoral thesis on world music in Australia which contained a detailed discussion of Australian world music festivals (Keogh 2014: 110–18).

Data and methods

There is a large number of jazz festivals in Australia that could have been selected for this analysis. For this study, I have chosen the Manly Jazz Festival, Wangaratta Festival of Jazz and Blues, Melbourne International Jazz Festival, Brisbane International Jazz Festival and Bellingen Jazz Festival.[1] One of the reasons I was attracted to these festivals was their high visibility. For example, Wangaratta has a reputation as the 'capital of jazz in Australia' (Curtis 2010: 105). This reputation has been built solely on the success of the festi-

---

1. For the purpose of brevity, I shall hereafter refer to these festivals by reference to the city, town or suburb in which they take place.

val itself, in spite of the apparent lack of a local jazz scene (Curtis 2010: 110). Wangaratta has become a significant mid-way point for musicians between the three major cities of Canberra, Melbourne and Sydney since its inauguration, encouraging collaborations between musicians who reside in different parts of the country (Curtis 2010: 104). Similarly, Melbourne International Jazz Festival has become one of the biggest jazz festivals in Australia. It regularly attracts major international bands/ensembles/groups (previous festivals have featured John Scofield, Kurt Elling, Charlie Haden, Chic Corea and Herbie Hancock) and highlights the strong local jazz scenes of Melbourne, holding events in both the major concert halls but also dedicated local jazz venues such as Bennett's Lane Jazz Club, Dizzy's Jazz Club and Uptown Jazz Café.[2]

Manly, a beachside suburb and major tourist destination in Sydney, is also a major annual jazz event, with a long history (37 years) and drawing around 100,000 visitors[3] over the course of the festival (Johnson 2003: 276). Brisbane was selected for this study, as it is the largest jazz festival in Queensland. It existed previously as the Valley Jazz Festival from 2004 until 2013 when it was re-launched under its current name. Since 2013, this festival has been attracting international artists such as Joshua Redman (USA), Julian Arguelles (UK) and Ernie Watts (USA). Finally, Bellingen was selected as it is one of the larger rural jazz festivals in Australia.[4]

One of the benefits of selecting these five festivals is that they provide a spread across urban, rural and beach settings of jazz in Australia. Johnson (forthcoming) has charted the transition of jazz in Australia from decadent, marginal and international musical form, to an institutionalized, local and central musical genre in Australia. Part of this shift in the discursive understanding of jazz and its connection to Australian identity has been the way jazz has been represented alongside powerful symbols of Australian national identity, such as the beach and the bush (ibid.). For this study, I have drawn on festivals spread across these three sites—urban (Melbourne and Brisbane), rural (Bellingen and Wangarratta) and beach settings (Manly)—of jazz in Australia. There are three festivals from major cities in Australia—Sydney, Melbourne, Brisbane—and two festivals from rural towns—Wangaratta and Bellingen. These festivals also represent a spread across the three States of NSW, Victoria and Queensland. As a result, there is a mainland, East Coast focus in this

2. http://melbournejazz.com/information/venues (accessed 14 May 2015).
3. This number is likely to have increased over the past ten years as the festival has moved from a three-day event to its current eleven-day format.
4. http://www.bellingenjazzfestival.com.au/about-the-festival (accessed 9 November 2014).

research; however the States and Territories of South Australia, Northern Territory, Tasmania and Western Australia are not featured.

A final guiding principle in the selection process has been that these festivals were running in the years 2004–2014. While each of the festivals has varying degrees of longevity (between Manly at 38 years to Brisbane at two years under its current name), each of the festivals selected ran during this period with slightly varying levels of frequency. For example, when Brisbane was called the Valley Jazz Festival, it ran biennially between the years 2005–2011.

Most of the data used in this analysis were able to be located through the various websites of the festivals chosen for analysis. For Melbourne and Manly, I also relied on the archival work of the Victorian Jazz Archive and Manly Library respectively. I also retrieved some of the programmes of past festivals through the archives at the NSW State Library, and was sent hard copies of past festival programmes of Bellingen direct from the festival organizers. As a result, this research draws on a total of 41 festival programmes between the years 2004–2014, featuring 1,740 bands/ensembles/groups and 2,080 performances.

In conducting this research, it must be acknowledged that there are some inherent limitations to this sort of data analysis. As Johnson (1987: i) has noted, the physical documentation of jazz in Australia cannot match the fluidity of its actual practice. This was evident when I received the raw data for Bellingen, which contained a corrected programme for the year 2013 so that the one that actually went to print was subsequently out of date. The choice of festivals is thus not meant to be a conclusive and exhaustive study of jazz festivals in Australia; rather these case studies provide a point of discussion regarding the role of festivals as cultural intermediaries. This study therefore should be taken as indicative and descriptive, drawing attention to the role of festivals as cultural intermediaries in contemporary Australian jazz.

Analysis and results

Origins of artists programmed

There are a number of trends that can be identified from the data concerning the origin of the artists who have been programmed at the five festivals in the period 2004–2014. By far the majority of bands/ensembles/groups that were booked across the five festivals over the ten-year period were based in Australia. Of the 2,080 performances analysed in this database, 1,597 bands/ensembles/groups could be identified as originating in Australia. There were a further 154 bands/ensembles/groups whose country of origin could not be identified. Table 1 demonstrates the number of groups that performed at these five festivals that did not originate from Australia.

Table 1: Number of ensembles/bands/groups not originating from Australia

Country	Number of Ensembles/Bands/Groups
USA	155
Italy	12
UK	9
Germany	7
Canada	6
France	6
Japan	5
New Zealand	5
Cuba	4
Spain	3
Ethiopia	2
Belgium	2
Indonesia	2
Brazil	1
Denmark	1
India	1
Korea	1
Portugal	1
Scotland	1
Switzerland	1

There were also a number of collaborations where the artists featured originated from two different countries. Firstly, there were a number of bands/ensembles/groups where artists originating from Australia collaborated with artists from other countries of origin. There were 25 collaborations between bands/ensembles/groups whose artists originated from both Australia and the USA; six collaborations between Australia and the UK; four collaborations between Australia and France; three collaborations between Australia and Argentina; and one collaboration between Australia and the following countries—Belgium, Israel, Japan, Norway, New Zealand, Canada, Denmark, Ethiopia, Ireland, Korea and the Netherlands.

Secondly, there were a number of bands/ensembles/groups in which the artists featured were collaborations between two different countries other than Australia. For example, there were bands/ensembles/groups in which artists originating from the USA collaborated with international artists outside Australia. There were two ensembles featuring collaborations from artists who originate from the USA and Germany; and Belgium, Canada, Greece,

India, Israel, Ireland each featured one ensemble which collaborated with artists from the USA. Additionally, there was one act from Norway and France; one from Sweden and the UK; one from Germany and the Netherlands, and one from Germany and Austria. There were also bands/ensembles/groups in which the collaboration occurred between artists originating from three different countries. There were three ensembles originating from Belgium, Germany and Luxembourg; two from Australia, Germany and Singapore; one from Germany, USA and Australia; and an act from the UK, Denmark and Sweden. Finally, there were a handful of bands/ensembles/groups that featured members originating from four different countries. There were two ensembles from Australia, Germany, USA and Argentina, and one from the UK, Denmark, Sweden and Australia respectively.

This data also demonstrates which festivals booked the most international groups in comparison to groups that originated from Australia. Of the 489 groups programmed at the Manly, 464 originated from Australia, equating to 94.88 per cent of the total groups programmed. The countries of New Zealand, France, Indonesia, and a collaboration between the UK and Australia, each featured one act. Italy, the USA and the UK featured two groups while Japan featured three. There was also a single collaboration between Australia and Cuba, and one between Australia and the USA. There were also 13 bands/ensembles/groups where the origin of the artist could not be identified.

Bellingen and Brisbane also demonstrated a small number of international artists programmed. Of the 298 bands/ensembles/groups used for analysis at Bellingen, 281 groups were from Australia, equating to 94.29 per cent of the total groups programmed. There were two collaborations from Australia and France, one ensemble from France and one from America exclusively. Of the 205 bands/ensembles/groups performing at Brisbane, 173 originated from Australia, equating to 84.39 per cent of total groups programmed. There were four groups originating from the USA, one collaboration from Australia and the USA, and Canada, Finland, France, Germany and the UK each had one group programmed. There were 22 bands/ensembles/groups from Brisbane that could not be identified.

Of the 576 bands/ensembles/groups used for analysis at the Wangaratta, 425 groups originated exclusively from Australia, equating to 73.78 per cent of the total groups programmed. The USA was the next largest country of origin, with 47 bands/ensembles/groups followed by the UK with five. A small number of ensembles originated from countries such as Sweden, Spain, Scotland, Norway, Portugal, New Zealand, the Netherlands, Italy, Germany, Austria, France, Finland, Denmark, Cuba, Canada, Belgium, Luxembourg, Japan, Argentina, Singapore and Amsterdam. Of the

576 bands/ensembles/groups at Wangaratta, there were 53 whose origins could not be accounted for.

Melbourne was particularly interesting, as it had the largest percentage of international groups programmed over the ten-year period in comparison to the other festivals. Of the 517 bands/ensembles/groups, 263 were exclusively of Australian origins, equating to 50.87 per cent. The next closest country of origin was the USA with 93 groups. 2004 was the biggest year for international artists, with 106 groups hailing from overseas.

Frequency of artists programmed

There were a number of groups that were frequently programmed at these festivals over the ten-year period analysed. One of the difficulties in highlighting the frequency with which a person performed at a given festival is that these musicians often perform in multiple ensembles. Sometimes the name of the musician is highlighted in a band/ensemble/group, sometimes the band/ensemble/group has its own name distinct from the members who constitute it. In this research, I have chosen to demonstrate the frequency of a particular act as it features on the programme, rather than demonstrate the frequency with which a particular musician performed throughout this period. So, for example, rather than calculate the number of times Allan Browne performed over the period, I have identified 15 different groups in which Allan Browne featured as a leader/featured soloist and the number of times each act performed across the five festivals.

Obviously, there is some crossover between the number of times a musician performs and the number of times an act appears; however, for the purpose of increased accuracy, I have chosen to highlight the latter here. It should be acknowledged that there would be a much larger pool of musicians and data to analyse if all the band members were included in the analysis. However, due to the difficulties associated with obtaining and analysing this data, and the fluidity of jazz music practice, I have instead decided to limit this research by highlighting the bandleaders and featured soloists on the programme as this information is more easily available. It is possible that this approach more accurately bridges the gap between the data and what actually occurs in practice, for the make-up of the band is likely to be more fluid than the featured soloist/bandleader featured on the programme.

There were a number of artists who featured in multiple ensembles/bands/groups as band leaders or whose names featured on the programme. The following musicians featured in four or more different ensembles/bands/groups (for background on the performers listed, see for example Johnson 1987: index):

- Allan Browne featured in 15 different groups;
- Sandy Evans and Paul Grabowsky featured in 13 different groups;
- Carol Ralph featured in ten different groups;
- Mike Nock featured in nine different groups;
- Dale Barlow, James Morrison, Joe Chindamo and Paul Williamson featured in eight different groups;
- George Washingmachine, Jamie Oehlers and John Morrison featured in seven different groups;
- Jeff Duff and Roger Burke featured in six different groups;
- there were six different groups from Monash University;
- Aaron Choulai, Bob Sedergreen, Charles Lloyd, Ingrid James, Stephen Magnusson, Andrea Keller and James Muller featured in five different groups;
- Barney McAll, Charlie Haden, Dan Barnett, Geoff Bull, Geoff Power, Jason Moran, Julien Wilson, Mark Isaacs, Michelle Nicolle, Sam Keevers, Phil Slater, Rob Burke, Ray Beadle, Scott Tinkler and Tony Gould featured in four groups.

There were also a number of bands that featured regularly at the same festival over different years. From the data, it is possible to observe the number of groups who performed five times or more over the ten-year period. Akabella were booked in five successive years at Bellingen Jazz Festival from 2010–2014; the Allan Browne Quintet performed eight times with a fairly even spread across the festivals; the Bernie McGann Quartet were programmed six times across Manly, Melbourne and Wangaratta; the Blue Riff Big Band performed five times exclusively at Manly; Dr V's Swing Thing were programmed seven times at Manly; Jim Conway's Big Wheel performed twice at Bellingen and four times at Wangaratta; The catholics performed five times spread over Wangaratta, Manly and Bellingen; the Vampires were programmed five times across Manly, Wangaratta and Melbourne; the View From Madeleine's Couch played four times at Brisbane and once at Manly; Vince Jones performed five times spread across these festivals excluding Manly; Misinterpotato performed five times with a fairly even spread across the festival; and Way Out West were programmed five times across Brisbane, Melbourne and Wangaratta.

Gender and Australian jazz festivals
From the above data on the frequency of groups programmed, one starts to see the gender distribution of groups favouring male artists that begins to emerge. In this section, I consider more closely the gender distribution of the groups programmed across these five festivals. In the database I collated, I

assigned where possible the gender of the bandleader(s) that had been programmed at the festival and, where relevant, the featured soloist. If an individual member of a group/act was particularly featured on the programme then I have correspondingly noted the gender of that person. An example of this is the act Fiona Boyes and the Fortune Tellers. Where there has been any ambivalence concerning the gender of the bandleader in a given act, rather than identifying them as male or female, I have chosen instead to leave it blank. Where two people of different genders are identified, I have labelled that with 'M/F'. An example of this is Allan Browne's performance with Margie Lou Dyer at the 2014 Wangaratta.

In constructing these categories, it is not my intention to impose a binary, especially one that privileges the 'male' side of set binary (see Moi 1988: 104); rather this method of identification is simply used to provide an insight into the gender distribution between male and female with regards to band leaders and the names of people featured on the programme. My purpose is to try to provide some insight into the distribution of the sexes as they are represented in the groups that have been programmed across these five festivals in the ten-year period. In the same way that the analysis of the frequency of artists could be well served to consider all the members of the band/ensembles/groups, so too would the study of gender distribution. However, as per the analysis of frequency of artists, I have chosen to limit this research to highlight the bandleaders and featured soloists for reasons of accuracy and the difficulty in sourcing the necessary information.

Table 2 therefore demonstrates the distribution of gender across the festivals insofar as the gender of the band leader, and/or an individual featured on the programme, could be identified.

Table 2: Gender distribution across the five festivals, 2004–2014

Row Labels	Bellingen	Brisbane	Manly	Melbourne	Wangaratta	(Blank)	Total
Unknown/F			1		3		4
Unknown/M			1	1			2
F	36	40	48	56	65		245
M	155	90	152	314	387		1098
M/F	44	19	11	31	26		131
(Blank)	62	56	275	112	92	3	600
Total	297	205	489	514	572	3	2080

From this table, there are a few observations that can be made. Of the 2,080 ensembles/bands/groups analysed, 1,098 were identifiably male, with only 245 groups being identifiably female. Thus 52.78 per cent of the total groups had a band leader/name on the programme that was identifiably male; in comparison 11.77 per cent of total groups had a female band leader/name on the programme. There were 131 identifiably mixed groups equating to 6.29 per cent of total groups. There were six collaborations where one gender could be identified, but the other side of the collaboration could not. In these cases the number of Unknown/Female groups were four as opposed to the Unknown/male, which was two. There were also 600 groups where the gender of the bandleader/name on the programme could not be identified from the data, which equates to 28.84 per cent of total groups. It is also possible to observe the number of bands that featured both male and female band leaders/names on the programme. Compared to the total number of groups at each festival, Bellingen had the highest proportion of mixed groups at 14.81 per cent, followed by Brisbane at 9.26 per cent, Melbourne at 6.03 per cent, Wangaratta at 4.54 per cent, and finally Manly at 2.24 per cent. Table 2 also gives an indication of the comparative gender distribution across the five festivals. If we compare just the categories of identifiably Male/Female band leader/name on the programme, Brisbane had the most balanced gender distribution over this time period with 44.44 per cent of groups having a female band leader/female name on the programme. Manly 31.57 per cent had the second highest gender distribution, followed by Bellingen, 23.22 per cent, Melbourne with 17.83 per cent and finally Wangaratta with 16.78 per cent.

There are some limitations in this research with regards to an analysis of gender in Australian jazz scenes. Firstly, it is difficult from this data to ascertain the nuances involved in gender studies from a festival programme. For example, there are some bands that I am aware of which feature members who identify as transsexual (for example The Sirens Big Band). Unfortunately, this research has not been able to account for the degrees and nuances of gender/sexuality in current Australian jazz scenes. Thus the sample that I have drawn on has instead focused on the gender distribution across the groups that appear to identify as male or female.

Jazz and world music crossovers
I stated at the beginning of this study that I was interested in the crossover between artists who perform at jazz and world music festivals. My approach to the data collection in this regard was to only identify the jazz/world music connection where a group had been described as world music on the programme. Table 3 demonstrates the number of ensembles/bands/groups that featured world music as a genre description in each year, according to each festival.

Table 3: Number of ensembles/bands/groups that featured 'world music' in their description

Festival	2004	2005	2006	2007	2008	2009	2010	2011	2012	2013	2014	Total
Bellingen	1	1					1	3	2	3	3	14
Brisbane						2		4		2		8
Manly	1	1		1		1		1				5
Melbourne	5						1			2		8
Wangaratta	1			1						1		3
Total	8	2		2		3	2	8	2	8	3	38

A few observations can be made from this table. The largest number of world music groups programmed at a festival occurred at Melbourne in 2004 and Brisbane in 2011. The biggest years for world music groups occurred in 2004, 2011 and 2013 respectively. The years 2006 and 2008 featured no world music groups. The most notable aspect of this table is the small number of groups that actually used world music to describe themselves, or cases where the festival had labelled them as world music. There were a total of 38 groups that were identified in the data with the label 'world music', which equates to only 1.82 per cent of the total number of groups analysed. It is my suspicion that the number of crossover groups would increase if the data analysed extended to past programmes of world music festivals around Australia, as musicians tend to be more fluid than genre categories imply and tend to modify their description depending on the performance context (Keogh 2014: 218–33).

Discussion

There are a number of key insights that can be drawn from these data concerning jazz festivals as cultural intermediaries. One trend that can be detected is a preference towards programming artists of Australian origin. The vast majority of artists programmed at these festivals originate from Australia. Manly was the least likely to programme international artists, followed closely by Bellingen, whereas Melbourne demonstrated a fairly even distribution between international and Australian artists.

Across these five festivals, bands/ensembles/groups originating from the USA were the second highest country after Australia. Where acts originating from the USA numbered 155, the nearest competing country of origin, Italy, featured only 12 acts. It is certainly plausible, if not probable, that the overwhelming tendency towards programming artists originating from the USA is influenced by the narrative of America as the original and authentic source of jazz to which diasporic jazz is compared, a narrative perpetuated by tertiary institutions since the 1970s (Johnson 2008: 114, 124).

There was a preference towards programming male-led featured acts/groups. The closest gender distribution across the festivals still favours the male sex by 56 per cent. The data support Johnson's (2000: 64; 2010: 53) discussion of the historical and cultural shifts in attitude towards jazz in Australia, from the perception of it as dangerous, effeminate divergent noise, to cerebral, masculine and implicated in national identity. It is worth considering whether the gender of the artistic/musical directors of these festivals contributes at all to the gender representation at these festivals. For example, the artistic directors of Melbourne have been male over the past ten years with the exception of Sophie Brous during the years 2009–2011.[5] Additionally, the current artistic/musical directors at Wangaratta[6] and Bellingen[7] are male. Manly and Brisbane are different in that they are currently directed by females (Caroline Speight[8] and Lynnette Irwin[9] respectively). It is noteworthy that the data analysed here demonstrate that Manly and Brisbane had the highest representation of groups with female bandleaders/featured soloists. This correlation highlights the role and importance of the artistic/musical director as cultural intermediaries contributing to issues of gender in Australian jazz.

These data demonstrate some of the ways in which festivals function as gatekeepers of taste and their role in framing discourses of genre. Here the 'search and selection' function of festivals is instrumental in framing the discourses of jazz in Australia, what is called jazz and what is permissible to include in a festival programme. This is demonstrated most clearly with respect to the colour coding system used on a number of Manly programmes indicating in broad-brush strokes the kind of genre of a particular act. For example in 2011 there were six broad genre categories that an ensemble/band/group would be classified under—Big Band and Students Groups; Mainstream and Swing; Vocal and Instrumental; Funk, Latin, Blues, Boogie, Zydeco; Contemporary and Modern; and Traditional and Classic jazz. These diverse and changing genre categories reflect the proliferation of genres away from the taxonomy of traditional and modern that was prevalent into the 1980s (Johnson 2008: 126), though the trace of this distinction can still be detected.

While contemporary jazz categories in Australia could be characterized by a certain stylistic eclecticism (ibid.), it appears that festivals are either reluctant to programme world music artists at jazz festivals, or alternatively there is a reluctance to use world music as a genre description for artists. Very few

5. http://melbournejazz.com.au/about-us/history (accessed 13 November 2014).
6. http://wangarattajazz.com (accessed 13 November 2014).
7. http://bellingenjazzfestival.com.au (accessed 13 November 2014).
8. http://jazz.org.au (accessed 13 November 2014).
9. http://brisbanejazzfestival.com.au (accessed 13 November 2013).

artists featured on the programmes considered in this research were associated with the label of world music. Notably, some artists have responded to this seeming reluctance by positioning themselves differently depending on the context in which they receive patronage. The flamenco guitarist Damian Wright is one example of an artist who, while associated with world music as a flamenco guitarist, has also attracted the attention of jazz festival programmers with his fusion group the Translators.

Another example of an artist who repositions himself according to context is the Egyptian/Australian *oud* player Joseph Tawadros. In an interview I conducted with him, Tawadros explains that he intentionally aligns himself with Western classical music in Australia (Tawadros, interview with author, 14 July 2010), but he is also just as comfortable operating in the discursive category of jazz. In this interview he defined world music as 'jazz with ethnic instruments' (ibid.). While this definition is open to criticism, it does resonate to some degree with the approach Tawadros has taken to composition and improvisation, and the musicians he has performed and recorded with. Tawadros has performed and recorded with a number of prominent jazz musicians such as guitarist Mike Stern, double-bassist Charlie McBride, guitarist John Abercrombie, drummer Jack deJohnette and bassist John Petatucci. In 2010, his album featuring John Abercrombie, John Petatucci and Jack deJohnette was nominated for an Australian Record Industry Award (ARIA) in the category of Best Jazz Album. In that same year, he was nominated in the category of Best World Music album for his recording *The Hour of Separation*. Tawadros thus provides an example of a musician who works across the genre categories of World and jazz music, and positions himself differently depending on the context in which he plays (Keogh 2014: 227).

Conclusion

The research presented in this study uses Australian examples of music festivals (specifically jazz festivals) to focus on a number of activities and trends of these cultural intermediaries. One of the noticeable trends in the data is the tendency towards following predictable patterns, where festivals follow 'established routines' and 'standardized formulas' (Negus 2002: 512–13) in their role as seekers and selectors. This is most notably seen in the predictable programming and visibility of male musicians as bandleaders and featured artists. It is also demonstrated in the repeated programming of certain artists. This paper has highlighted the tension between the predictability of the programming and selections that work across organizational boundaries. Festivals as cultural intermediaries position artists according to genre categories that reflect specific histories of jazz in Australia, but these categories are also characterized by a certain dynamism and fluidity. From the changing genre descriptions that appear at the Manly and Melbourne festivals, jazz as a genre appears as an extraordinarily complex and dynamic constellation of subgenres and music styles. Where there has been a historical trend towards eclecticism in Australian jazz (Johnson 2008: 126), the data suggest that within the constellation of subgenres, world music seldom features as a description of programmed acts. However, musicians have also responded and capitalized on the amorphous nature of genre categories and have been able to position themselves differently depending on the context of patronage. These genre categories are also further problematized by the changing nature of the musicians and the musical projects they are involved in.

Johnson (2008: 125) has noted that with the influence of feminism since the 1980s, there has been an increase in the number of female jazz instrumentalists. In the data analysed here, it appears that cultural intermediaries tend to conform to predictable patterns; however, there are also instances that suggest subtle disruptions to these patterns. Manly and Brisbane festivals demonstrate a correspondence between higher rates of female artist programming where the selection is being made by a female programme director, organizer or curator. It will be interesting to see if the increased number of female instrumentalists suggested by Johnson is reflected in future programming trends, and if this correspondence between the gender of the cultural intermediary and the artist continues to be characteristic of jazz festivals in Australia.

To conclude, music festivals are important sites for studying contemporary popular music. Where scholars have developed a number of approaches to the study of music festivals, I have focused on the role of festivals as cultural intermediaries that play an important function in connecting producers to consumers. Festivals act in a number of significant ways: as producers of symbolic goods (marketing, advertising, promotion) and as seekers, selectors, tastemakers and co-producers. I have drawn particular attention to the importance of the 'search and select' function of these cultural intermediaries, and the implications this has regarding the programming of local and international artists, the frequencies of artists programmed, the representation of gender at festivals and the construction of genre. This study of Australian jazz festivals has demonstrated the crucial in-between role that festivals play as mediators and co-producers; this role is characterized by the tensions of anxiety and celebration, homogeneity and heterogeneity, freedom and conformity, as jazz comes into being in the connection of sounds to audiences (Johnson 2008: 126).

Acknowledgements

The author wishes to thank Mauri Thomas of the Bellingen Jazz Festival, Jim Budd from Jazz Queensland, Katherine Lindsay of Melbourne Jazz Festival, Marika Jones of the Manly Jazz Festival, Ralph Powell at the Australian Jazz Museum, and James Woodhams, for their assistance in the preparation of this chapter.

References

Alter, A., and B. Keogh (2013) 'Some Preliminary Thoughts on Patterns of Programming in Australia's World Music and Folk Festivals'. In *Proceedings of the 2012 ANZ-IASPM Conference*, ed. Oli Wilson and Sarah Attfield, 5–15.

Bennett, A. (1999) 'Subcultures or Neo-tribes? Rethinking the Relationship between Youth, Style and Musical Taste'. *Sociology* 33/3: 599–617.

Bourdieu, P. (1984) *Distinction. A Social Critique of the Judgment of Taste*. London: Routledge.

Cummings, J. (2007) 'Selling the Indie Scene: Music Festivals, Neo-tribes and Brand Communities'. In *Refereed Proceedings of the Joint Australian Sociological Association (TASA) and the Sociological Association of Aotearoa New Zealand (SAANZ) Conference 2007, Auckland University, New Zealand, 4–7 December*.

Curtis, R. A. (2010) 'Australia's Capital of Jazz? The (Re)Creation of Place, Music and Community at the Wangaratta Jazz Festival'. *Australian Geographer* 41/1: 101–116. http://dx.doi.org/10.1080/00049180903535618

Dunn, J. (2013) 'Sirens, Yes. But the Music Always Comes First'. *Australian Jazz.net*. 23 February. http://australianjazz.net/2013/02/sirens-yes-but-the-music-always-comes-first/ (accessed 8 November 2014).

Evans, S. (2008) 'Sandy Evans—In Conversation with Michael Webb'. *Extempore* 1/1 (November): 23–39.

Foster, P., S. P. Borgatti and C. Jones (2011) 'Gatekeeper Search and Selection Strategies: Relational and Network Governance in a Cultural Market'. *Poetics* 39: 247–65. http://dx.doi.org/10.1016/j.poetic.2011.05.004

Gibson, C. (2007) 'Music Festivals: Transformations in Non-Metropolitan Places, and in Creative Work'. *Media International Australia incorporating Culture and Policy* 123 (May): 65–81.

Gibson, C., and J. Connell (2012) *Music Festivals and Regional Development in Australia*. Farnham: Ashgate.

Isar, Y. (2012) 'Global Culture'. In *International Relations: Perspectives for the Global South*, ed. Bhupinder S. Chimni and Siddharth Mallavarapu, 1–12. New Delhi: Pearson.

Johnson, B. (1987) *The Oxford Companion to Australian Jazz*. Melbourne: Oxford University Press.

—(2000) *The Inaudible Music: Jazz, Gender and Australian Modernity*. Sydney: Currency Press.

—(2003) 'Jazz Festivals'. In *The Currency Companion to Music and Dance in Australia*, ed. John Whiteoak and Aline Scott-Maxwell, 276. Sydney: Currency House.

—(2008) 'Australian Jazz—An Overview'. In *Sounds of Then, Sounds of Now—Popular Music in Australia*, ed. Shane Homan and Tony Mitchell, 113–29. Sydney: UNSW Press.
—(2010) 'The Australianisation of Jazz—A Strange Outcome of Media Convergence'. In *Proceedings of the 2010 ANZ-IASPM Conference*, ed. Jen Cattermole, Graeme Smith and Shane Homan, 53–56.
—(forthcoming) 'Gaining Citizenship: Jazz and Local Identity'.
Keogh, B. (2014) 'Analyzing World Music Discourse in Australia'. PhD dissertation. Sydney: Macquarie University.
Kernfield, B. (1988) 'Festivals'. In *The New Grove Dictionary of Jazz*, ed. Barry Kernfield, 360. London: Macmillan.
Maffesoli, M. (1995) *The Time of the Tribes: The Decline of Individualism in Mass Society*, vol. 41. London: Sage.
Moi, T. (1988) *Sexual/Textual Politics*. London: Routledge.
Negus, K. (2002) 'The Work of Cultural Intermediaries and the Enduring Distance between Production and Consumption'. *Cultural Studies* 16/4: 501–515. http://dx.doi.org/10.1080/09502380210139089
Riley, S. C., C. Griffen and Y. Morey (2010) 'The Case for "Everyday Politics": Evaluating Neo-tribal Theory as a Way to Understand Alternative Forms of Political Participation, Using Electronic Dance Music Culture as an Example'. *Sociology* 44: 345–63. http://dx.doi.org/10.1177/0038038509357206
Smith, G. (2005) *Singing Australian: A History of Folk and Country Music*. North Melbourne: Pluto Press.

Interviews with the author
Tawadros, J. (2010) Interview with author. 14 July.

Jazz festival programmes
Brisbane International Jazz Festival programmes, 2013–2014.
Bellingen Jazz Festival programmes, 2004–2014.
Manly Jazz Festival programmes, 2004, 2005, 2007, 2009, 2010, 2011, 2013.
Melbourne International Jazz Festival programmes, 2004, 2005, 2007, 2008, 2009, 2010, 2011, 2012, 2013, 2014.
Valley Jazz Festival programmes, 2004, 2005, 2007, 2009, 2011.
Wangaratta Festival of Jazz and Blues programmes, 2004–2014.

10 'I wouldn't change skins with anybody'

Dulcie Pitt/Georgia Lee, a pioneering Indigenous Australian jazz, blues and community singer

Karl Neuenfeldt[*]

This chapter explores the career and music of Indigenous Australian singer and musician Dulcie Pitt, also known as Georgia Lee.[1] She had a distinguished career as an internationally recognized jazz, blues and folk singer and versatile entertainer (1940s–1970s), performing extensively in Australia and Britain. Although there are currently other Indigenous jazz and blues artists,[2] Dulcie Pitt/Georgia Lee is unique, a pioneer at a time when Indigenous peoples in general were the objects of widespread, legislated race-based discrimination.[3] Through hard work and talent she set an example for other Indigenous performers to follow.

Importantly, she also came out of a tradition of Indigenous community musicians, singers and dancers. Music and dance within Indigenous communities helped, and still help, create group cohesion. Along with providing a creative outlet for musicians and singers, it was also vital for socio-cultural

---

[*] Karl Neuenfeldt trained in Anthropology (Simon Fraser University, Canada) and Cultural Studies (Curtin University of Technology, Australia) and is active as a music researcher, producer and performer. In 2009 he was awarded the 'Sound Heritage Award' by the Australian National Film and Sound Archives.

1. Some archival items cited herein are from Dulcie Pitt's personal collection and may lack full citational details. When there is a lack of identifiable source or specific pagination, these are noted respectively as 'n.s.' (no source) and 'n.p.' (no pagination).

2. Indigenous jazz and blues orientated artists include 'Seaman' Dan (born Henry Gibson Dan), John Nicol (born George Roy Nicol), Cindy Drummond (born Cynthia Walters), Jess Beck, Crystal Mercy and Liz Cavanaugh.

3. Kidd (1997) and Beckett (1990) delve into the different yet broadly analogous experiences of Aboriginal and Torres Strait Islanders regarding discrimination.

events. This was especially true historically in non-urban areas. Aboriginal and Torres Strait Islander people in remote and regional Australia were specifically excluded from urban areas and mostly confined to rural or remote missions, reserves and home-islands. The long-term and draconian legislation was the Aboriginals Protection and Restriction of the Sale of Opium Act of 1897, with amendments in 1934 and ensuing legislations (Donovan 2002). Dulcie Pitt grew up at a time when most Indigenous people were 'living under the Act'. Although Australian Indigenous peoples had been mostly shunted 'out of sight', they were not silenced and community music provided one enriching, artistic means to socio-cultural and sometimes political ends.[4] Over the course of Dulcie Pitt/Georgia Lee's long career, the community folk music of her Indigenous heritage was something she would revisit recurrently amidst her success as one of the doyennes of jazz, blues and the entertainment industry of Australia in the mid-twentieth century.

Starting in the early decades of the twentieth century, as elsewhere in Australia (Whiteoak 1999), one peripheral strand within the Indigenous community music was jazz, although arguably only some stylistic elements of what was characterized as 'jazz' at the time predominated. That was for several possible reasons. Firstly, Australian Aboriginal and Torres Strait Islander ancestral music historically was vocally rather than instrumentally oriented, thus song lyrics and melodies took precedence over instrumental virtuosity or complex arrangements.[5] Secondly, some relatively expensive instruments utilized in jazz such as piano, saxophone, trombone or trumpet could be unavailable because Indigenous peoples' wages, if they received any, were controlled by the 'Protector' or government agencies.[6] Thus an Indigenous person wanting to purchase an expensive instrument could be refused if the request were deemed frivolous, even if affordable. Thirdly, much more common and affordable were instruments such as guitars, mandolins, banjos, ukuleles and accordions. Fourthly, aside from some Indigenous community brass bands,[7] instrumental instruction and notation training were not readily available. Fifthly, mission-based choirs were commonplace, inexpensive and directly connected

---

4. For Indigenous non-ancestral popular music in Australia see Breen (1989), Walker (2000), Ryan (2003), Dunbar-Hall and Gibson (2004), Barney (2006), Patten (2007), Neuenfeldt (2008) and Corn (2010).

5. See Barwick (2000) and York (2000) for comments on Indigenous ancestral music.

6. For this race-based restriction and the resulting Stolen Wages controversy, see the Australian Human Rights Commission (2006).

7. For a revival of some Indigenous community brass bands, see Queensland Music Festival (2014) and Ridsdale (2005).

to the processes of pacification and Christianization.[8] Consequently, singing either without accompaniment or with affordable chordal instruments such as guitars was common.

For our purposes here, we will neither attempt to define the equivocal term 'jazz' nor particularize its plethora of styles. Nonetheless, whilst its styles include Dixieland, Big Band, Free Jazz, Bebop, amongst others, a missing style in Australia is Indigenous jazz, if in fact such a style can be said to exist.[9] However, for heuristic purposes towards putting forward a description, if not a definition, it may be useful to draw an analogy with the criteria currently used officially to determine Indigenous status in Australia. These criteria are commonly accepted by community organizations and governmental agencies. They are: being of Aboriginal or Torres Strait Islander descent, identifying as an Aboriginal or Torres Strait Islander, and being accepted as such by the community in which you live, or formerly lived. Thus, analogically, if a musician or singer traces their musical heritage to jazz, identifies as a jazz musician or singer, is accepted as such by the broader community, then they *are* jazz musicians and singers. Admittedly such criteria are somewhat open to interpretation, but no more so than the innumerable attempts to define and particularize the many global styles of jazz.

Demographically, Australia has two Indigenous peoples, Aborigines and Torres Strait Islanders. The estimated total population in 2013 was 670,000 people or 3 per cent of Australia's total population (Australian Bureau of Statistics 2011). In the last decades there has been a substantial increase in people who identify as Indigenous. This is partly owing to societal and political changes brought about by the decline and eventual demise of overt, legislated race-based discrimination, the recognition of some Indigenous Native Title rights and the integration of more Indigenous peoples into 'mainstream' Australian society and its economy. However, covert discrimination and racism remain entrenched in Australian society. Indigenous peoples' health, employment, incarceration and educational statistics reveal they still occupy the bottom rung of most indices of opportunity, income and individual and communal wellbeing (Australian Productivity Commission 2014).

---

8. Magowan (2013) and Reigersberg (2013) consider dynamics and uses of Indigenous religion-based choirs.

9. See Johnson (2008) for a concise overview of Australian jazz and Bisset (1979) and Whiteoak and Scott-Maxwell (2003) for expanded coverages. For Indigenous jazz and blues see Walker (2000). See Campbell and Puruntatameri (2014), Curkpatrick (2013) and Australian Art Orchestra (http://www.aao.com.au) for examples of recent Indigenous/non-Indigenous collaborations.

Dulcie Pitt/Georgia Lee
Northern Queensland
Clinton Walker, in *Buried Country: The Story of Aboriginal Country Music* (2000), offers a plausible explanation, albeit demographically no longer accurate, of why jazz historically was and remains a peripheral music for Aborigines and also by extension Torres Strait Islanders: 'Aborigines couldn't identify with jazz because in Australia it was a white music, and a sophisticated city phenomenon at that.' He goes on to suggest, apropos Dulcie Pitt/Georgia Lee:

> But if black Australia has a great popular music tradition alternative to country (prior to the emergence of outback settlement bands in the eighties [1980s]), it is the jazz/blues/soul diva from the Deep North... Queensland's Deep North is comparable, of course, to America's Deep South, not only for its redneck racism and steamy heat but also as a musical melting pot (Walker 2000: 52).

One such 'diva' from the 'Deep North' was Georgia Lee. Born Ramer Lyra 'Dulcie' Pitt in Cairns on 22 February 1921, she passed away there in a nursing home on 21 April 2010 at the age of 89 (*Funerary Prayer Service Booklet* 2010). Her father was Douglas Pitt Junior, whose father, Douglas Pitt Senior, was from the West Indies and whose mother, Sopa Kalemo, was from the Loyalty Islands in New Caledonia. Douglas Pitt Junior (ca. 1877–1926) was born in the Torres Strait region.[10] Dulcie's mother was Myra Kemple-Hopkins whose ancestors were Scottish as well as Afghan and Aboriginal Kalkodoon from the Cloncurry area of western Queensland.[11] As a singer and dancer,[12] Dulcie was but one of several musically talented children in the immediate and extended family. During the World War Two era she and her sisters Heather and Sophie formed the Harmony Sisters and with brother Walter began branching out musically to include jazz and blues, which were particularly popular with the African-American military personnel stationed in the Cairns area.[13] As well

---

10. See Shnukal (2001) and Watkin Lui (2012) for the diaspora of Queensland's Torres Strait Islanders.

11. Hodes (1998) notes that the status of Dulcie Pitt's immediate family was an anomaly to some extent because her father had a public profile because of his sporting prowess. Furthermore, the family's skills as entertainers were well regarded by the non-Indigenous community. See Hodes (2000) for the inconsistent application of raced-based legislation experienced by some mainland Torres Strait Islanders.

12. See Costigan and Neuenfeldt (2007) regarding the 'Torres Strait hula', based on filmic depictions.

13. See Peter Dunn's comprehensive website (http://www.ozatwar.com/usarmy/africanamerican.htm) for an overview of the roles of and restrictions on African-American troops in Australia during World War Two.

as her contributing to the war effort by packing parachutes, she and her siblings entertained troops, touring as part of the US Service Organization (USO) Shows. At the time there was strict racial segregation in the United States military so a local scene of mostly racially segregated private 'house-parties' and 'non-white' musical events and dances evolved that involved Cairns' different racial and ethnic groups, Indigenous Australians and African-Americans.

North Queensland newspaper accounts document some of her early public music and dance performances, although the Indigenous community music would usually not have been remarked on because it took place outside mainstream 'white' society. Her performances were not noted as being directly connected to jazz or blues per se, but more popular and folk music oriented. As the *Cairns Post* noted: 'Trocadero Dance Palais. Tonight will be swing time, South Sea Serenade at the Trocadero. The feature of the evening will be the appearance of Miss Dulcie Pitt, who will be featured in popular song hits' (1942: 3); and, 'The Trocadero Dance Palais management will conduct a Night in Honolulu on Saturday. The special of the evening will be the appearance of Miss Dulcie Pitt dancing the Hula' (ibid.).

As the *Cairns Post* recounted, Dulcie and family members also performed at community events such as a Victory Show for the Australian Comforts Fund (ACF). Along with the Australian Red Cross, it provided aid to Australian and USA World War Two military personnel and regularly organized entertainment for fund raising:

> Two of the most popular artists of the evening, Heather and Dulcie Pitt, sang two songs, accompanied by Walter [Pitt] and Victor [Graham] on guitars... This quartette also gave an item in the second half of the programme consisting of two popular songs, and on both appearances they were most enthusiastically applauded (*Cairns Post* 1943: 4).

The Harmony Sisters also broadcast on Atherton, Queensland radio (*T.S.I.M.A. Newsletter* 1984). During her early career in North Queensland, Dulcie continued to gain valuable entertainment industry experience. In 1944, Dulcie and some of her siblings relocated to Sydney to try their luck in a larger market. Public acknowledgement that their contributions to the local 'white' community as entertainers were appreciated is reflected in the following *Cairns Post* report of a Red Cross event: 'Best of luck from us went with Dulcie Pitt when she took off Friday to join sister Heather in Sydney on a singing tour' (1944: 1).

Southern Australia
When Dulcie and several of her siblings travelled to southern Australia in 1944, there were definitely more opportunities including a stint at the Tivoli Thea-

tre as 'The Hawaiian Trio'. A later account remarked they performed under the pseudonyms 'Lahni, Luahana and Layah. Few people realised that they were Dulcie, Heather and Wally Pitt, of Cairns' (Storr 1953: n.p.). In Sydney, performances at the Tivoli Theatre and elsewhere lead to other engagements in southern Australia.[14] Although some of her siblings returned eventually to Queensland, Dulcie remained in southern Australia, and adopted her professional name, Georgia Lee. It was in southern Australia that she began to develop increasingly as a jazz and blues singer, although she was advertised under a plethora of stylistic descriptions. For example, *Canberra Times* advertisements described her as: 'Miss Georgia Lee, a Sydney croonette will also give special numbers' (1947a: 6) and as a 'Sensational Hit Parade Vocalist' (1947b: 6). A photograph of her in a Northern Territory newspaper, *Centralian Advocate* (1948: 10), is captioned 'GEORGIA LEE, attractive young blues singer'. *Music Maker* (1949: n.p.) described her as a 'Dusky Bombshell.' In the Sydney area, she performed at numerous venues such as Gleneagles and the Roosevelt Club in the Kings Cross entertainment district and with well-regarded ensembles such as Graeme Bell's Jazz Band, the Port Jackson Jazz Band, the Jazz Rebels and the bands of Jack Brokensha and George Trevare.[15]

Newspaper reports of the day in southern Australia also provide a glimpse not only of her burgeoning musical career but also her involvement in an influential circle of artistic acquaintances. The *Sunday Herald* noted: 'Torres Straits folk songs sung with guitar by MISS DULCIE PITT (Miss Georgia Lee) and MR. DONALD FRIEND were a highlight of the party given by Mr. and Mrs. Russell Drysdale' (1949: 14).[16] In 1948 Friend had sketched her and she has been described as a 'habitué of the bohemian world of artists like Donald Friend and Russell Drysdale' (Australian Broadcasting Corporation 2010).[17] She was also becoming somewhat of a celebrity as someone reported on in the media for extra-musical activities. An item in a *Radio Roundabout* column in the *ABC Weekly* recounted:

> Georgia Lee, coloured singer with the Port Jackson Jazz Band, is a dignified young woman with a cultured speaking voice. Recently she visited Canberra. A politician in the hotel accosted her and, in pidgin English, demanded: 'What for you missy come along this fella town? Where you from?' Miss Lee replied with hauteur: 'I have come from

---

14. They also toured with regional tent-shows in New South Wales and Queensland under the aegis of promoter Rex St. Louis.
15. For background on most of the Australian musicians referred to, see Johnson 1987: index.
16. Friend and Drysdale were pre-eminent Australian painters of their generation.
17. See the Art Gallery of New South Wales for the sketch.

Papua to investigate your bank nationalisation scheme [of 1948]' (Thomas 1948: 4).

An indication of her ongoing disquiet for and involvement in issues concerning racial discrimination is her performances of the dirge-like song 'Strange Fruit', generally associated with singer Billie Holiday. First recorded in 1939, it was written by Jewish-American songwriter Abel Meeropol (Lewis Allan). The lynching of two African-American men in 1930 inspired the song. 'Will Sing Banned Song' is the title of a newspaper item prior to a performance in Sydney:

> COLORED [sic] BLUES singer Georgia Lee...will sing a banned number about negro lynching at the Town Hall tonight. The song, 'Strange Fruit', is on the radio prohibited broadcasts list.[18] Georgia said: 'this song is true, and the truth hurts' (n.s. 1948: n.p.).

Georgia relocated to Melbourne from Sydney in 1949 and eventually performed with various jazz ensembles including Frank Johnson's Fabulous Dixielanders and Graeme Bell's bands. In her first jazz concert there she was advertised as: 'Jamaican Blues Singer Georgia Lee "Beauty in Sepia"' (Celebrity Jazz Concert 1949: n.p.). Performing with Bruce George's band at Claridges' nightclub, *The Beat* (1949: n.p.) reported: 'Georgia is really all out in front with any number she tackles and the boys of the band have nothing but praise for her.' She was also with a resident band for a two-year engagement at Ciro's nightclub. Jazz guitarist and arranger Bruce Clarke commented on those gigs: 'We used to sit next to each other on the bandstand. She was very glamorous, always well dressed, very popular, very good' (Walker 2000: 58). In 1951 in Melbourne, she performed at a unique event for its era: the *Aboriginal Moomba*.[19] It combined Indigenous music, drama and stories and highlights her personal and musical engagement with issues of Indigeneity. Along with the Aboriginal singer Harold Blair, whose wife she played, the event garnered positive reviews such as

> 'White Men Coo-ee Blacks at Aboriginal Concert': Applause that grew to cheering and climaxed in cooees [an Aboriginal holler] was the tribute of a packed house at the Princess Theatre on Saturday to an Australian aboriginal caste... The night was a personal success for Georgia Lee as an entertainer, and triumph for the charm and dignity of the aboriginal (n.s. 1951: n.p.).[20]

18. The banning of the song in Australia has not been verified.
19. See Ramsland and Mooney (2007) on the *Aboriginal Moomba* and Kleinert (1999) for the role of such events in fashioning Indigenous identity.
20. The use of the word 'caste' rather than 'cast' in the review is perhaps inadvertent

Another review dealt overtly with the marginalization of Indigenous peoples at the time:

> Moomba took us by storm... 'Out of the Dark' was, in the main, extraordinarily well done... The pity of it was that it was all such a revelation to the majority of us. We were delighted—because we had suddenly discovered, in a white man's theatre, something that had been in existence for thousands of years... These [stories] should be part of our own folklore. They belong to this country, and children should learn them as American youngsters learn of Pocahontas and English children of St. George and the dragon. As it is, they know far more about Sitting Bull and the Sioux, the Navajos, and the Apaches than they do about their own Australian native tribes (Doherty 1951: 15).

Approximately a month after the *Aboriginal Moomba*, she featured in a newspaper report in the *Argus* of a cultural event of a different sort: a meeting of a theatre appreciation group, under the title 'An Old Aussie can teach us':

> Miss Georgia Lee, Australian aboriginal singer...was guest of honor... She enthralled her audience with a group of Torres Island folk songs, sung in the native tongue. One was the song of a pearl diver, a song about the Barrier Reef, calling on 'big winds' to speed the boat. The third was composed by native women during [World War Two] when they saw their sons going away in khaki uniforms (1951: 5).

Before Georgia Lee left Melbourne for overseas engagements she presented a farewell recital. The breadth of her musical skills is illustrated by a detailed account of the Downbeat event (Storr 1953: n.p.).[21] The recital's content is worth presenting in some detail because it summarizes her background as a jazz, blues and folk singer:

> GEORGIA LEE With the Quintones [—] It is a pity that, to a large degree, Miss Lee's singing of the type of songs included in this group has been heard mainly in the rarified atmosphere of the night club and smart restaurant. It was decided, therefore that her first appearance on this programme should bring a selection of melodies which have proved to have been so successful in that sphere.

---

but might also unconsciously reflect the immutability of prevailing notions of race; that is, something you are born into cannot alter and will always define you as a person.

21. There are recordings of Torres Strait Islander songs she performed at the event held in the Australian Jazz Museum (Victorian Jazz Archive), Melbourne.

> GEORGIA LEE With Special Rhythms arranged by Charles Blott. [—] This group of FOLK SONGS OF THE TORRES ISLANDS have their beginning lost in history, being part of the long history of traditional music handed down by races. As a child, Georgia Lee became familiar with them for as far back as she could remember. Two or three nights in the week, the family would gather together to sing and dance to the songs which were an integral part of people performing them... She will introduce the folk songs and their stories.
>
> GEORGIA LEE With Frank Johnson's Fabulous Dixielanders [—] Songs in the Jazz idiom of the American Southern States are in ideal hands when Miss Lee and the Fabulous Dixielanders join forces. One of her most sensational appearances was when she sang in the Sydney Town Hall 'Strange Fruit', which was written [sic] by blues singer Billie Holiday, and created a storm of controversy when it was first sung in America. Tonight's choice, however, is in different vein. It is the uninhibited freedom of Dixieland, essentially in the traditional mood of the Deep South, which brings Georgia Lee's final appearance.

It also noted:

> When the famous English entertainer and folk-lore authority, Jon Pertwee,[22] visited Australia, he enlisted my [John Storr] aid in tracking down a Dulcie Pitt. Jon had been told by Allan [sic] Lomax,[23] who, with his father, John Lomax, was responsible for the collection of the American Library of Congress folk music section—the biggest in the world—to find this woman, who was known overseas to have the biggest repertoire of Torres Island folk-songs...[24] He was recording some traditional songs at the Jubilee and he met Georgia Lee. He asked her if she could tell him where he could find the woman he was seeking. She replied that he would not have to look very far—she was Dulcie Pitt.

The content and intent of the 'Folk Songs of the Torres Islands' segment noted above is of particular interest. It reinforces the notion of Georgia Lee as not

---

22. Actor Jon Pertwee played the title role of *Doctor Who* in the iconic British television series from 1970–1974.
23. The USA recordist, researcher and performer Alan Lomax lived and collected folk music in the United Kingdom and Europe for almost a decade (1950–1959) (Szwed 2011). It is unknown if Lomax and Georgia Lee ever made contact during their overlapping years in Britain.
24. There is also a Torres Island in Micronesia, but what are meant here are undoubtedly Australia's Torres Strait islands.

only a jazz and blues singer but also a community musician performing Indigenous music to urban non-Indigenous audiences. Overall, the farewell recital was indicative of her esteem in the Melbourne entertainment industry, given that such a diverse group of performers joined together to give her a musical sendoff.

Performing overseas

As the previous playbills, advertisements and reviews attest, by the mid-1950s Georgia Lee was regarded by Australian audiences, musicians, booking agents and event producers as experienced and versatile. Being ambitious, however, it was perhaps predictable she would want to expand her career by performing overseas. The diversity of her performance and musical experiences in Australia augured well for continuing her career's successes and that proved true.

After a stint performing in Colombo, Ceylon with Max Wildman's Quintet at the Copacabana nightclub, as a Queen Elizabeth the Second Coronation attraction (*Lankadipa* 1953), she travelled to Britain. The British theatre impresario Harold Fielding represented her and she promptly gained notice for her well-honed musical and performance skills. The influential British weekly music newspaper, *Melody Maker*, noted her signing with renowned bandleader Geraldo:[25]

> Georgia from 'Down Under'. Geraldo has signed up Georgia Lee, the Australian Aborigine singer who made a highly successful debut with the Geraldo Orchestra at last Sunday's jazz concert at the Festival Hall. Geraldo told the MM [*Melody Maker*]: 'I think Georgia has the greatest personality of any singer we've had in this country for years. She has terrific quality' (*Melody Maker* 1954: 1).

Britain's *New Musical Express* newspaper had a front-page photograph of Georgia Lee with Geraldo announcing her signing and directly opposite was a photograph of Billie Holiday captioned 'Billie Holiday is coming here' (1954: 1). Physically, in the photograph the two women resemble each other as to similar clothing, hairstyles, make-up and 'race' and appear to be, perhaps accidentally, gazing across the front page at each other. Such a visual juxtaposition is a possible indication of where she was being located musically and also being marketed image-wise as a singer and personality.

---

25. Born Gerald Walcan Bright (1904–1974), he led popular British orchestras and also booked musicians on trans-Atlantic cruises as an employment contractor. Highly accomplished jazz musicians, singers and arrangers he worked with included Ted Heath, John Dankworth and Walter Stott/Angela Morley.

A popular magazine, the *Australian Women's Weekly*, ran an enthusiastic article on her successes, which also mentions her use of community music:

> In her first appearance in England after she arrived last October, Georgia sang Torres Island folk songs to a sophisticated night-club audience. This was the famous Astor Club, where the announcer insisted in introducing her as a girl from Trinidad, in the West Indies. 'I was indignant,' Georgia said, 'I wanted to be known for what I was—an aboriginal girl! I'm proud of it!' (Strutton 1954: 7).

After recounting details of her background of growing up in Cairns and her many jobs while awaiting a break in the music industry ('nursemaid, waitress, sort of female roustabout—everything') the article recounted she observed: 'I don't think they realised what a long trip it has been for me from Cairns, Queensland, to London, England' (ibid.).

Return to Australia

Returning to Australia after a long stint in Britain, she took advantage of career opportunities when they arose. A major opportunity was touring with American jazz pianist and popular singer Nat King Cole on his third Australian tour in 1957.[26] Notwithstanding the professional successes she had enjoyed overseas, when back home in Australia its abiding and still legislated racial prejudices were exhibited in some journalistic accounts. One particularly egregious, albeit untraceable, public account bizarrely but tellingly mixes personal praise for her with denigration of Indigenous peoples in general—and her parentage in particular.

> When I met Georgia she was packing 'em in at Lennons Broadbeach [Hotel at Queensland's Gold Coast tourism area] and I can say I was frankly charmed. Not only is she an artist, but she's as clever as a kookaburra [Australian bird], too. Georgia in no way resembles what she genetically claims to be—the daughter of a full-blooded aboriginal. She's beautiful, tall, the possessor of a provocative figure and she moves like a leopardess. Almost before we'd been introduced I asked her—'Are you an abo because you resemble rather more, a native of Haiti?'[27] In answer to my brusque questioning, she took me through the mazes of her genealogy. Like many theatricals, Miss Lee comes of lowly parentage (n.s. ca. post 1956: n.p.).

26. It was advertised as the *Big Show* and featured Nat King Cole supported by Georgia Lee, the Gill Bros, Yolanda and Antonio Rodrigues, Joe Jenkins and Joe Martin.
27. In Australian English, 'abo', a shortening of Aborigine, and 'boong' are analogous to other racist terms such as 'nigger' (USA) or 'kaffir' (South Africa).

The Australian launch of television in 1956 also presented performance opportunities, something she was well placed to excel at because of her extensive broadcasting experience. She performed on influential television shows such as the musical variety show *Bandstand* and entertainer Graham Kennedy's *In Melbourne Tonight*.[28] In 1961 she had a leading role in a television movie, *Burst of Summer*, as one of three Indigenous actors. Although she had previously recorded individual songs as a band vocalist, in 1962 she finally had the chance to record a full album as the featured artist. Her melding of jazz and blues is highlighted in a review in the *Australian Women's Weekly*:

> JAZZ: With 'Georgia Lee Sings the Blues Down Under' (Crest LP), you're hearing possibly the most professional member of Australia's small group of stylish jazz singers. In a selection that includes both 'Pete Kelly's Blues' and 'Basin Street Blues', there are two local compositions in the blues idiom—the 'Yarra River [Blues]' and 'Down Under [Blues]'. Georgia sings as though she understands what it's all about (Baker 1963: 71).

The album, although garnering positive reviews, was aimed at jazz and blues audiences that were losing market share as rock'n'roll increasingly dictated record sales and subsequent performance opportunities.

Due to her extensive entertainment experiences, in 1976 she was able to come out of what was in effect semi-retirement to take on a major music theatre role: the Wicked Witch of the West in *The Wiz*, an African-American re-imagining and re-working of the L. Frank Baum novel *The Wonderful Wizard of Oz* and only tangentially related to the iconic Judy Garland movie of 1939, *The Wizard of Oz*. Reviewers suggested her role as Evillene was successful, 'stereophonically funny and coarse' (Jillett ca. 1976: n.p.), although to one reviewer 'the Wicked Witch of the West, seems to have turned into a Red Hot Mama' (Thomas 1976: n.p.). Obviously, directors guide an actor but her performance skills were noteworthy within the ensemble.

As perhaps a final gesture for her contributions and career as a jazz singer, in 1977 she was crowned Melbourne's *Queen of Jazz*. A newspaper picture caption noted: 'The Melbourne King of Jazz, Graeme Bell, hands over his crown to the new jazz monarch, Georgia Lee, at the fifth annual Jazz Day in the Fitzroy Gardens yesterday' (*Age* 1977: n.p.). It may have been belated recognition as by then rock'n'roll, soul and singer-songwriter folk music had become central to popular culture in Australia. Arguably, jazz became somewhat peripheral to mainstream tastes although not to its advocates and its diminished yet still

---

28. *Bandstand* was broadcast from 1958–1972; *In Melbourne Tonight* from 1957–1970.

enthusiastic audiences. What Georgia Lee had excelled at—cabarets, radio, revues and nightclubs—was no longer in as high a demand.

Retirement and belated national recognition

Dulcie Pitt eventually returned to Cairns, where she resided in her latter years in a pensioner's flat. She performed occasionally at informal and formal events. In an email message to the author (15 November 2014), jazz guitarist Michael Knopf recalled that he had performed with her on numerous occasions and although she no longer played guitar, she still sang: 'Whenever we played together informally the tunes were [songs such as] "Summertime", "Nature Boy". When she did perform for small community gatherings, her stage presence was still strong with gestures and vocal boldness, etc.' He also recalled she would sometimes reminisce: 'Occasionally she would speak generally about being well regarded... I remember her eyes lighting up with enthusiasm when she did talk about the past. It was obviously of importance to her but she did not have enthusiasm for re-entering performance at her age.' However, she still did some formal performances, as he recollected: 'In 1986 she did a show under my coordination at the [Baha'i] Peace Expo in Atherton [Queensland] with jazz musos [musicians] from Cairns.' An account of the event and its international concert observed: 'Georgia Pitt, local Baha'i jazz and blues singer, was a tremendous hit, being called back for encores' (*Baha'i News* 1986: 676).

There were commendable, if somewhat belated, forms of national recognition. In 2010 the National Film and Sound Archive (NFSA) of Australia added *Georgia Lee Sings the Blues Down Under* to its Sounds of Australia register of historically important Australian recordings (NFSA Title 511557), only shortly before she passed away. Also in 2010, the Australian Broadcasting Corporation presented a radio documentary on her life and music, *Introducing Miss Georgia Lee*, on *Awaye*, the Indigenous Art and Culture programme (Australian Broadcasting Corporation, 2010).[29] Her album was also belatedly recognized in 2010 by the inclusion of her recording of 'Blues in the Night' on Australia's QANTAS Airline's *The Spirit* in-flight entertainment service (QANTAS 2010: 141).

Details of Georgia Lee's private life remain vague in contrast to her well-documented professional life. However, in the re-released *Georgia Lee Sings the Blues Down Under* liner notes (Aztec Music VIBE1), Walker (2009) said: 'Little

---

29. Daniel Browning and Phil McKellar produced. The author assisted with research and supplied information and photographs from Dulcie Pitt's personal collection, which she had given him to scan electronically in 1999 (Pitt 1999).

is known about Georgia Lee's personal life, save that in 1958, after the "King" Cole tour, she suffered a nervous breakdown.' The original liner notes also allude to stress leading to a breakdown. In an obituary Browning (2010: 10) commented on her private life: 'She was an exotic and glamorous beauty, yet shy and nervous... Lee never married. Unsurprisingly there were many offers, all politely refused.'

Discussion

Discussing, especially briefly, a long, multifaceted and eventful career and life such as lived by Dulcie Pitt and her professional alter ego Georgia Lee can be a challenge. Therefore, it is useful to pose several questions as a way of providing some structure and focus. Firstly, does the musical style of Indigenous jazz exist in Australia? Secondly, why is she an important and pioneering performer in Australian and Indigenous jazz? Thirdly, how did music, race and gender intersect in her career? The questions overlap to some degree because the musical and the extra-musical are two complex strands in her career and life.

For historical reasons, jazz has not had a major influence on Indigenous music for some of the reasons noted earlier. Thus it is not currently a readily identifiable style of Australian jazz. However, with increased access to formal musical education and a predominantly urbanizing population, there is no reason Indigenous musicians cannot chose jazz as their musical style—if it can substantiate and validate their life experiences and socio-cultural preferences. Direct involvement by non-Indigenous jazz musicians in community music projects may stimulate that process. Having role models is an important element in fostering interest in any musical style and accomplished jazz musicians such as James Morrison, Paul Grabowsky and members of the Australian Art Orchestra can provide that kind of personalized inspiration.

Regarding the second question, it is obvious Dulcie Pitt/Georgia Lee's musical accomplishments are noteworthy. Performing with top-notch Australian and British jazz musicians and bandleaders and across a range of performance formats demonstrates that she had the necessary talent, skills and work ethic. Similar to Harold Blair (opera) and Jimmy Little (country) in their particular styles, she was arguably the first Indigenous singer to be treated as an equal when it came to jazz and blues: that is, equally talented and equally capable of performing with musical proficiency and emotional honesty, holding audiences' attention and entertaining them. However, the difficulty of categorizing her music is indicated by varied designations over the course of her career such as: 'croonette', 'Sensational Hit Parade Vocalist', 'colored [sic] blues singer', 'Australia's Lena Horne', 'Queen of the Night Clubs'. Arguably, categorization was complicated by her eclectic musical tastes and how that impacted on her professional image.

In regard to the third question, music, race and gender undeniably intersected in Dulcie Pitt/Georgia Lee's career and in complex ways. Regarding music, as a musician nurtured in the context of community music, she regularly integrated the music of her childhood into her performances, even in unlikely settings such as Australian and British nightclubs. Newspaper accounts and advertisements make it clear she did not hide key parts of her cultural heritage; rather, she featured them.

Regarding 'race', it was also a site of some complexity, and confusion. Arguably her heritage of Aboriginal, Afghan, Scottish, West Indian, New Caledonian and Torres Strait Islander ancestors was too multifaceted for the desired monochromatic world of the White Australia Policy and race-based legislation.[30] This complexity and confusion are shown in descriptions of her 'race' as variously: 'Jamaican', 'Jamaican-Australian', 'Negro', 'black', 'abo', 'coloured', 'quartercast', 'daughter of an Indian mother and Jamaican father', 'a girl from Trinidad' and 'Dusky Bombshell'. Concerning Indigeneity per se, Weare (2010) observed: 'She was quite a well-known performer of jazz around Melbourne and Sydney. But in those days her indigenousness wasn't really concentrated on. It was the sort of thing that she was more or less just a dark skinned woman who could have been from the Caribbean or America or anywhere really.'

Regarding gender, there is also a plethora of varied descriptions of her physicality, attire and comportment, some which reiterate racialized stereotypes. For example, 'tall, amply-curved with creamy brown skin. Her eyes are black and expressive, her crinkly hair is drawn back into a bun' (*Big Show* 1957: n.p.); 'Beauty in Sepia' (Celebrity Jazz Concert ca. 1949: n.p.); and, 'Her dark eyes and shapely brown hands are so impressive, it's a pity her public can't see as well as hear her' (Lethbridge 1954: 2). Such descriptions tend to the exotic, especially in an era when racial 'purity' was a governmental and societal obsession in Australia.

Conclusion

Dulcie Pitt/Georgia Lee's career and life exhibit two key roles: firstly, as an entertainer and singer of high quality and wide experience; and secondly, as

---

30. See Reynolds (2003) and Ganter (2006) on race relations in Australia's tropical regions, apropos someone of mixed heritage from north Queensland such as Dulcie Pitt. See Lake and Reynolds (2008) for how European settler colonies dealt globally with issues of race.

an advocate for Indigenous peoples via her public profile. One of her most telling comments of the complementarity of the dual roles, and a realistic if somewhat discouraging assessment of making a change in Australian race-based attitudes, is contained in the following quotation:

> 'I feel that if I can make my name as a singer I might be able to help others... aborigines here have been ignored and drifted into obscurity. It is only in the last few years that the white people have really discovered the culture of aborigines and realised they are human beings. I do want to help on this change, if I can'. 'But', she added sadly, 'I am afraid it will not be completed during my lifetime' (Goddard 1949: n.p.).

Achieving a level of success allowed her to make those kinds of statements in public in Australia in the mid-twentieth century when Indigenous peoples were still living 'under the Act'. For that reason alone she was, and is, important as an Indigenous musical and extra-musical pioneer. Arguably, for Dulcie Pitt/Georgia Lee jazz, blues and folk were about more than merely the music. They were also about an opportunity to live a life as a professional entertainer, where even though racial and societal equality were more aspirational than reality in her era, it was 'the only profession in which whites and colored [sic] people can meet on equal ground' (n.s. ca. 1948: n.p.). Finally, when Indigenous peoples were literally and figuratively on the fringes of Australian society, Dulcie Pitt/Georgia Lee was centre stage. As she said in the interview above: 'Incidentally I'm deeply proud I'm colored [sic]. I wouldn't change skins with anybody.'

References

Age (Melbourne) (1977) 'Royalty...and all the Jazz'. 17 January.
Argus (Melbourne) (1951) 'An Old Aussie can Teach us'. 20 July.
Art Gallery of New South Wales. Georgia Lee by Donald Friend. http://www.artgallery.nsw.gov.au/collection/works/8089/ (accessed 25 January 2015).
Australian Art Orchestra (2014) http://www.aao.com.au (accessed 25 January 2015).
Australian Broadcasting Corporation (2010) *The Awaye Program*. http://www.abc.net.au/radionational/programs/awaye/introducing-miss-georgia-lee/3670634 (accessed 25 January 2015).
Australian Bureau of Statistics (2011) *Estimates of Aboriginal and Torres Strait Islander Australians*. http://www.abs.gov.au/ausstats/abs@.nsf/mf/3238.0.55.001 (accessed 25 January 2015).
Australian Human Rights Commission (2006) *Submission to the Senate Legal and Constitutional References Committee Inquiry into Stolen Wages*. Human Rights and Equal Opportunity Commission, Sydney. https://www.humanrights.gov.au/inquiry-stolen-wages (accessed 25 January 2015).

Australian Productivity Commission (2014) *Overcoming Indigenous Disadvantage: Key Indicators 2014.* http://www.pc.gov.au/research/recurring/overcoming-indigenous-disadvantage/key-indicators-2014 (accessed 25 January 2015).
Baha'i News (1986) 'Australia Peace Expo "Overwhelms" Atherton'. August.
Baker, Ainslie (1963) 'Listen Here with Ainslie Baker: "Jazz"'. *Australian Women's Weekly.* 27 March.
Barney, Katelyn (2006) 'Women Singing Up Big: The Growth of Contemporary Music Recordings by Indigenous Australian Women Artists'. *Australian Aboriginal Studies* 1: 44–56.
Barwick, Linda (2000) 'Music'. In *The Oxford Companion to Aboriginal Art and Culture*, ed. Sylvia Kleinert and Margo Neale, 328–48. South Melbourne: Oxford University Press.
Beat, The (Melbourne) (1949) 'Georgia Lee at Claridges'. 25 October.
Beckett, J. (1990) *Torres Strait Islanders: Custom and Colonialism.* Melbourne: Cambridge University Press.
Big Show (1957) [Nat King Cole 3rd Australian Tour] Playbill.
Bisset, A. (1979) *Black Roots, White Flowers: A History of Jazz in Australia.* Sydney: Golden Press.
Breen, M., ed. (1989) *Our Place, Our Music.* Canberra: Aboriginal Studies Press.
Browning, Daniel (2010) 'Trailblazing Indigenous Singer Belatedly Crowned Queen of Jazz'. *Age* (Melbourne). 15 May.
Cairns Post (1942) 'Trocadero Dance Palais'. 16 May.
—(1943) 'A.C.F. [Australian Comforts Fund] Victory Show'. 4 October.
—(1944) 'Round the Red Cross Clock'. 11 November.
Campbell, Genevieve, and Teresita Kilapayu Puruntatameri (2014) 'When Performance Comes before Research: Reflecting on a Tiwi/Non-Tiwi Musical and Research Collaboration'. In *Collaborative Ethnomusicology: New Approaches to Music Research between Indigenous and Non-Indigenous Australians*, ed. Katelyn Barney, 129–46. Melbourne: Lyrebird Press.
Canberra Times (1947a) 'What People are Doing: Diggers' Ball'. 19 November.
—(1947b) North Canberra R.S.L. Memorial Fund. Display Advertising. 16 December.
Celebrity Jazz Concert (ca. 1949) 'First Appearance in Melbourne of Jamaican Blues Singer Georgia Lee [:] "Beauty in Sepia"'. Display Advertising.
Centralian Advocate (Alice Springs) (1948) 'Georgia Lee'. 8 October.
Corn, Aaron (2010) 'Land, Song, Constitution: Exploring Expressions of Ancestral Agency, Intercultural Diplomacy and Family Legacy in the Music of Yothu Yindi with Mandawuy Yunupingu'. *Popular Music* 29/1: 81–102. http://dx.doi.org/10.1017/S0261143009990390
Costigan, Lyn, and Karl Neuenfeldt (2007) '"Doing the Torres Strait Hula": The Adaptation and Perseverance of "Hula" in an Australian Performance Culture'. In *Oceanic Encounters: Essays in Honor of Mervyn McLean*, ed. Richard Moyle, 97–108. Auckland: Research in Anthropology and Linguistics, University of Auckland.
Curkpatrick, Samuel (2013) 'Productive Ambiguity: Fleshing out the Bones in Yolngu Manikay "Song" Performance, and the Australian Art Orchestra's "Crossing Roper Bar"'. *Critical Studies in Improvisation* 2. http://www.criticalimprov.com/article/view/2694/3265 (accessed 27 January 2015).

Doherty, Frank (1951) 'Moomba Took us by Storm'. *Argus* (Melbourne). 30 June.
Donovan, V. (2002) *The Reality of a Dark History: From Contact and Conflict to Cultural Recognition*. Brisbane: Arts Queensland.
Dunbar-Hall, P., and C. Gibson (2004) *Deadly Sounds, Deadly Places: Contemporary Aboriginal Music in Australia*. Sydney: University of New South Wales Press.
Dunn, Peter. http://www.ozatwar.com/usarmy/africanamerican.htm (accessed 27 January 2015).
Funerary Prayer Service Booklet: Ramer Lyra 'Dulcie' Pitt (2010) St. John's Anglican Church, Cairns, Queensland. Father John Simmons officiating. 29 April.
Ganter, R. (2006) *Mixed Relations*. Crawley, Western Australia: University of Western Australia Press.
Goddard, Anthea (1949) 'Meet Georgia Lee'. *WOMAN*. 11 April.
Hodes, Jeremy (1998) *Torres Strait Islander Migration to Cairns before World War II*. Master's of Literature. Rockhampton: Central Queensland University.
—(2000) 'Anomaly in Torres Strait: Living "under the Act" and the Attraction of the Mainland'. *Journal of Australian Studies* 64: 166–72. http://dx.doi.org/10.1080/14443050009387568
Jillett, Neil (ca. 1976). 'The Wiz of the Wicked West' (n.s.).
Johnson, Bruce (1987) *The Oxford Companion to Australian Jazz*. Melbourne: Oxford University Press.
—(2008) 'Australian Jazz: An Overview'. In *Sounds of Then, Sounds of Now: Popular Music in Australia*, ed. Shane Homan and Tony Mitchell, 113–30. Hobart, Tasmania: Australian Clearinghouse for Youth Studies.
Kidd, R. (1997) *The Way We Civilize*. St. Lucia, Queensland: University of Queensland Press.
Kleinert, Sylvia (1999) 'An Aboriginal Moomba: Remaking History'. *Continuum* 13/3: 345–57. http://dx.doi.org/10.1080/10304319909365806
Lake, M., and H. Reynolds (2008) *Drawing the Global Colour Line: White Men's Countries and the International Challenge of Racial Equality*. Cambridge: Cambridge University Press. http://dx.doi.org/10.1017/CBO9780511805363
Lankapida (Colombo) (1953) 'August Festivities Supplement'. 4 August.
Lethbridge, Ann (1954) 'Australians can All be Proud of Georgia Lee'. *Courier-Mail* (Brisbane), Letter to the Editor Section, 28 December.
Magowan, Fiona (2013) 'Mission Music as a Mode of Intercultural Transmission, Charisma and Memory in Northern Australia'. In *The Oxford Handbook of Music and World Christianities*, ed. Suzel Reily and Jonathan Dueck, 45–68. Oxford: Oxford University Press. http://dx.doi.org/10.1093/oxfordhb/9780199859993.013.001
Melody Maker (London) (1954) 'Georgia from "Down Under"'. 6 February.
Music Maker (1949) 'Dusky Bombshell'. Display Advertising.
Neuenfeldt, Karl (2008) '"Ailan Style": An Overview of the Contemporary Music of Torres Strait Islanders'. In *Sounds of Then, Sounds of Now: Australian Popular Music*, ed. Shane Homan and Tony Mitchell, 167–80. Hobart, Tasmania: Australian Clearing House for Youth Studies.
New Musical Express (London) (1954) Front Page. 5 February.
n.s. (no source) (ca. 1948) 'Will Sing Banned Song'.
n.s. (1951) 'White Men Coo-ee Blacks at Aboriginal Concert'.

n.s. (ca. post-1956) [Lennons Broadbeach Hotel Queensland] Review of Georgia Lee performance.

Patten, Herb (2007) 'Stories of Aboriginal Heritage through a Multi Media Exploration of Gumleaf Music'. Master's Thesis, RMIT (Royal Melbourne Institute of Technology), Melbourne.

Pitt, Dulcie (Georgia Lee) (1999) Interview with Karl Neuenfeldt and Nelson Conboy. 2 October, Cairns.

QANTAS: The Australian Way Magazine (2010) Inflight Entertainment. Sydney: ACP Magazines. July.

Queensland Music Festival (2014). 'Yarrabah Band Festival: Celebrating the Sounds of Yarrabah'. Promotional poster. http://www.qmf.org.au/public/?id=300 (accessed 22 October 2014).

Ramsland, John, and Christopher Mooney (2007) 'Out of the Dark: The First Successful All-Black Musical: Aboriginal Celebrity and Protest'. *Victorian Historical Journal* 1: 63–79.

Reigersberg, Muriel Swijghuisen (2013) 'Christian Choral Singing in Aboriginal Australia: Gendered Absence, Emotion and Place'. In *Performing Gender, Place and Emotion in Music: Global Perspectives*, ed. Fiona Magowan and Louise Wrazen, 85–108. Rochester, NY: University of Rochester Press.

Reynolds, H. (2003) *North of Capricorn*. Crows Nest, NSW: Allen and Unwin.

Ridsdale, G. (2005) *Blow'im: The Story of the Yarrabah Brass Band*. Brisbane: Queensland Arts Council.

Ryan, Robin (2003) 'Jamming on the Gumleaves in the Bush "Down Under": Black Tradition, White Novelty?' *Popular Music and Society* 3: 285–304. http://dx.doi.org/10.1080/0300776032000116969

Shnukal, Anna (2001) 'Torres Strait Islanders'. In *Multicultural Queensland 2001: 100 Years, 100 Communities, a Century of Contributions*, ed. Maximilian Brandle, 21–35. Brisbane: Queensland Government.

Storr, John (1953) 'An Appreciation: Farewell Appearance of Georgia Lee'. Playbill, 8 May.

Strutton, Bill (1954) 'Dreamtime for Georgia: Aboriginal Girl Singer's Success in London'. *Australian Women's Weekly*. 24 March.

Sunday Herald (Sydney) (1949, no other date) 'Artists' Farewell: Parties of the Week' [The World of Women section].

Szwed, J. (2011) *Alan Lomax: The Man who Recorded the World*. New York: Viking.

Thomas, Helen (1976) '"The Wiz" without that Rainbow'. *Age* (Melbourne). Showscene section, 1 January.

Thomas, Wilfred (1948) 'Radio Roundabout'. *The ABC Weekly*. 3 April.

T.S.I.M.A [Torres Strait Islander Media Association] *Newsletter* (1984) 'Georgia Lee Story'. 5 December.

Walker, C. (2000) *Buried Country: The Story of Aboriginal Country Music*. Sydney: Pluto Press.

—(2009) Liner notes for Re-release of *Georgia Lee Sings the Blues Down Under*.

Watkin Lui, Felecia (2012) 'My Island Home: Re-presenting Identities for Torres Strait Islanders Living outside the Torres Strait'. *Journal of Australian Studies* 2: 141–53.

Weare, Nick. (2010) 'Indigenous Artist Celebrated after 50 Years'. Australian Broadcasting

Corporation (Radio National, *The World Today*). Reporter Annie Guest. Broadcast 9 October.

Whiteoak, J. (1999) *Playing Ad Lib: Improvisatory Music in Australia 1836–1970*. Strawberry Hills, Sydney: Currency Press.

Whiteoak, J., and A. Scott-Maxwell, eds. (2003) *Currency Companion to Music and Dance in Australia*. Sydney: Currency House.

York, Frank (2000) 'Torres Strait Islander Music'. In *The Oxford Companion to Aboriginal Art and Culture*, ed. Sylvia Kleinert and Margo Neale, 340–44. South Melbourne: Oxford University Press.

Discography

Lee, Georgia. *Georgia Lee Sings the Blues Down Under*. 1962. Crest Records. CRT 12-LP004. Album.

—*Georgia Lee Sings the Blues Down Under* [re-release]. 2009. Aztec Music. VIBE1. CD.

—*Three Torres Strait Islander Songs*. 1951. Australian Jazz Museum (Victorian Jazz Archive, Melbourne). Archival 7-inch tape.

—Bruce Clarke Quintet. *St. Louis Blues*. 1951. JZT JA-62.

—Bruce Clarke Quintet. *Blue Moon*. 1951. JZT JA-61.

—Graeme Bell Jazz Concert Radio Series. *Basin Street Blues*. 1950. SWG S-4504. Episodes 1 and 5.

—Graeme Bell Jazz Concert Radio Series. *Mean To Me*. 1950. PMDO-7518. Episodes 1 and 5.

—Graeme Bell Jazz Concert Radio Series. *Nobody Knows You When You're Down and Out*. 1950. SWG S-1004. Episodes 1 and 5.

—Graeme Bell Jazz Concert Radio Series. *It Had To Be You, Careless Love Blues, One and Two Blues, Tuxedo Junction*. 1949. SWG S-4511, S-1268, S-1268, FEST FL-31642, CAL R66-119. Episodes 10 and 14.

—Graeme Bell Jazz Concert Radio Series. *You Made Me Love You*. 1949. SWG S-1004. Episodes 19 and 23.

—Graeme Bell Jazz Concert Radio Series. *Sleepy Time Gal*. 1949. SWG JCS-33753. Episodes 19 and 23.

—Graeme Bell Jazz Concert Radio Series. *I'll See You In My Dreams*. 1949. SWG S-1004. Episodes 19 and 23.

—Graeme Bell Jazz Concert Radio Series. *Time On My Hands*. 1949. SWG S-1004. Episodes 19 and 23.

Musicians

11 Examining the legend and music of Australian saxophonist, Frank Smith

Ralph Whiteoak*

Introduction

The reputation of Frank Smith as one of the most talented, influential and original-sounding musicians of his time has been legendary in Australian jazz circles. Despite the breadth of his musical career, musical interests and influence on others, he was best known as a jazz saxophonist. Bruce Johnson suggested in 1983 that 'The legendary Frank Smith...deserves a chapter, if not a book, in the history of Australian jazz' (Johnson 1983: 15). The 'legend', however, exists primarily in the memories of his contemporaries, in the scattered fragments of his recorded musical output (held for the most part in private collections) and in comments sparsely distributed throughout various print sources on jazz in Australia.[1] There has always been a natural tendency in jazz history to exaggerate the attributes and achievements of those whose lives are least documented by confirmed facts. This tendency can be traced back in jazz to its first major figure, Buddy Bolden, who is the subject of many grandiose stories and claims, but far fewer confirmable facts (Marquis 1978). Legendary tales, some of them seemingly contradictory, are also told and retold about Smith, even though many of his contemporaries are still alive and performing today.

This chapter briefly sketches out Smith's career before critiquing certain stories and claims about his life, career, talent and contribution to jazz in Aus-

---

* Ralph Whiteoak is a PhD candidate at Sir Zelman Cohen School of Music Conservatorium, Monash University. He received a Masters in Music Performance in 2005 at Melbourne University—Victorian College of the Arts. Previous publication related activity include: 'Saxophone' in *Currency Companion to Music and Dance in Australia* (Currency House Inc., 2003) and the preparation of musical examples for John Whiteoak, *Playing Ad Lib: Improvisatory Music in Australia, 1836–1970* (Currency Press, 1999).

1. The most informative published sources are Johnson (1987: 254–55, see also Index) and Bisset (1987: 105–109).

tralia in an attempt to clarify uncertainties that have so far shrouded his past. Three primary questions are addressed in this process: why did Smith gain a reputation for originality in an era in which sounding like white or black American modern jazz legends was the benchmark of success? What was it about his approach to music (in particular his engagement with Hindemith's theories) and saxophone playing that created so much peer respect and 'legend' status and what was the special nature of the influence he is said to have exerted over many talented musical colleagues of his era? Smith's place in the pantheon of pioneer modernists in Australian jazz is based on a very considerable, diverse and often anecdotal range of recollected strengths and idiosyncrasies. These range from strictly musical qualities, including his extraordinary ear, his virtuosic execution his harmonic innovativeness and his mentoring generosity, to more personal characteristics including a notoriously dishevelled instrument and casualness about its treatment. It is impossible to cover the full range of the Smith legend here, so although I encompass a number of aspects of his reputation, my primary analytical musical focus will be on the one aspect of his musicianship, for which there happens to survive documentary evidence in the form of a body of hitherto unpublished sound recordings.[2]

Career

Frank Smith was born Francis Percival Schmich in Sydney on 30 July 1927 and died of a heart attack at his flat in St Kilda in Melbourne on 18 February 1974 at a mere 46 years of age.[3] The first documented reference to Smith entering the Sydney music scene dates to 1946,[4] which was the same year that Australians first began to become aware of the revolutionary new form of jazz called 'bebop' (Norman 1946: 1), a term that rapidly became the rallying cry for a self-aware Australian modern jazz or 'boppers' movement (Bisset 1987: 88–113). Over the remainder of the 1940s he engaged in the transient work available to professional musicians of that period, including dance-band circuits, nightclubs and Sydney jazz concerts[5] and, in 1950, he performed and recorded with the visiting American trumpeter Rex Stewart[6] (Mitchell 1988: 197). Through this paid work and private jam sessions, Smith undoubtedly

2. The Smith family entrusted me with Smith's archive of more than 200 reel-to-reel studio tapes which I continue to analyse and digitize.
3. See the biographical entry in Johnson (1987: 254–55) for additional detail.
4. *Music Maker*, 20 December 1946: 24. He is listed as the tenor player with the 12-piece band, Reg. Pederson and his Colossal Casuals.
5. *Music Maker*, January 1949: 33. Smith performed in Ralph Mallen's Orchestra 'Accent on Jive' concert, Sydney Town Hall.
6. *Music Maker*, December 1949: 3.

gained a modicum of fame among Sydney musicians and the dancing, night-clubbing and jazz concert-going public as a leading modernist. A bout of Bell's Palsy in late 1951[7] briefly threatened his advancement, but by 1954, in addition to leading club and jazz concert work, he was making regular appearances at the Australian Jazz Club in Sydney,[8] leading the 'Frank Smith Cool Quartet' at the Rivoli Ballroom[9] and playing at the Sydney Trocadero under the leader/trombonist often described as the 'Father of Australian Jazz', Frank Coughlan.[10] In 1957, Smith won the *Music Maker* poll for best alto saxophonist[11] and towards the end of the 1950s he was making impressive and influential appearances at Sydney's most progressive jazz venue, El Rocco (Johnson 1983: 15), gaining regular radio and television work[12] and backing visiting headline acts, including the American bop band leader, Billy Eckstine.[13]

In 1960 Smith relocated to Melbourne to take up a residency at the prestigious Embers nightclub in Toorak. He was soon engaged in Melbourne television orchestra work and sessions at the Jingle Workshop, which was run by the modern jazz guitarist, Bruce Clarke. He then formed his own sound and film production company, Frank Smith Productions that, like Clarke's Jingle Workshop, employed leading jazz and studio musicians.[14] By the late 1960s, Smith was doing very few public performances but, after winding up Frank Smith Productions in the early 1970s, he resumed professional music-making until his premature death in 1974 whilst on tour with Johnny Mathis.[15]

Smith and the saxophone

From a jazz history perspective, by far the most important aspect of the Smith legend is the technical brilliance and originality of his saxophone playing and

---

7. See 'Sydney Spotlight', *Music Maker*, September 1951: 22. Confirmed in personal communications with Beverly Smith, 7 November 2004.
8. J. Edgecombe, 'Australian Jazz Club', *Music Maker*, July 1954: 32.
9. '"Metronome" on Fridays', *Music Maker*, April 1954: 6.
10. 'Frank Coughlan Returns', *Music Maker*, September 1954: 6.
11. '"M.M." Readers Name Winners in 1957 Australian Musicians Poll', *Music Maker*, July 1957: 1. See also Example 1 below.
12. '"Jazz for Pleasure" from A.B.C.', *Music Maker*, June 1958: 2.
13. *Music Maker*, November 1958: 35. Eckstine and his band were reportedly billeted at Smith's parent's house because hotels in Sydney would not accept coloured people as guests. Taped interview with Ken White, Victoria, 8 May 2004. The White Australia Policy was not fully abandoned until 1973.
14. Reel-to-reel tape annotations from Frank Smith Productions' tape archive in possession of author.
15. Personal communication with Reg Walsh, Melbourne, 17 February 2004.

improvisations. What then was his actual approach to saxophone playing and how do (or did) his contemporaries perceive his abilities as a jazz saxophonist?

Smith received lessons from the Australian saxophone guru, Rolf Pommer (Johnson 1987: 324), at the beginning of his career, along with tips on breathing from pioneer Australian jazz trombonist and later Professor of Trombone, Harry Larson (Bisset 1987: 107). Furthermore, his enquiring mind compelled him to seek advice by correspondence from the world-famous classical virtuoso and Professor of Saxophone at the Paris Conservatory, Marcel Mule.[16] Through his communications with Mule and the study of recommended recordings, methods and, no doubt, some related literature, Smith developed a classical approach to saxophone playing that was radically different from that generally taken by Australian jazz saxophonists. On Mule's advice he adopted a mouthpiece 'setup' using a shaved-down number one reed. This is a very soft reed since most professionals use sizes ranging from strength two and a half to four. The theory is that a light reed requires less air to make it vibrate. Smith's approach meant that it was impossible to use any embouchure pressure: the embouchure had to be constant all over the range of the saxophone. So all Smith had to do was breathe.[17]

Smith used a Martin Committee alto saxophone[18] with an average sized Berg Larsen mouthpiece,[19] and even had an endorsement deal with Berg Larsen dating back to 1949.[20] He was able to produce an enormous amount of volume when required, regardless of the mouthpiece on his shaved-down number one reed, and he also had every recording of the Decca series *Marcel Mule Demonstrates the Mark VI*. His former student, Graeme Lyall, said that, by 1960, he was more interested in Mule than jazz saxophone giants such as Charlie Parker and Cannonball Adderley.[21]

Smith was renowned for having little regard for the maintenance of his instruments. Unsubstantiated tales of Smith leaving his alto in the pond at The Embers overnight in preference to packing it up are given some credence in other reports.[22] Bob Bertles recalls becoming curious about the strange way he had of standing when he played:

16. Taped interview with Graeme Lyall, Western Australia, 14 April 2004. Also see Bisset (1987: 107).
17. Taped interview with Graeme Lyall, Western Australia, 14 April 2004.
18. This saxophone is still held by the Smith family.
19. Taped interview with Graeme Lyall, Western Australia, 14 April 2004.
20. 'Advertisement for Berg Larson saxophone mouthpieces', *Music Maker*, July 1949: 25.
21. Taped interview with Graeme Lyall, Western Australia, 14 April 2004.
22. Personal communication with Smith enthusiast/researcher, Mal Eustice, South Australia, 13 October 2004.

> Frank was playing on a silver Martin and he had this funny stance, all bent over. So after the set finished I went over and introduced myself and I said; 'That's an interesting way you have got of playing, why do you play like that?' And Frank replied; 'Well I...have to because I've got no springs on the horn so I'm relying on gravity to open the keys'.[23]

Australian jazz legend Don Burrows recalls that:

> His sax was a web of elastic bands, almost no springs. He loved to be sent up about it. He would turn up to jobs with this sax barely holding together and people would say, 'Shit! Frank!' in horror at the state of his horn. But it made no difference, as it never hampered his playing at all.[24]

Despite Smith's seeming contempt for the welfare of his instrument, by the mid-1950s he was considered to be the best modern jazz saxophonist Australia had ever produced. Bob Bertles, who in the 1960s became one of a younger generation of hard boppers, evocatively describes the first time he heard Frank Smith playing as follows:

> He was about 12 years older than me and well established in the Sydney music scene. I remember that I walked in and he was playing 'All the Things You Are' at one hundred miles an hour and, in those days, 'All the Things You Are' was considered to be a very difficult tune. He was flying, like Bird, he was Australia's answer to Charlie Parker and I thought: 'Jesus'.[25]

Smith was also admired by his American counterparts and, in particular, Oscar Peterson. During Peterson's stint at The Embers he would sit at the front of the stage listening to Smith play. One night Peterson and his rhythm section of Ray Brown and Ed Thigpen seamlessly pushed the house band off the stage to play with Smith.[26] When Peterson went back to America, he warned alto saxophonist Benny Carter that there was a guy down there by the name of Frank Smith who could blow him off the stand.[27] When Carter finally arrived at The

---

23. Taped interview with Bob Bertles, Victoria, 11 December 2004. Also confirmed in Bisset (1987: 106).
24. Telephone interview with Don Burrows, 13 April 2005.
25. Taped interview with Bob Bertles, Victoria, 11 December 2004. See also Bisset (1987: 106) and Sharpe (2008: 159–60).
26. Taped interview with Professor Ted Nettelbeck, South Australia, 13 October 2004.
27. Taped interview with Graeme Lyall, Western Australia, 14 April 2004. Also see Bisset (1987: 109) citing Lyall.

Embers he burst into the club looking for Smith. Upon finding Smith he said 'So you're the guy who is going to blow my arse off!' (Bisset 1987: 109).[28]

Despite his jazz scene status as one of the 'first Titans of Australian modern jazz' (Johnson 1983: 15) and a gifted saxophone teacher, Smith was unable to gain much financial reward from playing or the academic recognition needed to get a teaching position at the Sydney Conservatorium (Bisset 1997: 107). When the 1957 *Music Maker* poll winners recorded a poll-winners' album for EMI Parlophone,[29] Smith was driving a taxi to make ends meet.[30] Bruce Clarke said of Smith that 'he knew he was a great musician, but no one had asked him to be great, and that was a particular frustration to him'.[31] It was probably why he advised his students to leave Australia before it was too late.[32]

Smith and Hindemith

Frank Smith attributed his formidable skill as a jazz musician to studying the teachings of Paul Hindemith under the tutelage of the composer, Raymond Hanson, at the Sydney Conservatorium.[33] Hanson graduated from the Sydney Conservatorium in 1947 and started teaching aural training there the following year, later teaching harmony, counterpoint and composition (Murdoch 1976: 112). It is not clear when Smith began studying with Hanson, but *Music Maker* of October 1952 sardonically alludes to Smith's studies under Hanson as overly progressive:

> Frank Smith, studious alto stylist at present studying theory with Ray Hanson at the Con, has bought a block of land at Springwood in the Blue Mountains, where he can further his meditation on flattened fifths and strangulated eighteenths.[34]

Hanson often sat in with the local jazz players in the late 1940s, including Smith. He apparently only knew a few ballads, but the changes he employed were so advanced that Smith was the only one capable of following them.[35]

---

28. Taped interview with Graeme Lyall, Western Australia, , 14 April 2004. See also taped interview with Professor Ted Nettelbeck, South Australia, 13 October 2004 and Bisset (1987: 109).
29. *Music Maker 1957 All Stars*, Sydney, July 1957, Parlophone PMDO-7511.
30. Telephone interview with Don Burrows, 13 April 2005. Also see Bisset (1987: 105).
31. Taped interview with Bruce Clarke, Melbourne, 6 May 2005.
32. Taped interview with Barry Duggan, Victoria, 14 September 2010.
33. Taped interview with Graeme Lyall, Western Australia, 14 April 2004.
34. 'Petits Morceaux', *Music Maker*, October 1952: 22.
35. Taped interview with Graeme Lyall, Western Australia, 14 April 2004. Also see Bisset (1987: 107).

11 Examining the legend and music of Australian saxophonist, Frank Smith

Example 1: Transcription of Frank Smith's alto saxophone solo in 'Ockeration' (composed by John Bamford) from on the album '*Jazz in Australia*', *The Music Maker 1957 All Stars*, recorded Sydney, July 1957 (transcription by author)

Smith told Graeme Lyall that Hanson would 'sit in' wearing his bow tie and play the most 'unbelievable' changes to standards Smith had ever heard, likening it to the playing of the early avant-garde jazz pianist Lenny Tristano.[36] Under Hanson's tutelage, Smith worked through Hindemith's *The Craft of Musical Composition* (Hindemith 1945) which explains the hierarchical chromatic theory of a musical vocabulary capable of encompassing traditional and avant-garde harmonies within the one system. A large part of *The Craft* comprises an in-depth study of intervals and chromatic counterpoint. It is highly probable that Smith also developed his rhythmic approach through Hindemith's *Elementary Training for Musicians* (Hindemith 1946).

My analyses and transcriptions of recordings of Smith reveal some traces of Hindemith's influence, such as non-tertian melodic lines and harmonies as well as an example of complex rhythmic groupings of quintuplet quavers accented in groups of two (see Example 2). However, the evidence is not sufficient to say categorically that this is where Smith is incorporating Hindemith's method into his own work.

Example 2: Excerpt of Frank Smith's alto saxophone solo demonstrating advanced rhythmic groupings in 1957 on 'Ockeration' from the album *'Jazz in Australia'*, *The Music Maker 1957 All Stars*

Interviews with Smith's contemporaries and students have shed little light on the question of how Smith adapted and applied Hindemith's theory to his own jazz-based compositions and improvisations. One of Smith's students, renowned bebop alto saxophonist Barry Duggan, suggests that Smith's use of Hindemith's method was not noticeable on a surface level. He claims that, if you listened to Smith improvise, you would not be able to recognize Hindemith's influence:

> I can't really go with the thing of 'Oh Frank was avant-garde and he came through the Hindemith method and applied that to improvisation'. In all honesty, I just don't hear that. But for his overall level of musicianship he obviously did it, I would certainly like to hear what he had to say about it but I don't know anybody who can actually quote him saying anything too much about it.[37]

36. Taped interview with Graeme Lyall, Western Australia, 14 April 2004.
37. Taped interview with Barry Duggan, Victoria, 14 September 2010.

What is more likely is that through his in-depth study into Hindemith's theory, Smith internalized a deep understanding of tonal and intervallic relations and melodic and harmonic movement from *The Craft*, plus advanced rhythmic devices from Hindemith's *Elementary Training for Musicians* (Hindemith 1946). Armed with the suite of skills gained from his studies with Hanson, he was, no doubt, able to traverse innovations in the jazz language with relative ease compared to his Australian contemporaries who had chosen a more ad hoc approach to learning jazz. The possibility that Smith deeply internalized Hindemith's theory is backed up by Graeme Lyall who, on Smith's advice, also studied Hindemith's theory with Hanson. Lyall claims that he was able to apply Hindemith's method to improvisation in a similar way to Smith but that it had become mostly an intuitive process.[38]

The available evidence, drawn largely from hundreds of hours of aural analysis of Smith's archival recordings held in my possession, indicates that it was not so much Hindemith's method that made Smith the great musician that his contemporaries describe but, instead, his particularly intense and in-depth study and internalization of the building blocks of music drawn from Hindemith, in addition to other sources. A more subjective form of evidence is accumulating from my own daily systematic study, practice and internalization of Hindemith methodology as a means of enhancing my own jazz vocabulary and skills.

Experimental jazz

A final but very important aspect of Smith's approach to music-making that relates to his reputation for originality is his experimentalism. Jazz guitarist and visual artist, Ken White, who worked closely with Smith on animated film production in the 1960s, discussed various fascinating examples of his unorthodox approaches to producing sounds and textures required for studio sound and film productions.[39] Smith took delight in creating the types of sounds and textures that were being created electronically using conventional and invented instruments. Many hours of this experimental music-making survive on his production company studio tapes.

Smith was especially interested in using jazz and non-jazz improvising musicians to create mood music, some of which would be described today as 'ambient music'. He would ask musicians to improvise to imagined scenes.

---

38. Taped interview with Graeme Lyall, Western Australia, 14 April 2004.
39. Taped interview with Ken White by John Whiteoak, Melbourne, 12 October 1990. See Whiteoak (1999: 265–95) regarding the 1960s Melbourne experimental jazz and art music scene, including references to Smith.

An often quoted example is Bob Sedergreen being asked to imagine and play an 'Aborigine jumping out from behind a bush' (Jackson 1981: 22). Bruce Clarke recalls that when he would allow Smith to use Jingle Workshop time for his ensemble experiments, Smith would say things like: 'Let's imagine a woman walking beside a pool' and they would then record it. Then he might say: 'Let's imagine a woman walking along a fence' and they would play and record that until it was time to relinquish the studio for paid work.[40] Recorded examples of this approach are also heard on the tapes from Smith's own production studio. You hear Smith verbalize a scene for the musicians to improvise over and then count them in very quickly without allowing them any time to contemplate the scene. Examples of this on tape include 'Two Eyes Staring out of the Fog', 'A Portrait of [actor/comedian] Frank Thring' and 'Chaos, a Murderer, Broken Windows, a Horrified Look on a Girl's Face Going into Peace and Tranquillity'. Clarke implied that Smith enjoyed experimenting with improvisation for its own sake. However, the experimental creation of mood music through improvisation also saved a lot of time in writing music for films, television and advertisements and could produce complex musical textures and rhythms not achievable with written arrangements. Examples of this sort of improvising are also heard on the tracks 'Malta 11 a.m.', 'Malta 4.00 p.m.' and 'In a Dark Room' on the CD *Frank Smith—A Jazz Portrait* (CQCD-2761).

A variation on this experimental approach can be heard on Smith's opening soundtrack music for the television drama *Hunter* (1967).[41] In this music, which Smith recorded at Armstrong's recording studios in South Melbourne, experimental improvisation was framed within a written arrangement. The unusual, even revolutionary, feature of the *Hunter* music was the use of two jazz drummers, Graham Morgan and Billy Hyde, improvising simultaneously. Morgan explained how the session unfolded:

> He had everything notated and some of it was highly complex, because he knew a lot about drums and rhythms. Billy Hyde was a great player and he could read everything and they went off very well, with lots of freedom to [improvise]. He would say: 'This is a chase scene and I want you two guys to just solo ad lib. Off you go, the two of you.' There was structure but great freedom within the structure as well... [I was aware of] what Bill was playing, but certainly making my own stamp, as he would too.[42]

40. Taped interview with Bruce Clarke, Victoria, 6 May 2005.
41. *Hunter*, Crawford Productions, 1967–1969, Australia.
42. Taped interview with Graham Morgan, Victoria, 12 November 2004.

Other examples of Smith's musical experiments include free improvisations (including duets between Smith and Billy Hyde), electroacoustic music, experiments with non-musicians and, contrary to Hindemith's neo-tonal influence, mid-1960s evidence of Smith improvising on tone rows. Three pieces, 'Confirmation', 'Consolidation' and 'Circles', are superficially reminiscent of the music of Ornette Coleman. However, closer examination reveals a head arrangement drawn from a tone row (Example 3).

Example 3: Frank Smith, 'Consolidation'

The above examples of experimentalism are not meant to suggest that Smith was somehow committed to experimentalism for its own sake and that this commitment informed his own approach to improvisation on the saxophone. It does, however, show one reason why he became identified as very progressive and also indicates that he fully recognized and drew upon the potential of originality.

Influence

As already stated, an important part of the Smith legend is that he profoundly influenced many Australian jazz musicians. His direct influence appears to have begun in Sydney during the 1950s and continued until his untimely death. Smith always encouraged the next generation of modern jazz musicians (Johnson 1983: 15), providing insightful advice and free lessons to his students. Smith was reportedly the first Sydney jazz musician to discover the benefits of studying with Hanson (Bisset 1987: 107). As well as encouraging his peers and later his students to study with Hanson, he encouraged various Sydney jazz musicians to become interested in classical music. Referred to as the 'Chamber Music Society of Lower Penkivil Street',[43] Smith organized

---

43. 'Chamber Music Society of Lower Penkivil Street', *Music Maker*, April 1952: 15.

rehearsals and recitals of classical transcriptions that he had arranged for Sydney's modern jazz players.

Possibly the most important phase of Smith's influence was in the late 1950s when the El Rocco coffee lounge became a focus for progressive jazz in Sydney. Smith was by 1958 undoubtedly recognized as the most advanced saxophone player in the country, having just won the 1957 *Music Maker* poll for best alto. His playing stood in stark contrast to the modernists of his generation, transcending divisions between cool and hard bop musicians (Clare 1995: 60). Johnson points out that, at El Rocco, Smith's 'generous and open-minded musical attitude, together with the respect in which he was held, helped to create an atmosphere hospitable to the more advanced thinking of the younger musicians of the period' (Johnson 1983: 15). Smith's influence continued in Melbourne where he profoundly influenced young saxophonists, Barry Duggan, Graeme Lyall and Ken Schroeder. Duggan remembers that during his lessons Smith would play a dominant 7th chord with sharp and flat 9th and a flat 13th and say, 'Now Barry, I don't want you to think of this chord as strange'.[44] Smith's instruction came mostly in the form of in-depth discussion about music and involved very little playing. Ted Nettelbeck recalls Smith once telling him that 'if you want to play jazz you have to practise jazz'. Smith explained that everything he improvised, every concept he used, he had practised as if preparing for a classical music recital.[45]

It could be claimed that ripples of Smith's influence reached the Victorian College of the Arts Improvisation stream under the helm of Brian Brown, where improvisation students were encouraged to move away from the American model of playing jazz and search for their own ways of creating music through improvisation. In a revealing recorded attempt at free improvisation Smith coaches his fellow improvisers, encouraging them to 'make wonderful moments, don't laugh, don't make any noises, but keep playing, treat it as serious, no matter what happens, just imagine it could have been written by someone. Now don't go berserk, discipline is the main thing, not too many notes.'[46]

Conclusion

Most of what is interesting about Smith goes beyond the legend of the great jazz saxophonist. His engagement with classical music, Hindemith's theories, verbal scores, serial techniques, free improvisation, electroacoustic music,

---

44. Taped interview with Barry Duggan, Victoria, 14 September 2010.
45. Taped interview with Ted Nettelbeck, South Australia, 2004.
46. Frank Smith talking from a Frank Smith Productions reel-to-reel recording.

film and television scores, and even early recorded engagements with 'world music',[47] as well as his skill as a multi-instrumentalist, demonstrate that he profoundly educated himself in many aspects of music beyond the realm of jazz music and certainly well beyond the musical realm of most of his Australian jazz contemporaries. Smith's creative endeavours often took him beyond the world of music and into, for example, cartooning, filmmaking, astral travelling, writing children's books and creating complex board games.[48] He was a polymath who reportedly intensely investigated whatever concept he became fascinated with.[49]

From a jazz perspective, the tragedy of the Frank Smith legend is that, despite my discovery that over 200 reel-to-reel studio production tapes had survived, only a handful of these or other recordings reveal the greatness of Smith as a jazz saxophonist. The *1957 Music Maker All Star* recording stands out as a fine example of Smith's advanced harmonic and rhythmic understanding whilst certain Melbourne recordings, such as *The Embers* album and a few examples recorded for television, reveal him as a highly polished modern jazz stylist who would not have sounded out of place next to any of his American counterparts. Although these snippets more or less confirm the legend of Smith the saxophonist, they fail to represent the extent of Smith's capabilities, such as his remarkable self-developed aural skills and boundless imagination. Yet the free-flowing inventiveness with startling honks and squeals, break-neck tempos and seemingly impossible rhythmic groupings that are heard in his music represent the inspiring sound of modern jazz riding comfortably on the deeply internalized skills of a very advanced, experienced professional musician. This impressive 'sound', along with the challenges he set his fellow musicians, seem to be the primary essence of what became the legend of Frank Smith.

References

Bisset, Andrew (1987) *Black Roots, White Flowers: A History of Jazz in Australia*. Sydney, Golden Press.

Clare, John (1995) *Bodgie, Dada and the Cult of the Cool*. Sydney: University of New South Wales Press.

Hindemith, Paul (1945a [1937]) *The Craft of Musical Composition. Book 1: Theory*, rev ed. London: Schott & Co.

—(1945b [1937]) *The Craft of Musical Composition. Book 2: Exercises in Two Part Writing*, rev ed. London: Schott & Co.

47. *Jazz from Down Under*, Vol. 3. Cumquat Records, 1961/63 CQCD-2726.
48. Taped interview with Beverly Smith, Victoria, 2004.
49. Taped interview with Graham Morgan, Victoria, 2004 and personal communications 2004.

—(1946 [rev. ed. 1949]) *Elementary Training for Musicians.* London: Schott & Co.

Jackson, Adrian 1981. 'Bob Sedegreen Talks to Adrian Jackson'. *Jazz: The Australasian Contemporary Music Magazine* 1/6 (December): 22–24.

Johnson, Bruce (1983) 'The El Rocco: An Era in Sydney Jazz (Part 1)'. *Jazz: The Australasian Contemporary Music Magazine* 3/1 (January/February): 12–15.

—(1987) *The Oxford Companion to Australian Jazz.* Melbourne: Oxford University Press.

Marquis, Donald (1978) *In Search of Buddy Bolden: First Man of Jazz.* Baton Rouge, LA: Louisiana State University Press.

Mitchell, Jack (1988) *Australian Jazz on Record 1925–80.* Canberra: Australian Government Printing Service.

Murdoch, James (1976) *Australia's Contemporary Composers.* Melbourne: Sun Books.

Norman, Wally (1946) 'They Call it "Be-Bop": An Exciting New Style that will Replace Swing'. *Music Maker*, 20 August: 1, 14.

Sharpe, John (2008) *I Wanted to Be a Jazz Musician.* Canberra: National Film & Sound Archive.

Whiteoak, John (1999) *Playing Ad Lib: Improvisatory Music in Australia: 1836–1970.* Sydney: Currency Press.

Interviews with the author

Bertles, B. (2004) Taped interview with author. Victoria. 11 December.
Burrows, D. (2005) Telephone interview with author. 13 April.
Clarke, B. (2005) Taped interview with author. Victoria. 6 May.
Duggan, B. (2010) Taped interview with author. Victoria. 14 September.
Lyall, G. (2004) Taped interview with author. Western Australia. 14 April.
Morgan, G. (2004) Taped interview with author. Victoria. 12 November.
Nettelbeck, T. (2004) Taped interview with author. South Australia. 13 October.
Smith, B. (2004) Taped interview with author. Victoria.
White, K. (2004) Taped interview with author. Victoria. 8 May.
Whiteoak, J. (1990) Taped interview with Ken White. Melbourne. 12 October.

12 Lydia in Oz

The reception of George Russell in 1960s Australia[*]

Pierre-Emmanuel Seguin[†]

In his book about jazz analysis, Laurent Cugny confesses his scepticism regarding the actual influence of George Russell (Cugny 2009: 498) and notices the lack of any text that details concrete evidence of the use of Russell's *Lydian Chromatic Concept of Tonal Organization* (*LCCOTO*) (Russell 2001). Indeed, if several high-ranked jazz musicians have acknowledged and expressed a profound interest in Russell's music and musical conceptions since the late 1950s, there is very little research that has traced the results of this influence and given specific examples of it. Perhaps the reason for this situation comes from the reluctance or difficulty of jazz musicians to explain precisely in which way Russell influenced them.

The *LCCOTO*'s audience goes beyond that of jazz, touching pop, electronic music and classical contemporary music. For instance, Peter Burt uncovered deep aesthetic and musical links between Russell and Toru Takemitsu, who lauded the *LCCOTO* to the extent of translating it into Japanese (Burt 2002). Interestingly Takemitsu came to know the *LCCOTO* the same way the Australian-born Bryce Rohde came across it, through David 'Buck' Wheat, then bass player with the Kingston Trio. As improbable as it seems, the message of the *LCCOTO* was spread, in the early 1960s in Japan and Australia (and possibly in other places, where the band toured), by a successful American folk trio. Before looking at length into the music of Bryce Rohde, it seems important to establish the context in which this music evolved, therefore I

---

[*] This research was conducted for my PhD at Macquarie University. Musical extracts are reproduced by permission of Bryce Rohde; all solos transcribed by the author.

[†] Pierre-Emmanuel Seguin is a jazz scholar who is currently based in the UK, where he moved after being awarded his PhD from Macquarie University in Sydney. He is particularly interested in the transnational evolution of the vocabulary of jazz from a historical and analytical point of view while integrating elements of social research.

would like to follow a short introduction to George Russell with an overview of his reception in the Australian press.

George Russell's career as a jazz musician started in his teens, then in 1944 Benny Carter hired him for the position of drummer in his orchestra. His career as composer began soon afterwards, with a composition called 'New World'. Russell gained the recognition of critics with both the small ensembles and the big band he led from the late 1950s onwards. However his *Lydian Chromatic Concept of Tonal Organization* (Russell 2001), first published in 1953, attracted the attention of a small group of musicians at first before being widely regarded as the first music treaty born from a jazz musician and considered by many scholars as a precursor of the modal jazz approach (Berendt 1991; Tirro 1993; Kernfeld 2001; Monson 1998; Priestley 1987). The term modal jazz usually refers to a number of compositional and/or improvisational characteristics: a low density of chords, a structural use of scales, the use of vamps and pedal points. Ingrid Monson adds to these characteristics two others: 'the development of nontriadic vertical sonorities' and the integration of 'rhythmic feels and melodic gestures' from non-western sources (Monson 2007: 297). Despite its name Russell's *Concept* is not modal; it is rather a re-envision of our 12 tones tonal environment, a different conception of the relationship of scale degrees and chords to the tonic. However some of its principles, such as the pairing of a chord with a specific scale, were transposed by other musicians in their own, and sometimes modal, approach. Russell's focus on chord/scale relationship[1] also had an influence on Miles Davis's musical evolution which has been acknowledged many times (for example Kahn 2000; Nisenson 2000). From 1956 to 1964, Russell published a number of recordings for Riverside, mainly with his sextet but also with the Jazz workshop for RCA as well as two albums with a big band for Impulse and Decca. By the mid-1960s Russell had emigrated to Scandinavia where he found more support and opportunities to perform than in the USA.[2] There, he performed with Swedish, Danish and Norwegian musicians, and with American expatriates. He helped launch the career of Jan Garbarek and Terje Typdal, for example. In the same period,

---

1. The chord/scale theory should not be confused with the *Lydian Concept*, although early versions of that approach before it was formalized by Nettles and Graf (1997), which can be found in pedagogical works by David Baker (1969) and Jerry Coker (1964), were inspired by Russell (see Seguin 2011: 218–33).

2. See Heining 2010: 185–91. After a period of self-publication, Russell's recording output was published by Soul Note, followed in the 1980s and 90s by Blue Note and Label Bleu.

Russell's name started to be known amongst musicians and jazz listeners in Australia.[3]

As we will see below, Bryce Rohde's acknowledgment of the influence of the *LCCOTO* on his musical practice considerably widened Russell's audience in Australia. Russell wasn't completely unknown, however, as the few occurrences of his name in magazine and newspaper articles illustrate. An early appearance of his name in the Australian press can be found in *Music Maker*, December 1958, in a review of a record by Teddy Charles (1956). The reviewer wrote the following: 'worth special attention is George Russell's "Lydian M-1", a rather unusual piece which utilizes the principles of Russell's own recently developed harmonic theory, "The Lydian Chromatic Concept of Tonal Organization"' (G.H. 1958: 33).[4] The same LP was reviewed a month before the *Music Maker*'s review in the *Sydney Morning Herald* (SMH). The review was positive, describing the record as a 'modern jazz LP of real stature', representative of 'current jazz thinking' and played by a 'group of skilled and inspired musicians' (*Downbeat* 1958: 105). Of the seven pieces appearing on the LP the reviewer, known only by his penname 'Downbeat', singles out two of them: 'Quiet Time' by Jimmy Giuffre and 'Lydian M-1' by Russell. There is not a word about the other pieces, not even those arranged by Teddy Charles and the only musicians mentioned are the 'outstanding soloists': Art Farmer, Gigi Gryce and Jimmy Raney. Given the restricted size of the review it might not be surprising that the information is incomplete, which makes the insistence on two of the commissioned writers even more striking. The name of George Russell, who is mentioned as 'one of the bop school writers', is then preferred to Mal Waldron and Gil Evans, who also provided arrangements for the session, to illustrate the music on that record.

The mention of the *LCCOTO* is also intriguing: the first edition of the *LCCOTO* was self-published in 1953 and therefore directed to a limited audience. The second edition would not be published before 1959, which means that the reviewer was very well informed about recent jazz developments in New York. In reality, the author of the *Music Maker*'s review copied word for word the liner notes that Teddy Charles wrote for the album. That doesn't diminish the puzzling fact that Russell received more space than more widely recognized writers. Perhaps Russell's reputation was already important in Australia, due

---

3. For further information about Russell's life I would recommend Duncan Heining's book (Heining 2010).

4. The initials G. H. probably stand for George Hilder who was a correspondent in Australia for the magazine *Downbeat*.

to the success of his first record for RCA. There is no evidence in the press of this success, however, and I have found no review of Russell's records under his own name before the 1980s.[5]

Russell's stature then moved from a recognizable name to an acknowledged influence within a few years. In the *Music Maker* of January 1964 an article appeared about a series of documentaries on Australia's leading modern painters. Quoted in the article, the composer of the soundtrack, John Allen, establishes an aesthetic relationship between abstract painting, George Russell and modern jazz:

> We determined at the outset that as the films were documentaries dealing with painters of the abstract school, the [accompanying] music should be documentary and abstract also. Today's jazz that is related to this idiom is from the George Russell, John Coltrane, Charlie Mingus, Eric Dolphy, Ornette Coleman school. In the main the music I wrote was based upon Lydian and whole tone scales and certain other modes and was unarranged except for introductions and melodic sections which led into free improvisation passages (Allen, cited in Anonymous 1964: 3).

I have not been able to find this programme, but Allen's quote is an indication of Russell's status as a composer of the jazz avant-garde and of his influence on Australian jazz musicians at the beginning of the 1960s. Allen's use of free improvisation, Lydian and whole-tone[6] scale-based composition mirrors the approach of Australian piano player Bryce Rohde, who introduced the *LCCOTO* to Australian jazz musicians. Indeed it is in articles devoted to Bryce Rohde that the majority of occurrences of Russell's name appears. As a member of the Australian Jazz Quartet/Quintet (AJQ), Bryce Rohde toured extensively in the USA between 1953 and 1958 (McLeod 1994: 43; Johnson 1987: 90–91). After returning to Sydney he met David 'Buck' Wheat, the bassist of the folk group the Kingston Trio, who gave him two copies of the *LCCOTO*.[7] Bryce Rohde kept one for him and gave the second to Bruce Cale, the bassist of Rohde's ensemble. The AJQ was famous both in the USA and Australia and its success overseas was translated into covers, reviews and articles in the Australian

---

5. In the magazine *Jazz*, Bruce Cale wrote a review of the most recent records by George Russell published by the Italian label Soul Note.
6. We will see later that the whole-tone scale is also the Lydian Auxiliary Diminished scale in the *LCCOTO*.
7. Dave Guard, the founder of the Kingston Trio, supported financially the publication of the *LCCOTO* and built his colour-based guitar method on it (Veitch 1962).

press.[8] Rohde thus was already an active and respected member of the Australian jazz scene when he came back in 1958. He then returned to the USA between 1961 and 1962. In an interview with John Sharpe he says that he was 'installed as a guest in Buck Wheat's house for that twelve months, free of charge, and just did George Russell for twelve months' (Sharpe 2001). Back in Sydney again he set up another quartet with Bruce Cale (double bass), Charles Munro (alto sax) and Mark Bowden (drums), all musicians that were especially impressed by the *LCCOTO* and started building their own music around it. Together they recorded *Corners* (Rohde 1963), *Just Bryce* (Rohde 1965) and *More Spring* (Rohde 1962 [1990]). Bryce Rohde is an exception in the Australian jazz soundscape, as he is one of the few 'progressive' Australian jazz musicians, with perhaps Don Burrows and John Sangster, to have been largely documented before the 1980s. He recorded seven LPs with the AJQ for the Bethlehem label, and five LPs and two 45 rpm under his own name on CBS/Coronet in the 1960s.

In the following pages I would like to discuss the compositions that Bryce Rohde acknowledged as being influenced by the *LCCOTO*. Through the analysis of these compositions I will show that the *LCCOTO* did not necessarily result only in 'modal' compositions but was used in many different ways, which are encapsulated in Rohde's work. We will, then, discuss the influence of Russell on the other members of the group before closing with considerations about the place of Russell and Rohde with regard to modal jazz in jazz history.

Rohde talked at great length about his passion for the *LCCOTO* and on one occasion specifically mentioned three compositions about which he said: 'I can almost blame George [Russell]' (McLeod 1994). These compositions are: 'Corners Suite', 'Whatever Happened To Yesterday?' and 'Autocoptus'. Rohde compiled his compositions in a book bearing the same title as one of his records: *Turn Right At New South Wales*. Inspection of the collection of scores shows that more than the three compositions mentioned above refer to Russell's *Lydian Concept*. 'Dumbrille Was No Greek', 'Blues For Cyber', 'Capt. Kenney's Bathing Ship', 'Millstream', 'Opus 4/56', 'People Running', 'Stop the Bus' and 'Turn Right At New South Wales' also make visible use of the *LCCOTO*, either because Rohde specifies the use of Russell's Lydian

---

8. For example: 'What's New on Record', *Sydney Morning Herald*, 8 June 1958: 97; review of the first AJQ record in *Billboard*, 28 January 1956; 'What's New on Records', 8 June 1958: 97; 'Quintet in Jazz Recital', *Sydney Morning Herald*, 27 November 1958: 6.

scales or because the chord progression implies such scales.⁹ This is not the place for an extensive analysis of all these tunes, but I will concentrate on a few of them to illustrate Russell's influence and Rohde's approaches to using the *Lydian Concept*.

An early piece marking the influence of Russell's *Concept* and a good introduction to Rohde's approach to it is 'Blues For Cyber' (1962) that appears on *More Spring*. Russell's influence is explicit as this composition contains common features with Russell's 'Stratusphunk' (1960). To Bryce Rohde this influence was rather unconscious. He said to me:

> I used to listen to that... Gil Evans recording of that over and over trying to figure it out how he arrived at those intervals at this melody. So maybe in a way, it was influenced by that' (interview with the author, 24-25 October 2009).

The walking bass line and the melody possess quite the same contours and both numbers share the same leading pitches. There is a chord progression, that of a 12-bar blues, but the chords themselves indicate the Lydian quality of the song with an extensive use of sharpened 11th chords, which is similar to the construction of 'Stratusphunk' as described by Russell in the third edition of his book (1964: 36). Rohde's deep engagement with the *LCCOTO* resulted in a large questioning of the musical structures and vocabulary of jazz. Firstly, Rohde increasingly used unconventional forms and frames. Some melodies are 68 bars long ('Millstream') or 64 bars long ('Woolloomooloo'); others are complex arrangements of conventional and unconventional frames ('Corners Suite', 'Whatever Happened To Yesterday?'). Rohde also revised his approach to the relationship between harmony and melody, basing that revision on the *LCCOTO*. He applied three approaches to the use of Russell's Lydian scales: 1) Free improvisation based on a given Lydian Scale; 2) imposition of one or more Lydian scales on a chord structure; 3) derivation of a chord structure (and melody) from a Lydian scale. To illustrate these approaches let us focus on a composition that brings them all together: 'Corners Suite'.

'Corners Suite' is a seven-part suite of approximately 20 minutes' duration. According to Rohde it was composed in 1962, then recorded on 24 April 1963 and gave its title to the LP issued by CBS. Table 1 describes the organization of the suite as well as the type of approach used.

---

9. The Lydian scale was known and used before Russell's *Concept*, therefore a chord or a chord sequence implying the use of the Lydian scale wouldn't necessarily imply any relationship to Russell's *Concept*. However, Rohde suggests in the introduction to his book that even his use of the basic Lydian scale is a sign of the influence of Russell.

Table 1: Organization of 'Corners Suite'

Part	Time	Event	Form
1	0'	Bass solo	Free
	1'04"	Walking bass	
	2'00"	Piano solo	Free
	2'51"	Alto sax and drums duet	Free
	4'07"	Collective improvisation	Free
	5'00"	Cue. Unison	Notated
2	5'17"	Theme	Notated
	6'35"	Piano solo	
	7'56"	Theme repeat	
3	8'45"	Bass solo 2	
	10'05"	Ensemble unison/1 bar drums solo	Notated
	10'10"	As solo	
	10'15"	Ensemble unison/1 bar drums solo, repeat	Notated
	10'20"	As solo	
	10'26"	Ensemble unison 2	
4		Theme 2	Notated
		Theme 2 with piano 'churchy'	Notated
5	12'11"		12-bar Blues
	12'57"	Collective improvisation	Blues
	13'42"	Cue	
6	13'47"	Theme 3	Notated
	14'42"	Unison + As solo	Blues
	15'26"	Cue + Ensemble	Notated
	15'40"	Theme 4	Notated
	15'52"	Piano solo	Blues
	17'17"	Drums solo	Free
	19'16"	Ensemble unison + Drums solo 2 bars	Notated
	19'55"	End	

There are many elements of the suite that are built on the *Lydian Concept*, the most obvious one being the use of the *Concept*'s Lydian scales in improvisations (first approach). Bruce Cale clearly builds his two solo improvisations on these scales. The first one opens the suite (Figure 1). Cale's solo oscillates between the C Lydian Auxiliary Diminished scale (Cad) and the C Auxiliary Diminished Blues scale (Cadb) as shown by the large number of occurrences of the bII (Db), V natural instead of sharp (G) and bVII (Bb). It is possible to consider them as passing notes, notably in bar 6, but the numerous occurrences of Db and the systematic use of Bb instead of B natural lead me to think of this solo as based on the C Lydian Auxiliary Diminished Blues scale.

Figure 1: 'Corners Suite', first bass solo

Cale's opening melodic gesture serves as a melodic signature of the piece as the same motive can be found transposed on C (from F in Cale's solo) in parts 3, 4, 5 and 7 of the suite, as well as cited again by Cale in his second bass solo.

The solo by Bryce Rohde that follows Cale's intervention is strictly based on the C Lydian Auxiliary Diminished Scale (Figure 2). This contrapuntal solo only includes notes from within the scale. It closes with a perfect fifth (Ab – Eb) giving an impression of a perfect cadence with the D natural leading to the Eb in the ascending melody.

However, the *LCCOTO* is not only used to improvise but also to construct new music (3rd approach). The main theme for 'Corners Suite' is played in Part 2 (Figure 3). That theme and its piano accompaniment are entirely written out in Rohde's book (Rohde 1993: 29). The melody uses the most distinctive pitches of the C Lydian Auxiliary Diminished scale: it starts right on the raised fourth (F#), goes down to the flat third (Eb) and to the raised fifth which is the enharmonic flat sixth on Rohde's score (G#/Ab). It is also unusual in its frame: 13 bars.

Figure 2: 'Corners Suite', piano solo

Figure 3: 'Corners Suite', Part 2, theme (from Rohde 1993: 29)

I have attempted to analyse the score by reducing it to chord symbols, to understand the type of chord progression that underlies this theme (see Table 2). The result is extremely complex as most chords are dense with their superstructure altered. When organized in scale, all the chord roots represent 10 pitches of the 12 available in the chromatic scale. In fact the two missing pitches, D and B natural, appear in the melody, so in concrete terms this Part 2 theme contains the complete Lydian Chromatic scale on C. The fact that Rohde has written out the chords means he had a specific sound in mind, in which the C Lydian Auxiliary Diminished Blues scale acted as a repertory of sounds to organize as he wished rather than following a conventional harmonic route. The following solos are not based on the chord progression of the theme, but occur on a repeated section of five bars with one chord per bar (Rohde calls them clusters), again taken out of the Cadb scale.

Table 2: 'Corners Suite', Part 2, chord progression

A	$Cm^{\triangle+9+11} \mid Fm^{7+11\,13}$	$E^{\triangle+9} \mid F\sharp_{o}$	$G^{\triangle\flat9\,13} \mid F^{\triangle\,13}$	$E\flat^{\triangle+9\,13} \mid A\flat^{+11+13}$	$G^{\triangle\flat9\,\flat13} \mid F\sharp_{o}$	$E^{\triangle+9} \mid F\sharp_{o}/E\flat$	
B	$E\flat^{+9+11} \mid A\flat^{+9+11\,13}$	$G^{\triangle\,9\,11} \mid Am^{13}$	$B\flat \mid A\flat^{+11\,13}$				
A	$Cm^{\triangle+9+11} \mid Fm^{7+11\,13}$	$E^{\triangle+9} \mid F\sharp_{o}$	$G^{\triangle\flat9\,13} \mid F^{\triangle+11}$	$E^{\triangle+9} \mid E\flat^{+11}$			

Generally speaking, the musicians are left with quite a degree of freedom to improvise. There are short solos (a few bars) between ensembles such as in Part 3, or longer solos such as in Part 2, as we just saw, and in Part 4 where 12-bar blues, and blues are the only instructions given to improvise. In Parts 3, 4 and 6, the C Lydian Auxiliary Diminished Blues scale dominates but it is intercalated, as in Part 4, between written ensembles, in this instance:

'churchy' chords (on F and C), and then imposed on a blues chord progression (2nd approach) as in Part 6. In this part rather than letting the fourth degree clash with the Cadb scale, Rohde uses the level of VTG[10] and harmonizes all the chords individually so that the Cadb (Figure 4), Fadb (Figure 5), G Augmented scale (Figure 6) and F Augmented scale (Figure 7) blend harmonically with the blues chords.

Figure 4: C Lydian Auxiliary Diminished Blues scale[11]

Figure 5: F Lydian Auxiliary Diminished Blues scale

Figure 6: G Lydian Augmented scale

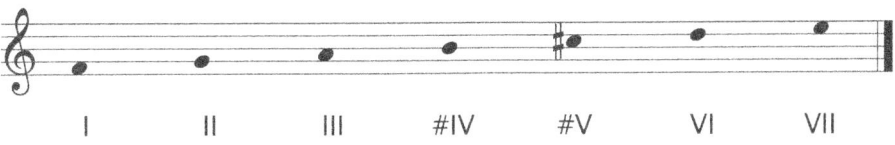

Figure 7: F Lydian Augmented scale

10. The level of Vertical Tonal Gravity (VTG) corresponds to the use of Lydian scales to accommodate each chord. There is an adequacy of scales and chords for the duration of each chord, hence the 'vertical' adjective.
11. All scales after Russell 2001: Chart A.

In 'Corners Suite' various uses of the Lydian scale are found: as material for free solo improvisation (Part 1), as a means to create an underlying harmony joined by two Lydian scales (at the level of HTG[12] in Part 2) and imposed on pre-existing chord progressions, such as blues progressions (at the level of VTG in Parts 4 and 6). By juxtaposing different approaches to composition and improvisation Rohde created a distinctive large jazz form that blends known jazz structures, such as the 12-bar blues, with completely original ones.

'Corners Suite' is peculiar in Rohde's output as its long form allows him to use all of his approaches in building music based on the *LCCOTO* within it. However, other pieces are based on one or two specific approaches. The second approach, imposing Russell's Lydian scales on conventional structures, is featured in 'Pickled Piper' and 'Opus 4/56'. They both feature an AABA form, although in 'Opus 4/56' it is preceded by two introductions, with a chord sequence based on ii – V – I progressions. At the time Rohde's band members were following his lead and studying Russell's *Concept*:

> Each member was devoted to the study of the concept exactly. We were doing my original tunes at that time and I would write the charts, and we discussed it. I tell them what chords they might want to use, what melody they might be inclined to use, I direct them to the Lydian conversion of those chords and that's the way we approached that particular part of our meetings (interview with the author, 24-25 October 2009).

There is evidence of this devotion in the music, with the extensive use of chords containing a raised fourth in the compositions and the use of Russell's scales in the solos. Charles Munro's solo, notably, leaves little doubt about his use of Lydian scales,[13] as, for example, in 'Pickled Piper' a semi-demi-quaver run features a C natural and an A natural, which would have been flattened if not using a Lydian scale (see Figure 8). In another version of the same piece, Frank Phipps's solo on bass trumpet is a literal enunciation of the Eb Lydian scale. In 'Opus 4/56', Charles Munro's alto sax solo is entirely built on the C Lydian scale (see Figure 9).

---

12. The level of Horizontal Tonal Gravity (HTG) is described by Russell as happening when a scale is used on a succession of chords.

13. Devising a solo based on Lydian scales would not necessarily mean that the musician is applying Russell's *Concept*, but in this context and following Rohde's quote about the group's interest in the *Concept*, I think it does.

Figure 8: Charles Munro's solo in 'Pickled Piper'

Figure 9: Frank Phipps's solo in 'Pickled Piper'

Another variation on Rohde's second approach, whereby the chord structure is taken from a well-known standard, in this case 'Sweet Georgia Brown', can be found in 'Whatever Happened To Yesterday?' (see Figure 10; Frampton and Johnson 1992: 73–77; interview with the author, 24-25 October 2009).

Figure 10: 'Whatever Happened To Yesterday?', main theme

The piece is a short suite, like a concise version of 'Corners Suite', containing five different segments. The first 12 bars of the theme are indeed similar to that of 'Sweet Georgia Brown' but the last 4 bars in Rohde's piece finishes on Ab13, instead of going through the circle of fifths (Bbm7; Eb7; Ab6; Gm7 and C7) or going down to Ab7 chromatically as in more conventional interpretations. The chord progression of the solos is a sequence of seventh chords following the circle of fifths from F to Ab, which is also the case for the theme's chord progression but starting on Gb.[14] A harmonic reading of these chord progressions based on the rules of 'common jazz practice' is possible: the final bVII can be seen as a double tritone substitute for V or a modal borrowing from the natural minor scale.[15] However, Rohde placed an annotation in his collection of compositions *Turn Right At New South Wales* (Rohde 1993: 156) which supports an interpretation based on Russell's *Concept*: on the last Gb chord he wrote: 'whole tone'. A whole-tone scale based on Gb is the equivalent to the Lydian Augmented scale. A possible explanation is that Rohde based his entire harmonic design on the *LCCOTO* and, therefore, looked for the parent scale of the Ab7 chord, which would be the usual tonic. According to the *LCCOTO* a seventh chord is always on the second degree of the Lydian scale (Russell 2001: Chart A). The Lydian tonic would then be Gb. Moreover, there are only three Lydian scales that contain a flat seventh on their tonic chord: the Lydian Augmented scale (whole-tone scale), the Lydian Auxiliary Diminished Blues scale, and the Lydian Flat Seventh. The latter scale didn't exist in the 1959 edition of the *LCCOTO*, which was the edition used by Rohde. In consequence the two remaining scales are those used in 'Whatever Happened To Yesterday?' Rhodes's improvisation is consistent with the Lydian Auxiliary Diminished Blues scale, but he seems to stay close to the chord progression, hitting notes such as the ninth (C), the thirteenth (G) and the sharp eleventh (E) on the Bb7 chord. His approach to the *LCCOTO* is much more varied and complex than the image that has been deduced from Miles Davis's so-called modal approach. Rohde's music didn't evolve into a vamp-based music that would use modes to construct its harmony but exploited the chromatic universe set by the *LCCOTO*.

After Rohde's departure for the USA, the musicians of his quartet continued to explore the possibilities of the *LCCOTO*. Bruce Cale also left Australia in 1965, going first to the UK where he worked with Tubby Hayes and John Stevens, then to the USA where he recorded for ESP with James Zitro, and with John Handy alongside the New Zealander Mike Nock. Cale divided his

---

14. This particular chord can be considered as a tritonic substitution for C7.
15. Thanks to one of the anonymous referees for pointing that out to me.

music between what has been called post-bop and free improvisation, but always kept Russell's *Concept* at the back of his mind and in 1981 he attended a ten-day seminar with George Russell himself (Myers 1985; interview with author, 8 August 2009). Interestingly, while Cale kept playing improvised music, he has devoted himself to composition for 'classical' ensembles since the late 1960s. George Russell also claims the status of composer, rather than arranger, exercising large control over his work and the way it should be played. It seems that most of Russell's compositions are fully scored (particularly from the late 1960s onwards, when he went to Europe) with only moments of possible improvisation, but the two are so intricate that it is very difficult for the listener to separate them. Bruce Cale has also worked on large scores both for jazz ensembles in which some space is left for improvisation and for orchestras and chamber ensembles for which everything is notated. This balance between improvisation and composition is a constant concern for both Russell and Cale, with the difference that while writing for classical or contemporary ensembles, Cale seems to leave this problem aside and everything is written down, with the improvisation/composition balance addressed more in his jazz work. Nevertheless the *Lydian Concept* remains at the core of Cale's work. In the score of 'A Century of Steps' (1977), for example, from bar 135, the scale A Lydian Augmented is indicated for the flute solo, then the trumpet, trombone and guitar are added with a D Lydian Augmented scale indicated. It is a perfect example of what Russell would have called poly-modalism, where two different Lydian scales are superimposed. Cale also extensively uses chords with a sharp eleventh, the mark of the Lydian scale, and the piece ends on a CM7/9#11 chord. In another composition for solo piano called 'Coalesce' (1992) (for which he was awarded the Jean Bogan Prize) Cale pushes to the extreme the logic of the *LCCOTO* by systematically opposing chords from the ingoing order to chords of the outgoing order; in other words, the two extremes of the Lydian Chromatic scale, its most consonant part and its most dissonant (Russell would not agree with these adjectives). Cale's compositional approach to this piano piece reveals, as well as Rohde's work, what the *LCCOTO* is really about: the systematic organization of consonance and dissonance, of tension and release.

Unlike Rohde, Charlie Munro's music took a more Coltrane-like turn and, though he still acknowledged the influence of Russell, he was progressively more interested in incorporating modes from different cultures. In 1967 Charles Munro recorded *Eastern Horizons* (Munro 1967), described by John Clare as 'the most striking and powerful album of Australian jazz' (Clare 1995: 72). Munro wrote most of the pieces on non-Western scales with a deliberate attempt of fusion between Western and Eastern music. In the liner notes of the record, Arch McKirdy (1967) explains:

> Munro readily acknowledges his debt to Bryce Rohde with whom he worked and experimented at length. Rohde's enthusiasm for George Russell's Conception of the Lydian mode excited an interest which Munro has extended to other forms of linear writing, and 'Eastern Horizons' evolved.

According to McKirdy, Munro's foray into the fusion of jazz and music from Japan and India is a direct consequence of Russell's influence. Australia saw further attempts of this kind of fusion. For example, the saxophonists Frank Smith and Dick Healey, in a band led by guitarist Bruce Clarke, recorded some free improvisation based on Indian ragas in 1961.[16] The saxophonist and flautist Brian Brown also explored modes but came from the perspective of having studied English folk music. According to Andrew Bisset, Mike Nock and Dave Levy, also a piano player, experimented with modes and then free playing in Sydney in the early 60s (Bisset 1987 [1979]: 144).[17]

As we saw earlier, Ingrid Monson expanded the definition of modal jazz and included the *Lydian Concept* as part of a broader musical, social and political context in which breaking the barriers of conventional structures of jazz based on the reduction of chords and the application of scales upon them as well as the introduction of drones and scales from non-Western music accompanies the fight of the civil right movements and the quest for spirituality. Musically, the context was similar in Australia in the 1960s: Munro's album is an expression of this context, as are the experiments of fusion with non-Western music evoked above, or John Sangster's inspiration from Sun Ra in his 'Sun Music' (Seguin 2011: 139). It is also possible that Russell's interest in the work by Gurdjieff and Eastern philosophy and spirituality in general influenced Munro, although Bisset specifically names a book by Sachs as a main influence (Bisset 1987: 146). Incidentally, Mike Nock was also influenced by Gurdjieff as the name of his group, The Fourth Way, and of his own record label testify (FWM for Fourth Way Music). The term modal jazz was, to my knowledge, never used in Australia to qualify the work of Miles Davis before the 1980s. The adjective modal was mainly used with regards to the music of Bryce Rohde and Russell's 'modal concept', or when talking about non-Western or church scales. It appears from the preceding analysis of Rohde's compositions that the only element that is related to modal jazz is the term Lydian. The same can be said about Russell's *Concept*, and Rohde's use of

---

16. The four pieces: 'That Old Calcutta Rag', 'The Delhi Belly Dancer', 'That Kama Sutra Feeling' and 'Back Home Again in Indian Annie' were published on Clarke's label Cumquat in the third volume of his *Jazz from Down Under* series.

17. In our interview Mike Nock dated his free-playing debut from the mid 1960s in New York while experimenting with Barre Phillips (Seguin 2011: 136–37).

the *Concept* confirms that it is an 'investigation into the tonal resources provided by equal tempered tuning' (Russell 1964: A), an organization of the tonal chromatic field around the Lydian tonic rather than a systematization of the relationship between chord and scales (Monson 1998: 149). As Russell puts it himself:

> The term 'Lydian Chromatic Scale' merely informs the practitioner of the tonal order existing within the chromatic scale. He may be far in (ingoing) within that order, or far out (outgoing) in relationship to it. He has the freedom to choose and create (Russell 1964: C).

Without denying the importance of this general context and the interest in modes shown by many musicians in Australia during the 1960s and after, my research has not revealed modal jazz as a term, a movement or even an attitude in which the musicians cited above recognized their music (Seguin 2011: 176, 247). Rohde, like Russell, stays firmly grounded in jazz history. The modification of conventional structures taken from jazz standards such as 'Sweet Georgia Brown' (in 'Whatever Happened To Yesterday?' by Rohde) or 'Love For Sale' (in 'Ezz-thetic' by Russell) is reminiscent of bebop, and the blues remains a pillar of the music by both musicians.

In the jazz literature, too much emphasis has been placed on the theoretical principles established by Russell from which the Chord-Scale Theory and modal jazz were derived. In Australia, Russell's influence did not result in the creation of a modal jazz school, even though it opened the door for some musicians like Munro to the discovery of a world of scales, but allowed musicians like Rohde and Cale to extend their musical vocabulary to extreme chromaticism, freeing themselves from the constraints of conventional structures of jazz, without forgetting their roots.

References

Anonymous (1964) 'Abstractions'. *Music Maker* 32/8 (January): 3.
Baker, D. N. (1969) *Jazz Improvisation: A Comprehensive Study for All Players*. Chicago: Maher Publications.
Berendt, J. E. (1991) *The Jazz Book: From Ragtime to Fusion and Beyond*. Brooklyn, NY: Lawrence Hill Books.
Bisset, A. (1987 [1979]) *Black Roots, White Flowers: A History of Jazz in Australia*. Gladesville, NSW: Golden Press.
Burt, Peter (2002) 'Takemitsu and the Lydian Chromatic Concept of George Russell'. *Contemporary Music Review* 21/4: 73–109. http://dx.doi.org/10.1080/07494460216666
Clare, J. (1995) *Bodgie Dada and the Cult of Cool*. Sydney, NSW: University of New South Wales Press.
Coker, J. (1964) *Improvising Jazz*. Englewood Cliffs, NJ: Prentice-Hall.

Cugny, L. (2009) *Analyser le Jazz*. Paris: Outre Mesure.
Downbeat (1958) 'What's New on Records'. *Sydney Morning Herald*, 16 November: 105.
Frampton, Roger, and Bruce Johnson (1992) *Australian Jazz*. Sounds Australian Music Resource Series for Secondary Schools. Sydney: Sounds Australian.
G.H. (1958) 'Teddy Charles's Tentet'. *Music Maker* 12: 33.
Heining, D. (2010) *George Russell: The Story of an American Composer*. Lanham, MD: Scarecrow Press.
Johnson, B. (1987) *The Oxford Companion to Australian Jazz*. Melbourne: Oxford University Press.
Kahn, A. (2000) *Kind of Blue: The Making of the Miles Davis Masterpiece*. New York: Da Capo Press.
Kernfeld, B. D. (2001) 'Modal Jazz'. In *The New Grove Dictionary of Jazz*, 2nd ed., ed. B. D. Kernfeld, 784–85.New York and London: Grove/Macmillan.
McKirdy, A. (1967) Liner notes in Charlie Munro, *Eastern Horizons*. Philips JS-020.
McLeod, J. (1994) *Jazztrack*. Sydney: ABC Books.
Monson, I. (1998) 'Oh Freedom: George Russell, John Coltrane and Modal Jazz'. In *In the Course of Performance: Studies in the World of Musical Improvisation*, ed. Bruno Nettl and Melinda Russell, 149–68. Chicago: University of Chicago Press.
—(2007) *Freedom Sounds: Civil Rights Call Out to Jazz and Africa*. New York: Oxford University Press. http://dx.doi.org/10.1093/acprof:oso/9780195128253.001.0001
Myers, E. (1985) 'Bruce Cale, Serialism and the Lydian Concept'. *APRA: Magazine of the Australasian Performing Right Association* 4 (October): 18–21.
Nettles, Barrie, and Richard Graf (1997) *The Chord Scale Theory and Jazz Harmony*. Rotterdam: Advance Music.
Nisenson, E. (2000) *The Making of Kind of Blue: Miles Davis and his Masterpiece*. New York: St Martin's Press.
Priestley, B. (1987) 'Modal Jazz'. In *Jazz: The Essential Companion*, ed. Ian Carr, Digby Fairweather and Brian Priestley, 343. London: Grafton Books.
Rohde, B. (1993) *Turn Right At New South Wales: The Compositions of Bryce Rohde*. Mill Valley, CA: Bryce Rohde.
Russell, G. (1964) *The Lydian Chromatic Concept of Tonal Organization for Improvisation*. Brookline, MA: Concept.
—(2001) *The Lydian Chromatic Concept of Tonal Organization: The Art and Science of Tonal Gravity*. Brookline, MA: Concept.
Seguin, Pierre-Emmanuel (2011) 'Modal Jazz in Australia in the 1960s: Challenging the Jazz Canon'. PhD Thesis. Sydney: Macquarie University.
Sharpe, J. (2001) Interview with Bryce Rohde. *Oral History of Australian Jazz*. Canberra: National Film and Sound Archives.
Tirro, F. (1993) *Jazz: A History*. New York: W. W. Norton.
Veitch, Jock (1962) 'The Happy American Who Made it Young'. *Sydney Morning Herald*. 16 December: 75.

Interviews with the author

Cale, B. (2009) Interview with author. 8 August.
Rohde, B. (2009) Interview with author. 24-25 October.

Discography

Charles, T. (1956) *Teddy Charles Tentet*. Atlantic, LTZA 15034.
Davis, M. (1959) *Kind Of Blue*. Columbia, CL1355.
Munro, C. (1967) *Eastern Horizons*. Philips, JS 20.
Rohde, B. (1962 [1990]) *The Bryce Rohde Quartet: More Spring*. MBS JAZZ, 6.
—(1963) *The Bryce Rohde Quartet: Corners*. CBS, BP-233046.
—(1965) *The Bryce Rohde Quintet: Just Bryce*. CBS, BP-233196.
Russell, G. (1960) *Stratusphunk*. Riverside, RLP 341.

13 Expressive identity in the voices of three Australian saxophonists: McGann, Sanders and Gorman

Sandy Evans[*]

> McGann's saxophone: 'hoarse and terse...choppy yet liquid... declamatory... big... raspy, rangy, across-the grain... a throaty growl... soaring cry... gentle whisper... honks... barks... yelps... scrambles... whips and hurtles... pops and smears' (Schonfield et al., in Page 1997: 11–12).
>
> Sanders's saxophone: 'warms the blood: a big, braying, honking beast of a thing that could unexpectedly whisper sweet nothings in your ear' (Shand 2002).
>
> Gorman's saxophone: 'enchanting tambers [sic] of cold starlight, robot-like motives [sic], seagulls' cries of despair and whatnot' (Erm 1990).

Bernie McGann, Kim Sanders and Tony Gorman[1] are three Australian saxophonists with distinctive sounds. The expressive power of their musical voices is reflected in the catalogue of poetic and metaphorical phrases, such as the examples cited above, that journalists have used to describe their playing. McGann and Sanders passed away in 2013, and Gorman is no longer active as a saxophonist due to chronic illness.[2] Honouring, understanding and docu-

---

[*] Sandy Evan teaches at the University of New South Wales and Sydney Conservatorium of Music. She is also a saxophonist, composer, music researcher and teacher. She has been a member of many Australian jazz groups since the early 1980s, toured extensively and published over 50 recordings including 'Testimony', a collaborative work with Yusef Komunyakaa, published by Wesleyan University Press. Sandy's research interests include Indian jazz intercultural music, Australian jazz and improvisatory practices.

1. As a disclosure of my position, please note that Tony Gorman is my partner.
2. Gorman still performs as a solo alto clarinet player, in a duo with tabla player Bobby Singh, and in The Monday Club.

menting their creative contributions to Australian jazz culture takes on a particular urgency and importance in the silent space left by the absence of their saxophone voices. Ulanov writes: 'As in almost no other art, individual identity shapes the structure of jazz. It obsesses the player or singer and haunts his or her audience' (1979: 245). The lives and music of McGann, Sanders and Gorman exemplify three different ways that individual identity shaped the structure and sound of jazz in an Australian[3] context. McGann is a bop-inspired modern jazz alto saxophonist, Sanders is a multi-instrumentalist who integrated world music influences with jazz, Scottish-born Gorman is a saxophonist and clarinetist with roots in jazz, funk, progressive rock and Western classical music. I am a saxophonist who has played with each of these musicians. I will investigate what musical materials and processes they use to express their identity; how their music reflects their cultural, social and personal histories, and aesthetic preferences; and what insights their creative work might offer into understandings about musical thought and practice, and identity in Australian jazz culture.

I will analyse and discuss a composition and improvisation from a seminal recording[4] by each saxophonist: McGann's 'Playground', Sanders's 'Gnome Chomsky's Deep Focus Boogie-Woogie' and Gorman's 'Spice Island', supported by material from interviews with the saxophonists where available. My objective is not to compare the relative merits of each saxophonist, but to identify some of the key factors in the conception, development and realization of their expressive identity.

The terms culture, identity and jazz have been used to signify, bound and investigate a range of complex phenomena and ideas, resulting in a web of confusing and sometimes contradictory meanings. The ideological viewpoints adopted here are informed by Hall (1989), Appudurai (1996), Feld (2005) and Sarath (2013) among others. Appudurai (1996: 12) prefers the adjectival form 'cultural' to the use of 'the word culture as a noun'. His ideas have led me to view culture as a process rather than something defined by a particular set of things or properties. Hence, by 'Australian jazz culture' I mean the process of playing and listening to jazz in Australia. Hall writes: 'cultural identities are the unstable points of identification or suture, which are made, within the discourses of history and culture. Not an essence but a *positioning*' (1989: 226; original emphasis). In music, 'positioning' occurs through a complex, multi-layered cycle of

3. Or, more specifically, a Sydney context.
4. Each track is from a CD that was either an ARIA (Australian Recording Industry Association) Award winner (McGann and Gorman), or a finalist (Sanders). For reviews of McGann and Gorman's recordings see http://www.rufusrecords.com.au/awards.html. For Sanders, see http://kimsandersworldmusic.com/kims-cds/.

listening and response, depicted in Feld's model of the 'musical encounter' (Feld 2005: 86), between the performer(s), the audience and 'discourses of history and culture'. In the discourse about jazz, my thinking aligns with Sarath, who writes: 'the point is not to endorse jazz as a self-confining destination but as a self-transcending gateway that connects musicians with the central creative and aesthetic pulse of today's musical world' (2013: 9).

Analysing jazz is not straightforward. Complex layers of individual and group[5] expression and interaction interweave with compositional and improvisatory processes in every performance. Much analysis in jazz has focused on the relationship between melody and harmony, as Potter's (1990) review found. Since then, Berliner (1994), Cooper (1996), Monson (1996), Lewis (2002), Keil (2005) and others have done much to develop effective analytical models for jazz. My analysis is guided by consideration of four interrelated parameters: form, timbre, musical language, and feeling,[6] building on a model developed by Cooper (1996: 127–29).

The case studies of McGann, Sanders and Gorman are presented in chronological order based on the ages of the saxophonists. Each track is composed by the player, is characteristic of important aspects of their compositional and improvisatory practice, and is repertoire I played with them. Each case study features some of their long-term collaborators. While the totality of each player's expressive language cannot be understood through the study of only one example,[7] this analysis will help identify some distinctive features of their musical materials and processes.

Bernie McGann

Alto saxophonist Bernie McGann[8] (1937–2013) was born in Sydney where he lived for most of his life. His father, a fitter and turner and accomplished dance-band drummer, was influential in developing his early interest in music

---

5. Due to the focus of this chapter on individual identity, the important area of group interaction is not foregrounded.
6. The rubric 'feeling' encompasses the affective qualities of music, including both emotive and engendered (groove-based) responses. See Keil (2005) for explication about 'engendered feeling' relating to groove-based elements in participatory and improvised music.
7. Recorded examples are only one snapshot of a player's work. As Hicks writes: 'recordings prove that a creative process occurred but can never represent the totality of that process' (2011: 13).
8. Page's (1997) biography of McGann includes interviews with McGann, musicians, family and friends. Also see Clare (1995), Johnson (1987), Shand (2009) and the documentaries *Beyond El Rocco* (Lucas 1991) and *Dr Jazz* (Perry 1998).

(Page 1997: 17). McGann was drawn to bebop by the passion, momentum and swing he heard in players such as Miles Davis, Art Blakey and Horace Silver on the radio show *Voice of America* (Ford 2012). He acknowledges Paul Desmond as an early inspiration and cites Charlie Parker, Sonny Rollins, John Coltrane and Dexter Gordon as important influences (Page 1997: 128). McGann's professional career commenced in the mid 1950s and continued until 2013. He led his own groups The Bernie McGann Trio and Quartet, and was a member of many jazz ensembles including The Heads, Kindred Spirits, The Last Straw, Ten Part Invention and duo and quartet projects with Paul Grabowksy.

'Playground'

'Playground' is the title track from a CD (1996) McGann recorded at Sony Studios, Sydney, released on Rufus Records. The musicians are McGann (alto saxophone), Sandy Evans (tenor saxophone), Lloyd Swanton (bass) and John Pochée (drums). Pochée[9] recollects that McGann wrote 'Playground' for The Last Straw[10] in approximately 1976, although the group didn't perform it at that time. McGann loved the repertoire of the American jazz songbook (Ford 2012). The form and musical language of 'Playground' exemplify how McGann simultaneously expresses his connection to this canon while extending genre boundaries. The formal structure of the chorus to 'Playground' is shown below.

> A1:   10 bars
> B: 9 bars
> A2:   12 bars
> B: 9 bars

The chorus is 40 bars long[11] whereas the usual chorus length for a jazz standard is 32 bars (De Veaux and Giddins 2009: 37–41); A1 and A2 are different lengths in 'Playground' while sections in a jazz standard would usually be the same length, organized in 4 or 8 bar phrases.[12] McGann uses common harmonic devices such as II–V–I chord progressions, pedal points and chromatically ascending dominant 7th chords placed extrinsically within the atypical architecture of 'Playground' to nudge the borders of convention. The II-V-Is move rapidly through eight of twelve possible tonal centres, and each of

---

9. J. Pochée, personal email to author, 1 October 2014.
10. See Page (1997: 48–51) for more information about The Last Straw.
11. McGann's well-known composition 'Spirit Song' also has an unusual chorus length of 76 bars.
12. There are other jazz compositions with atypical chorus structures such as 'Infant Eyes' (Wayne Shorter) and 'Stablemates' (Benny Golson).

the A1 and A2 sections begins and ends in a different tonal centre. McGann's sophisticated melodic development is evident throughout. For example, Figure 1 illustrates relationships between the opening phrase of A1 and A2. The rhythm of each phrase is identical, creating continuity. In A2, contrast is created with the inversion of the melodic contour and the transposition of the tonal centre down a tone.

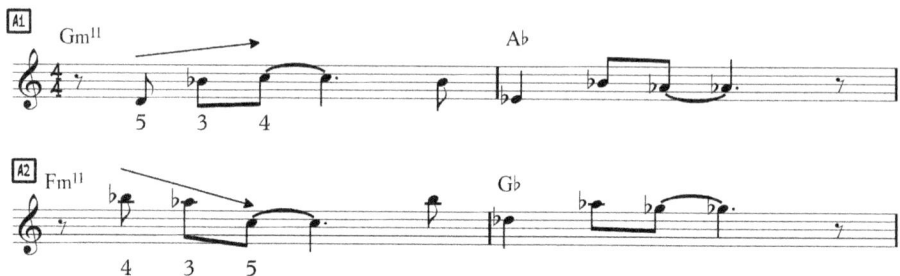

Figure 1: 'Playground', melodic inversion of A1 and A2

McGann's two-chorus improvisation is characterized by relatively simple, consonant harmonic language. His note choices consist predominantly of chord tones, sometimes linked by step-wise scalar movement or a chromatic approach note to a chord tone. Figure 2 illustrates these features in the opening phrase of the solo.

Figure 2: 'Playground', opening phrase of solo (Eb transposition)

McGann uses alterations of the 9th and 5th on dominant 7th chords sparingly, playing only two alterations in the first chorus.[13] In the context of the bebop genre that 'Playground' references, this is an interesting feature. As a point of comparison, there are 13 notes that could be considered alterations[14] of the 9th or 5th in the first chorus of Charlie Parker's (1951) solo on 'Anthropology', as transcribed in *The Charlie Parker Omnibook* (Aebersold 1978: 10–13).

13. The notes are the B and F# (concert pitch) over the B♭ pedal in Bar 37 of the solo.
14. See Levine (1989: 62–84) regarding alterations of the 5th and 9th in bebop melodic language.

It is likely that both aesthetic and practical considerations guided McGann's melodic conception. When Ford (2012) asked McGann what he learned from Desmond, he replied: 'I'm going to say taste', and extrapolates that taste is 'being selective in what you play'. McGann's note choices in his improvisation on 'Playground' illustrate how he 'selected' strong harmonic sounds to create tasteful melodies whose apparent simplicity belies a sophisticated artistry, much in the way Desmond's melodic conception does. Pochée comments that 'Playground' was challenging to play because there weren't 'too many signposts to latch onto in the blowing'.[15] McGann may also have maintained a consonant, diatonic relationship to the harmonic structure to maximize clarity and provide signposts throughout this complex form.

McGann said: 'The best thing you could want for is to surprise yourself when you play' (Ford 2012). In this musical 'playground', harmonic and rhythmic structures that are familiar enough to be comprehensible, but unusual enough to disrupt habitual improvisatory processes, give McGann ample opportunity to surprise himself. One of the ways he does this is by exploiting the timbral qualities of different registers of the saxophone, sometimes moving quickly and unexpectedly between registers. He plays five phrases in the altissimo register, moving from altissimo to other registers throughout the solo rather than building to a single climax.

Entries in one of McGann's practice notebooks[16] provide insight into his conceptual, creative, aesthetic and technical processes and goals. The notebook includes exercises, most likely composed by McGann, transcriptions of classical compositions by composers such as Bartok, piano voicings and timetables for practice routines. There are a few annotations throughout the notebook such as 'Long, Loose, Taste and Groove'. One entry reads 'Tongue and Sound'. Tonguing and sound are two of the main areas almost any saxophonist would study and practise, so in itself this is not remarkable. The variety, nuance and originality of McGann's articulation and sound are, however. Perception of saxophone timbre is affected by the attack, duration and ending of each note, as well as the way one note connects to the next in a phrase. McGann's solo contains many examples of his unique approach to articulation, whereby he chisels a highly textured stream of sound into his melodic inventions. A wide spectrum of heavy and light staccato and legato attacks imbued with different phonetic inflections drive the rhythmic momentum. Figure 3 illustrates the variety of articulations McGann uses in bars 34 and 35 of his solo (1:38).

15. Pochée, personal email to author, 1 October 2014.
16. McGann gave one of these notebooks to saxophonist Jeremy Rose who shared the contents with the author for this research. The date of the notebook is unknown.

Figure 3: 'Playground', articulation bars 34 and 35

Vibrato is an integral part of McGann's timbral palette. For example, vibrato on the last note of the phrase in bar 33 (1:36) follows a cracked altissimo register note to give the phrase a colourful texture (see Figure 4).

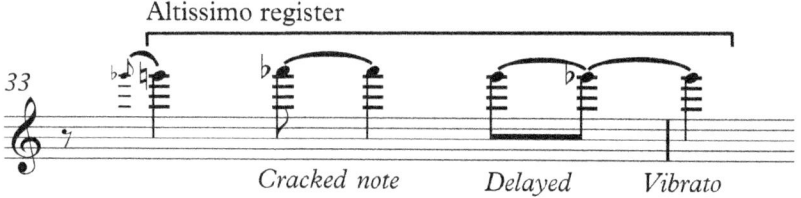

Figure 4: 'Playground', timbral variation

McGann also uses growls, such as that heard in bar 6 of the first chorus (1:00), for expressive effect.

McGann's fast tempo swing phrasing is another mark of his individuality. This can be heard in the double-time passage at 1:51 in bars 4 and 5 of the second chorus of his solo. One trope in discussions of swing holds that quavers are phrased in the ratio of 2:1 (a crotchet triplet followed by a quaver triplet).[17] Friberg and Sundström's (1997) empirical study found that the ratio varies from 1:1 to 3.5:1, contingent primarily on tempo, with more even ratios typically occurring at faster tempi. McGann's swing phrasing doesn't always become more even at faster tempi. This creates a distinctive, 'choppy, yet liquid' (Schonfield in Page 1997: 11) time feel.

McGann has been hailed as a player with a distinctly 'Australian' sound (Grabowsky in Nicholson 2005: 188; Shand 2009: 24). This is sometimes attributed to his outdoor practice sessions in the Royal National Park near Bundeena,[18] south of Sydney. McGann (Ford 2012) says he worked very hard to develop his own sound. Playing outdoors gave him a space to work

---

17. Time ratio is only one of many factors that delineate a swing feel. Other factors include articulation, accent and dynamics.

18. See Page (1997: 44–48) for information about McGann's time in Bundeena where he worked as a postman.

undisturbed, and helped him find a 'core' in his sound 'and enlarge that'. He acknowledges that his 'dry, crackling sort of a sound' may partly reflect a subconscious osmosis of elements from the natural environment, but downplays the significance of this.

Physical factors such as McGann's unconventional embouchure and unusual set-up, a 10 star metal Otto Link mouthpiece (Page 1997: 132–33), contributed to the sound he made. He suggests there was also a certain inevitability about the development of his sound: 'I'd play, and I thought that's not coming out like Paul Desmond...it's coming out like me...so I'd better work on me' (Ford 2012). McGann developed a strong, clear, precise aural concept, or 'tone imagination' (Rascher 1983: 8),[19] and made a single-minded, life-long commitment to realizing it.

Kim Sanders

Kim Sanders (1948–2013) was born in Sydney and grew up in Avalon on Sydney's northern beaches (Wockner 2008). He was a multi-instrumentalist[20] and 'a pioneer of what has come to be known as "world" music... [He] was also regarded as a formidable jazz player' (Jordan 2013). Sanders's interest in music was awakened, in part, by listening to his father's record collection, including jazz by Dave Brubeck and John Coltrane. The saxophone sound and ballad playing of Archie Shepp was an important influence (Wockner 2008). Sanders attributes his interest in world music partly to the 1960s work of jazz musicians such as Don Cherry and John Coltrane. Sanders lived in Dulwich Hill, Sydney. He travelled widely, studying and performing music in many countries including Turkey, Bulgaria, Macedonia, Greece, Gambia, Senegal, Indonesia and China. He led his own groups Kim Sanders and Friends, and Brassov, and was a member of many world music ensembles.[21]

---

19. Saxophone pedagogue Sigurd Rascher writes: 'Without a precise concept of the music to be reproduced, we are unable to render it in a convincing manner... The deliberate "imagination" of a tone is as concise an activity of the mind as is the imagination of a triangle with clearly defined properties, such as size, shape, colour, etc.' (1983: 8).

20. As well as tenor saxophone, Sanders played Macedonian, Bulgarian and Turkish gaidas, aardvark, kaval, ney, tin whistle, saluang, mey, duduk, zurna, guanzi, darabukka and tapan (http://kimsandersworldmusic.com/kims-instruments/).

21. 'Kim was co-leader (with Linsey Pollak) of Australia's first World-Jazz band (Rabadaki, 79) and has since played with... Flamenco Dreaming, Nakisa, Okapi Guitar Band, Seaweed & Wire, Chichitote, Davood Tabrizi, Descendance and Balcano' (Sanders 2014). See Virtue (2010: 46–56) and Welsman (2010: 199–200) for more information about Sanders's career in world music.

'Gnome Chomsky's Deep Focus Boogie-Woogie'

Sanders recorded two versions[22] of 'Gnome Chomsky's Deep Focus Boogie-Woogie' ('Chomsky'). The original version is on the Brassov CD *Chronic Rhythmosis* (1997). The version used in this analysis is from the CD *You Can't Get There From Here* (2002) recorded by Kim Sanders and Friends at Megaphon Studios, Sydney in 2002. The musicians are Sanders (tenor saxophone), Peter Kennard (darabukka) and Steve Elphick (bass). The story behind the composition exemplifies Sanders's characteristic humour, imagination, philosophical musing and gentle rebellion against authority:

> Kim has a garden gnome. It's obviously a thinking sort of gnome because he has his chin on his fist, contemplation-like. So he called it Gnome Chomsky. Unfortunately the CIA, using agents disguised as cats and small children, twice smashed the top off Gnome's head; but Kim glued it back on, and Gnome's still out there, keeping the bastards honest (Brassov 1997: CD liner notes).

Boyd[23] recollects that Sanders composed 'Chomsky' for Brassov in 1996. Brassov was modelled on Romani (gypsy) brass bands of the Balkans, but incorporated influences from jazz, West African, Latin-American and reggae music, as well as musical conceptions unique to the members themselves. The composition is in 17/8, grouped 2 2 3 3 2 2 3. There are long asymmetric meters in Balkan dance music[24] that Sanders was familiar with, but the 17/8 meter in 'Chomsky' is most likely his own invention.[25] The meter is outlined by a bass (or baritone saxophone) riff shown in Figure 5.

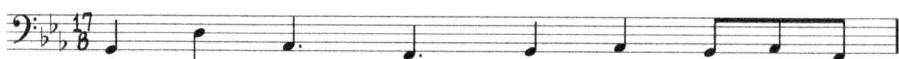

Figure 5: 'Chomsky', bass riff (concert pitch)

The contour of the tenor saxophone melody (Figure 6) also outlines the metric groupings.

22. Both recordings produced by Tony Gorman.
23. Boyd, personal email to author, 3 October 2014. Boyd is a multi-instrumentalist (baritone and bass saxophone, and bass and contra-bass clarinet) who was one of Sanders's colleagues in Brassov. The other musicians in Brassov were Robert Guzmanyi (trumpet), Christine Evans (alto saxophone), Peter Kennard (percussion) and Jamie Pattugalan (drum kit).
24. For example 'Sandansko Horo' in 22/8 grouped 2 2 2 3 2 2 2 3 2 2, and 'Jovino' in 18/8 grouped 3 2 2 2 2 3 2 2.
25. Verified by P. Kennard and M. Kiek, personal emails to author, 1 October 2014.

Figure 6: 'Chomsky', tenor saxophone melody (Bb transposition)

The pitch material used in the composition and improvisation incorporates ideas and approaches from modal jazz and Balkan brass band music. The influence of Sanders's knowledge of Bulgarian and Macedonian gaida (bagpipe) traditions and *makam*[26] in Turkish classical music is also apparent. The notes in 'Chomsky' come from the Phrygian dominant scale, shown in Figure 7, which has some similarity to the *makam Hijaz*.

Figure 7: Phrygian dominant scale

Sanders adds a harmonic element to the composition by using two notes from the mode—G and F—as bass notes to create different tonal centres. He develops this into a 4-bar solo form of 2 bars of G7♭9 followed by 2 bars of Fm7#11. Throughout the composition and improvisation Sanders only uses notes that belong to the scale. This contrasts with most modal jazz improvisations where players would typically employ some degree of chromaticism.[27] Sanders's melodies move almost exclusively in a step-wise scalar fashion, rarely using wide intervallic leaps. In these regards, Sanders's melodic conception is more similar to *makam* and traditional Balkan music than modal jazz,

---

26. *Makam (maqam)* is a complex, subtle and sophisticated melodic system used in the music of many Middle Eastern cultures. Although some correspondences between *makam* and mode can be identified, *makam* includes many dimensions that do not easily equate to Western conceptions. These include 'tonal spatial organization of a fixed number of tone-levels' (Touma 1971: 47) and interplay between compositional and improvisatory processes. Intonation in *makam* differs from equal temperament and includes many microtonal intervals. See Marcus (1993) regarding intonation in Arabic music.

27. Such as the technique of sideslipping developed by Coltrane and others, where a melodic cell is transposed (often by a semitone), and superimposed over the original tonality to create tension.

although, as Kennard says: 'it is testimony to how seamless his fusing of all this became; that we might struggle to unpick and identify individual elements'.[28]

Sanders's conception is informed by confluences he perceived between genres, as well as differences. He observes: 'The blues is really a *makam*...it uses the scale and bends between notes, and there are certain characteristic phrases' (Jones 2013).[29] Sanders uses bends between notes in his improvisation on 'Chomsky', and often ornaments phrases with grace notes. He uses a characteristic wide vibrato, particularly on long notes, that references Balkan vocal and bagpipe styles. His timbral concepts reflect both his passion for the sound of Archie Shepp and his study of Turkish ney: 'there are only six holes on the ney, so awareness of the overtones and mix of overtones in the sound helps with your tenor playing' (Sanders in Wockner 2008).

Sanders liked the rhythm section to provide a 'solid locked-in groove'[30] that he could phrase freely over. He instructed Kennard to 'concentrate on playing the riff...rather than counting the divisions'.[31] The riff established 'a specific constant ground/character/reference—against which the *makam* he was exploring would reveal itself, not just melodically but also rhythmically'.[32] Sanders moves between precisely outlining the rhythmic subdivisions of the 17/8 metre and more rubato phrasing. The rubato phrases most often occur towards the end of the rhythmic and harmonic cycle, creating a surge of new energy spiralling into the start of the next cycle.

The piece evokes a surreal, majestic grandeur, at once whimsical and passionate. Long melodic lines unfold in an asymmetric but sinuous flow, climaxing with an interlude Sanders christened 'James Brown horns'.[33] The CD title, *You Can't Get There From Here*, gives a cryptic clue about Sanders's musical philosophy. He travelled widely, both physically and musically. In 'Chomsky' he integrates feelings and ideas about form, timbre and musical language from a diverse range of sources encountered during these journeys without trying to be someone, or somewhere, he isn't.

Tony Gorman

Tony Gorman (1955–) was born and raised in Greenock, Scotland. He migrated to Sydney, Australia in January 1988 where he still resides. His father was a

---

28. P. Kennard, personal email to author, 1 October 2014.
29. See El Shibli (2007) for research into links between Islamic musical practices and the blues.
30. Kennard, personal email to author, 1 October 2014.
31. Ibid.
32. Ibid.
33. The title of the passage on Sanders's original manuscript.

13 Expressive identity in the voices of three Australian saxophonists

high-school teacher and a professional jazz and dance-band pianist. Listening to artists such as Count Basie, Dave Brubeck and Miles Davis in his elder brothers' record collections was a catalyst for Gorman's passion for jazz and the saxophone. Like McGann, Gorman cites Paul Desmond as an important early influence. Funk players such as Dave Sanborn and Tom Scott also influenced him. A formative teenage experience was playing in 666, a band inspired by progressive rock groups King Crimson and Van Der Graff Generator. During the same period,[34] Gorman studied Western classical music at the Royal Scottish Academy of Music and Drama, where clarinet teacher Janet Hilton was an important mentor. Gorman is best known for playing alto and tenor saxophone, and clarinet and alto clarinet. He is a versatile musician who performed in many jazz, world music, rock, classical and improvising ensembles. He observes: 'coming from Scotland, you had to be very versatile and play a wide variety of styles. It wasn't uncommon to play bebop, Keith Jarrett, Scottish country dancing and the Top Ten in the one gig'.[35] He was co-leader of Clarion Fracture Zone and the Original Otto Orchestra, and was a member of Chelate Compound, Mara!, and the Australian Art Orchestra.[36] Gorman has travelled extensively, once spending 18 months working as a musician on cruise ships in the Caribbean.

'Spice Island'

'Spice Island' is from the Clarion Fracture Zone (CFZ) CD *Blue Shift* (1998)[37] recorded at ABC studios, Sydney in 1990. The musicians are Gorman (alto saxophone), Sandy Evans (tenor saxophone), Alister Spence (piano), Steve Elphick (bass) and Andrew Dickeson (drums).[38] Gorman wrote 'Spice Island' in 1988 when CFZ was formed. 'Spice Island' is one of a series of 'long trek journey pieces'[39] that emerged from a passion for Horace Silver, and experience playing in

---

34. On the website 'Scotbands' a banner says: 'During 666's break at the [Burns'] Howff [rock venue in Glasgow] Tony Gorman stands up with his clarinet and plays Stravinski—a tumbleweed moment while the bemused silent audience think they've smoked one too many—conversation only returning as the band restarts' (Lawrence 2014).
35. Gorman, interview with author, 23 August 2014.
36. See *Dr Jazz* (Perry 1998) and *Extempore* (Zolin 2008) for more information about Gorman's career.
37. *Blue Shift* was released by ABC Music in 1990 and reissued by Rufus Records in 1998.
38. Alister Spence, Sandy Evans and Tony Gorman were co-leaders of CFZ. Bass player Lloyd Swanton and drummers Toby Hall, Tony Buck and Louis Burdett were subsequent members of the rhythm section.
39. Gorman, interview with author, 23 August 2014. 'Moshoeshoe The First' and 'Moshoeshoe The Second' are other examples of Gorman's compositions in this genre for CFZ.

Scotland with African drum band Atsimevu.[40] In 'Spice Island' Gorman wanted to evoke 'super hot emotion', a spirit he associated with Caribbean calypso bands that helped him develop 'an appreciation for "simple" ways of playing music'.[41]

'Spice Island' has a 20-bar form. The saxophone parts and chord sequence are shown in Figure 8.

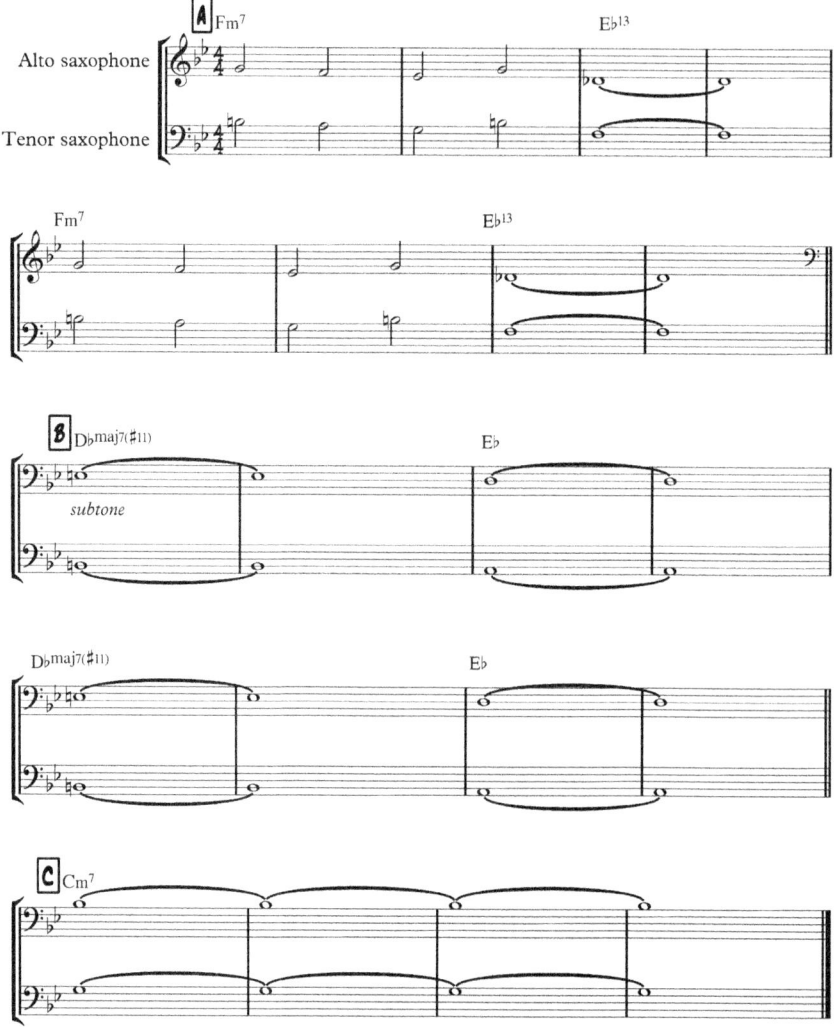

Figure 8: 'Spice Island', form and saxophone melodies (concert pitch)

40. Ibid.
41. Gorman, interview with author, 30 September 2014. 'Eternal Frost' is a companion piece to 'Spice Island' where Gorman says he wanted to evoke 'super cold, unemotion'.

13 Expressive identity in the voices of three Australian saxophonists

Elements from twentieth-century Western classical music, modal jazz and blues converge in Gorman's melodic and harmonic language in 'Spice Island'. The saxophone parts move homophonically in parallel harmonies (a 6th apart at letters A and C, and a 4th apart at letter B), reminiscent of orchestration techniques Gorman admires in Bartok's 'Concerto for Orchestra'.[42] The texture created by the harmonic and timbral meshing of the two parts is often more important than the melody of the upper part. This is particularly evident at letter B (Figure 9) where alto and tenor saxophone play identical notes (on the instrument) subtone in the low register.

Figure 9: 'Spice Island', B melody (Eb and Bb transposition)

Figure 10 illustrates the pitch material in this bar in concert pitch.

Figure 10: 'Spice Island', first bar of letter B (concert pitch)

Gorman's use of dissonance in the composition and improvisation is a striking feature. The melody notes—E and B—appear to be dissonant, or even wrong, in the harmonic context of the D♭maj7 chord.[43] The harmony could perhaps be

---

42. Gorman, interview with author, 7 September 2014.
43. The minor 3rd (in this case E) is usually considered an 'avoid' note on a major 7th

analysed as a D♭m7♭5 with an added major 7th (in the piano part) and natural 5th (in the bass part). However, this analysis forces Gorman's conception into a paradigm where it doesn't entirely belong. The timbre, feel and groove of the three-note voicings in the piano ostinato form one stream of sound whose independent journey as blocks of colour cannot always be explained in terms of a jazz harmonic approach. Heble speaks of dissonance as sounds 'that are "out of tune" with orthodox habits of coherence and judgment' (Heble 2000: 9). Gorman's use of dissonance, both in the composition and improvisation in 'Spice Island', owes as much to his passion for the music of Stravinsky and Messiaen, as to orthodoxies of jazz harmonic language with which, at times, it is 'out of tune'. Gorman draws inspiration from several sources to form his own unique melodic and harmonic language. The dissonant sounds have an intriguing and subtle beauty in the context of the soft and gentle dynamic, the breathy subtone timbre of the saxophones, the consonant relationship between the two saxophone parts, and the hypnotic groove.

Of his improvisations on 'Spice Island', Gorman says: 'I was always trying to express intense relaxation... In a piece like that, that's when I say my prayers. Although it's slow, it's not meant to be the least bit sad. It's a very optimistic piece.'[44] He uses vibrato to create 'hotness and warmth'.[45] Gorman expresses affinity with powerful forms of vocal expression, including both European opera and African-American oratory.

> I have an operatic approach to playing melodies... I seek to follow the rhythms of natural breathing; to have the oratory commentaries of Martin Luther King, or Roland Kirk...the rise and fall of the voice. I am talking about a subject I'm extremely passionate about and will end screaming, or proclaiming my love of God.[46]

The architecture of improvised solos is a prime consideration for Gorman.[47] He recalls that he learned to consider the architecture of short (typically 8-bar) solos 'in relation to the rest of the song'[48] when he played in rock, funk and show bands. Rock guitarists were Gorman's main models for this aspect of his improvisatory process, particularly in relation to rhythmic phrasing. He often leaves a few bars silent at the end of a chorus to gather his thoughts for

---

chord in jazz theory. For example, it isn't listed as a choice in any scale for a major chord in Aebersold's scale syllabus (1974: ii).

44. Gorman, interview with author, 30 September 2014.
45. Ibid.
46. Ibid.
47. Gorman, interview with author, 7 September 2014.
48. Ibid.

the next chapter. He says 'Each chorus is another chapter where I flex more muscles, including the diaphragm'.[49] His solo builds to a climax over six choruses. The intensity in his sound increases and he uses a high tessitura progressively more, opening out into a raft of soaring melodic proclamations in the altissimo register. Gorman realized he 'didn't want to be a bebop player. Everything had already been done, so why bother? I looked for ways to take different sized steps.'[50] Gorman takes 'different sized steps' from one chorus to the next in his solo on 'Spice Island' creating emotional intensity and a carefully constructed architectural contour.

Expressive identity

Intersections and differences between the lives and music of these three saxophonists provide insight into ways individual identity shapes the 'structure of jazz' (Ulanov 1979: 245). Their music speaks in some ways to generational difference: McGann's bebop roots; Sanders's interest in world music and the avant-garde of the 1960s; Gorman adding the influence of 1970s funk and progressive rock. The Dave Brubeck Quartet was influential on the early development of all three musicians; for McGann and Gorman this was to do with the sound and style of saxophonist Paul Desmond; for Sanders, Brubeck awakened his interest in playing asymmetric rhythms. The multiplicity of small but significant communities of musicians and listeners, whose overlapping and fluid membership organically develops around bands, venues and music organizations, are of primary importance in the work of all three saxophonists. They all recorded for the Sydney jazz label Rufus Records, performed for the Sydney Improvised Music Association and appeared at the Strawberry Hills Hotel during the 1990s. Their presence in local subcultural communities[51] contrasts with a relative invisibility on the international jazz stage, although all three musicians performed internationally and did receive a degree of international recognition. Australia's geographic isolation and relative invisibility in the international jazz scene afforded some freedom to traverse, explore and reimagine genre boundaries and stylistic conventions in innovative ways.

McGann's 'Playground' expands on formal structures and harmonic language from bebop; Sanders's 'Chomsky' develops a new Balkan inspired meter and explores confluences between modal jazz and *makam*; Gorman's

49. Gorman, interview with author, 30 September 2014.
50. Ibid.
51. This did not equate to financial sustainability, recognition in mainstream Australian culture, or certainty or regularity of performance and recording opportunities for any of the saxophonists.

'Spice Island' integrates melodic and harmonic approaches from twentieth-century Western classical music with jazz and rock. Timbral manipulation such as vibrato, articulation and register shifts are important for each player. Sanders's vibrato is a mark of his identification with Balkan vocal and bagpipe traditions; McGann makes bebop sound fresh with his unique articulation, sound and time feel; Gorman uses the expressive qualities of different registers of the saxophone to shape the architecture and intensity of his improvisation. They each harness the saxophone's expressive potential to 'identify' and 'disidentify with...inherited forms [and] playing procedures' (Ulanov 1979: 256) in a range of diverse, overlapping and unique ways. Their creative choices result in a *'positioning'* (Hall 1989: 226; original emphasis) of their sonic identities in relation to other like and unlike music-sound events. Depending on the perspective of the listener, the positioning of the players' choices might be interpreted differently. For example, the integration of Balkan elements into Sanders's expressive language could be read as part of the 'necessary movement of jazz to expand its resources' (Ulanov 1979: 256), or disidentification with 'inherited forms and playing procedures in jazz' (ibid.), or identification with inherited forms and playing procedures in Balkan music.

McGann, Sanders and Gorman use form, timbre, musical language and feeling in compositional and improvisatory processes in diverse, overlapping and imaginative ways. Jazz is a gateway connecting them to the aesthetic and creative pulse(s) of the world (Sarath 2013: 9), pulses emanating from bop, cool, swing, post-bop, avant-garde, Latin-American, blues, rock, funk, calypso, West African, Balkan, Turkish and Western classical musics. From Gnome Chomsky ruminating on Boogie-Woogie in his garden in Dulwich Hill to McGann's post-bop 'Playground' to Gorman's 'Spice Island', the work of these three saxophonists gives voice to distinctive expressions of identity. The differences between them, and the wide variety of global musical source cultures they draw from, indicate the breadth and diversity of Australian jazz. It is imperative to consider Australian jazz identity as multiply-constituted, and to undertake critical enquiry to understand and document the musical practices of the individuals and groups who create and inhabit Australia's richly nuanced musical spaces: a 'Playground' you **can** get to from here.

References

Aebersold, Jamey (1974) *The II-V7-I Progression*. New Albany, IN: Jamey Aebersold Jazz, Inc.
—(1978) *The Charlie Parker Omnibook*. New York: Atlantic Music Corp.
Appudurai, Arjun (1996) *Modernity at Large: Cultural Dimensions of Globalization*. Minneapolis: University of Minnesota Press.
Berliner, Paul F. (1994) *Thinking in Jazz: The Infinite Art of Improvisation*. Chicago: University of Chicago Press. http://dx.doi.org/10.7208/chicago/9780226044521.001.0001

Clare, John (1995) *Bodgie Dada and the Cult of Cool: Jazz in Australia since the 1940s*. Sydney: University of New South Wales Press.
Cooper, John Burnie (1996) 'An Aesthetic Inquiry into a Process of Composition for the Jazz Orchestra'. PhD thesis, New York University.
De Veaux, Scott, and Gary Giddins (2009) *Jazz*. New York: W. W. Norton.
El Shibli, Fatima (2007) 'Islam and the Blues'. *Souls: A Critical Journal of Black Politics, Culture, and Society* 9/2: 162-70. http://dx.doi.org/10.1080/10999940701382615
Erm, Anne (1990) 'A Band of Lovers'. *Eesti Ekspress* (Estonian Express), 27 July.
Feld, Steven (2005) 'Communication, Music, and Speech about Music'. In *Music Grooves* by Charles Keil and Steven Feld, 77–95. Tuscon, AZ: Fenestra Books.
Ford, Andrew (2012) 'Bernie McGann: Alto Saxophonist Turns 75'. ABC Radio National, http://www.abc.net.au/radionational/programs/musicshow/bernie-mcgann/4418266 (accessed 6 September 2014).
Friberg, A., and A. Sundström (1997) 'Preferred Swing Ratio in Jazz as a Function of Tempo'. *TMH-QPSR* 38/4: 19–27.
Hall, Stuart (1989) 'Cultural Identity and Diaspora'. *Framework: The Journal of Cinema and Media* 36: 222–37.
Heble, Ajay (2000) *Landing on the Wrong Note: Jazz, Dissonance and Critical Practice*. New York and London: Routledge.
Hicks, Tony (2011) 'The Path to Abstraction: A Practice Led Investigation into the Emergence of An Abstract Improvisation Language'. MMus thesis, Victorian College of the Arts and Music, University of Melbourne.
Johnson, Bruce (1987) *The Oxford Companion to Australian Jazz*. Melbourne: Oxford University Press.
Jones, Anthony Linden. (2013) 'Kim Sanders—a Casual Conversation with Anthony Linden Jones'. musicinaustralia.org.au, http://musicinaustralia.org.au/index.php? (accessed 22 August 2014).
Jordan, Seth (2013) 'Kim Sanders: World Music Pioneer was Also a Top Jazz Performer'. *Sydney Morning Herald*, 21 December.
Keil, Charles (2005) 'Motion and Feeling through Music'. In *Music Grooves* by Charles Keil and Steven Feld, 53–76. Tuscan, AZ: Fenestra Books.
Lawrence, Brian (2014) 'Scotbands: Musicians G'. http://www.scotbands.moonfruit.com/musicians-g/4532511282 (accessed 6 October 2014).
Levine, Mark (1989) *The Jazz Piano Book*. Petaluma, CA: Sher Music Co.
Lewis, George (2002) 'Improvised Music after 1950: Afrological and Eurological Perspectives'. *Black Music Research Journal* 22: 215–46. http://dx.doi.org/10.2307/1519950
Lucas, Kevin (1991) *Beyond El Rocco*. Lucas Produkzions and FFC. DVD.
Marcus, Scott (1993) 'The Interface between Theory and Practice: Intonation in Arab Music'. *Asian Music* (University of Texas Press) 24/2: 39–58. http://dx.doi.org/10.2307/834466
Monson, Ingrid (1996) *Saying Something: Jazz Improvisation and Interaction*. Chicago: University of Chicago Press.
Nicholson, Stuart (2005) *Is Jazz Dead? (Or has it Moved to a New Address)*. New York and London: Routledge.
Page, Geoff (1997) *Bernie McGann: A Life in Jazz*. Armidale, NSW: Kardoorair Press.
Perry, David (1998) *Dr Jazz*. Artfilms. DVD.

Potter, Gary (1990) 'Analyzing Improvised Jazz'. *College Music Symposium* 30/1: 64–74.
Rascher, Sigurd M. (1983) *Top-Tones for the Saxophone*. New York: Carl Fischer.
Sanders, Kim (2014) 'Kim Sanders World Music'. http://kimsandersworldmusic.com (accessed 22 August 2014).
Sarath, Edward W. (2013) *Improvisation, Creativity and Consciousness: Jazz as Integral Template for Music, Education, and Society*. Albany, NY: SUNY Press.
Shand, John (2002) 'Cooking up Multicultural Treats in a Musical Fantasy Land'. *Sydney Morning Herald*, 14 November.
—(2009) *Jazz: The Australian Accent*. Sydney: University of New South Wales Press.
Touma, Habib Hassan (1971) 'Tha Maqam Phenomenon: An Improvisation Technique in the Music of the Middle East'. *Ethnomusicology* 15/1: 38–48. http://dx.doi.org/10.2307/850386
Ulanov, Barry (1979) 'Jazz: Issues of Identity'. *Musical Quarterly* 65/2 (April): 245–56. http://dx.doi.org/10.1093/mq/LXV.2.245
Virtue, Therese (2010) 'The Compelling Tug of Asymmetric Rhythms: Balkan, Gypsy and Klezmer Sounds in Australia'. In *World Music: Global Sounds in Australia*, ed. Seth Jordan, 46–56. Sydney: University of New South Wales Press.
Welsman, Kate (2010) 'The Global Drop: Cross-cultural Hybrids and World DJ Culture'. In *World Music: Global Sounds in Australia*, ed. Seth Jordan, 199–195–211. Sydney: University of New South Wales Press.
Wilson, Peter Niklas (2001) *Sonny Rollins: The Definitive Musical Guide*. Berkeley, CA: Berkley Hills Books.
Wockner, Peter (2008) 'Interview with Kim Sanders'. Jazzandbeyond. http://www.jazzandbeyond.com.au/sound/KimSanders.mp3 (accessed 23 August 2014).
Zolin, Miriam, ed. (2008) *Extempore*. Kew, Victoria: Extempore Pty Ltd.

Interviews with the author
Gorman, T. (2014) Written notes, 23 August, 7 September and 30 September.

Discography
Brassov (1997) *Chronic Rhythmosis*. Rufus Records, RF032 CD recording.
Clarion Fracture Zone (1998) *Blue Shift*. Rufus Records, RF040 CD recording.
McGann, Bernie (1996) *Playground*. Rufus Records, RF023 CD recording.
Parker, Charlie (1951) *Anthropology*. Columbia.
Sanders, Kim (2002) *You Can't Get There From Here*. Kim Sanders. CD recording.

14 *Sex* and the sonic smorgasbord

The Necks—extending the 'jazz' piano trio format

Jane Galbraith[*]

Introduction

The Necks—Chris Abrahams (piano) Lloyd Swanton (bass) and Tony Buck (drums)—are one of Australia's leading trios of improvised music. This publication explores how the international achievements of The Necks over a 25-year-plus career have established them as one of the most important and distinctive Australian jazz groups. *The Guardian*'s (UK) John Walters describes them as:

> Entirely new and entirely now... They produce a post-jazz, post-rock, post-everything sonic experience that has few parallels or rivals... They may be teaching us to listen in a new way, but they communicate a fierce energy and warmth at the same time. Their music is a thrilling, emotional journey into unknown territory... Like seeing a world in a grain of sand, The Necks permit us to hear a whole new world of music in a sliver of sound (Walters 2001).

In the light of their extraordinary international reception, this chapter presents an overview of their approach to improvisation, combining discussion of significant aspects of their music as preserved on recordings. The focus is on how The Necks expand the 'jazz' piano trio format. Central to the argument is the enigmatic nature of their work where the parameters are both simultaneously open and restricted. What originally began as a collaborative personal project between the three musicians evolved into an eventual display of public performance, establishing many of the elements that characterize

---

[*] Jane Galbraith is a Sydney-based jazz pianist, educator and writer. She studied jazz piano with Mike Nock at the Sydney Conservatorium of Music before embarking upon a successful career as a performer. Jane completed her Doctor of Creative Arts at the University of Technology, Sydney, on the music of the Australian free improvising trio The Necks. She has a particular interest in approaches to creating new and experimental art works.

much of their work: the one-hour sets in which they explore the unknown using strict guidelines; no rehearsals; no discussion of a gig in advance; the players taking it in turns to begin each piece and setting up a groove using repetitive motifs and a minimalist approach on which to base a performance. The Necks subvert a number of established jazz conventions. They established a formula early on and this hasn't changed. Characteristic is the eschewal of the overt 'virtuoso' profile and the abandonment of 'theme...solo improvisations...theme' in favour of a less formally structured, reflective or meditative approach (which is also reflected in the live performance dynamic—no 'solo...applause...solo'). They are less inclined to play 'outside' conventional harmonic structures. Whilst they incorporate cross-generic influences, this is now a well-established fashion or 'fusion' in jazz, and does not on its own distinguish the band.

Despite these established elements, The Necks explore new ideas about rhythm, form and instrumentation. Characterized by a fusion of jazz, ambient and world music influences, their diverse body of work ranges through studio and live performances. They have recorded 17 albums, composed music for film (*The Boys*), television (*In the Mind of the Architect*) and worked on live, installation-based projects (including *Life After Wartime*, and improvised accompaniment to the play *Food Court*).

Photograph by Holimage—The Necks website

Global and local—free improvised music, the minimalists and exploring sonic boundaries

Jazz is constantly evolving, absorbing external influences and expanding its horizons geographically. Whilst jazz critics and writers on Australian jazz differ in terms of the degree to which post-bebop bands have forged new ways of improvising and experimenting with the production of sound, there is general consensus regarding the importance of The Necks as leading exponents of a new type of free improvised hybrid fusion. The Australian jazz writer and critic John Shand argues that 'Australia has become a creative center of jazz, rivalling the Scandinavian and Western European countries that have steadily diluted New York's pre-eminence over the last three decades' (Shand 2009: 2). Certainly a fusion of styles has occurred in Australia, particularly in post-1960s jazz, resulting in the emergence of some highly original performers and bands.

There are a number of examples of Australian musicians exploring free improvisation; however, none exhibits the characteristics and processes adopted by The Necks. It is beyond the scope of this chapter to explore in detail other Australian jazz bands and their relationship (or not) to The Necks; however, a brief discussion of some of the key protagonists follows. I include some who have connections with extending the 'jazz' piano trio format as a foundation and new ways of creating sound.

One of the first to explore new directions in improvised music is Charlie Munro whose ground-breaking album from 1967, *Eastern Horizons*, is an early example of world music and free jazz, with its influences from Indian, Arabic, Japanese and other sources. Munro explores modes, textures, polyphony and sounds prevalent in these cultural contexts. Pianist and saxophonist Roger Frampton pioneered acoustic and electronic music in a free improvised way in the early 1970s with the bands Teletopa (1970) and the Jazz Co-Op (1972). He was influenced by avant-garde minimalists such as John Cage and his philosophy:

> In Teletopa we sometimes used conventional instruments, but we tried to find other ways of producing sounds from them. We wanted to disguise the instrument and go beyond its role. And we used found objects, to which we attached little microphones, and just tried to find other sound sources. One of the most amazing sounds I heard was a vacuum cleaner with a balloon over the end, used as a membrane. You could control the pitch and it was incredibly loud (Clare 1995: 145).

Jon Rose,[1] an Australian violinist born in the UK, has been at the forefront of experimental improvised music and media since the 1970s. One of his celebrated works is the worldwide Fence project—an environmental performance based on bowing fences in the Australian outback. Rose is an internationally recognized exponent of free improvisation and sound art, new instrument design and interactive electronics. Both Chris Abrahams and Tony Buck have

---

1. www.jonroseweb.com (accessed 25 September 2014).

collaborated with Rose on a number of inventive projects (Abrahams with the trio Artery and Buck with The Exiles). At the extreme end of the free improvised spectrum pianist Serge Ermoll's Free Kata 'was one of the few bands in the world that improvised at all times with no predetermined structures or guidelines whatsoever—no tune, no chord sequence; not even a drone or a rhythmic pattern' (Clare 1995: 149). The arrival of British double bass virtuoso and keyboardist Roger Dean in 1989 saw him form the group AustraLYSIS with Sandy Evans and Tony Buck which explored:

> a kind of rarified lyricism of wide intervals and silences, to dense, polyrhythmic, high-energy cataclysms. When Buck has been in the band he has used a sampler at high speed while drumming—greatly expanding the sonic range. Dean not infrequently uses the acoustic piano and synthesizer simultaneously, sharing Buck's ability to 'program' on the run (Clare 1995: 187–88).

Jazz writer John Clare argues that there has been a general lack of innovation in Australian jazz.

> My feeling is that Australian jazz has not created any profoundly new idioms, but has found its own slant on several jazz styles. Roger Dean, who played for years at the highest levels of European jazz and new music, tended to agree: 'There is a lot of stuff around that is distinctive and separate in some ways from the American thing—just as there is in Europe... In the newer idioms, I think to a degree The Necks are original. What they do is related to Californian things, like Terry Riley, but I think it has something of its own' (Clare 1995: 201–203).

John Shand further explores a connection between The Necks, American and UK minimalists:

> There were obvious precursors for their concept of slow motion, evolving repetition in the work of minimalist composers such as Steve Reich and the loop-based ambient dreams of Robert Fripp and Brian Eno. But the minimalists were working with strict notation rather than improvisation, and Fripp and Eno with the aesthetics of sound more than with human interaction (Shand 2009: 97).

In a global context there is a connection with American minimalists Terry Riley, Steve Reich, Philip Glass and Charlemagne Palestine, but there is also a European influence in their work, similar to the work produced by the Munich-based ECM label, as well as a distinctively Australian identity to their music, which I discuss below.

To exemplify the connections just alluded to, there are similarities in The Necks' use of minimalist and repetitive pitch patterns, and a definable tonality not unlike Riley's *In C*. The concept—an innovation consisting of 53 separate modules of roughly one measure apiece, each containing a different musical pattern but each, as the title implies, in the key of C—contains parallels with the way The Necks explore and manipulate groups of sounds (as will be shown in *Drive By* [2003]). The anchoring of a steady pedal point based on 'C' is a frequently employed repetitive device used by Swanton. Steve Reich's exploration of samples and loops are techniques The Necks have incorporated into their work (as heard in *Silent Night* [1996]) and *Drive By* which are discussed below). Reich's *Come Out* with its continuously looped vocal patterns gradually slipping out of sync and widening to become vague references to the original rhythmic and tonal speech patterns resulting in a conglomeration of sound, is similar to The Necks' use of related processes. Philip Glass's use of repetition and minimalism is often apparent with The Necks' music. The use of pitch patterns in *Music in Fifths*, which explore aspects of the interval of a 5th (open, sparse), along with repetition and minimalism, are frequently employed techniques by The Necks. There are similarities between Charlemagne Palestine's ritualistic style, although not his flamboyance, and Abrahams' work. *Strumming Music* (1974), for example, perhaps Palestine's best known work, features over 45 minutes of forcefully playing two notes in rapid alternation that slowly expand into clusters. The sustain pedal is depressed for the entire length of the work and the music swells and leads to the detuning of the piano. Subsequently the overtones build and create a variety of timbres rarely produced by the piano. As will be discussed below, Chris Abrahams experiments with a range of sonic capabilities and a number of different keyboard instruments.

Since the 1980s and the establishment of jazz courses at leading tertiary institutions such as the New South Wales State Conservatorium of Music (1973) and the Victorian College of the Arts (1982), a number of contemporaries of The Necks have made invaluable contributions to current improvised music scenes in Australia including Clarion Fracture Zone, The catholics, Wanderlust, Alister Spence, Jackie Orszaczky, Sandy Evans, Matt McMahon, Mark Simmonds, Phil Slater and Mike Nock.

Between the head and the shoulders

Chris Abrahams describes the origins of the band's name: 'The Neck. It's one of the more functional parts of the human body. It's quite modest. And it's something that in some ways lacks a kind of identity. It's between the head and the shoulders' (Galbraith and Mitchell 2005: 11). This quote captures significant features of The Necks. Onstage they are modest and unassuming. The 'lack of identity' parallels the difficulty in categorizing their music. Despite a number of key features being discussed here that set them apart from other Australian jazz groups, there is an ambiguity and abstractness in their work—difficult to define and amorphous: 'Between the head and the shoulders.' Some critics, and indeed The Necks themselves, refer to 'blurred boundaries' in relation to jazz. Chris Abrahams speaks of the difficulty in categorizing their music:

> I've hopefully ceased to get really hung up on being categorized. To me it's totally human. If you don't have the music to play people you've got to actually try and describe it somehow. No one's ever going to describe it how it really is. Most people think of us still as a jazz band and that's the way it is (Galbraith and Mitchell 2005: 5).

Certainly the piano trio format and the inclusion of standard jazz harmonic devices (7ths, 9ths), and rhythmic feels such as swing and syncopated accenting, pedal points and modes are consistent with the jazz genre. Absent, however, is the overt 'theme…solo improvisations…theme' structure, superseded by a progressive, linear structure. Buck sees 'Miles Davis's *In a Silent Way* and *On the Corner*, where the ensemble sound took precedent over the virtuoso soloist' (Buck in Shand 2009: 97), as also exerting a significant influence on The Necks. It is the juxtaposition of The Necks' approach to free improvisation with conventional musical traditions that adds to the difficulty of categorizing their music.

Background

The Necks' genesis is described by Chris Abrahams:

> We've all known each other and played together. Even though the band was formed in 1986 Lloyd and I played in a group between 1980 and 1985. Tony and I grew up in the same suburb. I first played with him when I was about seventeen so we have quite a large shared musical relationship (Galbraith and Mitchell 2005: 8).

The Necks began in 1986 as a collaborative personal project between the three musicians. When the band formed they were adamant they weren't going to play in public. Rather, the experience was more an outlet away from other projects they worked on as individuals. The longevity of their musical association is sustained by a specific rapport. The Australian jazz writer and academic John Whiteoak describes this as a 'unique ensemble syntax and sound' (Whiteoak 2004: 5). All of the members are in equal partnership in the creative process and direction. Chris Abrahams has explicitly stated that if any one of The Necks members was unable to continue with the group, it would cease to exist (Galbraith and Mitchell 2005: 6). They subvert the common hierarchical band leader scenario by adopting a shared approach and the band members take turns in starting a performance.

Individually Abrahams, Buck and Swanton have pursued highly successful careers working with other performers locally and internationally, bringing a wide diversity of experience from other contexts into the group ranging from fairly conventional rock music to extreme avant-garde practices. In 1991 Buck moved to Japan where he played and co-founded the Australian/Japanese experimental, post-punk, hardcore, improvised noise outfit PERIL, an improvising group with a rock/noise focus. Not ready to return to Australia, he moved to Amsterdam in 1994 and immersed himself in the European improvisation scene. In 1997 Buck based himself in Berlin, which remains his current home in between frequent touring, and he finds the supportive arts community there inspiring. Abrahams, too, has forged connections on an international scale through his increasing participation in the Berlin Echtzeitmusik free improvisation scene. The term 'Echtzeitmusik' translates as real time, in the sense that the decision about what one plays happens in the moment of playing.

Sex (1989): the beginning

The Necks' first studio album *Sex* displays many distinguishing characteristics that already set them apart from other Australian jazz bands. Firstly, it establishes the hour-long format adopted in live performances and most of their studio albums. They have also explored a variety of other structural formats (e.g. shorter pieces as heard in their second album *Next* [1990]). *Sex* is based on an idea by Swanton which subverts the soloist/accompanist model that is so entrenched in contemporary jazz practice. Titled 'The Wheel' (1983), it was inspired by Indian music and based on a concept with

> all members gradually transforming the ensemble part, rather than there being soloists and accompanists, but the piece did not work. When The Necks recorded for the first time they used the rhythm parts to 'The Wheel', but dispensed with the melody (Shand 2009: 98).

This exemplifies the abandonment of the traditional jazz dynamic of themes and solos that is a feature of their work. *Sex* sets up a format in which each instrument enters as a strongly differentiated timbral, rhythmic and motivic presence, creating a framework on which to develop individual ideas such as small pitch sets and motifs. The trademark trance-like mantra is created through this build-up of texture, staggered entries and the repetition and gradual transformation of subtle rhythmic and melodic shadings. The 'jazz' piano trio format is extended in *Sex* to include a plethora of electronic samples and other sources suggesting the idea of a sonic smorgasbord. A conglomeration of sounds—sawing, woodblock, finger cymbals, temple bells, bongos, maracas and ratchet noises—emerges with the addition of environmental sounds such as wood and water that are multi-tracked and cleverly woven into the piece. These are used very quietly, allusively, almost subliminally, rather than being ostentatiously foregrounded, forming part of a background sonic fabric.

Whilst in subsequent recordings The Necks experiment with asynchronous rhythm, a defined rhythmic pulse and restricted parameters which are a common feature of their work, a moderate steady tempo and 4/4 time signature are established and maintained throughout *Sex*. In creating a minimalist, repetitive and hypnotic piece the band overdubbed a dual take whilst using a two-bar motif as a basis on which to construct their improvisations. The bass sets up the opening with an octave A↑A' two-bar ostinato (A minor tonality), forming a relentless, minimalist platform to which Abrahams provides contrast through a diverse array of piano registers, pitch patterns and rhythmic variants. These include sustained cluster chords based on 4ths and 5ths, sparse, angular descending chords based on 4ths, and rapidly descending semiquaver scale passages. Closely entwined with this is Buck's repetitive and meticulous drumming characterized by a constant, driving, swing pulse. *Sex* is hypnotic and repetitive, blending simplicity with experimentation. The frequently used one-hour format characterized by subtle and gradual change is already established alongside other features that set The Necks apart from other Australian jazz bands.

Aquatic (1994): cross-generic fusion

The Necks incorporate cross-generic influences, although this is now a well-established convention in jazz, so it does not on its own distinguish the band in the history of Australian jazz. An example is heard in The Necks' third album *Aquatic*. The sonic horizons are expanded through a Renaissance-meets-world music festival of multi-tracked sound effects, wild animal sounds, 1980s organ, Hendrix-inspired wah-wah pedals (on track 1), as well as tremolos and heavy reverb used on the piano. Subverting the typical one-hour format, the album comprises two half-hour tracks, each titled 'Aquatic'. The inclusion of hurdy gurdy played by Stevie Wishart on track 2 contributes to a defamiliarizing effect that evokes sonic images of untempered Renaissance music. This is emphasized by the prominent status afforded Wishart in the form of a highly exposed reedy, distorted improvisation—cadenza-like in its execution. Abrahams explores a range of techniques and melodic material in the form of repeated single notes in the opening section, ascending, fragmented scale passages, heavily pedalled and hammered piano, pentatonic triplet motifs, chant-like motifs and extensive use of trills. Swanton precedes the hurdy gurdy solo with a double bass solo, exploiting a repeated minimalist two-note F → F# pitch pattern.

An unusual approach to rhythm is adopted. In the opening section of track 2, polyrhythmic effects are explored between the constant 4/4 pulse of the two-note octave jump in the double bass (this interval featuring predominantly in Swanton's bass motifs in numerous Necks' performances including *Sex*). This is juxtaposed with a contrasting tambourine rhythm which, initially giving the illusion of being out of time, is actually a layering of triple time. Both feels, however, seamlessly combine to create a robust 12/8 rhythm recalling the form of a Renaissance folk dance. Whilst demonstrating many common elements used by The Necks including minimalist pitch patterns and Abrahams's use of trills, triplet motifs, chant-like in their execution (further discussed below), *Aquatic* explores new ideas in terms of structure and the addition of instrumentation borrowed from the Renaissance era.

The sonic smorgasbord—techniques, sampling and multi-tracking

In The Necks' output, the boundaries of the 'jazz' piano trio are extended further both through the exploration of acoustic instrumental techniques as well as through the addition of other instrumentation and electronica. Citing Cecil Taylor as an influence, Abrahams employs trademark piano techniques such as the use of pounding clusters created by hitting the forearm horizontally on the piano keys and extending the use of the pedal to fine-tune the subtle, sustained sonic capabilities of the instrument. Extreme tremolos, trills and other embellishments are also frequently used devices. He also uses his elbows and crossing over hands on the keyboard.

> Lately I've been interested in the keyboard as a kind of distancing mechanism. Even though it's presumably an interface with which you play the piano in a standard way by pressing the keys, I'm interested in trying to find ways of making the keyboard kind of problematic or in some way indeterminate as to what's going to happen with the instrument (Galbraith and Mitchell 2005: 7).

Like Charlemagne Palestine, Abrahams is renowned for his experimental approach to creating new sounds out of the acoustic piano and often tries effects that violate 200 years of piano tradition. He often subverts traditional techniques by trying to get the piano to distort in ways that piano makers don't necessarily anticipate. He has explored microtonality in tuning by pressing the sustain pedal down and playing very fast notes, which creates an effect whereby the wildly vibrating string sympathetically resonates every other string on the piano. This in turn creates a type of distortion, not unlike the effects pedal on an electric guitar. Keyboard sounds and techniques are also explored and incorporated into various multi-tracked studio albums. His armoury of keyboard instruments includes the DX7 synthesizer, audio samples, organ and Hammond organ.

Swanton explores the sonic capabilities of the bass using a variety of techniques. Repeated single plucked notes and octave jumps are commonly used as a foundation. Sustained notes and drones are frequently used, contributing to a spatial effect of suspension of sound. Pizzicato, arco, glissando, heavy vibrato, tremolo and percussive slides are also featured, often used as a subtle means to vary motifs and riffs. Double stopping (often bowed) thickens and intensifies the sound and is used to amplify the role of the bass. Although Swanton's usual instrument is the double bass, he also uses piccolo bass (pioneered by legendary Australian bassist Jackie Orzaczky) and electric bass. Sometimes in studio albums, both electric and double bass are used concurrently (such as on *Next* and *Silent Night*).

Buck experiments extensively with percussive effects such as using circular saws on the skin and rim of the floor tom to create a variation on using brushes resulting in a thicker, harsher, more intense sound. Orchestral techniques are common, with soft mallets often used to add timbral contrast via cymbals and floor tom. He even plays electric guitar on a number of Necks' albums (he made his debut on the instrument on *Chemist* [2006] and also plays it on *Silverwater* [2009] and *Open* [2013]).

Sampling and multi-tracking
Two examples highlighting The Necks' extension of the 'jazz' piano format and enhancing this with a diverse array of sonic material through multi-tracking— *Silent Night* and *Drive By*—invite analysis in this context.

Silent Night (1996). This album subverts the mood of the well-known Christmas carol *Silent Night*—all is not really calm or bright in the two dark and brooding tracks 'Black' (1:03:27) and 'White' (53:49). The Necks' fourth album, *Silent Night*, was released on the Fish of Milk label as a double CD, each track featuring the hour-long format. The *Rolling Stone* (Australia) review of the album describes The Necks as creating: 'mood music of the highest calibre. Compelling and beautiful music that repays repeated listening'.[2] *Silent Night* epitomises The Necks' foray into extending sonic horizons. Using an ambient bed of pre-recorded film sound (closing doors, footsteps, creaking, unzipping

---

2. http://www.thenecks.com (accessed 12 August 2012).

a bag, clunking, more footsteps, moving stands, paper, unscrewing the lid off a bottle, pouring a drink and laughing) independently as an introduction to track 1, 'Black', the piece morphs into a film noir soundscape featuring Abrahams on piano, organ and samples, Swanton on acoustic and electric bass and Buck on drums and samples. The piece embeds small audio grabs of classic films Abrahams had recorded off Special Broadcasting Service (SBS) television on VHS cassette over a number of years. Abrahams sees 'Black' as a homage to his favourite films and a soundtrack to a film that has been shot using small sound samples. Sustained Hammond organ lines drift in and out and extremes of registers are explored in the piano. The 'Mary Had A Little Lamb' motif (often used in other works such as *Next*, track 2 'Nice Policeman Nasty Policeman') gives the impression of Abrahams practising a distorted, warped version of the nursery rhyme. Extremes of register and minimalist pitch patterns are explored. Many electronic sound effects in the form of industrial and warped, phased sounds are used, the effect contrasting with both the traditional acoustic sounds of piano, bass and drums and the pre-recorded film excerpts. The use of modes and a tonal centre is demonstrated through the use of E minor tonality in track 1 and the use of a G Aeolian mode on track 2.

Drive By (2003). *Drive By* is The Necks' eleventh album and received the Best Jazz Album award in the Australian Recording Industry Association (ARIA) Music Awards of 2004. It was described by John Walters in the UK *Guardian*:

> If *Drive By* is a hitch-hike, it's an hour-long ride through William Gibson territory in a sleek limo, blurred shapes barely visible through the tinted windows. A triple-time electric piano figure provides a click track against which several different versions of The Necks fade in and out (Walters 2004).

According to Swanton:

> The concept of the album was to have discrete instrumental groups in different polyrhythms recorded simultaneously and move between them gradually. There's a couple of weeks of recording involved there. Most of the overdubs went for an hour—it's just that in the final mix, we may have only used a few minutes (Swanton in Walters 2004).

As usual, much more material was recorded than was utilized in the final mix, which condensed the material dramatically in the way hour-long dubs were reduced to a few minutes' duration. Abrahams describes this process:

> We do a lot of mixing and editing—not so much in terms of mixing the album tracks—particularly with *Drive By*. That was a situation where we just loaded it up. In all I think we ended up with 30 tracks. Each of us had an idea and we just did that for an hour on a piece of tape and then when we came to mix it, it became more of a performance phase (Galbraith and Mitchell 2005: 5).

This distinctive process whereby sounds were chosen, recorded and edited now becomes woven into the fabric of the improvisation. Buck reinforces the significance of this stage of mixing: 'The mixing is more important than the recording. After we finished recording we took away "rough mixes" with everything on them, they were really dense. At the mix the multi track becomes like playing a huge sampler with hour long samples' (Walters 2004).

A tonal centre of C is evident (this, however, is manipulated through the addition of Eb and Ab in the piano). There is some exploration of time through the use of 3/4 and 4/4 time signatures. *Drive By* begins with an electronic bass sound playing a repeated syncopated tonic/dominant pattern (C → G) followed by a constant electronic beeping sound and brief L → R panned radio signal effects. Intermittent grabs of sound effects appear as brief sonic punctuations in the form of helicopter and phased synthesizer sounds. More sound effects are incorporated in the form of electronic wind-up sounds, phased, tinny bell-like sounds and a Moroccan hand drum. The noises of children playing suggest a sonic narrative behind the music, followed by radio sound effects and electronic sounds (war-like sounds and gun shots). Sounds of swirling radio tuning, locusts, Hendrix-style organ and cockatoos flying overhead are heard. *Drive By* is very meditative, mesmerising and transfixing, exemplifying not only an experiment with sound, but is also an example of their distinct impact on the Australian jazz landscape.

Repetition: stuck in the groove or evolving the groove?

The way The Necks approach repetition is a key feature that sets them apart from most Australian improvising groups. The abandonment of 'theme…solo improvisations…theme' (or ternary form) is similar to a through-composed structural process, albeit made of subsections of material which gradually evolve. The Necks have often stated that change eventuates only as a result of being unable to tolerate further repetition of a musical idea. Brian Eno sums up the minimalist ethos in terms of repetition as a form of change (Ross 2009: 556) where each layering of repeated material is altered gradually, so that the initial statement of a motif is received differently from subsequent repeated material. This is significant in interpreting how The Necks' works are constructed and is an example of the subtle nuances and transitioning of ideas prevalent in their approach. Whilst repeated motifs and patterns are evident in their work, The Necks' music is not a simple conjunction of these, but it is about how these gradually metamorphose into something else.

This process is described by Chris Abrahams in terms of the Australianness of The Necks' music:

> The size of Australia—I see a real relationship in that. I found in about 93/4 I drove from Alice Springs to Darwin and I thought that was actually like a Necks experience. To see just this gradual, constant landscape that looks the same but then you're somewhere else (Galbraith and Mitchell 2005: 13).

The Boys (1998) and *Open* (2013)

Two examples of The Necks' work—*The Boys* and *Open*—particularly exemplify The Necks' idiosyncratic use of repetition.

The Boys—film music
The Boys is an Australian film directed by Rowan Woods released in 1998. The plot is loosely based on the Anita Cobby murder, although the murder is never graphically represented, and is a powerful and disturbing portrait of three brothers and the women in their lives. The Necks' approach to film composition is ambient, stark and minimalist, based on subtly shifting nuances. The music is characterized by mesmerising repetition, stillness and silence.

A long-time fan of The Necks, Rowan Woods invited them to be involved in the creation of music for the film in 1997. He was particularly impressed with *Silent Night*, in particular the film noir aspects of 'Black' and the incorporation of the 'narrative' of movie samples. 'Black' contained elements Woods sought in conveying the disturbing masculine violence and drama in *The Boys* and played it on set during rehearsals and filming as a means of psyching the actors into their parts and creating atmosphere. Unlike the traditional approach to film composition, The Necks didn't wait for a locked-off final cut to compose to. Instead, exposed to all aspects of the film, they entered the studio and simply played (Woods in Mitchell 2005: 7). In Necks tradition, large swathes of music, most of which were not used in the film, were recorded. From the 90 minutes of music presented to the editor less than 10 minutes were used in the film.

A dichotomy exists in The Necks looking for 'ways to establish the music as both a separate entity from the film and a commentary on it, which would exist on its own terms' (Mitchell 2005: 8–9). The music released on the soundtrack CD (their sixth) differs considerably in format from the majority of releases by The Necks: 49 minutes of music consisting of seven tracks of varying lengths (from just over three minutes to 20 minutes and 20 seconds), most of which evoke dark and menacing undertones. Four tracks not featured in the film occur on the CD. The original 1997 *Boys* soundtrack was deleted, which saw Abrahams and Swanton remixing and repackaging a version of their own in 2004 on their label Fish of Milk. Some additional less threatening, more lyrical pieces were added to the album.

'The Boys 1' (main theme) (04:28)
The opening credits, one of the three sequences in the film that use music, begin with black and white footage tracking shops, houses and the road—complete with white lines—as seen through the eyes of the main character from a moving car. Myriad sounds like buzzes are created by a DX7 synthesizer, electric machines contorting and malfunctioning and 'subaudible sounds emitted from high tension wires' (Woods in Mitchell 2005: 11). Mitchell cites the origin of these sounds as from Alan Lamb's 'Beauty' (from his 1995 album *Primal Image*). Lamb recorded ambient sounds by attaching microphones to telegraph wires in various locations and under various weather conditions over a seven-year period. The resultant foreboding white noise then merges using an overlapping fade into The Necks' music.

The minimalist main theme exhibits a tonal centre of G minor and is composed of a simple piano fragment DDD to Eb followed by repeated G/D two-note chords based on exposed 5ths which fade out. Repetition of a semitone fragment creates a Hitchcock-like tension. Mitchell (2005: 3) draws parallels between Bernard Herrmann's cinematic representations of violence and minimalism in the music from *Psycho* (USA 1960) and The Necks' music used in *The Boys*. Herrmann's use of high-pitched, screeching, repeated string motifs is a widely referenced early example of cinesonic minimalism. Within the 4:28 framework the motif is repeated 15 times. When music is present, it is 'confusingly allusive, disconnected, detached, often enhancing the disturbing indeterminacy of the film's mood by confusing the distinction between noise and music' (Johnson and Poole 2005: 104). Nick Meyers, editor and sound editor of *The Boys*, recalls:

> The Necks also did atmosphere effects... We were chasing the tonal quality of the sound effects...you're not quite sure where the effects stop and the music starts because a lot of the effects have a musical quality and some of the music is used like sound effects (Johnson and Poole 2005: 105).

The role of music in the film is 'never mere accompaniment, but operates as an underscoring pulse which taps into the unspoken violence simmering beneath the surface of the protagonists' conversations and behavior' (Mitchell 2005: 3). It is interesting how The Necks have used repetition, albeit in a condensed framework compared with their frequently used one-hour format, to create a stark and minimalist film score. One of the most distinctive aspects is the blurred boundaries between the music and sound effects.

Open (2013)

The Necks' seventeenth album, *Open*, demonstrates how the group has established certain conventions yet also manages to create a discrete, original sound work. I wish to focus on two key aspects: structure and instrumentation. Compared to *Sex*, a more inconsistent structural approach is adopted. Their seventeenth album returns to the hour-long format:

> The previous record, *Mindset* [comprising 2 x 21 minute tracks] reached some pretty intense levels at times, and though we never overtly discussed it, I think that on *Open*, by contrast, all three of us were taken by the idea of working in a field of significant stillness. At least, after a couple of days' recording, it became clear that the music was leading us in that direction (Swanton 2013).

A hammered, dulcimer-like piano sets up a meditative presence, followed by the addition of tinny chimes and cymbals, and a monochord, played by Buck, provides a thick, distorted overblown harmonic sound adding intensity and a thicker dynamic. A monochord is an:

> ancient one-stringed instrument originally built by Pythagoras in which an open-tuned string was stretched over a wooden plate and used for harmonic experiments... The instrument was built and provided by Emma Nilsson, and played by Tony Buck to striking effect at the beginning of the piece, combining with the drummer's Tibetan-like cymbals to produce a raga-like effect (Mitchell 2014).

Abrahams is featured on organ and synthesizers, Swanton on bass and Buck, as well as the monochord, on drums, percussion and electric guitar. The double bass features simple, repetitive crotchet patterns; however, this differs from the role of the bass in *Sex*. Instead of a constant, repeated bass figure, *Open* is characterized by an interrupted rhythmic flow, with each instrument interspersing with silence, stillness and space. There is a more erratic, inconsistent flow which is more fragmented and, for example, less reliant on the continuous repetition of the bass riff used in *Sex*. This creates a type of shifting matrix. As is prevalent in some of their other work such as *Silent Night, Aether* (2001) and *Mosquito/See Through* (2004), complete silence is used around the mid-point (32:18) creating a type of orchestral interlude, a resting place of stillness and meditation.

Following on from the extreme use of layering featured on many of their studio albums, *Open* makes considerable use of textural variation and overdubs. Present in the electronica are:

> floating arco harmonics, minimalist funk, iterative piano figures, subliminal and luminal pulses, twittering electronics and at one point an arco bass choir. It is unequivocally a studio work, with layer laid on layer, while still, miraculously, remaining architecturally spare.[3]

In some ways *Open* displays similarities with their first album *Sex*. The one-hour format, the use of minimalist pitch patterns, repetition and drones (as heard in the use of the monochord) are frequently used devices in their work. There is an extension and exploration of elements such as the addition of new and unconventional sound sources and continual shifting of techniques (as heard in Abrahams's use of the dulcimer-like piano and Buck's monochord). The use of space and silence is a key point of difference from The Necks' more common use of a consistent rhythmic approach.

Conclusion

The Necks extend the parameters of the 'jazz' piano trio, exploring free improvisation, adopting a particular format of performance and incorporating influences from world music, art music, jazz, rock, funk, electronic music and minimalism. Despite the common view that their work is characterized by hour-long pieces which state an idea, explore it, expand it, and then 'bring it back down to land', as Swanton puts it (Shand 2009: 100), their work contains a diverse set of sonic landscapes reflecting a range of cultural and social trends. The highly original use of instrumentation, exploration of sound sources and the way sampling and multi-tracking are used in their work parallels a type of sonic smorgasbord. They have set themselves apart from other Australian jazz groups by adopting a distinctive approach characterized by shunning the typical overt 'virtuoso' profile, abandoning the 'theme…solo improvisations…theme' and are less inclined to play outside conventional harmonic structures which had itself become a convention of contemporary jazz performance. There are connections with US and UK minimalists and the European jazz scene. They have been prolific in exploring other genres of music including music for film, television, installation-based projects and improvised projects.

Lloyd Swanton captures the spirit of their approach:

---

3. Birdland, review of *Open*, http://www.birdland.com.au/catalogue/category634/p66222 (accessed 23 September 2014).

It was more like therapy for all the other things we were doing. But I guess we found a foolproof way of generating music and just thought we should try putting this in front of people (Walters 2004).

Chris Abrahams elaborates further:

This way of playing was there from the start and we haven't changed it. We are constantly finding new things: ideas about time, about structure, about the sonic possibilities of the instruments we play. All these things come from a simple approach into which we can plug many different genres of music (Walters 2004).

The Necks have begun to influence subsequent improvisatory trends in Australia and internationally, creating new sonic spaces and forging new communities based on an experimental dialogue created through the extensive use of repetition and minimalism. The fascination lies in how they create individual, discrete, original sound works, characterized by a clearly focused, improvised narrative. Their musical trajectory parallels a large-scale version of one of their performances, creating a kaleidoscopic aural effect.

References

Clare, J. (1995) *Bodgie Dada and the Cult of Cool*. Sydney: University of New South Wales Press.
Galbraith, J., and T. Mitchell (2005) 'Interview with Chris Abrahams—The Necks'. Sydney: Unpublished.
Johnson, B., and G. Poole (2005) 'Scoring: Sexuality and Australian Film Music, 1990–2003'. In *Reel Tracks: Australian Feature Film Music and Cultural Identities*, ed. Rebecca Coyle, 97–121. Eastleigh, UK: John Libbey Publishing.
Mitchell, T. (2005) 'Minimalist Menace: The Necks Score "The Boys"'. *Screening the Past* 18. http://tlweb.latrobe.edu.au/humanities/screeningthepast/firstrelease/fr_18/TMfr18a.html (accessed 20 October 2014).
—(2014) Review of *Open*. www.musictrust.com.au (accessed 13 December 2014).
Ross, A. (2009) *The Rest is Noise*. London: Harper Perennial.
Shand, J. (2009) *Jazz: The Australian Accent*. Sydney: University of New South Wales Press.
Swanton, L. (2013) Review of *Open*. http://northernspy.11spot.com/the-necks-open.html (accessed 10 December 2014).
Walters, J. L. (2001) 'The Necks. Ocean 2, London'. www.theguardian.com/culture/2001/apr/13/artsfeatures (accessed 10 December 2014).
—(2004) 'Necks Big Thing'. *The Guardian*. http://www.guardian.co.uk/music/2004/jan/09/2 (accessed 14 August 2014).
Whiteoak, J. (2004) 'VCA Forum Improvised Music: A Challenge for Tertiary Education'. 14 September 2004, Victorian College of the Arts.

Discography

Davis, Miles (1969) *In a Silent Way*. Columbia Records. CD.
—(1972) *On the Corner*. Columbia Records. CD.
Lamb, Alan (1995) *Primal Image*. Glen Waverley, Vic. Dorobo. CD.
Necks, The (1989) *Sex*. Spiral Scratch/Fish of Milk. CD.
—(1990) *Next*. Spiral Scratch/Fish of Milk. CD.
—(1994) *Aquatic*. Fish of Milk/Shock. CD.
—(1996) *Silent Night*. Fish of Milk/Shock. CD.
—(1998) *The Boys*—music for the feature film. Original soundtrack Wild Sound/MDS. Reissued on Fish of Milk/ReR Megacorp. CD.
—(2001) *Aether*. Fish of Milk/Shock/ReR Megacorp. CD.
—(2003) *Drive By*. Fish of Milk/Shock/ReR Megacorp. CD. Best Aria Music Awards–Jazz Category–2004.
—(2004) *Mosquito/See Through*. Fish of Milk/ReR Megacorp. CD.
—(2006) *Chemist*. Fish of Milk/ReR Megacorp. Best Aria Music Awards–Jazz Category–2006. CD.
—(2009) *Silverwater*. Fish of Milk/ReR Megacorp. CD.
—(2011) *Mindset*. Fish of Milk/ReR Megacorp. CD.
—(2013) *Open*. Fish of Milk/ReR Megacorp/Northern Spy. CD.

Film

Connolly, R., and J. Maynard (1998) *The Boys*, directed by Rowan Woods. Sydney, Arenafilm. Distributed by Roadshow Entertainment. DVD.

Television

Clark, T., and J. Ryan (2000) *In the Mind of the Architect*, episodes 1–3, directed by Tim Clark, ABC TV.

Collaborations

Gibson, R., and K. Richards (1998) *Life After Wartime*. Multi media.
Food Court (2009) Back To Back Theatre, 9 June 2009, Sydney Opera House as part of Luminous Festival curated by Brian Eno.

Index

ABC *see* Australian Broadcast Corporation/Commission
Abercrombie, John 188
Aboriginal Moomba 198–99
Aboriginal people 12, 193–207, 224 *see also* Indigeneity, Torres Strait Islands
Aboriginals Protection and Restriction of the Sale of Opium Act of 1897 194
Abrahams, Chris 13, 267, 269–75, 277, 279–82
Adelaide 5, 7, 41, 84–88, 90, 92–93, 95–96, 98, 100
Adderley, Cannonball 218
Adelphi Cabaret (Wellington NZ) 68
Adorno, Theodore 8
Aebersold, Jamie 262
Aether (recording) 281
Afghanistan 195, 206
Akabella 183
Albert, Prince 23
Albert's American Annual (sheet music) 36
Albert & Son's music house 38
'Alexander's Ragtime Band' (song) 23, 38
Alice Springs 279
Allan, Cameron 143
'All Coons Look Alike to Me' (song) 33
Allen, John 232
Alliance of Melbourne Women Improvising Musicians 163
'All the Things You Are' (song) 219
Alter, Andrew 177
Ampersand record label 88, 100
Amsterdam 181
Angel Heart (film) 139
Angels and Rascals (recording) 166
Angry Penguins (journal) 7, 90, 92–95, 97–99, 100
'Anthropology' (song) 251
Apollo Theatre (New York) 94
Aquatic (recording) 274–75
'Arabia Land' (song) 53
Arabic music 269
Archibald Prize 90
Ardell, Anita 123
Argentina 180–81
Arguelles, Julian 178
Aria Music Awards (Australian Recording Industry Association Music Awards) 166, 188, 249, 277
Armiger, Martin 142
Armstrong, Gillian 137, 147
Armstrong, Louis 94
ArtPlay, Federation Square (Melbourne) 162
Arts Victoria 163
Ascenseur pour l'échafaud (film) 140
Astor Club (London) 202
Astor Showcase (television programme) 122
Atkinson, Leon 84, 95
Auckland 71–73, 104
Australasian Performing Right Association (APRA) 160, 166
Australia Council 162–64, 166
Australian Academy of the Arts 90, 92
Australian All Stars (band) 123–26
Australian Broadcast Corporation/Commission (ABC) 9, 98, 117–18, 119–32, 161–62, 165–67, 204
Australian Comforts Fund 196
Australian Human Rights Commission 193
Australian Jazz Archive 10–11
Australian Jazz Bell Awards 166
Australian Jazz Club 217
Australian Jazz Convention 6, 94
Australian Jazz Museum *see* Victorian Jazz Archive
Australian Jazz Quartet/Quintet (AJQ) 11, 100, 232–33
Australian Music Centre 160, 166
Australian Red Cross 196
Austria 181

Baartz, Martha 163–64, 167–68
'Back Home Again in Indian Annie' (song) 244
Bailey, Buster 95
Bailey, Judy 159, 170
Baker, David 230
'Bakiff' (song) 93, 98
Balkans, the 256–57, 263–64
Bamford, John 220
Bandstand (television programme) 122, 203
Band Waggon (radio programme) 73
Banks, Don 91, 100, 138
Barlow, Dale 183
Barnard, Bob 11

Barnett, Dan 183
Barnett, Shannon 164
Barrett, Ray 141
Barry, Keith 119–20, 122, 125
Bartok, Bela 143, 253, 261
Basie, Count 259
'Basin Street Blues' (song) 203
Baum, Frank L. 203
Bay of Plenty (NZ) 70
BBC *see* British Broadcasting Corporation
Beadle, Ray 183
Beatles, The 118, 127
'Beauty' (song) 280
Beck, Jess 192
Beiderbecke, Bix 86
Belgium 180–81
Bell, Graeme 3, 6–7, 11, 41, 43, 85–89, 91–92, 94–97, 99, 124, 130, 166, 197–98, 203
Bell, Roger 3, 5–7, 11, 43, 85–89, 94–97, 99–100
Bellingen Jazz Festival 177–79, 181, 183–87
Bennett, Claude 79
Bennett's Lane Jazz Club (Melbourne) 105, 161, 165, 178
Benson, Ivy 159
Berardi, Kristin 164
Beresford, Bruce 143
Bergner, Yosl 91
Berlin, Irving 23, 29, 37–39
Bernhard, Paul 87
Bertles, Bob 218–19
Best, Peter 141
Bethlehem record label 233
Beyond El Rocco (film) 250
Big Sleep, The (film) 140–41
Bijou Theatre (Melbourne) 41
Bird of Paradise (stage musical) 54
Birth of White Australia, The (film) 36
Bishaw, Henry Peelua 54
Bjelke-Petersen, Joh 141
'Black' ('song') 276–77
Blair, Harold 198, 205
Blakey, Art 251
Bloom, Harry 80
Blott, Charlie 100, 200
Blue Note record label 230
Blue Riff Big Band 183
blues 157, 192–93, 195–98, 201, 203, 205, 207, 258, 261, 264
'Blues for Cyber' (song) 233–34
Blue Shift (recording) 259
'Blues in the Night' (song) 204
Blythe Waterland Minstrels 29

Body Heat (film) 139
Bolden, Buddy 215
Bonano, Sharkey 86
Bonython, Kym 86–88, 91
Boptet (band) 110
Bowden, Mark 233
Boyd, Arthur 99
Boyd, Peter 256
Boyes, Fiona 184
Boys, The (film) 138, 268, 279–81
Bradley, Reuben 109
brass bands 3, 28, 158, 194, 256
Brazil 180
Brisbane 60–61, 68, 74, 104, 166
Brisbane International Jazz Festival 177–79, 181, 184–87, 189
Britain *see* United Kingdom
British Broadcasting Corporation (BBC) 119–21, 159
Brokensha, Jack 197
Brous, Sophie 187
Brown, Alan/Allan 68–69, 79
Brown, Baden 71, 80
Brown, Brian 111, 113, 226, 244
Brown, Bryan 142
Brown, Ray 219
Brown, Tas 86
Browne, Allan 111, 182–84
Browning, Daniel 204
Brubeck, Dave 255, 259, 263
Brunswick Green venue (Melbourne) 108
Bryant, Gai 160
Buck, Tony 13, 259, 267, 269–70, 272–74, 276–78, 281–82
Buckley, Jim 70
Bulgaria 255, 257
Bull, Geoff 183
Bunyip, The (stage musical) 53
Burdett, Louis 259
Burke, Rob 183
Burke, Roger 183
Burnett, Fiona 162–63, 165–66, 168
Burrows, Don 11, 219–20, 233
Burst of Summer (television movie) 203
Burt, Peter 229
Byas, Don 94

Café Continental (television programme) 12
Cage, John 269
Cairns 195–96, 202, 204
Cale, Bruce 232–33, 235–36, 242–43
Campbell, George 71, 80
Campbell, Phil 80

Campion, Jane 144
Canada 180–81
Canberra 178
'Capt. Kenney's Bathing Ship' (song) 233
Carides, Zoë 145
Carter, Benny 219–20, 230
Carter, Howard 4
Cavanaugh/Cavanagh, Inez 93–95
Cavanaugh, Liz 192
Cave, Jenna 164
Celia (film) 144
'A Century of Steps' (song) 243
Ceylon 158, 201
Chamber Music Society of Lower Penkivil Street (Sydney) 225–26
Chapple, Frank 79
Charles, Teddy 231
Chatham Theatre (New York) 24
Chauvel, Charles 9
Chemist (recording) 276
Cherry, Don 255
Chicago 84–85, 89, 95, 100
'Chicken and Almonds' (song) 89
China 4, 47, 50–62, 255
'China Girl' (song) 52
Chinatown (film) 139
Chindamo, Joe 183
'Ching A Ling's Jazz Bazaar' (song) 57–58
'Ching Chong' (song) 53
'Ching Chong Jazz Arrangement' (song) 53
Choulai, Aaron 183
Christchurch (NZ) 104
Chronic Rhythmosis (recording) 256
Chu Chin Chow: A Musical Tale from the East (stage musical) 55
'Circles' (song) 225
circus 49
Ciro's nightclub (Melbourne) 198
'Clare the Kitchen' (song) 25
Claridge's nightclub (Melbourne) 198
Clarke, Bruce 43, 136, 198, 217, 220, 224, 244
'Clever Fellow' (song) 97
Cloncurry 195
Cloudstreet (film) 145
'Coal Black Rose' (song) 24
'Coalesce' (song) 243
Coates, Jimmy 68–69, 76, 79
Cocoanut Grove dance hall (Brisbane) 74
Coker, Jerry 230
Cole, Jeremy 146
Cole, Nat King 202, 205
Coleman, Ornette 100, 225, 232

Coloured/Colored Idea (Revue) 5
Coltman, W. Stan 'Tut' 65, 67–70, 74–79
Coltrane, John 232, 243, 251, 255, 257
'Come and See Her' (song) 138, 146
Come Out (recording) 271
Commonwealth Investigation Branch 5
'Confirmation' (song) 225
Connolly, Jerry 78
Connolly, Keith 67
'Consolidation' (song) 225
Contemporary Art Society 90–92
convict heritage 20, 24–26, 28, 34, 43–44
Conway, Jim 183
Coppin, George 24
Corbyn's Original Georgia Minstrels 31–32
Corea, Chic 178
Corners (recording) 233
'Corners Suite' 234–41
Coronet record label 233
Corris, Peter 141
'Corroboree Rag' (song) 53
Coughlan, Frank 11, 68, 76, 217
Coughlin, Jerry 80
Counihan, Noel 91
Countdown (television programme) 129
Courtney, Vince 53
Creary, Jim 79
'Crocodile Creep' (song) 98
Croydon Palais (Sydney) 71
Cuba 180–81
cultural intermediaries 174–75, 189
'Cunt Song, The' (song) 92
Curtis's Grand African-American Carnival 32–33
Czechoslovakia 43

Dallwitz, Dave 7, 88–89, 91–93, 95–100
Dallwitz, Joan 91
Dan, 'Seaman' 192
dance 3, 5, 9–10, 21–24, 28, 31–33, 35–39, 43–44, 53, 57–60, 62, 65–66, 69–72, 75–76, 85, 91, 120, 157–59, 192, 195–96, 216, 256, 275
Dandenong Mountains (Victoria) 86
Dankworth, John 201
Darwin 279
Davidson, Jim 76
Davies, Spadge 86
Davis, Miles 8, 13, 140, 230, 242, 244, 251, 259, 272
Dean, Roger 270
Debussy, Claude 93
Decca record label 230

Dee-Jays, The 8, 123–24, 127
De Heer, Rolph 8
deJohnette, Jack 188
'Delhi Belly Dancer, The' (song) 244
Delius, Frederick 93, 95
Denmark 180–81, 230
Desmond, Paul 251, 253, 255, 259, 263
Dickeson, Andrew 259
Diet Coke Women in Jazz Festival (New York) 161
Dingo (film) 8
Dizzy's Jazz Club (Melbourne) 178
Djin Djin the Japanese Bogie Man (stage musical) 55
Dobell, William 90
Dobson, George 76, 80
Does the Jazz Lead to Destruction? (film) 8
Dog (band) 109
Dolphy, Eric 232
Downes, Jim 79
'Down in Chinatown' (song) 52
'Down Under [Blues]' (song) 203
'Dreamy Honolulu' (song) 53
Drive By (recording) 271, 277–78
Dr Jazz (film) 250, 259
Drummond, Cindy 192
Dr V's Swing Thing (band) 183
Drysdale, Russell 90, 197
Duff, Jeff 183
Duggan, Bernie 80, 220, 222, 226
'Dumbrille Was No Greek' (song) 233
Dyer, Margie Lou 184
Dyn, Paul 113

Eames, Penny 99
Eastern Horizons (recording) 243, 269
Easybeats, The (band) 138, 146
'Eccentric' (song) 86
Eckstine, Billy 217
ECM record label 270
Ed Sullivan Show, The 118
education programmes, jazz 2, 10, 110–12, 159–60, 186, 271
Edwards, Billy 53
Edwards, Jimmy 120
Egan, Kev 80
Egerton, Norm 80
Egypt 4
Eldridge, Roy 95
Elling, Kurt 178
Ellington, Duke 85, 89, 91, 93–94, 98
Ellis, Lauren 109
Elphick, Steve 256, 259

El Rocco Jazz Cellar (Sydney) 159, 217, 226, 250
Embers nightclub (Melbourne) 217–20
Embers, The (recording) 227
Empress Ballroom (Sydney) 68
Empty Beach, The (film) 141–42
Eno, Brian 270, 278
Ermoll, Serge 270
Ern Malley Suite (recording) 99
ESP record label 242
'Eternal Frost' (song) 260
Ethiopia 180
Ethiopian Serenaders 29
Eureka Stockade uprising 26
Europe 4–6, 48–49, 58, 87, 95–96, 99, 170, 176, 200, 206, 242, 262, 269–70, 273
Eustice, Mal 218
Evans, Christine 256
Evans, Gil 231, 234
Evans, Sandy 160–62, 164, 168–71, 183, 251, 259, 270–71
'Everyone Loves a Jazz Band' (song) 41
'Ezz-thetic' (song) 245

Farewell, My Lovely (film) 140
Farmer, Art 231
Ferguson, Maynard 108
Festival Hall (London) 201
festivals, jazz 8, 10–11, 155, 160–71, 173–90
Festival Sextet (band) 164, 166, 169–70
Fielding, Harold 201
Fields, Noel 69, 79
film 1, 8–10, 49, 52, 55–56, 71, 76–77, 135–50, 157, 195, 223, 227, 268, 277
Finland 2, 181
Fisk Jubilee Singers 32
Fitzgerald, Ella 110
flappers 9, 39–40, 59, 157–58
Foo, Henry 58
Food Court (stage play) 268
Fox, Charles 95
Fox, Kerry 147
Fox, Rodger 108–109, 112
Fox, Roy 73
Frampton, Roger 269
France 2, 95, 180–81
Frank Smith – A Jazz Portrait (recording) 224
Frascati's Cabaret (Christchurch NZ) 70
Freeman, Dick 158
French, Lex 108
French, Syd 68, 78–79
Friend, Donald 197
Fripp, Robert 270

'From Here to Shanghai' (song) 53
Fujii, Satoko 164
Fuller, Ben 19, 68
Funston, Grace 158
Funstons, The (all women band) 157

Gambia 255
Ganz, Bruno 147
Garbarek, Jan 230
Garden, Steve 114
Garland, Judy 203
Garner, Errol 94
Garner, Helen 145
Gassman, Josephine 40–41
Gedson, Fred 80
gender politics 9–10, 12, 14, 145, 155, 157–61, 167–71, 176–77, 183–85, 187, 189, 206
George, Bruce 198
Georgia Lee Sings the Blues Down Under (recording) 203–204
Geraldo 201
Germany 180–81, 273
Gershwin, George 4
Ghana 103
Gibson, William 277
Gilday, Rube 80
Gill Brothers 202
Gillespie, Dizzy 94
Ginger Jar Cabaret *see* Oriental Cabaret
Girvan, Bob 69, 79
Giuffre, Jimmy 231
Glass, Philip 27, 271
Gleeson, James 91
Gleneagles Club (Sydney) 197
Globe Theatre (Sydney) 8
'Gnome Chomsky's Deep Focus Boogie-Woogie' (song) 249, 256–58, 263
Godbolt, Jim 96
Goffin, Robert 87
Gold Fever (recording) 99
Golson, Benny 251
Goodbye Paradise (film) 140–41
Goode, Morris 94
Goodman, Benny 72
Gordon, Dexter 251
Gorman, Tony 13, 248–50, 256, 258–64
gospel music 21 *see also* spirituals
Gould, Tony 42, 110, 113–14, 183
Gower, Jim 79
Grabowsky, Paul 94, 111, 137–38, 148, 205, 251, 254
Graham, Victor 196

Grainger, Percy 93–95
Granville, Nick 109
Great Depression, the 4, 9, 85, 158
Greece 180, 255
Greene, Gene 39–40, 53
Gryce, Gigi 231
Guard, Dave 232
'Gumbo Chaff' (song) 24
Gurdjieff, George 244
Guzmanyi, Robert 256

Haden, Charlie 178, 183
Halesworth, Tanya 131
Hall, Toby 259
Hampson, Roy 122
Hancock, Herbie 178
Hancock, Tony 120
Handy, John 242
Hanson, Raymond 220, 222–23, 225
Harley, Cathy 160
Harmon, Paul 137, 145
Harmony Sisters, The 195–96
Harris, Max 90, 92, 94, 99
Harrow, Lisa 147
Haskell, Jack 53
Havana venue (Wellington) 105
Hawaii 52, 54, 196–97
Hawkins, Len 80
Hay, Dean 86
Hayes, Tubby 242
Headhunters (recording) 109
Healey, Dick 244
Heath, Ted (bandleader) 201
Heatwave (film) 143
Heavy Weather (recording) 109
Hemmingsen, Colin 113
Henderson, Brian 122
Henderson, Jeff 111
Hendrix, Jimi 278
Herman, Woody 108
Herrmann, Bernard 280
Hester, Joy 90, 99
Hewson, John 144
'Hi Lee Hi Lo' (song) 53
Hershey, Burnet 1
Hick, Jacqueline 91
Hickman, Art 29
Hicks' Original Georgia Minstrels 31–33
Hicks-Sawyer Minstrels 32
'High Society' (song) 86
Hilder, George 231
'Hi Lee Hi Lo' (song) 57
Hills, Allan 80

Hilton, Janet 259
Hindemith, Paul 216, 220–23, 225–26
Hitchcock, Alfred 280
Hobart 7, 24, 44, 93, 100
Hogan, Ernest 33
Holiday, Billie 198, 200–201
Holyoak, William V. 87–88, 98
'Hong Kong Dream Girl' (song) 60
Horbelt, Sonja 162–63, 165, 167–68
Horne, Lena 205
Hot Club of France 95
Hounslow, Keith 98
Hour of Separation (recording) 188
Howard, John (politician) 143, 145
Hoyts Theatre circuit 70, 73
Hubner, Daphne 158
Hugo's Colored Minstrels 33–34
Hugo's New Minstrels 34
Hunter (television series) 224
Hustas, Anita 163–64, 166
Hyde, Billy 224–25

Icedreaming (recording) 166
Illawarra Flame (recording) 99
Images of Man (film) 138
Immigration Restriction Act *see* White Australia Policy
improvisation/improvisatory music 20–21, 27, 30, 52, 54, 67, 75, 87–89, 91, 93, 96–97, 105, 107, 142, 161–63, 223–24, 226, 232, 235, 242, 244, 252, 258, 267–68, 271–72, 278
In a Silent Way (recording) 272
India 62, 18, 181, 206, 244, 269, 273
Indigeneity 12, 34–35, 41, 192–207
Indonesia 180–81, 255
'In Dreamy Araby' (song) 53
'Infant Eyes' (song) 251
In Melbourne Tonight (television programme) 203
In the Mind of the Architect (television presentation) 268
Ireland 180–81
Irwin, Lynette 163, 187
Isaacs, Mark 183
Israel 180–81
Italy 180–81
'It Don't Mean a Thing If It Ain't Got That Swing' (song) 86
ITV 119

Jac, The (band) 109
Jackson, Martin 162–63, 166–67

Jacquet, Illinois 94
Jamaica 206
James, Ingrid 164, 166–67, 183
Japan 2, 32, 55, 103, 106, 180–81, 229, 269, 273
Jarrett, Keith 259
Jazz Action Societies 10
Jazzart record label 98
Jazzchord (journal) 10
Jazz Co-ordination Associations 10
Jazz in Australia: The Music Maker 1957 All Stars (recording) 222, 227
Jazz from Down Under (record series) 244
jazzing 20–21, 28, 35, 37, 39, 44, 50, 52, 54, 58, 62
Jazz Rebels (band) 197
Jazz Week, The 8
'Jazzie Jazz in Chinaland' (song) 57
Jenkins, Joe 123, 202
'Jim Along Josey' (song) 24
Jindyworobaks (literary movement) 92, 97, 99
Johnny O'Keefe Show, The (television programme) 129
Johnson, Frank 43, 198, 200
Johnson, Lucien 109, 111
Johnson, Wal 79
Johnston, Russ 53
Jones, David 166
Jones, Vince 111, 113, 183
Joye, Col 127
'Jump Jim Crow' (song) 19, 21–28, 44
'Jungle Blues' (song) 98
Just Bryce (recording) 233
Justin Firefly Quartet (band) 109

'Kama Sutra Feeling, That' (song) 244
Kaminsky, Max 5, 100
Kansas City 84
Keating, Paul 143, 149
Keevers, Sam 183
Keller, Andrea 111, 162–66, 169–70, 183
Kelly, Ned 53, 90, 99–100
Kemple-Hopkins, Myra 135
Kennard, Peter 256, 258
Kenton, Stan 88
Kerr, Donald 90
Kewe, Emil 79
Kind of Blue (recording) 13, 109
King Crimson (band) 259
King, Martin Luther 262
King, Tom 80
Kingston Trio 229, 232
Kirk, Roland 262

Index

'Kismet' (song) 52
Klute (film) 139
Knopf, Michael 204
Komunyakaa, Yusef 160
Korea 180

Label Bleu record label 230
La Mama Theatre (Melbourne) 164
Lamb, Alan 280
Lambert, Constance 89
Lanigan, Gordon 80
larrikin 19–20, 43–44
Larson, Harry 218
Last Days of Chez Nous, The (film) 137–39, 142, 145, 147–49
Lawrence, Harry 142
Lawrence, T. E. 4
League of Notions (stage revue) 68
Lee, Georgia (aka Dulcie Pitt) 12, 192, 195–207
Lee, Sun Moon 47, 59–62
Lennon, John 8
Lennon's Broadbeach Hotel (Gold Coast) 202
Levy, Dave 244
Lewis, Lou 70
Life After Wartime (installation project) 268
Lightfoots, The (all-women band) 157
Lilburn, Douglas 113–14
Lincoln Centre (New York) 161
Lindsay, Sir Lionel 90
Little, Jimmy 205
Litweiler, John B. 100
Lloyd, Charles 183
Logan, Freddie 121, 124
Lomax, Alan 200
Lomax, John 200
'Look Down the Road' (song) 97
'Love for Sale' (song) 245
Lumsdaine, Jack 53
Luna Park Palais de Danse (Perth) 71
Luter, Claude 95
Luxembourg 181
Lyall, Graeme 218–20, 222–23, 226

MacCunn, Andrew 53
Macedonia 255, 257
Magnusson, Stephen 183
Magpies Ladies Orchestra, The 157
Maitland (NSW) 24
Majestic Cabaret (Wellington NZ) 69, 71, 74, 80
Make Ours Music (television programme) 126
Maldon Coons 41

Malle, Louis 140
Mallen, Ralph 216
Malley, Ern 90, 92, 99
Manly Jazz Festival 177–79, 181, 183–87, 189
Marcel Mule Demonstrates the Mark VI (recordings) 218
Marston, Brian 80
Martin, Joe 202
Martin, Sal 80
'Mary Had A Little Lamb' (song) 277
Mastodon Minstrels 32
Mathis, Johnny 217
McAdoo's Genuine Georgia Minstrels and Alabama Cake Walkers 32–33
MCA/Freedman Foundation Jazz Fellowship 166
McAll, Barney 183
McAlpine, R. Alistair 99
McBride, Charlie 188
McClain, Billy 33
McGann, Bernie 13, 94, 183, 248–55, 259, 263–64
McKellar, Phil 204
McKirdy, Arch 243–44
McMahon, Matt 271
McMahon, Tiny 79
McPherson, Cluny 68, 79
McQueen, Humphrey 25
Meadmore, Clem 91
Meehan, Norman 112, 114
Meeropol, Abel (aka Lewis Allan) 198
Mehden, Len 79
Melbourne 5–6, 30, 37, 40–41, 57, 59, 73, 84–85, 88, 90–93, 95–96, 99–100, 104–15, 126, 136, 155, 161–71, 178, 198–99, 201, 203, 216–17, 227
Melbourne International Jazz Festival 165, 177–78, 182–87, 189
Melbourne Jazz Co-op 162
Melbourne Suite (recording) 99
Melbourne Women's International Jazz Festival (MWIJF) 10, 155, 161–71
Meldrum, Max 91
Mellish, Wally 146
Melly, George 86
Melrose Prize 90
Memphis record label 88, 98
Menzies, Sir Robert 90, 92
Meow venue (Wellington NZ) 105
Mercy, Crystal 192
Meredith, John 44
Merry Makers (all-women dance band) 62

Merzi, Gus 124
Messiaen, Olivier 262
Meyers, Nick 280
Midnight Crawl (recording) 99
Mikrokosmos: The Bartók Project (recording) 166
Miller, Henry 92
Miller, William H. 88, 93
'Millstream' (song) 233–34
Mindset (recording) 281
Mingus, Charlie 232
minstrelsy 3, 20–35, 40–41, 44, 49, 54
Misinterpretato (band) 183
Mitchell, Milton 123
Monash University 112, 183
Money Mowers (film) 143
Monroe, Patti 124
Monsbourgh, Ade 3, 6–7, 11, 85–86, 89, 96–100
'Mood Indigo' (song) 91
Moody, Belinda 164
Moran, Jason 183
More Spring (recording) 233–34
Morgan, Graham 224
Morocco 278
Morrison, Cec 6
Morrison, James 11, 104, 183, 205
Morrison, John 183
Morton, Jelly Roll 89, 96, 98–99
'Moshoeshoe The First' (song) 259
'Moshoeshoe The Second' (song) 259
Mosquito/See Through (recording) 281
'Mother Waratah' (song) 53
MTV 11
Mule, Marcel 218
Muller, James 183
multi-tracking 275–77
Munro, Charles 'Charlie' 78, 233, 240, 243–45, 269
Murn, Edith *see* Pardey, Edith
Murphy, Tamara 164–65, 170
Murray, Bill 53
Musgrove, Nan 123
Musicians' Unions 4, 54, 78, 126
Music in Fifths (recording) 271
'My Chinee Girl' (song) 53

Nance, Ray 98
Napier (NZ) 68
National Archives of Australia 118, 123, 125, 127, 130–31
National Film and Sound Archive 10, 122, 137, 204

National Gallery of Australia 90
National Library of Australia 56
National Theatre (Sydney) 19
'Nature Boy' (song) 204
Naylor, Mel 79
Necks, The (band) 7, 13, 138, 267–83
Ned Kelly Jazz Suite (recording) 99–100
Negro's Vengeance: A Tale of the Barbadoes, The (stage melodrama) 24
Neilson, Lee 123
Netherlands 180–81, 273
Nettelbeck, Ted 219–20, 226
New Caledonia 195, 206
New Jazz Studies 2–3, 135–37
New Orleans 1, 84–85, 88, 94–96, 98, 106, 108, 110
New Plymouth (NZ) 68
New South Wales State Conservatorium of Music *see* Sydney Conservatorium of Music
New York 84, 88, 94–95, 108, 161, 231, 244, 269
New Zealand School of Music 112
Next (recording) 273, 276–77
'Nice Policeman Nasty Policeman' ('song') 277
Nicholas, Jessica 167
Nicol, John 192
Nicolle, Michelle 108–109, 112, 183
Nilsson, Emma 281
Nock, Mike 11, 104, 113–14, 183, 242, 244, 271
Nolan, Sidney 90–91, 96, 99
Norway 180–81, 230
Noyce, Phillip 143
'Nulla-Nulla' (song) 53
Nullarbor (recording) 97, 99

'Ockeration' (song) 22, 222
Oehlers, Jamie 183
O'Hagan, Jack 53
O'Keefe, Johnny 8, 119, 121, 123–25
'Old Man's Beard' (song) 96
One, Ben Nee 57
On the Corner (recording) 272
Open (film/recording) 276, 280–82
'Opus 4/56' (song) 233, 240
Oriental Cabaret *aka* Ginger Jar (Sydney) 72, 80
orientalism 48–49, 53, 56, 60, 62
Orrell, Reg 80
Orszacky, Jackie 27, 276
Oxford (UK) 88

Page, Peter 127
Palestine, Charlemagne 270–71, 275
Panassié, Hugues 89
'Pan Yan and his Chinese Jazz Band' (song) 57–58
Papua 198
Pardey (aka Murn), Edith 53–54
Pardey, Laurel 53
Paris Cat venue (Melbourne) 105
Paris Conservatory 218
Parker, Charlie 160, 218–19, 251–52
Parrott, Lisa 160
Parrott, Nicki 160
participatory discrepancies 21, 27, 30, 40
'Passion Rag' (song) 98
Pattugalan, Jamie 256
Paying Bay, The (film) 138
Pearce, Cedric 87, 93
Pederson, Reg 216
Penman, Matt 104
'People Running' (song) 233
Perceval, John 90, 99
Perth 71
Pertwee, Jon 200
Petatucci, John 188
'Pete Kelly's Blues' (song) 203
Peter Pan Cabaret (Auckland NZ) 71–74, 80
Peterson, Oscar 219
Pfeiffer, Paul 90
Phillips, Barre 244
Pickering, Tom 89, 95, 98, 100
'Pickled Piper' (song) 240–41
Pilzer, Leigh 160
Pitt, Douglas 195
Pitt, Dulcie *see* Lee, Georgia
Pitt, Heather 195–97
Pitt, Sophie 195
Pitt, Walter 195, 197
'Playground' (song) 249, 251–55, 263
Pochée, John 251, 253
Pollak, Linsey 255
Pommer, Rolph 218
Porter, David 124–26
Port Jackson Jazz Band 197
Portugal 180–81
Pound, Ezra 93
Power, Geoff 183
Presley, Elvis 23, 39, 129
Primal Image (recording) 280
Prince's Theatre (Melbourne) 198
Pritchard, Billy 80
Provan, Felicity 164
Psycho (film) 280

Qantas airline 204
Queensland Music Festival 193
Quon, Alma 62, 158
Quon, Lorna 62

Ra, Sun 244
radio 1, 58, 65, 68–69, 71–75, 77–78, 88–89, 159, 196, 204, 217
Rae, John 111
Rage (television programme) 129
ragging 20–21, 28, 31, 33, 37, 39–40, 50
ragtime 3, 20, 29, 32–33, 39–40, 44, 57, 97
'Ragtime Goblin Man, The' (song) 40
'Ragtime Tuba' (song) 98
'Railway Overture' (minstrel act) 30–31
Rainey, Ma 157
Ralph, Carol 183
Raney, Jimmy 231
Rattle record label 114
Ravel, Maurice 93
RCA record label 230, 232
Real Swing, The (radio programme) 88
'Rebel Rouser' (song) 123
recording 1, 2, 43, 77–78, 85–88, 94–95, 159, 222, 224, 227, 230
Red Arrows, The (US service band) 5
Redman, Joshua 178
Reed, John 90
Reed, Sunday 90
Reeves, Splinter 100
reggae 142, 256
Reich, Steve 270–71
Revudeville and Rhythm (radio programme) 69
Rhapsody in Blue 4
Rhythm Changes project 2
Rice, Thomas Dartmouth 'Daddy' 22–25, 29, 35, 39
Rich, Buddy 108
Riley, Terry 270–71
'Riverboat Shuffle' (song) 86
Rivoli Ballroom (Sydney) 217
Roberts, Jackie 79
Roberts, Max 80
Roberts, Pixie 100
Robertson, Archie 80
Robertson, Ben 166
Robinson, Eric 120
rock 'n' roll 8, 21, 106, 117–19, 121, 123–32, 203, 249, 259, 262–64, 273 *see also* Six O'Clock Rock
RocKwiz (television programme) 129
Rodrigues, Yolando and Antonio 202
Rogers, Bob 128–29

Rogue and Vagabond venue (Wellington NZ) 105
Rohde, Bryce 12, 229–45
Rollins, Sonny 251
Romain, Abe 159
Romaine, Billy 59
Romeo is Bleeding (film) 139
Rooftop Rendezvous (television programme) 125
Roosevelt Club (Sydney) 197
Rose, Jeremy 253
Rose, Jon 269
Rosenkrantz, Timme 94
Roskolenko, Harry 94
Ross's Jazz Band 6 *see also* Three Australian Boys
Royal Hotel (Sydney) 29
Royal Prince Alfred Hospital (Sydney) 61
Royal Scottish Academy of Music and Drama 259
Rufus record label 251, 263
Russell, George 13, 229, 230–45
Rutherford, Jann 160–61, 165–66

Sam, Long Tack 59–60
sampling 275–77
Sanborn, Dave 259
'Sandansko Horo' (song) 256
Sanders, Kim 13, 248–50, 255–58, 263–64
Sangster, John 11, 86, 91, 138, 233, 244
SBS *see* Special Broadcasting Service
Schroeder, Ken 226
Schultz, Carl 140
Scofield, John 178
Scotland 180–81, 206, 249, 258, 260
Scott, Tom 259
Sedergreen, Bob 183, 224
Sellers, Roger 113
Semmler, Clement 120–22, 130
Senegal 255
Sex (recording) 267, 273–74, 281–82
Sharpe, Sammy 158
Shaw, Artie 5, 100
Sheik, The (film) 4
'Sheik of Araby' (song) 52
Shepp, Archie 255, 258
Sherlock, James 108–109, 112, 164
Shorter, Wayne 251
Shotgun Wedding (film) 137–38, 142, 145–47
Should a Girl Propose (film) 9
'Sich a Gettin up Stairs' (song) 24, 27
Silent Night (recording) 271, 276, 281
Silver, Alex 164–65

Silver, Horace 251, 259
Silverwater (recording) 276
Simmonds, Mark 271
Simpson, Roy 80
Singapore 181
Singh, Bobby 248
Sing Sing Sing (television programme) 129
Sirens Big Band 185
'Sittin' on a Rail' (song) 28
Six-Five Special (television programme) 121, 129
Six O'Clock Rock (television programme) 8, 117, 119–21
skiffle 121–22
Slater, Phil 183, 271
'Sleepy Seas' (song) 53
Smart, Jeffrey 91–92
Smith, Bessie 157
Smith, Frank 12, 215–27, 244
Smith, Lyn/Linn 59, 67–68
Smith, Mamie 157
'Somewhere South of Shanghai' (song) 53
Sonny Clay's Plantation Orchestra 36, 54
Soul Note record label 230
South Africa 2, 103, 202
Spain 180–81
Spanier, Muggsy 86
Special Broadcasting Service 119, 277
Speight, Caroline 187
Spence, Alister 259, 271
'Spice Island' (song) 249, 259–64
Spicks and Specks (television programme) 129
'Spirit Song' (song) 251
spirituals 29 *see also* gospel music
Squatter's Daughter, The (film) 136–37
'Stablemates' (song) 251
State Library of South Australia 88
State Theatre (Sydney) 56
St. Benedict's Old Boys' Music Company 41
Stern, Mike 188
Stevens, John 242
Stewart, Rex 98, 216
Stiles, Jack 79
St. Louis, Rex 197
Stompology (recording) 99
Stoneham, Reg 53
'Stop the Bus' (song) 233
Stott, Walter (aka Angela Morley) 201
'Strange Fruit' song 198, 200
Stratton, Tommy 68, 78–79
'Stratusphunk' (song) 234
Stravinsky, Igor 91, 259, 262
Strayhorn, Billy 94

Strumming Music (recording) 271
Styles, Edwin 125
'Summertime' (song) 204
'Sun Music' (song) 244
Surfer's Paradise 140–42
Swanton, Lloyd 1, 251, 259, 267, 271, 273, 275–77, 281
Sweden 157, 181, 230
'Sweet Georgia Brown' (song) 241–42, 245
Sweethearts of Rhythm, The (all women band) 159
Sweetie (film) 144
swing 5, 65–67, 70, 72, 74–76, 78, 85, 87–89, 159, 264
Swinn, Fran 164
Switzerland 180
Sydney 5–6, 8, 19, 24, 26–29, 33–34, 37, 44, 56, 59–60, 62, 67–68, 70–71, 77, 94, 104, 118, 126, 141–42, 145, 147, 149, 158–59, 161, 178, 196–98, 216–17, 219, 221, 225, 232, 244, 250–51, 254–55, 258, 263
Sydney Conservatorium of Music/New South Wales State Conservatorium of Music 159, 161, 220, 271
Sydney Improvised Music Association (SIMA) 160–62, 263
Sydney International Women's Jazz Festival 167
Sydney Town Hall 200, 216
Sylvia, Belle 3, 19
Symons, Red 142

Tabrizi, Davood 255
Takemitsu, Toru 229
Tall Timber film script 136–37
Tate, Nick 142
Tatum, Art 95
Tawadros, Joseph 188
Taxi Driver (film) 139
Taylor, Cecil 275
television 8, 117–32, 159, 203, 217, 224, 227, 268
'Tell the Boys You Saw Me' (song) 97
'That Old Calcutta Rag' (song) 244
'That Woodbourne Strut' (song) 96
Theatre Royal (Hobart) 24
Theolonius Monk Orchestra Live at Town Hall, The (recording) 109
'There's a Little Bit of Bad in Every Good Little Girl' (song) 40
Thigpen Ed 219
Third Reich 2
Thirteen Sketches (recording) 166

Thirty Years of a Gambler's Life (melodrama) 44
Thompson, Bill 79
Thomson, Chris 141
Three Australian Boys 6 *see also* Ross's Jazz Band
Tibet 281
Tinkler, Scott 183
Tivoli Theatre circuit 40, 57, 59, 67, 196–97
Tizol, Juan 93, 98
Torres Strait Islands (TSI) 192, 194–95, 197, 199–200, 202, 206 *see also* Aboriginal people, Indigeneity
Trevare, George 197
Tristano, Lennie 222
Trocadero ballroom (Sydney) 158, 217
Trocadero Dance Palais (Cairns) 196
Trumbauer, Frankie 86
Tucker, Albert 90–91, 99
Turkey 25, 257–58, 264
'Turkey in the Straw' (aka 'Zip Coon') 28
Turner, Ann 144
Turner, Geoff 'Dutchy' 76, 80
Turn Right At New South Wales (recording and song) 233, 242
Typdal, Terje 230

Uncle Tom's Cabin (novel) 35
United Kingdom 2, 5–6, 13, 23, 34, 48, 86, 88–89, 103, 119–20, 158–59, 180–81, 192, 201–202, 205–206, 267, 269–70
Unwin, Harry 80
Uptown Jazz Café (Melbourne) 105, 108, 178
US Service Organization (USO) Shows 196

Valley Jazz Festival *see* Brisbane International Jazz Festival
Vampires (band) 183
Van Der Graff Generator (band) 259
Vassilieff, Danila 91
vaudeville 2–3, 19, 49–50, 57–59, 62, 67–68
Ventura, Charlie 94
Victorian College of the Arts 112, 165–66, 226, 271
Victorian Jazz Archive (now Australian Jazz Museum) 179, 199
Victoria, Queen 23
Victoria Theatre (Sydney) 24
View From Madeleine's Couch (band) 183
Vincents Rhythm Roundup (television programme) 122
Virginia Minstrels 24
Vogelsang, Detective 90
Voice of America (radio programme) 251

Waldron, Mal 231
Walsh, Reg 217
Walsh, Winsome 75
Walters, John L. 13, 267, 277
Walters, Theo 65, 70–78, 80
Wangaratta Jazz and Blues Festival 165–66, 174, 177–78, 182–87
Warren, Jim 75
Washingmachine, George 183
Watson, George 80
Watters, Jimmy 80
Way Out West (band) 183
Webber, Bruce 126–27
Webster, Ben 94–95
Weimar Republic 87
Wellington (NZ) 68–69, 71–72, 104–15
Wellington Jazz Festival 109
Wellington Mingus Ensemble (band) 109
Westgarth Theatre (Melbourne) 59–60
West Indies 135, 202, 206
'Whatever Happened to Yesterday' (song) 234, 241–42, 245
Wheat, David 'Buck' 229, 232–33
'Wheel, The' ('song') 273
'When China Boy Meets China Girl' (song) 54
Where the Action Is (television programme) 129
Whidden, Jay 73
'White' ('song') 276
White Australia Policy 57, 206, 217
White, Ken 217, 223
White, Reverend James 38
Whiteman, Paul 4, 29
Why Jesse Learned to Jazz (film) 9
Wildman, Max 201
Wilkenfeld, Tal 104

Williamson, Paul 183
Willis, Tim 106, 111
Wills, Orm 80
Wilson, Julien 183
Wilson, Teddy 95
Wilson, Vern 80
Wintergarden Theatre (Brisbane) 60–61
Winton, Tim 145
Wishart, Stevie 274
Wiz, The (stage musical) 203
Wizard of Oz, The (novel/film) 203
WOMADelaide Festival 176
Women's Jazz Festival (Kansas City) 160
Wonder Years, The (film) 140
Woodford Folk Festival 177
'Woolloomooloo' (song) 234
world music 177, 185–88, 255, 263, 274
World War I 3, 85
World War II 5, 10, 90, 158, 170, 195–96, 199
Wright, Bob 98
Wright, Damien 188

'Yankee Doodle Dandy' (song) 26
'Yarra River [Blues]' (song) 203
Yellow Wave, The (novel) 36
You Can't Get There From Here (recording) 256, 258
Young, Aden 145
Young, Denise 129
Young, Lisa 164
Young Women's Jazz Workshops 16

Zavod, Alan 13, 138, 146
'Zip Coon' (song, aka 'Turkey in the Straw') 27
Zitro, James 242

CPSIA information can be obtained at www.ICGtesting.com
Printed in the USA
BVOW06*0226140216

436650BV00003B/5/P

9 781781 792803